Emerging Stock Markets

Emerging Stock Markets

A Complete Investment Guide to New Markets Around the World

Margaret M. Price

McGraw-Hill, Inc.

New York   San Francisco   Washington, D.C.   Auckland   Bogotá
Caracas   Lisbon   London   Madrid   Mexico City   Milan
Montreal   New Delhi   San Juan   Singapore
Sydney   Tokyo   Toronto

Library of Congress Cataloging-in-Publication Data

Price, Margaret M.
　　Emerging stock markets : a complete investment guide to new
　markets around the world / Margaret M. Price.
　　　　p.　　cm.
　　Includes index.
　　ISBN 0-07-051049-0 :
　　1. Investments, Foreign—Handbooks, manuals, etc.　2. Stocks—
　Handbooks, manuals, etc.　I. Title.
　HG4538.P685　1994
　332.6′73—dc20　　　　　　　　　　　　　　　　　　　　93-25979
　　　　　　　　　　　　　　　　　　　　　　　　　　　　　　CIP

1 2 3 4 5 6 7 8 9 0　DOC/DOC　9 9 8 7 6 5 4 3

ISBN 0-07-051049-0

*The sponsoring editor for this book was David Conti, the editing supervisor
was Jane Palmieri, and the production supervisor was Pamela Pelton. It was
set in Palatino by McGraw-Hill's Professional Book Group composition unit.*

Printed and bound by R. R. Donnelley & Sons Company.

This publication is designed to provide accurate and authoritative information in regard to the subject matter covered. It is sold with the understanding that the publisher is not engaged in rendering legal, accounting, or other professional service. If legal advice or other expert assistance is required, the services of a competent professional person
should be sought.

*—From a declaration of principles jointly adopted by a committee
of the American Bar Association and a committee of publishers*

This book is printed on recycled, acid-free paper
containing a minimum of 50% recycled de-inked fiber.

*Special thanks is due Robert Paul Molay,
managing editor of* The Bond Buyer Newsletters,
*for his extensive help with the editing of
this book.*

Contents

Preface

For many years, my husband and I have traveled to the developing countries of the world. This book combines my long-term personal interest in third world cultures and societies with my professional insights as a financial journalist. It was in Hungary in early 1991 that I first saw the need for a journalist's assessment of a brand-new market opening in a once centrally planned economy. The week after a failed coup in Venezuela in February 1992, I saw brokers standing listlessly in front of Caracas's stock exchange as many investors steered clear. But that summer, I saw Hong Kong ablaze with activity amid the excitement over the loosening of economic reins in China.

Although such markets certainly pose risks for the international investor, they also hold the greatest potential rewards for the future.

In the short term, events like the Persian Gulf War or the health of Deng Xioping will create uncertainties and jar markets. But in the long term, demographics and the increasing free flow of information and technology will prove to be more decisive. As we approach the millennium, and the world really does become more of a "global village," it is important to know where the risks and challenges are. The aim of this book is to point some of them out.

As my strategy in describing countries, I decided to take a "top-down," macroeconomic view, so that readers can understand why markets have been behaving in a certain way. As has been graphically seen in Latin America, decisions made in capital cities strongly influence the performance of companies and the stock markets. The markets I focused on were the ones of greatest investor interest and/or regions of economic importance.

For market performance data, I relied on statistics from the International Finance Corporation (IFC), the arm of the World Bank that assists the private sector in developing countries. While there are other fine performance indexes of emerging markets, the IFC's indexes are the oldest and are well known internationally. Although in 1993 the IFC unveiled a series of investable emerging markets indexes—limited to stocks foreigners can buy—these indexes were not available when I began my research for this book. I have thus relied on the IFC's older global market price indexes.

Among other research techniques, I surveyed 37 stock exchanges at the beginning of 1993. I am grateful to the 25 that responded. I would also like to thank the myriad of sources from around the world who so generously provided me with information. While data in this book are believed to be reliable, I did find "factual" discrepancies in some reports, which is certainly a hazard when dealing with developing nations and markets.

Finally, I would like to thank the people who provided me with research/editorial assistance in producing this book. Besides my husband, Arthur Nealon, I received assistance from, in alphabetical order, Phyllis Feinberg, Amy Friedman, Steve Hemmerick, Paula Horwitz, Elaine Klein, Robert Molay, Sal Nuccio, Linda Rolfus, and Richard Weissbrod. Amy Friedman provided invaluable research assistance throughout this project.

In addition, I would like to thank my editors at *Pensions & Investments*, Michael Clowes and Nancy Webman, for granting me the time to work on this extensive project and my McGraw-Hill editor, David Conti, and editing supervisor, Jane Palmieri, for their many contributions.

Margaret M. Price

1
Probing the New Frontiers

In mid-August 1991, six investment professionals, led by the Boston-based Batterymarch Financial Management, arrived in what was then called the Soviet Union. It was a hopeful time, as glastnost and perestroika seemed to pull Russia closer into the world's economic orbit. Optimists were calling Russia, with its rich resources and educated populace, "The New Yukon." Since 1989, Batterymarch had been working on a Soviet Companies Fund that was intended to invest in portions of Soviet military enterprises being converted to civilian use. In August of 1991, six mostly American investors came to explore the possibilities.

Hardly had they unpacked when news broke of a coup d'etat. Suddenly, a sense of danger descended, as civil war and detention in the country became possibilities. The group's concerns ranged from that of their own safety to the practicalities of keeping appointments. Would they still be welcome in the U.S.S.R.? Should they return home? Having come this far, the group chose to forge ahead and keep appointments. To do so they wove through gnarled traffic, intensified by the armored tanks rumbling into Moscow.

But far from terrified, some members of the Batterymarch group were evidently invigorated by the events. Word of an anticoup demonstration—the now-famous Boris Yeltsin–led showdown—drew some members of the Batterymarch group.

One of them—an exhilarated U.S. pension fund sponsor—climbed onto a Soviet tank and began shouting and cheering in unison with the dissident Soviets.

But although the coup swiftly fizzled, the U.S.S.R., now called the Commonwealth of Independent States (CIS), did not emerge stronger in the early 1990s. Continuing political and economic turmoil alarmed and deterred many portfolio investors. Even Batterymarch was unable to weather Russia's brutal economic winter; in 1992, its Soviet Companies Fund was subsumed by the European Bank for Reconstruction and Development.

However, as Russia's at least near-term prospects declined, China's star was rising. In 1992, the world's then fastest growing economy began to allow foreigners to participate in its nascent stock markets. Prospects appeared red-hot, as nominally communist China embraced ever more tenets of a market economy. "Paramount Leader" Deng Xioping was said to have extolled the merits of getting rich. Foreigners had good reason to be excited about prospects in China, where, as opposed to Russia, economic liberalizations were proceeding smartly without a simultaneous political overhaul. It seemed that so much more could be accomplished in a stable, albeit autocratic, political environment.

Other bright lights shined in other parts of Asia and parts of Latin America. The economic turnaround in Argentina, continued high growth in Southeast Asia, budding entrepreneurship in Eastern Europe, and the general firming of democracy in many parts of Asia have all caught the world's attention.

More and more countries—either because of lending institutions' requirements and/or their own inspiration—have come to embrace greater openness and free market strictures. They want access to the world's trading system and its capital flows. Their governments can no longer afford to run massive organizations, such as telecommunications companies and oil behemoths, that the private sector could run better. As more economically developing countries accept the private sector as their premier route to long-term growth, they see an important role for their stock market. More countries are trying to dust off these backwater casinos, trying to recast them as serious, well-regulated and operationally efficient institutions.

The trends are spawning impressive opportunities. "For the foreseeable future, there is a compelling case for investing, on a carefully selected basis, in emerging markets," maintains Peter Vermilye, senior advisor to Baring Asset Management in Boston. In early 1993, he observed that "China's economy is growing at 12 percent, India's 5 percent, Chile's 9 percent, Venezuela's 7 percent, Mexico's 3 percent, while Japan's economy is shrinking, Europe's is at best flat, and growth is 2.5 percent in the United States. It's perfectly clear to me that the seven Asian Tigers—Korea, Taiwan, Singapore, and Hong Kong, as well as Malaysia, Thailand, and China—will run economic rings around Japan" in the 1990s.

This focus on developing countries' markets is known as "emerging markets" investing. Money manager Antoine W. van Agtmael takes credit for coining the phrase "emerging markets" in 1981 when he was an official of the International Finance Corporation. Since then the name has caught on, although people's definition of "emerging markets" varies.

As a general rule, however, these are markets in economically developing countries, and/or those that have restricted foreign investments. The World Bank defines "developing" countries as those with modest per capita annual incomes. In 1990, that was defined as countries with a gross national product per capita of less than $7620. Although stock markets exist in more than 50 such countries, this book studies most of the 20 markets tracked in the Composite Index of the International Finance Corporation (IFC), the unit of the World Bank that aids private sector development. These 20 markets are those of Argentina, Brazil, Chile, Colombia, Greece, India, Indonesia, Jordan, Korea, Malaysia, Mexico, Nigeria, Pakistan, the Philippines, Portugal, Taiwan, Thailand, Turkey, Venezuela, and Zimbabwe. The book's reach also extends to Eastern Europe and the republics of the former Soviet Union, as well as to the People's Republic of China. It also previews small markets that should gain greater attention later in this decade and beyond.

The characteristics of emerging markets vary widely. The degree of maturity among the group ranges from Mexico's adolescent market, which appears to be approaching developed market status, to Nigeria's nascent and hard-to-penetrate arena. Among countries in the IFC Composite Index, the markets of Mexico, Chile, Korea, and Taiwan are widely viewed as among the most operationally sophisticated, compared with those of Indonesia, Jordan, Nigeria, and Zimbabwe.

The Risks

Although emerging markets share a potential for big gains, they are also fraught with risks. On their dark side, emerging markets have volatile performances and suffer from thin trading activity, dubious investor protections, and, often, a dearth of solid corporate information. Inflation and high interest can singe stock prices, as can political turbulence. Venezuela's market endured both problems in 1992, and consequently fell 42.7 percent in U.S. dollar terms, according to the IFC Price Index for Venezuela. In 1992 a disastrous flood, coupled with political upheavals, jarred Pakistan's market, while a drought ravaged sub-Saharan Africa.

For those trying to explore investment possibilities, transportation and communications can be frustrating, and some situations can be personally dangerous. One of Batterymarch's research assistants, a Chinese citizen, was arrested in Shenzhen, China, while traveling with other Batterymarch personnel. The problem centered on her passport, which was missing a necessary stamp from the Chinese embassy in New York to convert it from personal to business use. The woman was jailed overnight in Shenzhen until it was ascertained that her passport was legitimately issued, and was subsequently detained in the country for four weeks until the matter was fully sorted out.

Driving via jeep to the Harrison Malaysia plantation in the mid-1980s, Thomas Tull, principal of Gulfstream Global Investors Ltd., Dallas, Texas, and his companions were stopped by two armed men who turned out to be plantation guards. Unable to communicate in Malay, Tull's group remained captive for about 20 minutes until they were rescued by a plantation executive. To Tull, "it was the longest 20 minutes we'd ever experienced."

The Attractions

Such traumas pale in comparison to the potential opportunities of emerging markets. At times powerful performers, the markets can soar to breathless peaks, as dramatized by Argentina's 393.8 percent boom in 1991 in U.S. dollar terms. They can also tumble to deep troughs, as did Turkey's market. After falling 44.1 percent in 1991, it dove another 54.8 percent in 1992, according to the IFC's indexes.

As a group, emerging markets can significantly outpace the returns of developed markets, but that depends on the time period being considered. Almost any given year is likely to bring at least some glittering individual performers among emerging markets. In 1992 returns, in dollar terms, ranged from a high of 202 percent for Jamaica's market to the 61.6 percent plunge for Zimbabwe's, according to the IFC (see Fig. 1-1).

Although emerging markets' performances can swing fast and furiously, long-term investors still stand to profit handsomely if they are in the right markets. Take the case of Argentina. After its nearly 400 percent surge in 1991, that market fell 27.5 percent in dollar terms the following year, the IFC's data show.

But investors who stayed this stomach-churning course pocketed hefty returns—a net gain of 257.9 percent over the 2 years ended in 1992.

Moreover, the low similarity of emerging markets' returns—with each other's and with developed markets' returns—helps to cushion overall portfolio risk. As was seen in 1992, for example, Venezuela's market fell sharply, while Colombia's neighboring market climbed significantly. This dissimilarity of returns reduces the overall volatility of a globally invested portfolio, as some experiments have shown. BARRA, a Berkeley, California–based investment technology firm, compared the results of mixing varying portions of five-year returns of the IFC Composite Index into a portfolio that was invested according to the Financial Times Actuaries' World Index. BARRA found that emerging markets weighing up to 20 percent in that portfolio would decrease its overall performance risk.

Why? Because of the low correlation of returns among emerging markets, and between them and developed markets. As

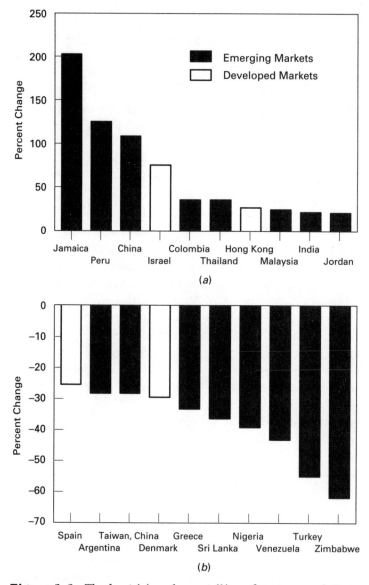

Figure 1-1. The best (*a*) and worst (*b*) performing markets in 1992 based on U.S. dollars and indicating the percent change in price indexes. (*Source: International Finance Corporation*)

BARRA points out, not only had many of these countries restricted outsiders' participation in their markets, but their insular economies were also disconnected from the global trading system and international capital flows.

Perhaps not surprisingly, emerging markets investing has become more lucrative since the mid-1980s—about the time that international investors seriously began to consider these nascent arenas. IFC data on nine developing markets dating to 1975 shows that six of those nine performed better between 1984 and October 1992 than they did between 1975 and October 1992.

High-flying emerging markets reflect the fast economic growth—usually from a low base—of their underlying economies. That trend should continue, especially in Asia with its exceptional growth prospects. According to the Organization for Economic Cooperation and Development (OECD), the Asia–Pacific region, which in this case includes the developed countries of Japan, Australia, and New Zealand, should post average annual growth in the 5-to-6-percent-a-year range in the 1990s and beyond, while its slice of world income could leap from 24 percent in 1989 to more than 50 percent by 2040.

The region is benefiting from a convergence of favorable developments. As production costs in Japan and the "Four Tigers"—Korea, Hong Kong, Singapore, and Taiwan—have climbed, these countries redirected their low-end production to cheaper locales, including Thailand, Malaysia, and other countries of Southeast Asia. Recipient countries consequently enjoyed rises in industrialization and export opportunities. Economic growth began to feed on itself, as stronger economies saw increased consumerism and planned expanded spending for infrastructural development. In addition, Asian countries have formed their own strong regional trading group. The growing opportunities for dealing in and with China enhance economic prospects for Asian nations. Evidently, such developments have not been lost on the Japanese, the long-time powerhouse in the region; according to press reports, in his 1993 New Year's statement, Japan's then-Prime Minister Kiichi Miyazawa dubbed Asia "the world's brightest spot over the next century."

Latin America, where some countries have emerged from the "lost decade" that was the 1980s, continues to bode well. Trade pacts, lowered tariff barriers, debt restructuring, relaxed currency controls, slashed government budgets, and privatizations were among the hallmarks of a region that has widely come to embrace free-market economics. During the 1990s, the OECD projects that Latin America will post an average annual economic growth rate of about 3 percent, which would still surpass the expected 2.5 percent range for North America during the period. Even more graphically, the WEFA Group, an economic forecasting firm, in Bala Cynwyd, Pennsylvania, projects that between 1990 and 1997 the gross domestic product (GDP) of developing countries will advance 40.45 percent, compared with 17.94 percent among developed countries and 1.3 percent growth among centrally planned economies.

Growing Investor Interest

International investors have been seizing the moment. A 1992 survey of 30 institutional investors—mainly money managers—by the consulting firm of Kleiman International Consultants Inc. in Washington, found that between 1989 and 1992 those managers on average had quadrupled their emerging markets allocations to 10 percent of assets. "Latin American and Asian markets are now attracting funds not only from blue-chip securities firms and international brokers but also from conservative pension fund investors," Kleiman International found. Other regions also seem destined to catch on, survey participants held. Kleiman reported that "as Central America, Africa, the Middle East, and the former East Bloc continue to liberalize their economies, these regions will also begin to attract international institutional investment, many survey participants believe."

Daniel Smaller, executive director of the emerging markets products group at Lehman Brothers International in London, estimates that international investors have already put more than $65 billion in emerging markets; that figure should swell to $200 billion by the end of the century, he believes, as developing stock markets grow in size, importance, and attractiveness. According to experts' assessments, emerging markets represent 85 percent of the world's population but only 19 percent of its GDP and 7 percent of the world's stock market capitalization (see Figs. 1-2 through 1-4).

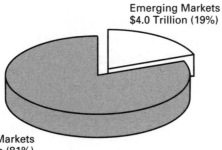

Emerging Markets
$4.0 Trillion (19%)

Developed Markets
$17.1 Trillion (81%)

Figure 1-2. World gross domestic product, 1991. (*Source: International Finance Corporation and SEI Corporation*)

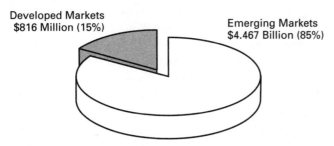

Developed Markets
$816 Million (15%)

Emerging Markets
$4.467 Billion (85%)

Figure 1-3. World population, 1990. (*Source: World Bank and SEI Corporation*)

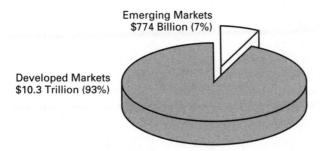

Emerging Markets
$774 Billion (7%)

Developed Markets
$10.3 Trillion (93%)

Figure 1-4. World market capitalization, 1992. (*Source: International Finance Corporation and SEI Corporation*)

Institutional investors have been the major participants in emerging markets investing. At year-end 1992, 10 of the 40 pension fund clients of consultant Frank Russell Co. in Tacoma, Washington, were allocating money to emerging markets. By the turn of the century all 40 clients are likely to be doing so, projects Mark Castelin, a senior research analyst with the firm. In a 1992 survey of U.S. pension funds with more than $100 million in assets, the consulting firm of SEI Corporation, Wayne, Pennsylvania, found fully one-third, or 74 of the 200 respondents, invested in emerging markets. Their mean allocation to emerging markets was 2.3 percent of total holdings in equities. Of those not invested in emerging markets, 35 percent of respondents said they would consider doing so.

In early 1992, the $28 billion Wisconsin Investment Board expanded its emerging markets holdings to about $128 million. The allocation represented almost 10 percent of the fund's $1.3 billion in international investments. As of the beginning of 1993, the £6 billion British Gas Pension Funds had about £20 million sterling, or about $30 million, invested in emerging markets. The fund "would still look to increase that by another £10 million over the next six months. Twice that allocation is not beyond realistic expectations," says David Stuart, the fund's investment manager, who points out that beginning-of-the-year outlays were still less than 0.5 percent of total assets. "In five years' time, we could have 5 percent of our money invested in what are now considered 'emerging markets'—although some of them, such as Mexico, Korea, and Thailand—may no longer be considered 'emerging' at that time," he said.

Increasingly, individual investors are showing interest in nascent markets, in part because of publicity about high-flying markets and partly because of the growing number of vehicles and vendors pitching investment products to the retail sector. For example, Shearson Lehman has 8500 brokers who can include emerging markets among their offerings aimed at the retail market. (Lehman Brothers' sales force of over 300 is aimed at the institutional market.) Montgomery Asset Management, San Francisco, found ample interest in its Montgomery Emerging Markets Fund for retail customers that was launched in March 1992. By late January 1993, that vehicle had already attracted more than $100 million.

Characteristics of Emerging Markets

What are the hallmarks of emerging markets? Chiefly, they include countries experiencing or having the potential for high economic growth but facing substantial political, economic, and/or market-specific risks. As illustrated by emerging markets' returns, investors can be well rewarded for taking the risk. But they still present a plethora of worries. These range broadly from the possibility of a government overthrow or ouster, as was seen with Brazil's 1992 impeachment of its president, to the possibility of a prolonged recession, a surge in inflation, currency devaluation, and other economic woes. In the market, the panoply of problems includes insider trading, unclear accounting practices, and inadequate disclosure of crossholdings by majority shareholders.

The monthly *International Country Risk Guide* (ICRG), published by Political Risk Services, Syracuse, New York, ranks countries by political, financial, and economic consideration. (See Figs. 1-5 to 1-9 for countries grouped by regions.) Its December 1992 edition shows that the least attractive countries in their respective regions were all in the nondeveloped category: Haiti, Yugoslavia, Iraq, Liberia, and Myanmar, while the three highest scorers of all countries measured were, in descending order, the small countries of Luxembourg, Austria, and Switzerland.

Thomas Sealy, the ICRG's editor in the United Kingdom, points to some characteristics of stable versus risky countries. He holds that, while stable countries generally benefit from such characteristics as a sizable middle class—which has a stake in a country's future—some of the most potentially risky countries are those with wide, potentially revolution-inspiring gulfs between rich and poor. Or, Sealy points out, they may have been governed by a long-entrenched ruling party, which can spawn governmental complacency and corruption.

Ex-colonies, notably those of Britain, France, Spain, and Portugal, can be potentially risky. Among other deficiencies, few of the indigenous people in these countries have benefited from colonialism, and they have too rarely received the training and skills needed to operate their country after their colonial rulers' departure, says Sealy. In some cases prolonged strife ensued, as

Country	Current political rating 12/92	Current financial rating 12/92	Current economic rating 12/92	Composite ratings		
				Year ago 12/91	Current 12/92	F'cast 12/93
Angola	42.0	21.0	36.5	50.5	50.0	52.0
Botswana	69.0	39.0	42.0	73.0	75.0	76.0
Burkina Faso	45.0	25.0	37.0	50.0	53.5	51.0
Cameroon	46.0	24.0	31.5	53.5	51.0	53.0
Congo	44.0	20.0	28.5	51.5	46.5	45.0
Cote d'Ivoire	64.0	28.0	25.5	60.0	59.0	59.0
Ethiopia	18.0	15.0	18.0	29.5	25.5	28.0
Gabon	55.0	31.0	35.5	64.5	61.0	62.5
Gambia, The	63.0	34.0	34.0	60.5	65.5	67.0
Ghana	62.0	30.0	29.5	57.0	61.0	62.0
Guinea	46.0	22.0	31.5	48.0	50.0	49.0
Guinea-Bissau	44.0	20.0	16.5	43.0	40.5	42.0
Kenya	59.0	25.0	26.5	49.5	55.5	60.0
Liberia	9.0	8.0	11.5	15.5	14.5	15.0
Madagascar	46.0	20.0	25.5	50.5	46.0	50.0
Malawi	50.0	26.0	30.5	53.0	53.5	50.0
Mali	42.0	19.0	31.5	44.5	46.5	47.0
Mozambique	38.0	24.0	15.5	43.0	39.0	46.0
Namibia	65.0	27.0	39.0	54.5	65.5	68.0
Niger	36.0	24.0	31.0	46.0	45.5	46.5
Nigeria	54.0	30.0	31.5	58.0	58.0	60.0
Senegal	54.0	28.0	33.5	57.0	58.0	57.0
Sierra Leone	25.0	17.0	11.0	34.5	26.5	28.0
Somalia	10.0	10.0	8.5	19.5	14.5	14.0
South Africa	64.0	36.0	37.0	59.5	68.5	63.5
Tanzania	61.0	29.0	23.5	54.5	57.0	56.5
Togo	36.0	25.0	36.5	50.5	49.0	50.0
Uganda	39.0	21.0	14.0	31.5	37.0	40.0
Zaire	22.0	12.0	19.0	29.0	26.5	30.0
Zambia	59.0	24.0	23.5	43.5	53.5	55.0
Zimbabwe	61.0	30.0	16.5	52.0	54.0	55.0

Figure 1-5. Risk ratings indicating current assessments and a one-year forecast for sub-Saharan Africa. The lower the rating, the higher the risk. (*Source:* International Country Risk Guide, *December 1992, published by Political Risk Services, Syracuse, N. Y.*)

Country	Current political rating 12/92	Current financial rating 12/92	Current economic rating 12/92	Composite ratings		
				Year ago 12/91	Current 12/92	F'cast 12/93
Albania	52.0	26.0	8.0	43.5	43.0	43.0
Austria	90.0	48.0	39.5	87.5	89.0	85.0
Belgium	79.0	46.0	39.5	79.6	82.8	81.0
Bulgaria	69.0	30.0	21.5	57.5	60.5	58.0
Cyprus	79.0	45.0	39.0	73.5	81.5	80.0
Czechoslovakia	63.0	35.0	40.8	70.0	69.5	n.a.
Denmark	84.0	47.0	39.5	82.0	85.5	82.0
Finland	81.0	42.0	35.0	80.0	79.0	78.0
France	81.0	47.0	36.5	80.5	82.5	80.0
Germany, FR	77.0	49.0	40.5	86.5	83.5	80.0
Greece	65.0	36.0	32.0	62.5	66.5	66.0
Hungary	72.0	38.0	34.5	64.5	72.5	70.0
Iceland	80.0	41.0	36.5	79.5	79.0	77.0
Ireland	72.0	42.0	38.0	78.5	76.0	76.0
Italy	68.0	43.0	33.6	77.5	72.5	70.0
Luxembourg	93.0	49.0	40.0	89.5	91.0	88.0
Malta	76.0	43.0	43.0	70.5	81.0	78.0
Netherlands	83.0	48.0	40.0	86.0	85.5	84.0
Norway	79.0	46.0	44.0	87.0	84.5	82.0
Poland	69.0	35.0	36.5	61.0	70.5	70.0
Portugal	71.0	43.0	41.0	77.5	77.5	76.0
Romania	61.0	34.0	23.0	53.0	59.0	59.0
Russia	51.0	28.0	35.5	n.a.	57.5	47.5
Spain	75.0	43.0	38.0	75.0	78.0	75.0
Sweden	79.0	45.0	39.0	82.5	81.5	79.0
Switzerland	88.0	50.0	41.5	91.5	90.0	88.0
UK	76.0	46.0	36.0	82.0	79.0	80.0
Yugoslavia	26.0	15.0	24.5	36.0	32.5	45.0

Figure 1-6. Risk ratings indicating current assessments and a one-year forecast for Europe. The lower the rating, the higher the risk. (*Source: International Country Risk Guide, December 1992, published by Political Risk Services, Syracuse, N. Y.*)

Country	Current political rating 12/92	Current financial rating 12/92	Current economic rating 12/92	Composite ratings		
				Year ago 12/91	Current 12/92	F'cast 12/93
Australia	79.0	43.0	39.5	80.0	81.0	80.0
Bangladesh	44.0	26.0	33.5	39.0	52.0	50.0
Brunei	81.0	48.0	42.0	85.5	85.5	85.0
China, PR	75.0	37.0	41.5	61.0	77.0	76.0
Hong Kong	66.0	45.0	40.0	65.5	75.5	78.0
India	48.0	34.0	29.0	40.0	55.5	60.0
Indonesia	59.0	42.0	36.5	69.0	69.0	68.5
Japan	81.0	50.0	43.0	85.0	87.0	85.0
Korea, DPR	51.0	13.0	12.0	47.5	38.0	38.0
Korea, Rep.	75.0	47.0	39.0	73.0	80.5	80.0
Malaysia	70.0	45.0	42.0	77.5	78.5	77.0
Mongolia	59.0	30.0	16.0	64.5	52.5	48.0
Myanmar*	37.0	10.0	24.5	30.5	36.0	38.0
New Caledonia	43.0	20.0	38.0	46.0	50.5	56.0
New Zealand	81.0	46.0	38.5	79.5	83.0	80.0
Pakistan	40.0	30.0	32.0	43.5	51.0	54.0
Pap. N. Guinea	54.0	26.0	31.5	54.5	56.0	58.0
Philippines	55.0	34.0	34.0	46.0	61.5	58.0
Singapore	77.0	48.0	43.0	83.5	84.0	80.0
Sri Lanka	40.0	32.0	34.5	46.5	53.5	55.0
Taiwan	77.0	48.0	44.5	81.5	85.0	84.0
Thailand	63.0	43.0	39.0	66.5	72.5	74.5
Viet Nam	55.0	20.0	24.0	44.0	49.5	55.0

Myanmar = Burma

Figure 1-7. Risk ratings indicating current assessments and a one-year forecast for Asia and the Pacific. The lower the rating, the higher the risk. (*Source:* International Country Risk Guide, *December 1992, published by Political Risk Services, Syracuse, N. Y.*)

was the case with Angola and Mozambique—two former Portuguese colonies.

In remote markets, costs of investing are relatively high, and procedures—in some countries, including filing preinvestment registration applications with local authorities—can be cumbersome. Investment costs are discernibly higher in emerging mar-

Country	Current political rating 12/92	Current financial rating 12/92	Current economic rating 12/92	Composite ratings		
				Year ago 12/91	Current 12/92	F'cast 12/93
Argentina	68.0	37.0	24.5	63.0	65.0	67.0
Bahamas	67.0	39.0	37.5	71.0	72.0	70.0
Bolivia	54.0	36.0	27.5	60.0	59.0	60.0
Brazil	66.0	38.0	27.0	62.5	65.5	68.0
Canada	78.0	48.0	38.0	83.0	82.0	78.0
Chile	67.0	42.0	38.0	69.5	73.5	71.0
Colombia	58.0	41.0	37.0	68.0	68.0	67.0
Costa Rica	72.0	37.0	33.0	69.5	71.0	70.0
Cuba	58.0	20.0	14.0	40.5	46.0	50.0
Dominican Rep.	56.0	28.0	36.5	53.5	56.0	55.0
Ecuador	62.0	34.0	27.5	56.5	62.0	60.0
El Salvador	54.0	24.0	34.0	43.5	56.0	58.0
Guatemala	49.0	29.0	33.5	50.5	56.0	54.0
Guyana	53.0	29.0	22.0	50.5	52.0	50.0
Haiti	25.0	13.0	28.5	31.0	33.5	35.0
Honduras	51.0	30.0	32.0	53.0	56.5	55.0
Jamaica	69.0	39.0	28.0	66.0	68.0	68.0
Mexico	69.0	42.0	30.5	71.0	71.0	76.0
Nicaragua	47.0	28.0	22.0	44.0	48.5	47.0
Panama	48.0	33.0	35.0	55.5	58.0	56.0
Paraguay	69.0	40.0	37.0	58.5	73.0	70.0
Peru	44.0	25.0	25.0	51.0	47.0	45.5
Suriname	47.0	25.0	21.5	50.0	47.0	48.0
Trinidad/Tob.	62.0	36.0	31.0	64.5	64.5	68.0
United States	75.0	48.0	39.5	83.0	81.5	82.0
Uruguay	66.0	39.0	33.0	69.0	69.0	69.5
Venezuela	60.0	37.0	34.5	75.0	66.0	70.0

Figure 1-8. Risk ratings indicating current assessments and a one-year forecast for the Americas. The lower the rating, the higher the risk. (*Source:* International Country Risk Guide, *December 1992, published by Political Risk Services, Syracuse, N. Y.*)

kets. These reflect the higher costs of acquiring information and trading stocks in developing countries. According to Adam Spector, manager of SEI Corporation's emerging markets group,

Country	Current political rating 12/92	Current financial rating 12/92	Current economic rating 12/92	Composite ratings Year ago 12/91	Current 12/92	F'cast 12/93
Algeria	45.0	31.0	28.0	58.5	52.0	55.5
Bahrain	66.0	42.0	39.5	62.0	74.0	75.0
Egypt	60.0	38.0	33.0	59.0	65.5	67.0
Iran	60.0	36.0	26.5	55.5	61.5	66.5
Iraq	24.0	4.0	26.5	23.0	27.5	31.5
Israel	71.0	39.0	35.0	62.0	72.5	74.0
Jordan	65.0	34.0	36.0	49.5	67.5	68.0
Kuwait	66.0	43.0	34.0	52.5	71.5	72.0
Lebanon	40.0	22.0	34.0	43.5	48.0	50.0
Libya	59.0	30.0	34.5	56.0	62.0	68.0
Morocco	65.0	39.0	33.0	55.5	68.5	70.0
Oman	69.0	43.0	36.5	70.5	74.5	75.0
Qatar	61.0	42.0	42.0	64.5	72.5	75.0
Saudi Arabia	68.0	43.0	40.0	67.5	75.5	78.0
Sudan	27.0	12.0	11.0	23.5	25.0	31.0
Syria	58.0	31.0	31.0	55.0	60.0	62.0
Tunisia	66.0	36.0	35.0	55.5	68.5	68.5
Turkey	65.0	37.0	28.0	51.5	65.0	63.0
UAE	64.0	41.0	40.5	63.5	73.0	76.0
Yemen, Rep.	54.0	32.0	28.0	42.0	57.0	55.5

Figure 1-9. Risk ratings indicating current assessments and a one-year forecast for the Middle East and North Africa. The lower the rating, the higher the risk. (*Source:* International Country Risk Guide, *December 1992, published by Political Risk Services, Syracuse, N. Y.)*

for pension funds, investment management fees for emerging markets can range from about 100 to 125 basis points (a basis point is $1/100$ of a point) on the size of the amount being invested. That would compare with fees of about 80 basis points, depending on size, paid for an internationally invested account in developed markets. Not only are such costs as brokerage commissions higher in the third world, but so are custodial fees. According to Spector, custodial fees are up to 50 basis points on the value of assets under custody. Costs are "doubly expensive" for retail investors, he says. This sector is unable to capitalize on economies of scale available to large institutional investors, such as pension funds.

Still in their developmental stages, emerging markets can manifest some risky and/or unsavory investment practices. In the 1980s, one investor recalls watching brokers in Indonesia photostating stock certificates in a backroom. These days, common complaints center on the existence of unsubstantiated rumors that can still drive prices; insider trading; market/company information that may be sketchy, out-of-date, or questionable or incomprehensible; unclear relationships and crossholdings among companies; and general lack of concern about minority shareholders by families or other groups holding the majority interest in a company.

According to Kleiman International, Indonesia's market is cited most often for overt manipulation and lack of regulatory oversight, although some incremental progress has been made. The markets of Turkey, Brazil, Venezuela, India, and Pakistan are also problem areas for institutional investors, Kleiman's survey shows, while investors rate Mexico's market the best supervised and most transparent of the emerging markets.

The IFC's *Emerging Stock Markets Factbook 1993* points out some of the differences in emerging markets' developments. Its analysis shows that only 10 out of 23 emerging markets reviewed require quarterly company results to be published. Accounting standards earned a "good" rating in only 8 of the 23 countries, and a poor rating in 2 of them—those of China and Indonesia. Only 6 markets received a "good" rating on investor protection.

However, progress is being made in upgrading those markets. As evidence, participants in Kleiman International's 1992 survey of 30 money managers cited a vast improvement over the previous four years in the quality of information emanating from emerging markets, especially from local brokers in Latin America and Asia. This group is "now an important source of market and company information," holds Kleiman, even if their stock analysis is still not top-notch by developed markets' standards.

Although restrictions to foreign investment have been declining in many markets, quite a few countries maintain some controls. These range from limiting the size stakes foreigners can

Table 1-1. Entering and Exiting Emerging Markets
A Summary of Investment Regulations* (at March 31, 1993)

Are listed stocks freely available to foreign investors?	Repatriation of:	
	Income	Capital
Free Entry		
Argentina	Free	Free
Brazil	Free	Free
Colombia	Free	Free
Greece	Free	Some restrictions
Malaysia	Free	Free
Pakistan	Free	Free
Peru	Free	Free
Portugal	Free	Free
Turkey	Free	Free
Relatively Free Entry		
Bangladesh	Some restrictions	Some restrictions
Chile	Free	After 1 year
Costa Rica	Free	Free
Indonesia	Some restrictions	Some restrictions
Jamaica	Free	Free
Jordan	Free	Free
Kenya	Some restrictions	Some restrictions
Korea	Free	Free
Mexico	Free	Free
Sri Lanka	Some restrictions	Some restrictions
Thailand	Free	Free
Trinidad & Tobago	Free	Free
Venezuela	Free	Free

*It should be noted that some industries in some countries are considered strategic and are not available to foreign/nonresident investors, and that the level of foreign investment in other cases may be limited by national law or corporate policy to minority positions not to aggregate more than 49 percent of voting stock. The summaries above refer to "new money" investment by foreign institutions; other regulations may apply to capital invested through debt conversion schemes or other sources.

Key to Access:
Free Entry—No significant restrictions to purchasing stocks.
Relatively Free Entry—Some registration procedures required to ensure repatriation rights.
Special Classes—Foreigners restricted to certain classes of stocks, designated for foreign investors.

SOURCE: International Finance Corporation.

take to imposing high taxes that discourage repatriation of earnings, especially on short-term investments. (See Table 1-1 for the IFC's assessment of markets' openness.) Until 1990 and 1991, respectively, Taiwan and Korea barred direct foreign investments in their stock markets. While those rules were lib-

Table 1-1. Entering and Exiting Emerging Markets (*Continued*)
A Summary of Investment Regulations* (at March 31, 1993)

Are listed stocks freely available to foreign investors?	Repatriation of:	
	Income	Capital
Special Classes of Shares		
China	Free	Free
Philippines	Free	Free
Zimbabwe†	Restricted	Restricted
Authorized Investors Only		
India	Free	Free
Taiwan, China	Free	Free
Closed		
Nigeria	Some restrictions	Some restrictions

†At the end of April 1993, the government of Zimbabwe announced its intention to open the stock market on a limited basis to foreign investors.

Key to Access (cont.):
Authorized Investors Only—Only approved foreign investors may buy stocks.
Closed—Closed, or access severely restricted (e.g., for nonresident nationals only).

Key to Repatriation:
Income = Dividends, interest, and realized capital gains.
Capital = Initial capital invested.
Some Restrictions = Typically, requires some registration with or permission of Central Bank, Ministry of Finance, or an Office of Exchange Controls that may restrict the timing of exchange release.
Free = Repatriation done routinely.

SOURCE: International Finance Corporation, Washington, D.C., *Emerging Stock Markets Factbook 1993.*

eralized, as of this writing foreigners in total can buy only up to 10 percent of available shares in either of these markets. In China, the supply of "B shares" available to foreigners is still extremely limited. Kenneth King, head of international equity investments, Kleinwort Benson Investment Management Ltd. in London, reports that, in 1992, when his firm launched its China fund (a fund targeted to take direct stakes in Chinese companies instead of buying shares on the stock market), there were more funds for investing in China "B" shares than "B" shares in existence.

Other characteristics of emerging markets today include a high concentration of trading volume in a few stocks, overall thin trading liquidity, and sharp differences in the valuations of markets. The IFC's data show that, in 1992, price-earnings ratios

(P/E) among markets in its Composite Index ranged from a high of 37.99 for Argentina's market to a low of 2.03 for Zimbabwe's. These levels compare with a 1992 P/E of 18.47 for the IFC's Composite Index—which was still beneath the average of 23 for the world's developed markets. (See Fig. 1-10.)

Although many emerging markets are small, some of them contain a large number of listed companies. Most notably, with more than 6700 listed stocks, India has the second largest supply of listings in the world, after the United States' market. According to the IFC, other emerging markets with more than 500 listed stocks include the São Paulo exchange in Brazil, as well as the markets of South Korea, Pakistan, and Egypt. In total, at the end of 1992, the IFC counted a total of 13,217 listed stocks in 36 emerging markets, compared with 18,452 in 24 developed markets. Stock listings in emerging markets had grown sharply from the total of 6,764 in 1983.

The capitalization of emerging markets has ballooned, from $83.2 billion in 1983 to $774 billion in 1992—about an 830 percent increase. According to the IFC, in 1992 the three largest emerging markets in terms of capitalization were Mexico's ($139.061 billion), Korea's ($107.448 billion), and Taiwan's ($101.124 billion).

Market Improvements

Simultaneously, investment services in these markets, from international brokerage to custodial banking, have been rapidly expanding, making it easier for investors to penetrate the markets. Recent improvements have been substantial. Lehman's Daniel Smaller observes that as late as early 1992 "it was still difficult for institutional investors to obtain custodial services" in some emerging markets. "That process has since become much more easy. [Moreover,] when I first tried to buy stock in Peru in March, 1992," he recalls, "there was no forward market in foreign exchange, otherwise known to us as a 'spot' or, two-day delivery" foreign exchange rate. At that time, Lima only had a same-day exchange rate. As a result, foreign investors couldn't know how much money to send to cover the cost of local currency for stock purchases. To be safe

Market	Price–earnings ratio			Price–book value ratio			Dividend yield		
	End 1992	Relative to world*	End 1991	End 1992	Relative to world*	End 1991	End 1992	Relative to world*	End 1991
Latin America									
Argentina	37.99	1.65	− 405.97	1.20	0.63	1.68	1.93	0.69	0.33
Brazil	− 24.43	− 1.06	15.47	0.37	0.20	0.76	0.68	0.24	0.64
Chile	12.99	0.56	15.87	1.71	0.90	1.73	3.82	1.36	3.55
Colombia	27.95	1.22	40.15	1.73	0.92	2.35	1.89	0.67	2.26
Mexico	12.28	0.53	14.14	1.99	1.06	1.64	0.99	0.35	0.84
Venezuela	15.63	0.68	28.52	1.61	0.85	3.61	0.98	0.35	0.54
East Asia									
Korea	21.43	0.93	21.31	1.06	0.56	1.00	1.81	0.65	1.64
Philippines	14.13	0.61	11.29	2.45	1.30	2.58	1.02	0.36	0.76
Taiwan, China	16.57	0.72	22.27	2.15	1.14	3.27	1.77	0.63	0.87
South Asia									
India	33.74	1.47	25.43	4.74	2.51	3.91	0.73	0.26	1.27
Indonesia	13.19	0.53	11.63	1.60	0.85	1.65	2.06	0.74	0.00
Malaysia	21.84	0.95	21.35	2.53	1.34	2.49	2.36	0.84	2.37
Pakistan	21.86	0.95	23.88	2.55	1.35	3.14	2.55	0.91	1.88
Thailand	13.93	0.61	12.01	2.52	1.33	2.10	2.62	0.94	1.86
Europe/Mideast/Africa									
Greece	6.89	0.30	10.74	1.67	0.88	2.28	11.02	3.94	3.83

Figure 1-10. Comparative valuations of IFC global indexes for 1992.
(*Source: International Finance Corporation*)

(*Continued*)

Market	Price-earnings ratio			Price–book value ratio			Dividend yield		
	End 1992	Relative to world*	End 1991	End 1992	Relative to world*	End 1991	End 1992	Relative to world*	End 1991
Europe/Mideast/Africa (*Continued*)									
Jordan	14.49	0.63	9.98	1.61	0.85	1.40	2.51	0.90	8.73
Nigeria	8.98	0.39	10.58	1.74	0.92	1.58	5.10	1.82	6.81
Portugal	9.05	0.39	10.94	1.02	0.54	1.26	4.68	1.67	3.66
Turkey	6.95	0.30	13.74	1.29	0.68	2.30	8.14	2.91	4.45
Zimbabwe	2.03	0.09	6.99	0.31	0.16	1.04	6.13	2.19	5.83
IFC Regionals									
IFC Composite	18.47	0.80	20.27	1.70	0.90	1.82	1.92	0.69	1.42
Latin America	17.93	0.78	18.44	1.46	0.77	1.76	2.18	0.78	1.68
Asia	19.45	0.85	17.54	1.04	0.55	1.41	1.89	0.67	1.53
Developed Markets†									
France	15.80	0.69	12.70	1.50	0.79	1.51	3.50	1.25	3.50
Germany	14.30	0.62	15.10	1.65	0.87	1.82	3.90	1.39	3.70
Japan	38.90	1.69	35.30	1.77	0.94	2.42	1.00	0.36	0.80
United Kingdom	19.70	0.86	15.20	2.13	1.13	1.81	4.50	1.61	5.30
United States	22.70	0.99	21.70	2.36	1.25	2.32	2.50	1.04	3.00
World	23.00	1.60	21.10	1.89	1.00	2.01	2.80	1.00	2.70

*Relative to the MSCI World Index.

†Source for developed markets: MSCI.

Figure 1-10. (*Continued*) Comparative valuations of IFC global indexes for 1992. (*Source: International Finance Corporation*)

they had to send 5 to 10 percent greater amounts of money than current exchange rates dictated, to cover expected fluctuations in currency. But by later in the year, a spot market had been created.

As Smaller sees it, "All these bits and pieces of market development are significant."

Of course markets are developing at different rates, as the April 1992 issue of *Global Finance* magazine illustrated. Out of the 20 emerging markets reviewed, 12 had a stock settlement date that took place three days or less after a share was traded. However, according to *Global Finance*, trade settlements can take weeks in Zimbabwe and Nigeria. It can also "take a long time" in Pakistan, and in India procedures are "the worst in the world."

In contrast, Taiwan's market is already a model of operational efficiency. In some brokers' offices in Taiwan, investors can automatically call up their stock balances and transfer securities from one account to another. In China, trading and settlement systems are automated, and although the currency isn't convertible, experts say that repatriation of trading profits is relatively easy. In Shanghai, Chinese B shares (those available to foreigners) are quoted in U.S. dollars, and trades are settled in U.S. dollars; in Shenzhen as of June 1993, B shares are quoted in Hong Kong dollars, and trades are settled in the same currency.

To aid in establishing or enhancing their markets, many countries are seeking guidance from public and private sources. One important source has been the U.S. Securities and Exchange Commission (SEC), which in 1991 launched its International Institute for Securities Market Development. Although that program originally was targeted to assist in the development of Eastern Europe's markets, interest proved to be much wider. When the Institute held its first training conference on market development in 1991, 75 officials from 32 countries attended. In 1992 it drew 90 officials from 44 countries, "and we could have had another 40 to 50 people, because demand was so great," recalls Terry M. Chuppe, the SEC's associate chief economist and director of the Institute.

In 1992 the conference, one of five Institute programs, lasted two weeks and concentrated on three parts: policy framework for capital markets' development; the "practical side" of trading, clearance, underwriting, and other operations; and insights into the SEC's and other governments' experiences regulating capital markets' activities.

After the two-week session in Washington, about 60 participants went on brief internships. They visited such organizations as securities firms, stock markets, and clearing corporations around the United States. The payoff from these programs has already become evident in some cases. And, in general, Chuppe foresees markets developing "over the years with sound regulatory standards and practices."

When to Invest?

Clearly, the sooner investors get started the better for them. As Peter Jeffreys of Fund Research Ltd. in London points out, "Until now, it's been relatively easy to make money in emerging markets. In hot markets, even bad stocks went up almost as much as good stocks. But increasingly, the marketplace is becoming more discriminating, and in the future, making money in emerging markets will be tougher."

In some emerging markets, big booms may already be over. After their scorching 1991 performance, some Latin American markets in 1992 looked as melted as used dinner candles. Brazil's is seen as the last of the big economies whose market could still rocket. Of course there will still be smaller markets opening up over the next two decades, some experts say, and Eastern Europe's now-nascent markets probably may not catch many international investors' fancy until the 1996–2000 period. But at this point many of the perceived attractive developing markets, especially in Latin America and Asia, have been identified. Dean LeBaron, chairman of Batterymarch Financial Management, even believes that "we're running out of emerging markets. Mexico's and Chile's markets, once underdeveloped, are now developed and accepted....In 20 years, Pakistan's market may not be distinguishable from others." He expects that over time, markets will become increasingly similar as "technology worked out in a developed market is extended to others."

Clearly, the race is on to capitalize on the opportunity. In search of the next hot arenas, at least some money managers have been opportunistically shifting money from one region to the next. After Latin America's markets boomed in 1991, at least some managers significantly reduced their exposure to that area, in many cases relocating it to Asia. William E. Morfeld, a vice president with the brokerage firm of Lynch, Jones & Ryan Inc. in New York, feels that such market rotations could last until the middle 1990s, by which time he expects that most of the major economic shifts to have occurred, with more markets sharing characteristics.

For those seeking clues as to timing their entrance into an emerging market, analysts typically cite signs of cooling inflation, easing of credit conditions, falling interest rates, legislative approval of economic reforms, and the advent of a political leader who inspires confidence, both locally and abroad.

In his "gloom, boom, and doom" report, Dr. Marc Faber of Marc Faber Ltd. in Hong Kong provides some long-range guideposts. Faber identifies seven phases in emerging markets' life cycles, based largely on economic, political, and market conditions in these developing countries. From Phase Zero, where no market yet exists, as in Cuba and parts of China, formerly stagnant economies awaken in Phase One amid improved social, political, and economic conditions. Perhaps an important discovery is made, or prices of important local commodities climb. In Phase Two, capital spending soars, unemployment falls, credit expands quickly, and market prices leap to overvaluations, as was seen in Thailand between 1987 and 1990 and Kuwait from 1978 to 1980, he says.

In Phase Three, markets reach their peak, before sliding backward. Manifest signs are a boomtown mentality in a country's business capital, even as infrastructural problems emerge along with excess capacity in some sectors, and slowed growth in corporate profits. Today, while very few emerging countries with established stock markets are still in Phase One, according to Faber, some, such as those of Brazil, Colombia, and Argentina, may be in Phase Two or in the early part of Phase Three.

Countries in Phase Four manifest such troubles as slowing credit growth, deteriorating corporate profits, and a falling stock market that temporarily rebounds amid the still strong economy. Among Phase Five's characteristics are credit deflation, badly deteriorated social, political, and even economic conditions, the bankruptcy of a "big market player, " as well as withering stock prices. Finally, in Phase Six, investors give up on stocks. According to Faber, "Phase Four will occur 6 to 18 months after the market's high, while Phase Six comes on usually much later—frequently 4 to 6 years after the market's top...when pessimism is rampant as a result of a total wealth destruction."

Faber recommends buying stocks during Phase Zero, when the potential for gain is greatest. To avoid being caught at a market's peak in Phase Three, Faber prefers to exit it during Phase Two. "Purchasing an emerging market in Phase Three is comparable to buying one stock or an entire industry group at the peak of its popularity," he has written. "Investors who bought the 'nifty-fifty,' Hong Kong stocks in 1972, oil stocks in 1980, high-technology stocks in 1983, or real estate in 1988, had to endure a miserable performance for many years. For this reason, it is important for anyone involved with investing in emerging markets to consider seriously and analyze in which phase of the cycle the emerging market finds itself."

2
How to Invest

You could say that Olumide Wilkey uses some "heavy artillery." To find attractive emerging markets, Wilkey, president of Key Investors Asset Management Inc., Greenwich, Connecticut, uses a program that was designed to detect the presence of Soviet submarines in the cold-war era. The program is called "vector auto-regression moving average" (VARMA). It was developed in the late 1970s at the University of Wisconsin with funding from the U.S. Defense Department.

In the post-Soviet era, Key Investors uses VARMA to evaluate 22 developing markets by identifying the economic factors that most accurately predict stock market returns. These factors can range from the direction of interest rates to the level of industrial production to the price of coffee.

Key's adaption of VARMA sifts through some 40 macroeconomic variables for each of the 22 emerging markets the firm follows. From these variables, the model projects returns for all the markets for the coming quarter. Based on the information on market conditions, VARMA recommends asset allocations, such as investing 10 percent in Mexico and 3 percent in Turkey.

The model also helps to identify attractive stocks via a "risk optimizer," which assesses 4000 equities and provides a risk/return profile of the stocks in which Key wishes to invest. After these computer-generated functions have been completed, Key Investors applies human judgment and its own analysis to the intended portfolio.

"This is a very powerful tool," says Wilkey. Unlike "some conventional econometric models—such as the capital asset pricing model or the arbitrage pricing theory—you don't have to have a preconceived notion about how the world works to use this model. VARMA finds relationships among variables by itself. You just supply the variables."

Does this work? Apparently, it has in the past. While employed by Matrix Capital Management, Hugh Neuburger, now executive vice president of Key Investors, used VARMA successfully to signal investment opportunities in developed markets in the 1980s. According to Wilkey, use of the model from 1988 to 1990 delivered average premium returns of 3.3 percentage points above the performance of the Morgan Stanley Capital International Europe Australia Far East (EAFE) index.

Wilkey expects even better results from VARMA's application to emerging markets. Why? Emerging markets themselves are likely to outperform EAFE, he says. Moreover, "most emerging markets managers are still using old-fashioned or traditional techniques," holds Wilkey. With his quantitative approach "we expect at least to exceed the median performance of our peer group."

While Key Investors isn't the only technologically sophisticated, quantitative firm in emerging markets, its debut in 1991 signals the heightening competition: More vendors are seeking ways to distinguish their services. One route to this goal is to extend to the new frontiers the use of tools used to evaluate developed markets.

Getting Started

Today, an array of funds and other instruments, including synthetic and derivative products, are available for emerging markets investments. But most investors still aren't ready for anything too exotic. Instead, many investors are choosing simple solutions as they gain market experience.

Typically, they make initial forays into developing markets by allocating proportionately small amounts to this sector. Often, these investments are in well-diversified portfolios. Moreover, many emerging markets investors do not yet use a portfolio dedicated to this purpose. In its 1992 survey of U.S. pension funds with more than $100 million of assets, SEI Corporation found that, of respondents who were already investing in emerging markets, two-thirds did so by allowing their international managers who invest in developed markets to expand into the third world.

Today, a growing legion of vendors help clients find the right emerging markets strategy. At year-end 1992, the consulting firm of Frank Russell Company counted some 35 money management firms worldwide that were offering emerging markets investing—although Russell was then recommending only 8 or 9 of these firms to its clients.

International brokerage firms, mainly those based in the United States and the United Kingdom, were rapidly expanding into emerging markets, as were global custody banks and consulting firms. The latter pair clients with managers and assess the capabilities of managers. Along with Frank Russell, some of the U.S.-based consultants providing services on emerging markets included, but were not limited to, SEI Corp. of Wayne, Pennsylvania, which in 1991 organized a full-time group dedicated to emerging markets investing; Rogers, Casey & Associates, Darien, Connecticut; InterSec Research Corporation, Stamford, Connecticut; the Chicago-based Ennis, Knupp & Associates; Asset Strategy Consulting, West Los Angeles, California; and Wilshire Associates of Santa Monica, California, which operates an emerging markets institute.

When shopping for a money manager, past performance is only one consideration, some consultants say. Other key issues range from evidence of a firm's financial stability to its contacts and experience in the developing world. Such qualities can exist in both specialist boutique firms, if participants have gained a track record elsewhere, or in an emerging markets arm of a larger organization.

Attributes to consider:

- A firm's ability to attract and retain talented investment professionals

- Its ability to provide its own research and analysis
- Its skill at articulating the firm's investment style and demonstrating how it is reflected in its investment activities

Most important, "you have to know how well emerging markets managers are plugged into a market. That's critical when dealing with huge economies, large numbers of people and changing and complex policies," points out Mark Ahern, managing director and chief investment officer, international investment, SEI Corp. To discern managers' familiarity with third world markets, Ahern suggests that potential investors inquire about their brokerage connections in local markets and their knowledge of second- as well as first-tier stocks. Investors could also probe managers' travel schedules, to see how often they visit developing countries and which important people they see.

Take Josephine Jimenez, managing director of Montgomery Asset Management. When visiting a country, this native of the Philippines not only calls on corporate officials, market participants and the like, but also looks in stores to "see what the local people are buying."

In selecting investments, the majority of emerging markets managers employs a top-down macroeconomic approach, reveals a 1992 survey by Kleiman International Consultants Inc. That technique of picking countries first has tended to work well in the developing world. As Fund Research Ltd. in London explains, "when investment sentiment turns positive toward a country, the inflow of money…causes the market to rise and all the constituent shares with it."

Sector and stock picking follow country selection in the top-down approach. After countries' sectoral strengths are assessed, stocks are chosen, often with an eye toward picking the more liquid larger capitalization issues that mirror a country's overall economic growth. These often include shares of the telephone company, a major brewery, banks, and big retailers, as well as equities of cement and textile producers in some countries.

Approaching the Markets Directly

Buying stocks directly in developing markets is the most common approach for many money managers. The technique is not only a pure play in developing markets, but offers investors the widest possible choices from which to tailor a portfolio to their particular needs. But emerging markets are rife with pitfalls, meaning that investors dealing directly in developing country stocks should first be savvy as to market rules and practices.

How should investors approach a market? Peter Douglas, with Latin American Securities Ltd. in London, advises against rushing with sizable sums into an emerging market. Douglas suggests researching a market, then building positions slowly to avoid moving the market against you. Necessary research includes firming up contacts and gathering market information.

While money managers would be expected to have intimate knowledge of markets and their operations, underlying investors such as pension funds or individuals would spend more time selecting vendors such as managers or custodians.

Key points investors need to know include the following:

- Some countries allow only foreign institutional investors, not foreign individuals, to buy shares directly in their markets.

- Some countries require foreigners to apply for permission to bring in money to invest.

- Foreign investment limitations vary from country to country.

- Investors need to determine on a country-by-country basis how and where their stocks are kept for them.

Other issues range from differences in local tax rates to corporate reporting requirements. Since the quality of stock analysis also varies among countries, it becomes useful to assess which organizations provide the best services. A survey of U.K. fund managers by Extel Financial Ltd., London, provides us with the names of some analysts preferred by British investors.

For Southeast Asian emerging markets—including Thailand, Korea, and the Philippines—the five best-rated investment analysts in Extel's 1992 survey, in order, were Baring Securities,

Carr Kitcat & Aitken, Robert Fleming Securities, Hoare Govett Investment Research, and James Capel.

For Latin America, the five highest scorers in Extel's 1992 survey were Baring, S.G. Warburg, Interacciones, Nomura Research Institute, and James Capel.

The top five brokerage firms in Asia, according to *Asia Money & Finance* magazine's 1992 poll, in order, were Baring, Jardine Fleming, W.I.Carr, Barclays de Zoete Wedd, and Peregrine.

Besides conferring with brokers and analysts, emerging markets managers also "kick tires" in faraway countries. In some cases they've trained local brokers as to the stock analysis and types of investments they want. Some managers employ their own or others' databases and, like Key Investors, may create computerized tools as a guiding light.

Montgomery Asset Management uses a three-pronged investment strategy, starting with a top-down quantitative approach to asset allocation. Sector analysis is the second phase, after which, says Josephine Jimenez, the firm zeros in on the most attractively valued companies in those industries.

Montgomery culls its stock ideas in part from its database on over 400 companies, among other sources. Hands-on activities include reclassifying each company's financial data to make it conform to accounting practices in the United States, generally accepted so that Montgomery can then assess companies on a global basis.

When inflation roars, Montgomery attempts to capitalize on the situation. For countries with hyperinflationary economies, including Brazil and Turkey, Montgomery adjusts corporate earnings and other financial data to reflect inflation-adjusted values. Stock portfolios in hyperinflationary markets need to be rebalanced more often than those in other markets, Jimenez maintains.

Trading practices are also adjusted, since inflationary markets swing more dramatically than others, and local interest rates can gyrate widely and rapidly, helping to alter the local stock market's path, according to Jimenez. "For Latin American investments, sometimes I change my limit prices on buy and sell orders three times a day" to capture opportunities or avoid losses. In Turkey, daily stock price moves of 4 to 10 percent are normal; in the markets of Argentina and Brazil, "a stock's price at the end of the week could be 50 percent below its level on Monday," she notes.

Sector Analysis

As emerging markets gain popularity, more investors are finding the need for sector analysis to help steer them to the most promising markets.

Sector analysis identifies specific economic strengths of a country. In emerging economies, these strong points vary dramatically, reflecting countries' diverse underlying political, economic, and social orientations and development as well as their unique demographics.

For instance in India, with its huge 200-million-strong middle class, consumer sectors would be among the more promising investment prospects. However, in neighboring Pakistan the "big push" is "for electrification of villages and infrastructural development," reports Lehman's Daniel Smaller, pointing to possible investment themes in that South Asian land.

In 1992, Bruce Johnson, global research director at Baring Securities Ltd. in London, assessed the manufacturing advantages of emerging markets. Using data mainly from the United Nations Industrial Development Organization, Johnson studied sectors in 110 countries to find out which excelled. Johnson assessed which countries were outstanding in 1989 in which industries, based on their degree of value-added in manufacturing per capita. He also looked at which sectors were growing the fastest on a global basis in terms of value-added in manufacturing, and which sectors were the fastest-growing within a particular country.

To make these determinations, Johnson compared countries' GDP per capita with their level of value-added in manufacturing (MVA) for 16 sectors. He used data for 1975, 1980, and 1988, as well as the amount of MVA change from 1980 to 1989. To evaluate the growth of sectors within a particular economy, Johnson excluded countries with 1 percent or less annual GDP growth from 1980 through 1989. That eliminated much of Latin America.

The study showed Japan and Germany to be among the current leaders, especially in the more advanced manufacturing sectors. Sweden and Ireland also currently score well. In terms of future potential, Korea has a dominant position in more advanced sectors, while, according to Johnson, Sri Lanka, Mauritius, and Egypt "show future potential in the less advanced sectors" such as textiles, food products, and building materials. (See Fig. 2-1.)

What conclusions can be drawn? Sector growth is robust, albeit often from a low base, in several developing countries. The challenge lies in identifying tomorrow's tough international competitors. Although Hong Kong's strength in textile manufacturing is well known, Johnson points out that investors may have missed Sri Lanka's growth from a small base. That's where his analysis can help. As he explains, "assessing the change in the rate of value-added in manufacturing per capita helps find countries that are in their beginning stages of industrialization."

Alternatives to Direct Stock Investments

Buying stocks directly in an emerging market certainly has its advantages. Not only do participants gain a familiarity with a market and its companies, but they may also find this to be an easy way to custom-tailor investments. But this expertise does come at a price. As Mark Ahern of SEI Corporation points out, those who "buy shares directly have to know what they're doing. Not only do these investors face custody costs that are tremendously high, but also high overall transaction costs, a substantial risk of fraud, and hard-to-manage corporate actions.

"Investors seeking to eschew some of the complexities of emerging markets investing can seek simpler solutions. The two most obvious choices are depositary receipts and investment funds, both of which can be appropriate to both individual and institutional investors." For sophisticated institutional investors, synthetic or derivative products could be a consider-

Best of the Best—Present and Future			
Sector	Present 1989 extreme outlier	Future I 1980–89 high MVA growth	Future II 1980–89 high growth relative to GDP
Manufacturing	Belgium Singapore Austria Ireland Japan West Germany	Mauritius Korea Taiwan Thailand Japan	Mauritius Ireland Indonesia Malaysia Japan
Food Products	Iceland Ireland	Sri Lanka Egypt Korea	Sri Lanka Egypt Japan
Textiles	Hong Kong	Iran Korea	Sri Lanka Mauritius
Apparel	Hong Kong Mauritius	Turkey Indonesia Sri Lanka	Turkey Indonesia Sri Lanka
Wood Products	Sweden Finland	Iran Ghana	Indonesia
Paper	Finland Sweden Canada	Korea Taiwan	Korea Taiwan
Industrial Chemicals	Belgium West Germany	Singapore Malaysia Iran	Singapore Malaysia
Petroleum Refining	Saudi Arabia Iran	New Zealand Peru	Austria Netherlands
Plastics	Taiwan Japan	Korea	Korea
Building Materials	Iran Ireland	Iran Egypt Korea	Egypt Korea
Nonferrous Metals	Norway Chile	Iran Egypt	Egypt Korea

Figure 2-1. Analysis of sector strength. (*source: Baring Securities Ltd.*)

(Continued)

Sector	Present 1989 extreme outlier	Future I 1980–89 high MVA growth	Future II 1980–89 high growth relative to GDP
Iron/Steel	Japan Austria	Indonesia Korea	Indonesia Korea
Metal Products	Sweden Israel	Korea	Korea Egypt
Non-Electrical Machinery	Japan West Germany Ireland	Iran Korea	Korea Ireland
Electrical Machinery	Singapore Japan West Germany	Korea Ireland	Korea Ireland
Transportation Equipment	Sweden West Germany	Korea Egypt	Korea Egypt
Professional/ Scientific Equipment	United States Switzerland	Korea Taiwan	Korea Taiwan

Figure 2-1. (*Continued*) Analysis of sector strength. (*source: Baring Securities Ltd.*)

ation when approaching a hard-to-penetrate market or trying to hedge stock holdings. Or, in addition to third world stocks, investors could try the backdoor route: buying shares of companies in developed markets that have sizable third world exposure.

Depositary Receipts

Depositary receipts are securities tradeable in an investor's home country that represent a given number of shares of companies whose underlying stock trades abroad. Depositary receipts are usually listed on an internationally recognized exchange.

Investors can convert these receipts into a company's underlying equities. But the compelling attraction of depositary receipts is that they don't trade in remote countries. Instead, they trade and settle on such major exchanges as New York or London. For issuing companies, depositary receipts provide entrée to new markets, giving them access to capital outside their own territory. Through this indirect channel, issuing companies gain some additional visibility and recognition in the foreign markets, which can lead to higher sales.

American depositary receipts, or ADRs, are by far the most commonly issued version of depositary receipts, according to the New York–based Bankers Trust Co., a depositary bank. Bankers Trust publishes *ADR Universe,* a guide to this market. Bankers Trust looks particularly at sponsored depositary receipts, in which a company appoints one sole depositary bank to issue the security and perform other depositary functions. At year-end 1992, 96 percent of sponsored depositary receipts were settled in the United States, according to Bankers Trust.

However, a growing number of companies are also issuing DRs elsewhere. Those issued in Europe are called either *European* or *international depositary receipts,* while the versions issued in the United States and some other countries are called *global depositary receipts* or *GDRs.*

ADRs now have a substantial history. As Bankers Trust Co. describes, their debut came in 1927, in response to a law passed in England that prohibited British companies from registering shares overseas without using a British-based transfer agent. Since "U.K. shares were physically not allowed to leave the U.K., a U.S. instrument had to be created; it was called an ADR. The ADR business assumed its present form in 1955, [when the] Securities and Exchange Commission established its Form S12 for registering all depositary receipt programs," Bankers Trust explains.

The supply of depositary receipts is increasing, especially from companies in the developing world. (See Fig. 2-2.) Bankers Trust reports that the total number of depositary receipt issuers rose from to 1017 at year-end 1992, from 886 at the end of 1990. As of the end of 1992, 48 countries had at least one company that had issued DRs.

While the majority of these issuers were companies in developed nations, the fastest growth is coming from the developing

Country	Number of issues 1992	Number of issues 1993	Percent of change
Argentina	0	7	N/A
Australia	208	190	− 8.65
Austria	1	4	300.00
Belgium	2	2	0.00
Bermuda	9	11	22.22
Brazil	0	1	N/A
Botswana	1	1	0.00
Canada	1	0	− 100.00
Chile	1	3	200.00
Denmark	2	2	0.00
El Salvador	1	1	0.00
Finland	6	6	0.00
France	31	26	− 16.13
Germany	25	25	0.00
Gibraltar	0	1	N/A
Greece	2	3	50.00
Hong Kong	35	31	− 11.43
Hungary	0	1	N/A
India	0	1	N/A
Indonesia	1	1	0.00
Ireland	8	9	12.50
Israel	6	5	− 16.67
Italy	22	22	0.00
Jamaica	1	0	− 100.00
Japan	150	148	− 1.33
Korea	1	5	400.00
Luxembourg	3	4	33.33
Malaysia	9	15	66.67
Mexico	25	44	76.00
Netherlands	22	24	9.09
New Guinea	2	2	0.00

Figure 2-2. Depositary receipts breakdown by country.
(*Source: Bankers Trust Company, January 1993.*)

Country	Number of issues 1992	Number of issues 1993	Percent of change
New Zealand	3	5	66.67
Norway	14	13	− 7.14
Philippines	2	4	100.00
Portugal	1	1	0.00
Singapore	16	14	− 12.50
South Africa	97	92	− 5.15
Spain	9	10	11.11
Sweden	16	13	− 18.75
Switzerland	4	7	75.00
Taiwan	0	3	N/A
Thailand	2	4	100.00
Turkey	0	1	N/A
United Kingdom	234	232	− 0.85
United States	14	12	− 14.29
Venezuela	4	9	125.00
Zambia	1	1	0.00
Zimbabwe	1	1	0.00

Figure 2-2. (*Continued*) Depositary receipts breakdown by country. (*Source: Bankers Trust Company, January 1993.*)

world. In a breakdown by country, Mexico ranked fifth out of 48 countries, with 44 separate depositary receipt programs as of December 1992. The American depositary receipt of Telefonos de Mexico (Telmex) has greater trading volume in New York than Telmex's actual stock has in Mexico. The ADRs of Telmex and the British-based Glaxo are among the most actively traded issues on the New York Stock Exchange.

Among their risks, DRs can certainly be volatile. The price quoted by a broker or market maker is determined by the price of the underlying security, along with the foreign exchange conversion. That means that DR investors should track the direction of their own country's stock market as well as that of the country that had issued the DR. They should also take into account the expected movement in currency. From the American perspective, for example, a rise in the U.S. dollar against the British pound would negatively affect the price of Glaxo's ADR.

On the bright side, DRs have ample attractions, including the fact that they pay interest or dividends in local currency. Investors would find them advantageous in circumstances where they face restrictions on foreign ownership, or when an investor, such as a pension fund, is prohibited from buying foreign shares. DRs also are advantageous in circumstances where settlement practices make one market preferable to another, when foreign exchange rules or rates pose a problem, or—as may sometimes be the case—if an investor prefers a registered share to a bearer share.

DRs are also cheaper than stock purchased directly in a foreign market, considering the higher brokerage fees, taxes, and custody in the foreign country. As Bankers Trust spells out, "When an ordinary share is purchased abroad by a U.S. investor, the investor must pay a safekeeping charge on top of commissions of approximately 1520 basis points per year, charged monthly or quarterly. In addition, there is a fee charged by the custodian bank in the home country of the issuer ranging from $25 to $50 per trade."

Who buys DRs? Mainly institutional investors seeking to diversify their portfolio. Lack of knowledge about the instruments has limited participation by individual investors, according to Peter Duggan, assistant vice president in the ADR department of Bankers Trust. He notes that no more than 20 percent of outstanding ADRs are in the hands of individuals.

Depositary receipts can be purchased via brokers, and their prices are published by exchanges.

Investment Funds

Investing in funds is a convenient way to penetrate the emerging markets. A single outlay gives participants a diversified portfolio. Approved funds can also provide easier access to a market that is otherwise highly restricted. And investors can choose from a wide array of emerging markets funds.

In its debut edition in 1992, *The Wilson Directory of Emerging*

Market Funds, published by Wilson Emerging Market Funds Research Inc., Providence, Rhode Island, profiled 460 equities-oriented funds with assets of $22 billion (in U.S. terms). Most of these funds would be available to both foreigners and local investors. By June 1993, Ian M. Wilson, president of Wilson Emerging Market Funds Research, had uncovered 2119 funds for emerging markets, partly as he discovered many more funds for domestic investors in these countries.

Of the 460 funds originally profiled, about 65 percent are closed-end, meaning that they have a limited number of outstanding shares and often trade on an exchange. The remaining 35 percent represent open-end mutual funds that can expand with investor demand. While most of the 460 funds are single-country in scope, 46 invest globally in emerging markets, 67 are regional Asian funds, 24 target Latin America, 6 are African, and 3 are European regional. Of the countries covered separately in the book, Mexico, with 78 funds, was by far the leader; followed by Thailand and Korea, each with 34 funds; Pakistan and Taiwan, both with 26; and China with 22.

While many funds are open to both institutional and individual investors, about 10 to 15 percent of the funds require a minimum outlay of $100,000. That would put them out of the reach of most individuals, Wilson points out.

One of the attractions of funds is that they are a cheaper way of buying a diversified portfolio of stocks than buying the shares individually. Normally, closed-end funds also outperform a market index or similar mutual fund, says Thomas Herzfeld, author of *Herzfeld's Guide to Closed-End Funds* (McGraw-Hill). Since closed-end funds can be leveraged, Herzfeld explains, they can buy more stock than unleveraged funds. "Since many closed-end funds are leveraged, and markets generally rise over time, the average closed-end fund has outperformed the average market index," he says.

"Bear in mind that emerging markets funds are typically unleveraged. They should tend to outperform index funds with similar objectives, because managers don't have to worry about net redemptions and sales."

Emerging markets funds listed in London are more likely to be using leverage than those listed in the United States.

Although newly issued closed-end funds often trade at a premium to the fund's net asset value (NAV), that initial premium often dissolves into a discount. At that point, investors improve their risk/reward relationship, says Herzfeld, who is also president of Thomas J. Herzfeld Advisors Inc., Miami, Florida. As he explains, discounts provide a form of leverage, boosting the fund's price in a rising market and cushioning it in declining markets. Over time, a deeply discounted price is, like a stretched elastic band, likely to contract. In a declining market, this contraction would help to offset losses in the fund's underlying assets.

In 1992 many funds were trading at a discount. According to William McBride, international editor of Lipper Analytical Services, based in Summit, New Jersey, at year-end 1992, 139 funds were trading at average discounts of 17.6 percent to the NAV, among country and regional funds for which complete pricing data were available, while 25 traded at an average premium of 10.1 percent. However, 1993 brought a substantial narrowing of these discounts. As interest heightened in emerging markets, more investors seized the opportunity to buy funds at attractive prices.

Funds listed outside the United States have tended to have deeper discounts and more modest premiums than have American funds. Reviewing four Chilean funds, the London-based Fund Research Ltd. found, for example, that the U.S.-registered Chile Fund Inc. was trading in August 1992 at a discount of 3.9 percent, compared with discounts of 27.9 percent for the Five Arrows Chile Fund, 34.5 percent for Genesis Chile Fund, and 30.6 percent for the GT Chile Growth Fund.

Why the difference? Supply/demand and regulatory reasons play a part. While retail investor interest is said to be stronger in the United States, there are fewer of these funds within U.S. borders than offshore. In addition, operational practices and taxation rules have influenced investors. In the United States, closed-end funds typically distribute income and capital gains, a practice that attracts many investors and keeps discounts narrow, says Herzfeld. Since funds subject to U.K. tax codes retain their capital gains rather than distribute them, for many investors the U.K. funds become less attractive.

The U.S. government has seized on this difference in distributional practice. To discourage Americans from selecting foreign funds to avoid capital gains tax, the government created the passive foreign investment company rule. It essentially treats an increase in the value of these funds as taxable gains, regardless of whether the gain was actually realized, says Lipper's McBride. Uncertainty surrounding the effects of the rule has been a deterrent to non-U.S.-fund investing. In turn, lower demand contributes to the illiquidity and wider discounts in those non-U.S. funds.

With open-end mutual funds, the concern centers on the effect of redemptions. If, for example, a country's market begins to sink, surging demand for fund redemptions can force fund mangers to sell stock to pay investors. Such intensified selling would erode the market further, especially in thinly traded emerging markets. Some funds have addressed this problem by limiting possible redemptions. Institutional investors may consider using commingled funds as an option to an exclusively managed account.

Taking Direct Stakes through Funds

Institutional investors or wealthy individuals can most easily take direct stakes in companies via investment funds. So far, the number of these vehicles has been limited. Impediments have included the regulatory restraints against direct investments in some countries, as well as the difficulties involved in finding attractive unlisted companies in the third world. Ian Wilson, of Wilson Emerging Market Funds Research, counts 180 to 200 funds that take direct stakes in emerging markets companies. He estimates that another 40 to 50 emerging markets funds allow about 10 percent or more of assets to be invested directly.

According to Wilson, about 90 percent of the direct investment funds are located in Asia, with the remainder in Eastern Europe, Africa, and Latin America. Asian direct investment funds have attracted significant sums from Japan, Wilson reports. While many of the Asian funds are run from Hong Kong, Singapore, or Tokyo, they invest in companies through-

out the continent. Direct investment funds often lock in participants for a set number of years. In return, investors hope for
above-average and more stable returns than they can garner
from emerging stock markets.

Why better results? With fewer sources of capital at their disposal than public listed companies, private firms typically sell at
lower valuations, which, proponents say, ultimately means
higher returns for investors. The China Investment &
Development Fund Ltd., managed by KB China Management
Ltd., in Hong Kong, offers a case in point. This fund aims to
take direct stakes in private companies at much lower multiples
of earnings than those of listed Chinese 8 shares. China's "stock
markets are disgracefully unattractive," Kenneth King of
Kleinwort Benson Investment Management Ltd. in London
declared in early 1993. "This fund is a way to get exposure to a
hugely attractive economy at attractive multiples."

In spring 1993, Emerging Markets Corp., Washington, D.C.,
planned to begin marketing a fund for institutional investors
that would take direct stakes in companies in developing markets. The globally diversified fund would start with at least
$300 million in assets and would have an eight-year life.
(Eventually, the firm would set up a separate fund for investing
in stocks.) By targeting the perceived best companies and countries, the fund expects to log an annual return in excess of 20
percent, said EMC's chairman Moeen Qureshi (who was inter-
viewed before he became caretaker Prime Minister of Pakistan
in July 1993). "We offer lower risk and higher return potential"
than stock investors can expect, he held. "The IFC's index can't
be as selective as we can with our investments. The EMC's
vehicle will target established companies with good track
records, and at the appropriate time, in perhaps three or four
years, exit the investment."

Initially, the EMC's fund expected to consider investments in
Indonesia, Thailand, China, Malaysia, Chile, Mexico, and
Argentina. Other countries, including those of Eastern Europe,
would also be prospects, Qureshi had said.

Fund managers must have an intimate knowledge of their markets to find the best investments and to obtain regulatory
approvals to invest, said Qureshi. His background includes some

30 years with the International Monetary Fund and the World Bank. Before joining Emerging Markets Corp., he was the World Bank's senior vice president for operations; earlier, he was executive vice president of the IFC. Donald Roth, EMC's managing partner, was treasurer of the World Bank and, before that, chairman and chief executive officer of Merrill Lynch Europe.

Synthetics/Derivatives

When a seemingly attractive market is hard to penetrate for regulatory reasons or because of supply limitations, institutional investors can consider synthetic or derivative products. These vehicles can also be used to hedge a portfolio. While they are still novelties in emerging markets, some experts believe that the popularity of synthetics and derivatives should rise over time as their availability expands. James Chau, a senior managing director of M.D. Sass Investors Services Inc., New York, also sees cost advantages to using synthetics or derivatives, when everything from custody services to brokerage commissions in the developing world is taken into account.

With derivative or synthetic products, investors don't own underlying shares. Instead they purchase an option or a warrant on stock, or engage in a swap transaction. The option or warrant is on an index based on the value of a basket of stocks, or even a single stock. Typically, the resulting derivative trades over the counter, but it may also be listed on an exchange.

The investor profits in this transaction if the index on the underlying shares is higher than the exercise price of the call option at expiration date. In structuring the transaction, the agent bank or brokerage firm earns a placement fee of typically between 2 to 5 percent on the value of the deal. The counterparty that owns the stock profits from the premium paid him initially, minus the difference he has to pay out between the exercise price of the call option and the price of the index at the expiration date of the option.

Investors can also buy put options as a hedge against their portfolio, when they are bearish on the market. In a swap transaction, investors exchange the total return on a market index, presumably one in a developed market, such as the Standard &

Poor's 500 Stock Index for the total return of the Malaysian, Korean, or some other developing market's index. These deals are also arranged by an agent bank or brokerage firm. An expert on the use of synthetics and derivatives, Chau of M.D. Sass, notes that swap transactions have so far been more commonly used than options and warrants. "A swap transaction is a lot more popular because of the simplicity and the large size of transactions that can be arranged," he explains. Moreover, "people understand the concept more readily because interest rate swaps, now a $3 to $5 trillion market, have been around for years. The mechanism is similar for both the equities and the fixed-income markets."

Fees paid for options/warrants versus swap transactions vary according to the size of transaction. The choice between synthetics/derivatives and swaps depends on how much of a market commitment investors want, in terms of size and duration of transaction. While a swap doesn't require any cash outlay, investors would have to purchase an option or a warrant. The duration of a swap transaction tends to be longer than that of an option that can be renewed every six months.

Chief among the risks of these instruments is the possibility that the counterparty in the deal will be unable to pay monies owed. To avoid that potential problem, Chau advises investors to check the creditworthiness of the potential counterparty and the agent bank, when it serves as principal/counterparty in the transaction.

Synthetic/derivative offerings can be arranged in most of the Latin American and Asian markets, including China, according to Chau. However, they would be appropriate only for sophisticated institutional investors.

Backdoor Exposure to Developing Markets

To obtain exposure to the developing world, investors don't have to rely on third world markets. They can also buy stocks, such as Coca-Cola or Pepsi, with ample exposure to emerging countries. On the downside, some investors pooh-pooh the technique as a lazy investor's strategy for the third world, and one with lower potential, at least in the near term. In a hypothetical example, even if U.S. company X has a 50 percent exposure to Argentina's economy, its stock investors certainly won't fare anywhere near as well as investors who bought major Argentine companies in 1991, the year the market rocketed 392 percent in U.S. dollar terms.

Even the stocks of multinationals are heavily influenced by the market where they're listed. But as Giles Keating, chief economist of Credit Suisse First Boston in London, points out, emerging markets stocks can soar to "crazy premiums." He sees an attractive medium-term play in investing in companies in the developed world with ample third world exposure. While not a "pure play" on emerging markets, he considers this backdoor route to be an additional approach to emerging markets. "A company like Pepsi" can reap high returns "if it doubles the number of markets it sells into without having to invest in new products or develop a brand name," says Keating. "With Telmex [Telefonos de Mexico] you don't get that. Although Telmex gives exposure to growth in Mexico, it's a narrow play on one developing economy. It's not giving investors the benefit of taking established technology and a brand name to a whole new market."

Investors would find no dearth of multinationals to choose from. In one illustration, according to the U.S. Commerce Department, direct foreign investment in China's Guangdong province during 1991 amounted to $1.82 billion, up 24.9 percent over 1990, according to Guangdong's 1991 statistical bulletin.

A December 1992 article in *The New York Times* cited the extent to which foreign-branded soft drinks have infiltrated Vietnam. According to the *Times,* "Coca-Cola, Pepsi, 7-Up, and Sprite are being sold openly almost everywhere in Vietnam, north and south, city and countryside, smuggled in across the porous border from Cambodia."

How much of a portfolio should be devoted to emerging markets exposure? Keating suggests that "according to conventional portfolio theory, you might want to have a portfolio that was roughly proportional to the involvement of these companies in those emerging markets." Attractive companies should have a "substantial and rapidly growing proportion there." In his view, "the corporations that will do best are the ones that have a rolling strategy of responding to" this opportunity that "will be with us for decades. The corporations that succeed in this environment," he maintains, "will be those that continue to move and set up to take advantage" of the profit opportunities afforded by growth in the third world.

Nonetheless, picking companies would require attention to local market or economic conditions in the developed world. For instance, although Germany's Volkswagen and Britain's Imperial Chemical are well known for their international exposure, Keating pointed out early in 1993 that it was probably not then a good time to be buying such cyclical stocks.

Handling the Currency Exposure

Alan J. Brown, managing director and chief investment officer of Pan Agora Asset Management Ltd. in London, voices an oft-heard view about how to handle the foreign exchange aspect of emerging markets investing. "Think about currencies for about two minutes and then forget about them," Brown holds. Not only is currency hedging extremely difficult in developing markets, it is also seemingly unnecessary in light of investors' modest exposures. If, for example, a pension fund invested 3 percent of its assets in a half-dozen emerging markets, probably "no more than 0.5 percent of assets would be invested in any one of them," he says. That slight exposure wouldn't "impact a fund's overall volatility."

Although a falling currency hurts returns for foreigners invested in that country, the declining currency won't necessarily hurt the stock market. In 1992, for instance, Sweden's and the United Kingdom's stock markets soared after the Swedish Kroner and the British pound dropped. "When the currency and interest rates fall, the economy gets a breath of fresh air," Brown explains. It's not surprising that the stock markets would respond to such a net stimulus. Brown concludes: "If you do have a big currency devaluation, its effect could be offset by stock market appreciation."

Currency hedging, especially through the foreign exchange forward market, is possible in some third world countries. But it is likely to be expensive and can run counter to investors' objectives, points out David Wilson, a joint author of *Corporate Financial Risk Management* (Wiley and Sons). Because of the thin liquidity in these currency markets, a portfolio investor may not be able to match the maturity of the currency liability with the maturity of the stock portfolio. Typically, six months is the longest maturity investors can get from a currency market in a developing country, if even that is available, Wilson says.

Investors could also run into a change of regulations governing foreign exchange that could make unwinding a currency hedge extremely expensive, if not impossible. That very situation arose in Mexico in the 1980s, he recalls. Some U.S. money-center banks speculated heavily against the peso. Exploiting their customer bases, these non-Mexican banks sold pesos forward and, in turn, bought them forward at large profits, often from multinational corporations with Mexican operations. In doing so, the banks expected to earn a spread and/or a speculative profit.

To stem this speculation, the Bank of Mexico (the country's central bank) imposed a new regulation: Foreign banks could not receive Mexican peso payments unless those payments came from each foreign bank's own correspondent bank. Wilson, who is also a vice president in the New York office of GiroCredit Bank, reports that several U.S. banks resultingly incurred foreign exchange losses as they unwound their forward contracts. The unwinding involved selling pesos back to their multinational clients and purchasing the same amount of them from their own correspondent bank. Involved U.S. banks had to settle the dollar difference between the original forward contract and the new spot contracts with their multinational clients. They, in turn, had to sell the pesos in the spot market at whatever rate they could get from a Mexican bank. By changing the rules in the middle of the game, the Bank of Mexico effectively negated the value of the multinational corporations' hedges. Many of the involved banks and corporations incurred losses from unwinding these hedges.

According to Wilson, Venezuelan authorities followed Mexico's example. But Venezuelan regulations were more flexible, in that they distinguished between banks that speculated heavily against the Bolivar and those that used Bolivar accounts for routine commercial transactions.

Investors would certainly not want to confront any such complications. Rather than getting caught in a currency imbroglio, investors would be better off simply diversifying their portfolio as a natural hedge. As Wilson points out, diversification helps to control foreign exchange risk, since "some currencies will be rising in value at the same time as others will be falling."

3

The Best-Performing Money Managers

Recognizing new markets as fertile territory for value investing, the best-performing emerging markets managers were, not surprisingly, some of the earliest pioneers in this sector. Investing before the crowd poured in, they scooped up some of the best bargains and then waited—in some cases, not even as long as originally expected—until the market at large discovered these jewels. While this strategy was risky, it ultimately brought handsome returns.

Take the performance of the Templeton Emerging Markets Fund Inc., managed by the Templeton Worldwide emerging markets group in Hong Kong. For the three years ending with 1992, that fund posted a net asset value total return of 100.56 percent in U.S. dollar terms, according to Lipper Analytical Services, Summit, New Jersey, Templeton's performance compares with a negative 17.3 percent cumulative total return of the IFC's Composite Index over the period. The second best performer was the Templeton Emerging Markets Investment Trust, with its net asset value total return of 80.57 percent over the three years ending in December 1992.

Other stellar performers were the Genesis Emerging Markets Fund Ltd., managed by Genesis Investment Management Ltd., with its 67.25 percent gain, the Emerging Markets Growth Fund, managed by Capital International Inc., with its 66.91 percent net asset value total return, and the Emerging Markets Strategic Fund and the Emerging Markets Investors Fund, both managed by Emerging Markets Investors Corporation, with returns of 65.56 and 65.91 percent, respectively.

Top-performing managers were assessed according to their performance with global emerging markets funds. A three-year measurement period was used, because of the scarcity of global emerging markets funds with track records dating back even that far. This assessment reviewed the performance of 14 such global funds, with most data provided by Lipper Analytical Services. The London-based Micropal Ltd. also contributed some performance information.

Data show that the best-performing funds were all closed-end vehicles targeted to institutional investors. These funds were not subject to redemptions on demand, and if managers chose, could be fully invested. Naturally, investment styles varied from firm to firm. The common thread among the winners was a focus on value investing. Here's how the premier players addressed the opportunities in emerging markets.

Templeton Worldwide Inc.

From his headquarters in Hong Kong, J. Mark Mobius, head of the Templeton Worldwide emerging markets group, is demonstrating how attractive emerging markets can be. Its Templeton Emerging Markets Fund Inc. posted a net asset value total return of 100.56 percent over the three years ending in December 1992. The fund's performance trounced its competitors' offerings and soundly beat the second best performer, the Templeton Emerging Markets Investment Trust, with its comparable 80.57 percent return over the period.

How has Templeton fared so phenomenally well? Through careful research, adherence to a bottom-up, value-oriented investment approach, and its patient stock buy-and-hold process, all of which have paid off, especially in 1991. That year, the now six-year-old $226 million closed-end Templeton Emerging Markets Fund posted a 78.5 percent return. In other years, its respectable gains included: 29.2 percent in 1988, 47 percent in 1989, 2.2 percent in 1990, and 9.3 percent in 1992.

Savvy stock picking led Templeton to such winners as the Philippine Commercial International Bank, which gained 480 percent for the Templeton Emerging Markets Fund since it was first purchased in June 1987, as well as the Philippine Long Distance Telephone Company, which delivered a 360 percent return since it was first bought in March 1987, the firm estimated in early 1993. On average, 70 percent of the fund's stock investments have gained, while 30 percent produced losses.

Exposure to hot markets has certainly contributed to the returns. At its peak in 1991, the U.S.-registered Templeton Emerging Markets Fund had a 50 percent weighting in Latin American companies, including about 23 percent in Argentina and a similar 23 percent exposure to Mexico. That year the Argentine market rocketed almost 400 percent in dollar terms, while Mexico's soared about 100 percent, according to the IFC's price indexes for those markets.

At year-end 1992, the Templeton Emerging Markets Fund was invested in 17 countries, which was less than its allowable universe of 22 markets. But the firm has been expanding its horizons. In 1992 it invested in Sri Lanka's market for the first time, and, among its more exotic exposures was its 0.04 percent weighting in Swaziland. At the end of 1992 the Templeton Emerging Markets Fund was about 40 percent invested in Asia, with other major exposures being in Turkey, Greece, Portugal, Brazil, and Mexico. By industry, the fund's five largest sector investments—in banking, telecommunications, metals and mining, food and household products, and automobiles—accounted for 40.88 percent of holdings, while its 10 biggest stock holdings were 28.71 percent of total share investments.

Stock picking is a disciplined but flexible process for Templeton's emerging markets group, a unit of Templeton Worldwide Inc. The team, headed by Mobius, has four dedicated emerging markets analysts located in Hong Kong and Singapore, and it can also access the 23 other country-specific and industry analysts in the overall Templeton organization..

Although methodical, stock selection for the emerging markets team has been anything but humdrum. Over the years since the Templeton Emerging Markets Fund debuted, Mobius has had to pioneer investing in some markets, and in some cases "we've opened them up as we've gone along," he recalls. Visiting companies in remote locales has also been an adventure. In search of corporate information, Mobius has flown over mountains in small planes and ridden up rivers into jungle terrain.

His "war stories" include being in the Philippines during the attempted coup d'etat in December 1990. "We were stuck in a hotel for three days as bullets were flying outside," he recalls of the hair-raising saga. But once the stock exchanges had reopened, Mobius quickly capitalized on this "buying opportunity" by grabbing attractive stocks whose prices had fallen amid the political maelstrom. Among the stocks picked: those of Philex Mining Corp., Philippine Commercial International Bank, and the Philippine Long Distance Telephone Company.

The firm's basic investment approach calls for finding "bargain" stocks—issues with low prices relative to their long-term earnings potential or real book value. The firm buys these stocks cheaply, then waits for the market to discover them. This may mean holding them for at least two market cycles. "Once we make a long-term decision to buy a stock, it doesn't pay to move to another one, despite what may happen to it in the short term," Mobius explains. "If the company's long-term prospects remain intact, we hold its stock."

The group won't sell holdings unless they can be replaced by something at least 50 percent cheaper. That way, Mobius says, "you avoid selling things that you shouldn't."

Templeton generally finds attractive companies through two main sources: its worldwide network of research sources, including brokers, bankers, independent research firms, and other contacts, and screening of its database of over 2000 companies in the emerging markets. The firm assesses whether stocks are cheap according to: their own history, their overall market, their industry globally, and as compared with other stocks in the database.

In making these assessments, analysts look at a company's past performance as well as review five years' projected data. Among the factors they consider are a company's sales growth, new product introductions, the quality of management, financial restructurings, adjusted net asset values, global supply and demand for products, as well as the currency movements in a country, Templeton says. Companies that surface as ideal investments are placed on the "bargain list" from which the firm picks additional investments. Recommendations all come with pricing buy limits. While the ultimate decision to purchase stocks rests with Mobius, he says his actions reflect the analytical skills and processes of his entire team.

A well-known personality in emerging markets investing, Mobius is, in effect, carrying the pioneering torch once lighted by Sir John Templeton. In the 1960s, Templeton, now chairman emeritus of Templeton Worldwide Inc., became renowned for investing in Japan's market while it was still emerging. Remaining on the forefront of global investing, Templeton was among those in the mid-1980s that bid to become the manager of the Emerging Markets Growth Fund, the first globally invested emerging markets fund created by the IFC. Although Capital International was eventually chosen, Templeton pursued the idea by forming its own fund. It was the first publicly listed global emerging markets fund.

To take charge of the new venture, the firm tapped Mobius, a German raised in America who had then been living in Asia for more than 20 years. Mobius, who holds a Ph.D. in economics and political science from the Massachusetts Institute of Technology, had come to Hong Kong in the 1960s to work as a research scientist for Monsanto Overseas Enterprises Company. Later he formed a business consulting firm, before joining the securities firm of Vickers da Costa in 1980. At the time Templeton beckoned, Mobius was president of International Investment Trust Company Limited in Taipei, Taiwan.

Over his now six years at Templeton, Mobius has seen the firm's emerging markets assets swell from $100 million in 1987 to about $1.3 billion today. The number of emerging markets funds and accounts has also mushroomed. In addition to its original Templeton Emerging Markets Fund, Templeton Investment Management (Hong Kong) Ltd. today also manages 10 other emerging markets funds, including the Templeton Emerging Markets Investment Trust plc; the Asia Development Equity Fund for Japanese investors; the Templeton Asia Fund (also for Japanese investors); an Indonesia country fund; two open-ended funds, the Templeton Developing Markets Trust for

American investors and the Templeton Emerging Markets Fund for Canadian investors; three funds that are part of an umbrella family of funds registered in Luxembourg, and a series of com- mingled funds for institutional investors. As of April 1993 the emerging markets group was also handling six separately man- aged accounts of $50 million or more each.

As assets under management have increased, the emerging markets group has become more "systematic" in its investing, Mobius says. "When you have more money to invest, you get better at it." Increased assets have also helped to lower the costs of investing and have encouraged vendors, such as brokers, to enhance their services. As Mobius sees it, all these factors have contributed to the group's performance.

Looking ahead, an enthusiastic Mobius foresees more oppor- tunities unfolding in emerging markets—in locales such as Africa, Eastern Europe, and Russia. As more countries and com- panies reach for investors' capital, he sees investment barriers crumbling and more shares becoming available. As the embry- onic phase of emerging markets investments ends, Mobius believes that "we're on the threshold of a whole new era" in third world investing.

Genesis Investment Management Limited

In 1989, four British investment professionals with a longtime background in Asian investing decided to expand their hori- zons. Seeing opportunities ballooning around the world, the quartet wanted to apply their knowledge to new markets, to "invest in structural change and economic development." The four, Jeremy Paulson-Ellis, Richard Carss, Anthony Newsome, and Mark Lightbown, created Genesis Investment Management Limited. Partners say it was the first U.K.-based money manage- ment firm specializing in emerging markets.

Today the firm has six investment directors, having subse- quently added Jonathan Points and Karen Baldwin in the main London office. Partners together hold a 33 percent stake in the firm, with the remaining equity held by outside institutions and wealthy individuals. At year-end 1992, Genesis was managing a total of $646.8 million. That included $264.8 million in separately managed accounts for (mainly U.S.) institutional investors, as well as the assets of five listed emerging markets funds and the $21 million Genesis Japan Emerging Growth Investments plc.

The firm's four closed-end emerging markets funds are: the Genesis Chile Fund Limited; the Genesis Malaysia Maju Fund Limited; the Genesis Condor Fund Limited, which is a Latin American regional fund; and the firm's flagship Genesis Emerging Markets Fund Limited, which invests in emerging markets globally.

Debuting in July 1989, the Genesis Emerging Markets Fund was the firm's first offering. And thus far its performance has done the firm proud. Over a three-year period ending in 1992, the net asset value total return of the globally invested $102.9 million (year-end 1992) Genesis Emerging Markets Fund Limited was up 67.25 percent in U.S. dollar terms, according to Lipper Analytical Services. The fund thus ranked third among globally invested emerging markets funds in existence over that period.

Why has Genesis done so well? Principals cite both their managerial style as well as their extensive backgrounds in developing countries.

Operationally, the firm employs what its chairman Jeremy Paulson-Ellis calls a "lateral" structure. Each of the six partners does his or her own research. In addition, each partner serves as either the lead manager or the backup manager for every country the firm invests in and for each client relationship; in turn, managers have complete authority over the investment decisions in the countries they oversee. To avoid becoming too focused on any one region, principals all follow markets in different parts of the world.

Genesis selects investments through a bottom-up stock-picking approach. In its hunt for value stocks, the firm often seeks candidates in perceived attractive sectors, such as telecommunications, infrastructural development, financial services, even soft drinks. Principals expand on or gain ideas by visiting their markets at least twice a year to meet a range of contacts, from brokers to corporate executives. After choice stocks have been identified, they're compared on a global basis, using Genesis' proprietary database of some 300 emerging markets companies. To keep global portfolios broadly diversified, the firm limits every country's exposure to 15 percent of the fund's assets at cost (book value). As of February 1993, the Genesis Emerging Markets Fund was invested in 24 countries.

Collectively, Genesis' partners claim to have 90 years' experience with developing countries/markets, which they feel gives them a competitive edge. Paulson-Ellis, for instance, began to focus on the Japanese market in 1968, when it was still a backwater. Richard Carss worked in investment management in South Africa from 1967 to 1970. In 1970 he joined the brokerage firm of Vickers da Costa, as head of its international desk covering Southeast Asia and Brazil. Carss, who was the managing director of Templeton Investment Management in London before establishing Genesis, is today lead manager of the Genesis Emerging Markets Fund.

Partners say their experience has already been paying off handsomely. Their favorite illustration: the 1989 investment in Embotelladora Andina, the Coca-Cola bottling company for the Santiago region of Chile. While in Chile in 1989, Carss and several other Genesis partners had their curiosity piqued when they saw crates containing full Coke bottles stacked on the street corners of Santiago. Retailers would come to these corners to collect Coke supplies for their stores. Intrigued by this distribution process, the money managers paid a call on the bottling company. They found that Andina was indeed doing a robust business. The company already had a market share of over 60 percent, was growing at about a 25 percent rate, and had just finished a $20 million modernization of its facilities.

Although local brokers discouraged Genesis from investing in Andina, the firm recognized the signs—including rising personal incomes—that showed that Chile's soft drink business was about to surge. "Experience had taught that when a country reached a certain income level, soft drinks changed from luxury to commonplace items," explains partner Anthony Newsome. Andina was shrewdly gearing up to accommodate this rising thirst for Coke in Chile. For its Chile Fund, Genesis quickly bought 5 percent of Andina's stock, which was then selling for only four times earnings. Over the next three years the stock's value appreciated 25-fold.

The Genesis Emerging Markets Fund has benefited from a number of stellar investments. Among the more memorable: the holdings in Greece's Ergo Bank, whose value more than quadrupled between the time Genesis bought it in mid-1989 and when it sold most of it in May 1990. In addition, the peak price of Mexico's Cifra was 11 times higher than what Genesis initially paid for it in 1989. At its height, the stock price of Argentina's Perez Companc had catapulted to seven times what Genesis paid for it in 1989, reports Anthony Newsome.

Of course "we do make mistakes," says Carss, citing the firm's 1989 investment in Korea Long Term Credit Bank (KLTCB). Genesis bought the stock at a premium over what Koreans had to pay, since at the time only a few shares were available for purchase by foreigners. But eventually the premium on Korean stocks shrank. By early 1993, Genesis had still not broken even on the outlay.

As it happens, the Genesis Emerging Markets Fund performed best in 1991, the year a number of Latin American markets exploded. At its peak in early 1992, the fund had an approximately 55 percent exposure to Latin America. By year-end 1992, that weighting had dropped to to 40.58 percent but was still the largest regional bet. At year-end 1992, the fund's largest country exposure, of 17.71 percent, was in Chile, and its single biggest investment, of 16.65 percent of the fund, was in the Genesis Chile Fund Ltd. The fund's second largest bet was a much smaller 3.54 percent weighting in the Philippine Long Distance Telephone Company.

Why such a big investment in the Chile fund? In 1989, Genesis initially put 12 percent of the fund in this holding as a way of gaining exposure to the then cheap but highly attractive Chilean market. Genesis formed its own country fund for Chile, because of the difficulties foreigners faced in accessing the Chilean market. Although in early 1993 the Genesis Chile Fund was trading at a deep discount to its net asset value, the total return on the fund's underlying assets had exceeded 250 percent since its 1989 launch, the firm said.

Genesis invests small amounts in developed markets—such

as Hong Kong's and even those of the United Kingdom and the United States—but only in a disciplined way. Partners say they buy companies in developed markets only if more than 50 percent of their sales and/or profits come from third world countries, or more than 50 percent of their assets are located there. On this basis, the Genesis Emerging Markets Fund has been investing in the Hong Kong-listed Liu Chong Hing Investments Ltd., Tian An China Ltd., and Tomei Industries, all of which have substantial business dealings in China.

Looking forward, Genesis expects to pursue its quest for value stocks partly by continuing to explore new markets and by probing deeper into more familiar ones. In 1992 the fund's more unusual investments included: a 2.93 percent exposure to the Zambian copper industry; its investment in six stocks in Botswana, for a total 2.26 percent market exposure; a 0.73 percent weighting in The Vietnam Fund Limited; and exposure to Papua New Guinea, where it invested 0.34 percent in retailer Collins & Leahy Holdings Ltd. and 1.32 percent in Oil Search Ltd. In 1993, the fund began to invest for the first time in the markets of Bangladesh and Mauritius—in the latter case, through the new Mauritius Fund.

But however adventuresome its investment practices may be, the firm is not looking to grow large and shed its original structure as a boutique. It also doesn't plan to slacken up on client services. "We want to keep the firm as a small partnership," says Anthony Newsome. "The amount of assets under management shouldn't unduly strain our structure, individuals, or management style." The firm's business limitations include a ceiling of 6 client relationships per manager and a total of 36 client relationships—which includes public funds under management as well as separately managed accounts. With 15 client relationships in early 1993, the firm was in no danger of soon exceeding its quota. The firm has no set limit on the amount of money it will manage.

Genesis expects future business growth to come from taking on new separately managed accounts for global emerging markets investments. Current clients for this service are mainly American. They include: the Frank Russell Trust Company in Tacoma, Washington, the General Motors pension fund, the pension fund of Shell Oil Co. in Texas, and the Oregon Public Employees' Retirement System.

Capital International Inc.

In 1985, when the IFC asked Capital International if it wanted to apply to manage its new global emerging markets fund, the firm at first hesitated. Emerging markets, after all, were risky propositions. By straying into almost unchartered waters, Capital, a unit of the Capital Group, felt it might hurt its then over 50-year-old reputation in investment management.

But before long, Capital warmed to the idea. "Long-term, we knew we wanted to be in emerging markets," said David Fisher, chairman of the Capital Group and one of the portfolio managers of the Emerging Markets Growth Fund Inc. The perceived benefits of early entry began to outweigh the risks.

Ultimately, Capital applied for and won the right to manage the IFC's Emerging Markets Growth (EMG) Fund—the first global fund for developing markets; it was the start of what has been—at least thus far—a happy new venture. Between the fund's June 1986 inception and the end of February 1992, the now approximately $2 billion, closed-end EMG fund posted a cumulative total return of 584.14 percent. For the three years ended 1992, the fund's net asset value total return was up 66.91 percent, according to Lipper Analytical Services.

Over time, Capital International introduced other emerging markets funds, and today manages $2.7 billion of assets in this category. Besides the Emerging Markets Growth Fund, its other emerging markets funds are: the six-year-old Emerging Markets Investment Fund for Japanese investors; the SEC-registered New World Investment Fund, focused on Latin America, that debuted in 1989; and the Capital International Emerging Markets Fund for European investors, launched in 1990. In 1993, the firm also plans to launch a fund for investing in Eastern Europe. Capital International does not handle separately managed accounts for the emerging markets.

How has Capital International fared so well—especially with its Emerging Markets Growth Fund? Partly because of its early arrival in developing markets, partly because of its research-oriented investment approach, and also because of the support the firm receives from the organization at large. As the kernel of its success, the entire Los Angeles-based Capital organization—including the emerging markets "jungle" team, as Fisher calls it—relies on its own in-house research. In 1992 for example, the organization's 93 analysts traveled more than one million miles and conducted 5000 research calls, including 2000 meetings with non-U.S. companies in 50 countries, the firm said. In 1991, of the 5000 research calls made, 400 alone were for emerging markets, Fisher reported.

Capital's dedicated emerging markets group consists of 4 portfolio managers and 12 analysts. The group can also tap the firm's other global industry analysts as needed. The "jungle" group isn't lacking in analytical expertise. The well-known David Fisher, for example, has been part of Capital since 1969, when he joined as a financial analyst and then became research director for 10 years. Fisher was a guiding light in the development of Capital's emerging markets investing—a process that followed the style used elsewhere in the firm.

Capital's strategy is to invest from the "bottom up": first picking stocks, but then weighing macroeconomic factors affecting countries and markets. In analyzing stocks, the firm assesses a company's overall business, its market position, its competition, how it motivates its management, its labor situation, and generally, the popularity of its products, Fisher reports. Visits to companies, their suppliers, competitors, and other sources provide key sources of information.

Fact-finding can also take some novel twists. For instance, tapping her background in the arts, Nancy Englander, president of the Emerging Markets Growth Fund, visits prominent Latin American business and political figures who are also involved in that field. She brings back "a different perspective on what's happening politically and socially in Latin America," says Shaw Wagener, chairman of Capital's emerging markets investment committee and a portfolio manager of the Emerging Markets Growth Fund. From Capital's office in Washington, political analyst Joe Higdon—a former Peace Corps volunteer in the Philippines—assesses Asian politics and global trade issues.

At Capital, investment decisions are made through a multiple portfolio management system. In the emerging markets group, managers and analysts are each allocated a certain portion of the assets of each fund—with usually about one-third going to analysts and about two-thirds to portfolio managers. Each participant "handles his piece as he sees fit," Wagener explains. However, all involved gather weekly in an investment meeting to air specific investment intentions and explore macroeconomic developments.

Important support has come from Capital's administrative professionals. When some attractive markets were hard to penetrate, such as Chile's in the middle 1980s, Capital's lawyers and other administrative professionals would help unlock technical/legal blockades that could range from impediments to buying shares to settling stock trades. With the aid of administration, Capital was able to invest in Chile's market by 1988—ahead of the ensuing boom in that market. "The same thing happened in various countries, including Mexico," Wagener recalls. Before the creation of that country's Nafinsa Trust—as an additional way for foreigners to buy otherwise restricted shares in Mexico—"that market was heavily restricted to foreigners." Wagener says Capital was among the organizations advising—even prodding—Mexico to open its market further.

As of year-end 1992, the EMG fund was invested in 19 countries; its largest market exposure was a 20.7 percent weighting in Mexico.

How does Capital pick stocks? There are no hard-and-fast criteria, other than the obvious quest for companies with demonstrably rising earnings. However, as a U.S-registered fund, the Emerging Markets Growth Fund has some built-in limitations: no more than 35 percent of investments can be in any one country, and no more than 25 percent in any one industry. Individual stock holdings are capped at 5 percent of assets at the time of purchase.

Capital seeks to minimize stock turnover, which for the Emerging Markets Growth Fund was 16.01 percent in 1992. Even if their share prices have galloped, stocks will remain in the portfolio if the company is still performing strongly. In the Mexican market, for instance, "Telmex (Telefonos de Mexico),

Cifra, and Kimberly Clark have all been home runs for Capital because of our reluctance to let go of them," Wagener says. "These were companies that know their business well and know what growth means." In Cifra's case, for example, the company understood that President Salinas intended to reduce trade barriers and other governmental protections for business. For Cifra, that translated into a need to start emphasizing sales volume as opposed to profit margins, which could be hurt with the cutback in governmental protections. Unlike some of its competitors, Cifra smartly lowered its prices in 1991, says Wagener, and its profits climbed.

Cifra's sharp eye on trends and crucial issues encourages Capital to hang onto its stock. The payoff: on average so far, the Cifra stock held by the Emerging Markets Growth Fund has appreciated some 10-fold. Its Telmex holdings have spiraled more than 18 times higher.

But of course, not all investments have flourished. Shaw Wagener points to the Mexican holdings of Ericcson and Alcatel, suppliers of telecommunications equipment. Capital had expected these companies' earnings to rise on the coattails of Telmex's breakneck growth. But what the firm failed to calculate was that the privatized Telmex, with its aggressive new private sector management, would pressure suppliers to slash their costs, which trimmed the profits of Ericcson and Alcatel, even though sales volume remained strong. As of early March 1993, the value of Capital's investment in Ericcson had dropped by about 50 percent. But compared with Telmex's returns, that seemed no great tragedy. As Wagener put it, "At least we got the biggest part of that equation right: the investment in Telmex."

In fact, Capital has a sizable weighting in large-cap emerging markets stocks, because, as David Fisher reports, "some of our big-name investments have done awfully well." At year-end 1992, the 10 largest holdings of the Emerging Markets Growth Fund accounted for about 27 percent of total assets, but the figure has been as high as 40 percent, Fisher reports. Among the long-time holdings: Telecomunicacoes Brasileiras (Telebras), Telefonos de Mexico, and the Philippine Long Distance Telephone Company. At the end of 1992 their stocks comprised the three largest positions in the Emerging Markets Growth

Fund, for a total exposure of about 12 percent. The remaining seven largest issues, in order, were: Cifra, Bangkok Bank, Siam Commercial Bank in Thailand, Cemex in Mexico, Nortel in Argentina, Grupo Televisa in Mexico, and San Miguel Corp. in the Philippines.

While the firm remains loyal to good companies, it is not, however, adverse to making shifts. In 1992, as the firm became more enamored of Asia, it shifted assets eastward, while trimming back on Latin America. The most popular destinations were the markets of Korea and the Philippines and, in particular, the banking industry in Thailand. At year-end 1992, Philippine investments weighed in at 11 percent in the Emerging Markets Growth Fund, Korea accounted for 5 percent of the portfolio—up from zero a year earlier—while Thai banks together accounted for 7.5 percent—just shy of the entire Thai market's index weighting, Wagener says.

That strategy proved fruitful. After an extended trough, the Korean market rallied in the second half of 1992; for the entire year, the Philippines' market gained 17 percent in U.S. dollar terms, according to the IFC's price index for that market. In 1992, Thailand's overall market climbed 30.2 percent in dollars, according to the IFC's price index.

Emerging Markets Investors Corporation

When Emerging Markets Investors Corporation hung out its shingle in 1987, it embarked on two then-unusual ideas: investing in emerging stock markets, and using quantitative techniques to chart its course.

"We wanted to build a long-lasting business, and one that would be on the forefront of analytical investment techniques," explains Michael Duffy, one of the six partners of the Washington, D.C.-based Emerging Markets Investors' Corporation (EMI). Over the long term "we found that managers with disciplined, quantitative strategies were the better performers. They survived beyond a run of simple good luck and favorable periods in their markets."

Thus far the quantitative, computer model approach has also worked for EMI. Six years after the firm's debut, EMIC today manages some $1.2 billion in assets; operates five funds, including an umbrella vehicle; handles a number of separately managed accounts; and has rung up impressive performances. Over the three years ending with 1992, its $280 million flagship Emerging Markets Investors Fund posted a 65.91 percent net asset value total return in U.S. dollar terms, according to Lipper Analytical Services. Its Emerging Markets Strategic Fund posted a higher net asset value total return of 65.56 percent.

Behind the firm's successes are 20 skilled professionals, led by the well-known, affable, and intensely dedicated Antoine van Agtmael. A native of the Netherlands, van Agtmael serves as EMI's president. A recognized authority on developing markets, he has authored (coauthored in the second case) two books on investing in emerging stock markets. They are *Emerging Securities Markets,* published in 1984 by Euromoney Publications, and *The World's Emerging Stock Markets, Structure, Development, Regulations and Opportunities,* coauthored with Keith K. H. Park and published in 1993 by Probus Publishing Company. Van Agtmael's hands-on experience dates back to 1975, when he came to Thailand to head Bankers Trust Company's investment banking operation in that country. In 1979 he joined the IFC, eventually going on to create its emerging markets database. In the mid-1980s van Agtmael, along with David Gill, then the IFC's director of the Capital Markets Department, designed the IFC's Emerging Markets Growth Fund, the first fund for investing in emerging markets around the world. The fund has been managed by Capital International Inc. since 1986.

In 1987, van Agtmael and five officials of the World Bank "decided to be more entrepreneurial" with the rest of their lives, recalls the firm's president. Their plan was to create a business that would specialize in global asset allocation and emerging markets investing. These two ideas took shape as two separate firms, with the boutique EMI handling emerging markets investing. Although the concept of a specialized emerging markets firm has since been replicated, the number of quantitatively oriented emerging markets managers remains small.

At EMI, use of a computer model has been vital to the firm's value-oriented, top-down investment strategy. The firm begins its analysis by picking the most attractive countries with the help of a proprietary country allocation model. This "navigational tool," as van Agtmael calls it, recommends market weightings based on a host of economic/market factors that range from broad macro trends in the economy to data on specific companies. After crunching these numbers, the model can point to historically and currently cheap markets with good performance prospects. It also helps to forecast which markets will move in which directions and which markets are likely to move in tandem. With this information, EMI can better diversify its portfolios by avoiding markets that are all moving in the same direction at the same time.

The country allocation model has been a helpful guide, EMI's partners believe. For instance, in the late 1980s it helped steer the firm to Latin America in plenty of time to capture the 1991 booms in that region's markets. But as those markets became overboiled, the model began to point eastward instead of to the south. By late 1991, it saw better value in the Asian markets of Korea and Taiwan, and Hong Kong, as gateways to China.

Taking its cue, EMI undertook a significant asset shift in its global accounts, says van Agtmael. By the end of 1992, Latin American holdings in the Emerging Markets Investors Fund had dropped to 30 percent from an earlier peak weighting of 45 percent. But the fund's exposure in East Asia had risen to approximately 29 percent, including 12 percent in South Korea's market, 7 percent in Taiwan's, and 10 percent in China plays, especially through stocks listed on the Hong Kong exchange.

How has it paid off? The Korean stock market did, in fact, rally in the second half of 1992. For the year 1992, Hong Kong's market gained 27.4 percent in U.S. dollar terms. And after its prolonged slump, Taiwan's market surged in early 1993.

For EMI, stock selection is expected to become an increasingly important contributor to returns. Once attractive countries have been identified, the firm selects stocks in them, often through a bottom-up approach: the firm's analysts make recommendations to the investment committee. As chief portfolio strategist, van Agtmael ultimately signs off on all purchases.

To ensure that portfolios are diversified, the firm takes small positions in a large number of stocks. Ideas emanate from a myriad of sources: visits to companies and markets (every investment gets a visit at least annually); maintaining what van Agtmael calls "thick files on every investment"; engaging in "lots of homework" by the firm's professionals; and subscribing to "virtually every database under the sun."

EMI has also devised some intriguing nontraditional research methods. Says van Agtmael: "I'm probably well known for believing that you can gain information from visiting companies' bathrooms. It's a bad sign if they're not clean," as is often the case.

Early on, the firm also found a clever way around the problem of inadequate information on third world markets. Unwilling to invest "on the basis of fragmentary pieces of information," EMI, says Duffy, created an internship program to instruct brokers in developing countries about sophisticated market analysis. EMI invites a select number of broker/analysts from developing countries—including, so far, Korea, Brazil, Venezuela, Chile, Argentina, and Turkey—to Washington to work with EMI for about three months. While there, some participants have also enrolled in the Chartered Financial Analysts' program under EMI's sponsorship. As intended, brokers return home with a better understanding of analytical standards of developed markets, as well as of EMI's own investment practices.

But although these processes seem to be producing good results, EMI evidently is not resting on its laurels. "My goal," says van Agtmael, "is not to get fat and happy but to keep pushing the frontiers....I believe that if you get stuck in the mud you will sink."

To keep itself on the cutting edge, the firm is moving forward on various fronts. According to van Agtmael, changes and enhancements include: probing new markets; penetrating deeper into known markets to uncover opportunities; and "further upgrading our investment methodology."

Currently, the firm's product line includes the five-year-old Emerging Markets Investors Fund, an open-ended fund domiciled in Canada (the only one of EMI's funds available to U.S. institutional investors); the five-year-old Emerging Markets

Strategic Fund; the Asian Emerging Markets Fund; the Latin America Emerging Markets Fund; and an umbrella fund that can include a global emerging markets fund and a Latin American and/or an Asian emerging markets fund. It also manages a number of separate accounts.

In the works, as of this writing, is a fund for investing in Africa, excluding South Africa. Van Agtmaels says that other newer areas of interest include markets of Central America, Eastern Europe, and China. "A good portion of our research effort is directed toward the pioneering effort, even though it may not pay off for another eight years," he says. Since "emerging markets are becoming more discovered and efficient, you need to position yourself early (in new markets) if you want a big payoff."

In 1992, EMI invested in Hungary, Poland, and Bolivia for the first time, and it added Peruvian stocks to some accounts. Perceiving that "several Eastern European countries, including Hungary and Poland, are starting to get their act together," van Agtmael expects to see 10 percent of EMI's global funds invested in Eastern Europe within one to two years.

Stock selection has also been refined. The firm's "general rule is that the bigger the country, the smaller the stock," its president says. The firm has thus been "selectively" replacing blue chips with smaller capitalized stocks. In 1992 that process—along with the reduced exposure to Latin America—precipitated the biggest turnover of any year yet for the Emerging Markets Investors Fund. Of the 280 stocks in the Emerging Markets Investors Fund, 104 were added in 1992, while 41 were deleted. At the end of that year, the fund's 10 largest stock holdings had appreciably changed from the year before. In late 1992 they were, in order, C.P. Pokphand in agribusiness (Hong Kong); United Overseas Bank in Singapore; Philippine Long Distance Telephone Co; Telefonos de Mexico; Semi-Tech in Hong Kong; the ROC Taiwan Fund; Telebras; Thai Farmers Bank; Samsung in Korea; and Singapore Airlines.

What hasn't changed is EMI's commitment to maintaining a manageable size. "We want to grow slowly," explains van Agtmael. "I believe that if you grow too fast you get sloppy." In 1992 the firm accepted no new separate accounts, and in 1993 it planned to take in only two new accounts of this kind—including one from an existing client. "After that, we'll close the door again to separately managed accounts," said the firm's president in early March 1993. Van Agtmael wants to avoid becoming weighted down by administration. To him, the "fun" of EMI is not in the paperwork but in the investing.

4
Argentina

The dramatic turnaround in Argentina's economy since 1989 sent a "go" signal to investors outside its borders. Trading activity in the Buenos Aires stock market, riding on a strong economy, jumped up 393.8 percent in 1991—giving Argentina the top slot in the IFC index that year.

Through 1992, though, with pivotal social security and labor issues still to be resolved, reform seemed to have lost momentum. Investors had taken a much more worried view of Argentina's market opportunities that year, partly due to a conspicuous slowdown in the pace of privatization. After its stellar 1991 showing, the stock market toppled 27.5 percent in 1992. One factor in the decline was concerns about negotiations on the North American Free Trade Agreement (NAFTA).

President Carlos Saul Menem, who took office in 1989, seems committed to pushing forward the reforms necessary to stabilize the economy and attract investments. His accomplishments in 1993 were being closely monitored by potential investors outside the borders. For Argentine citizens, expanded privatization will bring a boost in personal savings that will also strengthen the financial markets.

Under Menem, the new Argentine peso made its bow among world currencies on January 1, 1992, with an exchange value firmly pegged at 1 peso equals 1 U.S. dollar. Each peso replaced 10,000 of the overvalued and rapidly fluctuating Australs (which had been introduced in 1985 to replace the peso). Although the structure of the new peso should have reassured investors, they greeted 1993 with smoldering fears of a possible devaluation.

The currency worries were rooted in overvaluation of the economy itself. As imports streamed in from Brazil and other key trading partners, it became increasingly apparent that Argentina's industries needed to become leaner and more competitive.

That's been easier said than done in this land of the potent unions. But Menem and his Harvard-trained Economy Minister Domingo Cavallo have been aggressively pushing reforms on various fronts—including labor law changes to promote competitiveness.

The background to the 1991 stock market rally was Menem's moves to stem inflation, control currency risk, privatize businesses, and encourage both foreign and domestic investment. Funds from international investors poured in, but midway through 1992, Argentina's economy began to slow.

Brazilian manufacturers, aided partly by tariff cuts in the Mercosur (Southern Common Market) pact, flooded Argentina with goods. Consumers grabbed them, since they had more spending power due to rising real wages. Overall, capital goods imports increased 129.7 percent in 1991, with imports from Brazil jumping 100 percent in 1991 and 80 percent in 1992.

The balance of trade had been positive from 1980 through 1991, but by 1992, Argentina faced a deficit of over $2.9 billion (versus a 1991 surplus of $3.9 billion), and a 17.5 percent inflation rate.

Cavallo responded by raising tariffs, especially on goods from Mercosur pact countries, to an average 15 percent (from 11 percent). The statistic tax on imports was also raised to 10 percent from 3 percent; for capital goods, however, the reporting tax was eliminated, and capital goods manufacturers were given a 15 percent rebate on their sales.

To remedy the sagging exports of key Argentine industries, outgoing duties were eliminated on mineral products, along with domestic taxes on fuels and the 1.5 percent flat tax on farm exports. As these moves intended, imposition of incoming taxes and elimination of outgoing taxes made Argentine exports cheaper and imports more expensive. These adjustments in 1992 effectively devalued the Argentine peso for purposes of international trade.

A run on the dollar was triggered by a rumor that Cavallo would resign. Cavallo responded by taking aim at the rigid labor market regulations that have stymied the Argentine economy for decades. Any threat of change has generally been met with a tightening grip by the powerful labor unions, and by labor troubles. He proposed new rules for wage bargaining (conducted for decades on an industry-wide basis), breaking the union monopoly on health benefits, reducing employer liability for accidents and sick leave, and making it easier for employers to hire and fire.

To quell the threat of a national labor strike, a Social Security Reform Project was created in November 1992, permitting unions and other nonprofit entities to manage their own pension funds. According to New York-based J. P. Morgan & Co. Incorporated, pension fund reform could add US$2 to $3 billion to Argentina's capital markets, beginning in 1994, and "will also increase the stability and professionalism of the market with greater institutional ownership."

In mid-1993, the bill that would create a private pension system was passed by the lower house of Congress. Among its attractions, the measure was ultimately expected to help rescue a system where debts were $6 billion, the annual operating deficit was $2.4 billion, and benefits to 75 percent of retirees were at more than $200 a month.

Some investors have been applauding Argentina's efforts to address social and economic ills. "We are very bullish on Argentina," Veronica Berger Collins of Latin American Securities Ltd., London, said in early 1993. "Its government has managed to control inflation so far and achieved a fiscal balance, which is an incredible change. It forced a crackdown on tax evasion and got a balance of revenues and expenses. Now there are clear financial accounts with government and business."

National Treasures

Argentina is rich in natural resources and its population is 95 percent literate. The educated sector enjoys relatively high per capita income. However, only one-fifth of the population fin-

ARGENTINA

Currency: Argentine Peso

Stock Exchanges: There are five stock exchanges in Argentina, located in Buenos Aires (95 percent of volume), Rosaria, Cordoba, La Plata, and Mendoza.

Indexes: The two main indexes are the Merval Index (19 blue chips) and the Bolsa Index (all listed stocks).

Types of Securities: Equities (common and preferred), corporate bonds, Treasury bonds, government bonds.

Regulatory Body/Stock Exchange Supervision: The Comision Nacional De Valores (CNV) regulates and controls the stock exchanges, banks, and brokerages houses. Additionally, banks are governed by The Central Bank of Argentina.

Depository: All equities and some OTC Government and Corporate Bonds are held at the Central Depository, Caja De Valores (CDV). Most foreign investors hold their fixed-income securities in physical form in their subcustodians vaults, to allow them to meet the TD and T + 1 settlement dates.

Settlement Information

Equities:

- T + 1 or T + 3.
- Physical or book entry (most commonly used).
- Receive/deliver versus payment available.
- Same-day turnaround trades are possible in a physical environment only.

Fixed Income:

- TD (peso-denominated), T + 1 and T + 2 (USD-denominated).
- Physical delivery only.
- Receive/deliver versus payment available (peso-denominated), free of payment (USD-denominated).

- Held in bearer form only.
- Same-day turnaround trades are possible.

Taxes: There is a 16 basis points stock market fee on every trade.

Restrictions for Foreign Investors: Investment in the broadcasting industry is prohibited.

Securities Lending: Permitted, but not frequently used.

SOURCES: The Bank of New York and Baring America Asset Management Co. Inc.

ishes secondary school, even though education is free through the university level.

With 1.07 million square miles of land, Argentina is the second largest of the Latin American nations. Covering most of South America's southern half, it stretches 2000 miles from the northern subtropics to Tierra del Fuego near the Antarctic Circle.

The bulk of its nearly 33 million population, 87 percent, resides in urban areas. And youth prevails: 67 percent are under 40 and 39 percent under the age of 19, which translates into abundant availability for the work force. Like other Latin American nations, Argentina's population is a multicultural melange of Spanish colonists and native peoples, enriched by waves of European immigration. The dominant culture is strongly Spanish.

Its 1853 federal constitution established executive, legislative, and judicial branches similar to those in the United States. Each of its 22 provinces, as well as the one national territory and one federal district, has its own constitution, governor, and judicial system. However, Argentine provinces have no meaningful role in national government. The disposal of tax revenues, in particular, is entirely at the federal level.

However, from 1930 to 1983, when Raoul-Alfonsin was named president, Argentina was ruled by military dictators. Menem's election marked the first time in 60 years that Argentina's civilian government changed hands through an election.

The Economy

Despite Argentina's rich reservoir of natural and human resources, its standing among similar-size economies such as Australia, Canada, and Italy has been slowly declining since 1930, when military dictatorships assumed power.

At the peak of the 1991 stock market frenzy, the major components were manufacturing, agriculture, construction, and mining. Agricultural products—"meat and wheat"—accounted for nearly 40 percent of total exports.

As 1993 began, Argentina was endeavoring to diversify its main sources of foreign exchange. Argentina is self-sufficient in oil, producing 70 percent of its needs. A major offshore fishery industry is slowly developing along the Atlantic coast. Exports of wine, fruits, and edible oils are also growing.

Major manufacturing industries are food processing, machinery and equipment, textiles, hides, and metallurgy. Import barriers and high subsidies have stifled modernization, and overall labor and component costs are about 20 to 25 percent above Brazil, its major competition in the Mercosur free trade zone.

The 1970s were a decade of economic hardship for Argentina. Undergoing two recessions, its per capita GDP dropped 22 percent overall that decade. The average annual inflation rate was 145 percent, peaking at 440 percent in reaction to the 1976 oil crisis, and ending the decade of the '70s at about 100 percent. The oil crisis of 1982 fueled worldwide inflation, culminating in a global recession. Argentine export revenues fell sharply.

With the economy in sorry shape, Socialist Raoul Alfonsin won the presidency on a plank of tight fiscal policy. A freeze on prices and wages generated improvements in the budget deficit, but Alfonsin failed to impose tough, long-term discipline. Argentina was teetering on the brink of ruin, with antiquated infrastructure and an economy still strongly dependent on foreign capital. Crushing poverty still oppressed large sectors of the population.

When Menem, leader of the Justicialist Party, was elected in 1989, the budget deficit was nearly 22 percent of GDP. And the staggering average annual inflation rate of the 1980s, 565 percent, looked good by comparison with 1989, when it soared to 3080 percent. His stabilization program, immediately implemented, engendered remarkable improvement: the fiscal deficit fell from 21.8 percent of GDP in 1989 to 1.8 percent of GDP in 1991, and inflation also fell sharply, with April 1993 inflation at 11.7 percent.

Menem's Convertibility Plan, which linked the U.S. dollar to the peso, took effect on February 1, 1991. It ended indexation of local currency contracts; eliminated controls on prices, interest rates, and exchanges; eased wage controls; linked wage increases above basic levels to productivity increases; and reformed tax regulations.

During the Plan's first 12 months, industrial output increased 30 percent. Gross domestic product grew by 8.5 percent in 1991, and by about 7 percent in 1992. Montgomery Asset Management expected GDP growth to reach 9.8 percent for 1993. A caveat for potential investors: the underground economy accounts for about 50 percent of Argentina's official GDP.

Menem also eliminated import restrictions on foreign investment and cut tariffs to about 14 percent in 1992 from a high of 200 percent in 1989. Public entities can now buy certain imports even when domestic substitutes are available. By 1993, customs duties had been simplified and most limits on quantity of imports had been eliminated. Also, domestic trade on goods and services was deregulated in 1991.

By 1992 the annual inflation rate had dropped to 17.5 percent, far short of Menem's target of 7 percent, but a vast improvement over the 84.1 percent rate recorded in 1991. In real-income terms, monthly wages rose to US$842 from US$618, boosting tax receipts but cutting international competitiveness.

Under the Convertibility Plan's full implementation on January 1, 1993, the doors are open wide to foreign (especially U.S.) investing. Individuals and companies can now open U.S. dollar current accounts with checking facilities. All financial transactions (except wages and taxes) can be satisfied in either pesos or dollars.

In an effort to improve revenues, Argentine citizens must now pay taxes on personal assets held in Argentina and abroad, in hopes of repatriating offshore capital worth an estimated US$40 billion or more.

In 1992, average monthly tax revenues were 27 percent ahead of year-earlier receipts, and more than 50 percent greater than in 1989. Total tax revenues stood at 24 percent of GDP in 1992, up from 15 percent in 1989—and the highest level in more than 20 years.

Trade

Argentina and Brazil, later joined by Paraguay and Uruguay, created Mercosur, the Southern Common Market, in 1991 via the Treaty of Asuncion. Mercosur aims to be a pole in the hemispheric trade market, dealing with NAFTA and other multi-country trade blocs. Mercosur cut average tariffs among member nations to about half the levels charged to outside nations. The maximum customs duty is now 35 percent. The Mercosur market comprises a total combined GDP of US$420 billion and a population of 190 million. At last report, though the goal was to create a unified sector market by 1995, it is now delayed due to difficulties with Brazil's insistence on greater import protection on sensitive industrial products.

Foreign Debt Reduction

In late 1992, the Menem administration reached a "detailed agreement" under the Brady plan to restructure its commercial bank debt, totaling US$23 billion in medium-term debt and US$8 billion in unpaid interest payments. It is the sixth Latin American country to undergo a Brady restructuring. The debt service ratio has been dropping steadily, from 100 percent in 1990 to 57 percent in 1992.

Menem's three-year economic plan, introduced in third-quarter 1992, is expected to generate a primary surplus of 2 percent of GDP a year and to maintain a stable exchange rate, and it assured full reserve banking for the monetary base.

Privatization

Privatization of state-owned enterprises began in November 1990 with the sale of 70 percent of Entel, the national telephone company, which was split into Telefonica and Telecom. A successful sale of 33 percent of Aerolineas Argentinas in 1991 would have reduced the national debt by US$2 billion, but minority shareholders were unable to meet their obligations, and the government repurchased the shares in July 1992. The 33 percent government stake was expected to be reoffered in 1993.

Segments of YPF (Yaciemientos Petroliferos Fiscales), the state-owned oil company, had already been sold before the hugely successful mid-1993 stock offering of about $3 billion. Other public sector sales have included parts of the railway system, a shipping line, three petrochemical companies, and two steel mills.

Through April 1993, privatization raised $5.4 billion in cash and erased $12.5 billion (face value) of government debt. But it also reduced the public sector payroll by more than 42,000 jobs, of which 66 percent were "voluntary" retirements. Argentine economist Miguel Broda told the *Financial Times,* he expected state employees to drop to 41,000 at the end of 1993.

The Stock Market

The Buenos Aires Stock Exchange or BASE, founded in 1854, was the first in Latin America. In 1937, a Securities Commission (Commission Nacional De Valores—CNV) was established (along similar lines to the U.S. Securities and Exchange Commission), and it became independent in 1989. In accordance with the Stock Exchange Law of 1969, it regulates the issue and trading of securities, including activity on the Mercado Abierto Electronico (MAE), a nonprofit private organization of over-the-counter brokers who mainly trade government securities. The MAE is in the process of obtaining approval to function as a self-regulating market.

The CNV reports directly to the Ministry of Economy. Governed by a five-member board, its chairman is appointed by the Argentine President to a five-year term.

Other CNV-related exchanges are in Cordoba, La Plata, Mendoza, Rosario, and Santa Fe, but BASE, by far the largest and most important, is the major market for foreign investors. It accommodates both traditional auction-floor trading and a computerized system.

As of year-end 1992, the exchange listed 170 companies, with the 10 largest accounting for 71 percent of market capitalized in 1992, according to G. T. Management: Telefonica de Argentina, Telecom Argentina, Perez Companc, Sevel Argentina, Astra, Renault Argentina, Banco de Galicia, Siduca, Banco Frances, and Messalin Particulares.

Market capitalization at the end of 1992 was US$18.6 billion, down precipitously from the May 1992 peak of US$31.97 billion. It is by no means a good proxy of the Argentine economy, representing only 12.1 percent of Argentina's GDP in 1992.

BASE's cash market is the most liquid, encompassing 70 to 85 percent of traded value. Stock options, developed in 1991, currently represent 5 to 10 percent of daily turnover, although foreign investors do not usually play an active role in this segment of the cash market.

The Buenos Aires Securities Market Association (Mercado de Valores de Buenos Aires, or Merval) furnishes the most widely used market benchmark. The 19 stocks in the Merval index portfolio cover 80 percent of the BASE's total traded value. Another benchmark used is the General index, comprised of all shares listed on the BASE weighted by proportional share of market cap. The Merval usually has more day-to-day fluctuation than the General Index.

The Exchange Information System (Sistema de Informaciones Bursatiles—SIB) provides real-time information on prices and volumes, and historical information on the financials of publicly traded companies. In the equities market, the same regulations apply to foreign and local investors. There are no restrictions on industries, companies, or types of shares available to foreign institutions.

Trading and Investing

Though government securities dominate trading, private issues are becoming increasingly important, particularly as the national economy improves and more industries are privatized. International liquidity should be improved in late 1993 with Argentina's inclusion in the Euroclear system for equity trades.

Many Argentine company stocks still have small floats of about 30 percent, because of the strong presence of their founding families.

Political and economic instability of the past three decades had created a hostile environment for investment in Argentina's equity market, which appears to be turning. The number of listed companies had declined steadily from its 1962 high of 669.

Beginning in November 1991, brokerage commissions were deregulated from a fixed 1 percent, and are now negotiated between investors and their brokers. Current fees range from 0.4 to 1 percent of traded value. A 36 percent withholding tax on stock market gains for foreign investors was eliminated.

In May 1992, the CNV encouraged initial public offerings by

allowing companies to issue up to 30 percent of their shares as *acciones de participation* (nonvoting shares). Most shares issued and traded are *acciones ordinarias* (common). Preferred shares (*acciones preferidas*) are also issued, but less frequently used. More recently, higher penalties have been indicated for insider trading infractions.

Other securities available include a wide range of bonds, debt instruments, and promissory notes from the government and the central bank, as well as corporate bonds, known as ONs (Obligaciones Negociables).

Foreign Investors

Foreign investors are clearly welcome in Argentina. Money for investments may be moved freely in and out of Argentina, and no prior approval is required. Foreigners may invest in the equity market under the same regulations as local investors, with hardly any restrictions on industries (mass media is still off-limits), companies, or types of shares available. But foreigners have been cautioned to use influential intermediaries if they hope to succeed—let alone survive—in a market that releases all too little essential investment information and is known for its extreme volatility.

Major international securities houses carry enough punch to arrange direct transactions on the Argentine market. But individuals might do well to invest indirectly. They might consider buying shares, for example, in the Argentina Fund listed on the New York Stock Exchange. Two other Argentine funds cited by *The Wilson Directory of Emerging Markets Funds*, 1992-1993 edition, are the Argentine Investment Company listed on the Dublin Stock Exchange and the Argentinian Investment Company SICAV, which trades in Luxembourg.

Foreigners can also purchase Depositary Receipts on Argentine stocks through their domestic brokers, or they can buy directly on one of the Argentine stock exchanges. To do so, it's advisable to open an account with an Argentine brokerage firm. Among the main firms in Buenos Aires are: Banco de Valores, Banco Tornquist, Groupe Credit Lyonnais, Banco de Galicia, Cohen Bursatil, Tutelar Bursatil, Banco Roberts-Roberts

Capital Markets, Banco Medefin, Mercado Abierto, Compania General de Valores Mobiliarios, Comafi, Banco Mayo, Banco Mariva, Banco Macro, and Pecunia.

Argentine Investment Opportunities

Argentina watchers with money to invest would do well to keep a close tab on "any efficient company that has gone through restructuring to compete in today's open market," says Patrick Boland, vice president of BT Securities Corp. in New York. "Argentina is going from a closed to an open economy; certainly, companies that were successful before will be successful in the new environment."

Boland includes retail banking and telecommunications in his list, as Argentina already has a broad middle class, which is growing in earning and saving power.

Telecom and Telefonica were two of the most profitable publicly owned companies in Argentina in 1992. Phone penetration in Argentina, only 11.4 percent entering 1993, is low by the standards of more industrialized countries. Through 1997 (and potentially 2000), the two have exclusive rights to their respective markets, and they are expected to invest US$5.5 billion through 1996 to expand and modernize the phone network and improve service. Telefonica is also the only Argentine company that pays quarterly cash dividends. "Both telecommunications companies (Telecom and Telefonica) have excess demand for their products; growth in per capita income will allow a greater portion of the economy to afford these services," he said.

In the banking sector, excess demand and household income growth are important, said Boland. "In the days of hyperinflation and high interest rates, new mortgage lending and consumer auto lending did not exist. Growth in family income will allow people to save more and use the banking system more than in the past." He likes Banco Frances del Rio de la Plata and Banco Rio. Banco Frances has been an important corporate bank, but now also does middle-market and consumer business of good quality. Both, he feels, are also on the strong side of asset quality.

A report from First Boston Corp. points out that Argentina's backlog in infrastructure development should make the construction sector thrive. And continuing privatization could bring big advisory fees to private banks.

"The biggest beneficiaries from the announced increases in import tariffs should be companies in the food industry, and those engaged in production of raw materials," First Boston predicts. In the energy sector, which First Boston expects to outperform the market in 1993, the companies they like are Perez Companc and Astra. Among food companies, Molinos is expected to benefit long term—especially at the retail level—from the economic slowdown.

Lehman Brothers chimes in with prospects of significant growth in agriculture and food processing; telecommunications or data processing; banks, insurance companies, and real estate developers; and transport, distribution, and construction companies.

Investment choices could be linked to the need of privatized industries for improved infrastructure. Since cement will be needed to reconstruct roads and sidewalks torn up to get at underground telecommunications lines and for mains for waterworks, Argentina's better cement companies also warrant consideration.

5
Brazil

Brazil "is the country of the next century," goes the familiar quip, "and it always will be."

This massive, beautiful, and richly endowed South American land has had the potential to be a powerful force in Latin America and the world. While many investors bet that it still will be, its promise remains unfulfilled.

Discovered in 1500 by Portuguese navigator Pedro Alvares Cabral, Brazil is today a nation of some 146 million people and the world's ninth largest economy. Among its attractions is its well-developed financial system, an abundance of natural resources, a sizable consumer base, and world-class, competitive companies. According to James Capel Incorporated, Brazil is the world's largest producer of coffee beans, sugar cane, and orange juice, and it is the second largest producer of iron ore, tin ore, soybeans, and cocoa. Aided by a competitive exchange rate, among other factors, its exports hit a record high of $36.2 billion in 1992, contributing to a $15.7 billion trade surplus.

But Brazil also suffers from economic, political, and social ills—among them its fractious democracy, its inflation-ridden economy, and its wide gap separating rich and poor. As Montgomery Asset Management describes it, "the wealthiest 10 percent of the population control 48 percent of the national income."

A key problem for Brazil has been its political fragmentation. As illustration, James Capel reported in July 1992 that "while only 10 political parties have members in [Brazil's] Senate, over

30 [parties] are currently represented in the Chamber of Deputies," the lower house of Congress. The effect of such competing interests has been to hinder consensus building and the ability to solve problems.

In 1992, charges of corruption leveled against President Fernando Collor de Mello rocked the nation and brought on his downfall. Collor resigned during his impeachment trial. But rather than heralding a more peaceful political era, his departure ushered in new political uncertainties—some of which had been expected, some not.

President Collor had been a proponent of economic liberalizations and reforms. He was replaced by his staid former Vice President, Itamar Franco, who, in contrast to the flashy, progressive Collor, had been known as an economic nationalist and an advocate of trade protectionism.

Although, as President, Franco has proved to be surprisingly pragmatic, his initial popularity ebbed in the face of worsening inflation in early 1993 and signs of indecisiveness about the remedy for it. Finance ministers were short-lived in their post, as Brasilia grappled for solutions.

Such uncertainty was most inopportune for a country that was facing important decisions in 1993: first, an April plebiscite on the form of government Brazil should have starting in 1995; then, work on constitutional reform that would begin in earnest in the third quarter.

The constitutional review was expected to tackle a number of thorny issues, including: revenue-sharing arrangements between the federal government and states and municipalities; whether the central government should be given the right to fire workers; whether certain strategic government-controlled industries can be privatized; and prospects for implementing a one-person-one-vote rule, to achieve better representation of southern Brazil in Congress.

In the April plebiscite, Brazilians voted overwhelmingly to maintain their presidential form of government. But that decision was not expected to lower the political temperature. After the plebiscite, contenders for president in the 1994 elections were expected to announce their candidacy. Many expected that their campaigns would erode support for Franco and his agenda.

The Economy

Brazil's economy has been suffering from such problems as inflation, high interest rates, and hefty debt levels. In the fourth quarter of 1992, economic activity began to stir again and should rise 2 to 3 percent in 1993. But in 1992, overall it fell 0.9 percent, after a 1.2 percent gain in 1991, a 4.6 percent drop in 1990, and a 3.2 percent rise in 1989. In 1992, according to Morgan Guaranty Trust Company, inflation zoomed to 1149 percent, compared with 475 percent a year earlier and 1585 percent in 1990. Total external debt, according to Morgan Guaranty, was estimated to be $126.7 billion in 1992. Progress toward completion of a Brady debt reduction plan was slowed by political and economic developments—although as of this writing, a plan is expected to be finalized by late 1993.

Brazil's economic problems developed over a number of years and seem unlikely to disappear soon. Starting in the late 1960s, Brazil fueled its economic growth through hefty external borrowing. That left the economy prey to a series of economic woes that surfaced in the late 1970s and early 1980s. High interest rates in the United States intensified the debt-service burden of countries such as Brazil, that had sizable amounts of floating-rate debt. Then came the 1981-82 world recession, which higher oil prices had helped to induce. Finally, after Mexico declared a moratorium on debt repayments in 1982, foreign lending to Latin America dried up, plunging the entire region into a black hole of indebtedness.

Brazil has never quite recovered. As James Capel describes it, the country's efforts to reduce foreign debt by devaluing its currency and reducing dependence on foreign oil were only briefly successful. Programs to bring the domestic budget into balance soon were more than offset by widespread adoption of indexation of prices, wages, and other economic components. Indexing, a band-aid treatment at best, seemed all the more essential as inflation spiraled from 100 percent in 1980 to 239 percent in 1985.

Since 1985 when democracy replaced 21 years of military rule, Brazil has had seven economic adjustment plans, including two proposed in 1993. Before 1993, plans typically included wage

BRAZIL

Currency: Cruzeiro real

Stock Exchanges: The two main stock exchanges are BOVESPA (Bolsa De Valores De São Paulo), which accounts for 70 percent of the total trading volume, and the BVRJ (Bolsa De Valores Do Rio De Janeiro), with 15 percent of the volume, while another seven regional stock exchanges account for the remaining 15 percent of the volume.

Indexes: The two main indexes are the BOVESPA Stock Index and the BVRJ's IBV Index. The BOVESPA Index represents the present value of a hypothetical stock portfolio organized at the beginning of 1968. As a result of the method of calculation, the BOVESPA Index is heavily weighted toward the government-owned oil- and tin-mining companies (with five companies comprising over 5 percent of the index).

In contrast, the IBV is a market-value-weighted index based on an initial value of 100.00 as of the close of trading on the last business day of 1983. The weight of each stock in the index is based on the stock's percentage of overall market capitalization, represented by the market value of the outstanding shares. Variations of the index accurately reflect movements of the overall market.

Types of Securities: Equities (common and preferred), corporate bonds, government fixed-income securities, options and futures.

Regulatory Body/Stock Exchange Supervision: The CVM (Comissao De Valores Mobilarios) is the equivalent of the U.S. Securities and Exchange Commission. The CVM regulates and supervises the securities markets, including all stock exchanges and the OTC markets.

Foreign investors are required to obtain investment approval by registering with the CVM. The CVM has 30 days from the registration application filing date to make a determination (i.e., approve, reject, or request additional information). If no determination is made (after 30 days) the application is automatically approved. Upon approval a formal notice is filed with the Federal Register. The Central Bank of Brazil regulates all banking institutions and monitors the inflow and outflow of all investment capital.

Depository: CALISPA is the depository arm of BOVESPA for all securities traded in São Paulo, while the CLC (Camara De Liquidacao E Custodia SA) is the depository arm of the BVRJ for all securities traded in Rio De Janeiro as well as for all securities traded on the other seven regional exchanges. The CLC is linked to the electronic SENN System, which is used by all stock exchanges except BOVESPA. CALISPA and the CLC have recently received "no action" letters from the SEC for use by U.S. Mutual Funds. Government securities settle via book entry at SELIC, while corporate bonds settle by book entry at CETIP.

Settlement Information

Equities:

- T + 2.
- Physical or book entry (most commonly used).
- Receive/deliver versus payment available.
- The delivering party transfers traded securities into the counterparty's blocked account at CALISPA or CLC on T + 1. Shares are unblocked on the same day as receipt of payment.
- Same-day turnaround trades are not possible.

Fixed Income:

- TD.
- Book entry delivery only.
- Receive/deliver versus payment available.
- On TD, securities are transferred by book entry at either SELIC or CETIP against bank check or interbank transfer.
- Same-day turnaround trades are not possible.

Taxes:

- A withholding tax of 15 percent is paid by foreign investors upon repatriation of income.

(Continued)

- There is no capital gains tax, nor is there a stamp duty.
- All tax payments and filings are paid through the local administrator rather than the subcustodian.

Restrictions for Foreign Investment: All foreign investors are required to appoint a local administrator (often a subsidiary of the subcustodian), who is responsible for filing the registration application with the CVM, for paying taxes, and for ensuring continued compliance with local regulations and foreign ownership limits. Additionally the administrator will assist with the registration and repatriation of investment capital with the Central Bank of Brazil.

Each foreign investor is limited to owning no more than 5 percent of any company's voting shares, or 20 percent of its total shares. No more than 10 percent of the assets of investment companies and investment funds may be invested in any one company's securities.

Securities Lending: None available at present.

SOURCE: The Bank of New York

and price controls and freezing of bank accounts, among other moves. President Collor's National Stabilization Plan in 1990 also included steps to reduce the budget deficit, stabilize foreign debt-service payments, establish deregulation and privatization programs, and liberalize foreign trade, says James Capel.

But structural problems in Brazil's economy have made it difficult to stamp out inflation. According to current provisions in the constitution, the federal government must return to states and municipalities almost 50 percent of its revenues, even though it still pays for such services as defense, education, and health. To shoulder its costs, the government has pursued such inflationary policies as printing money or issuing debt. Large amounts of short-term debt are issued at high interest rates. This raises the government's debt-service ratio and worsens its fiscal woes.

To lick inflation, the government needs to solve its fiscal problems. But in some cases, actions would require constitutional changes. For instance, constitutional reform would be needed to change the current mandate that more than half of federal revenues be returned to the states; privatization of certain strategic government-controlled companies, such as Telecomunicacoes Brasileiras S.A. (Telebras, the national telephone company) and Petrobras, the state oil company, would also require a change in the constitution.

Tackling these big issues would certainly take time. But by April 1993, as inflation inched toward the 30-percent-a-month mark, the Franco administration opted for an interim economic program that would stimulate the economy while battling inflation. Having disavowed wage/price freezes and other similar drastic measures, President Franco chose what many considered to be a more moderate course. Announced on April 24, a key element of his program was a plan to stimulate growth of up to 3.5 percent in 1993 by having the government increase allocations to the agricultural and construction sectors as a way to create jobs. At the same time, the government would cut spending in other areas and accelerate the privatization program.

However, that plan never had a chance to be passed by Congress before yet another new finance minister, Fernando Henrique Cardoso, unveiled a new economic plan in June 1993.

As reported in the *Financial Times,* the June plan, which as of this writing is still undergoing the approval process in Congress, emphasized cutting government spending by $6 billion and instituting "various revenue-raising measures." Its six main tenets: reducing interest rates; speeding up privatizations; cracking down on tax evasion; suspending revenue transfers to states and municipalities; implementing a tax on check writing that was also proposed by previous finance ministers; and imposing stricter controls on state banks.

Other Recent Reforms

Brazil's government has already taken several widely applauded moves. Besides reactivating the privatization process, other improvements include: modernizing the ports (which will lead to lower operating costs); changing the rate structure for telephone and electric utilities to allow for higher rates; and progress on fiscal and tax reform.

In mid-1993, the lower house passed a tax reform measure the key provision of which was an 0.25 percent tax on all transfers of funds through the banking system. Payment of wages and purchases and sales of securities were among the major exemptions to the plan. Once it becomes law this (most likely) temporary measure is expected to provide revenues to help the budget deficit. Full fiscal reform will be addressed during the constitutional review beginning in October 1993.

Privatization

In 1991, President Collor began Brazil's privatization program, designed primarily to reduce public debt with the proceeds of privatization sales, stimulate competition in the economy, and promote broader investor ownership of the companies.

The first firm to be privatized in 1991 was the steel company Usiminas. The specialty steel maker Acesita was privatized in October 1992 with the sale of 79.1 percent of its voting stock for the equivalent of U.S. $451 million. While private interests hold a minority stake in a number of large state-owned companies, including Telebras, the government retains a controlling interest.

After a three months' suspension of the privatization program, starting in December 1992, President Franco allowed the program to begin again—this time under the auspices of a new commission he appointed rather than the National Development Bank (BNDES) that had been overseeing the program.

In March 1993, Poliolefinas was sold, followed in April by the sale to a consortium of about 60 percent of Companhia Siderurgica Nacional (CSN), Brazil's largest steel mill. As expected, its selling price came in at $1 billion.

According to a May 1993 Salomon Brothers' report, the Franco government aims by year-end 1994 to raise $15 billion through the privatization of 51 state-owned companies although strategic sectors remain constitutionally off-limits. Some revenues from these privatizations are expected to be used to help trim domestic debt.

Freeing the Market

Serious efforts have been made, especially since 1990, to make it easier and more attractive to conduct trade with Brazil. Amid a tariff reduction program, the average tariff rates have fallen to 45 percent in 1989, 32.2 percent in 1990, 24.2 percent in 1991, and 21.2 percent in 1992.

Additional tariff reductions took effect on October 1, 1992, when the average import tariff rate dropped to 17 percent from 21 percent; another decline to 14 percent took place in July 1993. Several industries, particularly manufacturing of finished goods (like appliances or electronics), strongly urged postponement of the proposed tariff cuts. However, the new government instead chose to continue to reduce import duties under the planned schedule.

In 1991 Brazil signed the Treaty of Asuncion with Argentina, Paraguay, and Uruguay, which lead to the formation of the Southern Common Market, or Mercosur. Although plans for its full implementation have since slowed, Mercosur's objective is to augment economic growth by joining member countries into a single market of some 187 million people, with more than $614 billion in combined GDP.

Mercosur quickly stimulated foreign investment interest, and the expectation is that the region's enrichment will attract even more foreign investment, which in turn should get the attention of U.S. exporters, especially of capital goods. This may give Mercosur members leverage in eventual negotiations with NAFTA partners in the formation of an Americas market.

While Mercosur members still trade primarily with European countries and with the United States, commerce among members was $4.8 billion in 1991, compared with $2.2 billion in 1987. And growth continues at a smart pace.

The Stock Market

Brazil's economic and political gyrations are mirrored in its stock market, which is the second largest in Latin America, trailing only Mexico's.

In 1991 the market turned in a strong performance, reflecting investor confidence inspired by the Collor administration's economic reforms. It was the world's fourth best performer that year, with international investors helping it to post a 148.4 percent gain according to the IFC's price index in U.S. dollar terms.

In 1992, the corruption scandal that engulfed President Collor, and the resurgence of inflation, helped send stock prices sliding. In the first six months of the year the market rallied anew, only to reverse course and plummet later on, ending the year down 1.5 percent, in dollar terms, according to the IFC's Brazil index. The market's 1992 performance placed it ninth, or almost in the middle of the IFC's composite index of emerging markets.

In early 1993, the market was again on the move. Investors were cheered by the reactivation and expected speed-up of the privatization program and the perception that higher rates would improve the cash flow of such public sector companies as Telebras and Electrobras. In early June 1993, the IFC's global price index for Brazil was up nearly 48 percent in dollar terms. Since the first of the year, it had far outpaced gains in the other five Latin American markets tracked by the IFC.

The Brazilian market is more developed and sophisticated than those of other Latin American countries. It has cash, forward, and options markets, a commodities exchange, and a smooth clearing and settlement system. Banks and brokerage firms trading for their own accounts create much of the market's swings as they use derivatives, buy shares in the spot market and sell call options, or engage in basis trading in stock index futures. On the São Paulo Stock Exchange in 1992, financial institutions accounted for 41.9 percent of turnover, compared with 23.1 percent by institutional investors, 19 percent by individuals, and 15.2 percent by public and private companies. Foreigners accounted for 11.2 percent of activity in that cash market.

The Exchanges

Brazil has nine stock exchanges. Some 75 percent of the trading volume takes place on the São Paulo Stock Exchange (Bolsa de Valores de São Paulo—the Bovespa), about 20 percent on the Rio de Janeiro exchange. The other seven exchanges are located in Fortaleza, Recife, Salvador, Belo Horizonte, Santos, Curitiba, and Porto Alegre. Except for São Paulo's, the exchanges are hooked up via the SENN automated trading network.

Sweeping reforms of Brazil's capital markets via the Banking Reform Act of 1964 obliged the Rio de Janeiro exchange, formally founded in 1845, to modernize and significantly increase its membership. Members were compelled to organize into brokerage firms. Formerly membership was like a club, closed to all but the descendants of the original brokers appointed to trade before its formal founding. It is now owned by its 77 members.

Founded in 1890, São Paulo's stock exchange, at year-end 1992, had 565 listed companies. The listed companies' market capitalization was $45.3 billion. Trades on the Bovespa are made on the open-outcry system or via the computer-assisted trading system (CATS) derived from the system developed by the Toronto Stock Exchange. According to the exchange, "CATS ensures that an order will be executed at the established price or at a better one, and that the chronological priority among the bids/offers will be observed. On-line confirmation of execution is provided."

The major exchanges have annual, quarterly, monthly, weekly, and daily publications. There is international daily wire service coverage of the stock market. Price-earnings ratios and yields are published on a regular basis.

International brokers and analysts, and some Brazilian brokers, offer market commentaries and company reports in English. Consolidated audited annual accounts and quarterly statements must be provided by public companies. Accounting standards of the public companies were rated "good" by the IFC.

In 1992 the Bovespa's most actively traded stocks were: Telebras, with a commanding 54.79 percent participation; the mining company Vale do Rio Doce, with 7.69 percent; Electrobras, with 4.88 percent; the oil company Petrobras, with 3.98 percent; and the steel company Usiminas, with 2.78 percent.

The 10 largest brokerage firms authorized to trade on the Bovespa exchange are: SN Crefisul S/A Sociedade Corretora; Novoinvest S/A Corretora de Valores Mobiliarios; Citibank Corretora de Cambio Titulos e Valores Mobiliarios; Itau Corretora de Valores; Tendencia Corretora de Cambio Titulos Valores Mobiliarios; Corretora Souza Barros Cambio e Titulos; Bozano Simonsen S/A Corretora de Cambio e Valores Mobiliarios; Unibanco Corretora de Valores Mobiliarios; RMA S/A Sociedade Corretora; Fonte S/A Corretora de Cambio e Valores.

Regulations

Before May 31, 1991, foreign institutional investors could not invest directly in Brazil's stock market, and had to use mutual funds. But a change in government regulations opened the market to direct investment by foreign pension funds, brokerage houses, and other institutional investors. With the change in regulations, foreign investors "can now register as direct investors or through omnibus accounts held by other institutions," reports James Capel. As of this writing, most foreign individual investors are still not permitted to invest directly in Brazil. However, individuals or legal entities domiciled in the countries that signed the Mercosur Treaty (Argentina, Uruguay, Paraguay, and Brazil) have been permitted to invest freely on Brazilian stock exchanges.

Foreign institutional investors undertake several procedures before becoming eligible to invest. According to Mark Tajima, a consultant with Emerging Markets Consulting Group International, foreign institutions initially appoint a Brazilian local administrator—usually a bank or a brokerage firm—to represent them to the Comissao de Valores Mobiliarios (CVM), or the Brazilian Security Commission. Investors then fill out a CVM application to invest in Brazil that is completed in duplicate and must be approved by an office of the Brazilian embassy or consulate. The investor then sends the three forms to his global custodian, who in turn sends them to the investor's local administrator in Brazil. The local administrator files the application with the CVM, which then has 15 days to reject the application. However, the applicant can begin investing as soon as the application has been filed with the CVM.

In 1993, the CVM was expected to simplify rules for foreign institutional investors and harmonize them with those of some of its Latin American neighbors. It may also recommend allowing foreign individual investors to buy stocks directly in Brazil's markets. In 1993 the CVM allowed the first foreign company to be listed on its exchanges.

Each foreign institution may own no more than 5 percent of the voting stock (the same as Brazilian institutions) or 20 percent of the total shares of any Brazilian company. A maximum of 10 percent of the resources of investment companies and investment funds may be invested in securities issued by just one company. Cash dividends to nonresident shareholders are subject to a 15 percent tax.

Investments to Consider

For investors who can tolerate risk, Brazil's market presents a good long-term bet. Brazil's is seen as one of the few sizable markets that could still show explosive gains. Few, however, can forecast when that should occur.

"The market could go up 10-fold in the next few years if fiscal adjustments are made, the economy stabilized, and inflation brought down," holds David Lazenby, portfolio manager of the Equity Fund of Latin America and the Equity Fund of Brazil, managed by Batterymarch Financial Management. "That's a lot of ifs; but we're going on potential," he says. "Ultimately, Brazil will have to catch up with its neighbors and the global trend" toward economic reforms.

Lazenby views Brazil's market as "a long-term buy." In April 1993 he pointed out that "the market is cheap, said to be the cheapest in Latin America, reflecting political and economic concerns. Large stocks are trading at 25 to 50 percent of book value." Having weathered a severe recession, Brazilian industry is also "lean and mean," points out William Truscott, vice president and assistant portfolio manager for The Scudder Latin America Fund. Thus, "any decent policies coming out of the government would be beneficial for stocks."

Moreover, a rise in inflation isn't always poisonous to the market. On the contrary, higher inflation can be positive in the short term, as investors switch from fixed-income investments to equities. With stocks, investors "feel they are closer to owning a real asset; with fixed income, they see themselves as merely holding short-term government debt, when there's not a lot of faith in the government," explains Paul White, Latin American portfolio manager of Arco Investment Management Co., which manages the $2.5 billion pension fund of Atlantic Richfield Co. in Los Angeles.

In April 1993, White said he was "cautious" about the near-term prospects for Brazil's market—especially after the market's runup earlier in the year. White was "comfortable" with an underweighted position in Brazil for Arco's $40 million Latin America portfolio. In contrast, Batterymarch's Lazenby said his Equity Fund of Latin America had an overweighted position in Brazil, relative to weight by market capitalization. Among the attractive stocks he cites are: Telebras, Petrobras, and Electrobras, which feature relatively low valuations and ample trading liquidity. Eventually, if these companies are fully privatized, investors should benefit from better management and enhanced profitability.

To address Brazil's large consumer market, Lazenby recommends Brahma brewing company and Sadia Concorida, a food processor. Both companies "are well run, with large market shares," he says. And for those who can weather a "difficult time in the pulp and paper industry because of low prices" on the world market, he suggests Aracruz Celulose, a strong player in the paper industry. With its natural resource advantages, Brazil's production costs in this industry are lower than those of Canada, Sweden, and other producers. Thus when prices eventually rise, Brazil's pulp/paper industry stands to reap higher profits.

Observing the economic landscape of 1993, Marcelo Cabral, a vice president at First Boston Corporation, saw "two investment bets. If you're less concerned about liquidity [which implies taking smaller positions in Brazil] and want to build a portfolio of $20 to $50 million with a three- to five-year horizon, there could be great stock investment possibilities in domestic-oriented companies." He cited Souza Cruz, a tobacco company with an 80 percent share of the cigarette market in Brazil; and refrigerator manufacturer Consul and compressor manufacturer Embraco, both of which are controlled by Brasmotor, the largest home appliance producer in Latin American (and a subsidiary of Whirlpool Corporation).

But for those with short-term horizons, he suggests examining the popular liquid stocks, including those of Telebras, Electrobras, and Companhia Electricidade de Minas Gerais. "These react quickly and forcefully to developments in the country," Cabral said.

For investors who prefer not to invest directly in Brazil's markets, Wilson Emerging Market Funds Research Inc. reports that, as of 1993, there were 119 country funds for Brazil, for international investors. Among the latter are: the open-end Brazilian Investment Co. (SICAV); closed-end funds Brazil Fund Inc. and Brazilian Equity Fund Inc., which both trade on the New York Stock Exchange; and the Brazilian Investment Trust plc, which trades on the London Stock Exchange.

According to Bankers Trust Company, as of December 1992, Aracruz Celulose was the only company with an American Depositary Receipt program.

6
Chile

Chile has been in the vanguard of economic reform for 20 years. Many of its well-honed programs—from debt equity swaps to a privatized social security system—have been adopted by other nations in the region, often with the help of Chilean consultants.

Ironically, until 1990, Chile was ruled by a dictator, contradicting the historic truism that dictatorships generally favor protectionism and iron-fisted control of the national economy and its key enterprises. General Augusto Pinochet Ugarte became president in 1973, on the heels of a bloody military coup that toppled the left-wing government of his predecessor, Salvador Allende Gossens.

Pinochet lost power in 1988, when he permitted Chilean citizens to vote in a plebiscite. A presidential election followed in 1989, which was won by Patricio Aylwin Azocar. In an inaugural ceremony on March 11, 1990, Gabriel Valdes, president of the Chilean Senate, removed the presidential sash from Pinochet and placed it on Aylwin.

The three principal figures in this peaceful inauguration were well acquainted. During Pinochet's reign, he had twice jailed Valdes; and he had banned Aylwin's Christian Democratic party, which led the center–left political coalition that defeated Pinochet at the polls.

The politically dominant Christian Democrats, in late 1992, selected Eduardo Frei—the party leader and a former businessman—as their candidate for the December 1993 presidential election, making him a virtual shoo-in as Aylwin's successor.

Frei is the son of the Eduardo Frei who served as President of Chile for two terms in the 1960s.

The reforms for Chile begun by Pinochet, who still commands the army, have been diligently continued by Aylwin. Debt both foreign and domestic is being reduced. Fiscal and monetary policies are sound.

Most significant from the outsiders' perspective, the rules of foreign investment are being softened. International trade is being liberalized and expanded. Many other reforms have contributed to consistent economic growth.

Real growth in the gross domestic product averaged about 6 percent annually in the five years through 1991. In 1992, real economic growth was 10.4 percent—making it Chile's best year in three decades; about 6 percent growth was forecast for 1993. In the five years to 1992, per capita GDP climbed from $1734 to $2400, and at 5 percent, the unemployment rate stood at a 20-year low.

This upbeat news naturally won the attention of international investors. With their help, the Chilean stock market had become one of the world's best performers. In 1992, according to the IFC Price Index, Chile posted its eighth consecutive yearly gain—up 12.3 percent in U.S. dollar terms— after a 90 percent gain in 1991. Total market capitalization had more than doubled by year-end 1991, to almost $28 billion, from $13.6 billion a year earlier. At year-end 1992, it was $29.6 billion, according to the IFC.

Chile's economy has been getting hotter and hotter. But the glut of cash from foreign business and industrial investors, eager to share the prosperity, has threatened to stymie efforts to curb inflation.

To neutralize the impact of large capital inflows, Chile's central bank stepped up marketing of government securities. The peso was revalued about 10 percent in 1992. The inflation rate, which had been above 30 percent in the mid-1980s, was 13 percent in 1992.

Topping the list of long-term problems was poverty, which spawned other social blights; among them: illiteracy, alcoholism, out-of-wedlock births, and a high death rate. An estimated 40 percent of Chile's 13.4 million people live in poverty, and four out of five workers do not earn enough to support a family. But Housing Minister Alejandro Foxley announced at year- end 1992 that real wages were up 5 percent and that Chile had succeeded in lifting about 700,000 people out of poverty. Elections are not likely to alter Chile's economic course.

Government and Politics

In 1970, Allende became Latin America's first elected Marxist President, but only with the support—in a close race—of non-communist political parties desperately seeking relief from decades of economic problems. Allende pursued his goal of making Chile a socialist state by nationalizing banks, copper mines, and a broad range of industrial enterprises. He imposed price controls and guaranteed workers real wage increases.

Not surprisingly, Allende's approach further disrupted the economy. The results were hyperinflation, widespread short-ages, and a balance-of-payments crisis aggravated by capital flight. In September 1973, purportedly with the tacit approval of rightist parties, a brutal military coup deposed Allende and suspended congress indefinitely. A ruling four-man junta named its leader, Pinochet, as president. Leftist political parties were banned, and all other parties were declared to be in "indefinite recess."

Under Pinochet, labor unions and strikes were outlawed. Press censorship was imposed, and elected local officials were replaced by the junta's appointees. Thousands of Allende sup-porters were imprisoned, and many were executed.

In the beginning of his regime, Pinochet received strong sup-port from the United States, which had actively opposed the Marxist Allende. Relations became strained, though still tenable, after the 1976 car-bomb murder in Washington of Orlando Letelier, Allende's friend and foreign minister.

In 1980, a new constitution extended Pinochet's presidency for eight years, after which a partial return to civilian govern-ment would begin. But this constitution also provided the presi-dential plebiscite of 1988, which permitted voters to approve or reject the single presidential candidate nominated by the junta.

Pinochet lost the plebiscite by a wide margin, compelling him to

CHILE

Currency: Chilean Peso (CLP)

Stock Exchange: Chile has three stock exchanges: the Santiago Stock Exchange (Bolsa De Comercio De Santiago), with 80 percent of the total volume, the Electronic Stock Exchange (Bolsa De Valores De Chile), with 15 percent, and the Valparaiso Stock Exchange (Bolsa De Comercio De Valparaiso), with the remaining 5 percent of the volume. The three stock exchanges are not linked to one another and they compete for listings.

Index: The main market index is the General Index for Stock Prices (IGPA). The IGPA was created in 1958 and represents a variety of market sectors, with 1980 used as the current base year. The Index includes all stocks with a presence in the Chilean market. The other important market index is the Selective Index of Stock Prices (IPSA), which represents the 40 most important publicly traded stocks in terms of volume and market presence.

Types of Securities: Equity, government securities, corporate securities, time deposits, repurchase agreements, swaps, options, and futures.

Regulatory Body/Stock Exchange Supervision: All banking operations and securities markets are regulated by the Superintendency of Securities and Insurances (Superintendencia De Bancos E Instituciones Financieras). In addition, foreign investors are regulated by the Central Bank, the Foreign Investment Committee, and the Internal Revenue.

Depository: Although no central depository currently exists in Chile, one is being developed by market participants with a target implementation date of early 1994.

Settlement Information

Equities:
- T + 2.

- Physical delivery only.
- Receive/deliver versus payment available.
- On SD, a due bill invoice along with a certificate of transference of ownership (*traspaso*) is signed by both buyer and seller and is sent to the company's registrar for reregistration into the new owner's name. A bank check or interbank transfer is exchanged when the *traspaso* is signed by both parties.

Fixed:

- TD (OTC market) T + 1 (exchange traded)
- Physical delivery only
- Receive/deliver versus payment available
- Physical certificates are exchanged on SD against a bank check or interbank transfer.

Restrictions for Foreign Investors

Foreign Investment Laws: Decree Law 600 and F.I.F. Law 18,657 are the most common methods by which foreign investors enter the Chilean market. The main components of these regulations are as follows:

Decree Law 600

- Allows for investment in all economic sectors.
- Requires authorization from the Foreign Investment Committee.
- Requires contract to be signed with the Republic of Chile.
- Guarantees access to the formal foreign exchange market.
- Restricts capital repatriation to one year.
- Imposes no restrictions on profit/capital gains remittances.
- Assesses remittance tax at a rate of 35 percent.
- Requires a local/legal representative, tax adviser, and accountant (may be one person).

F.I.F. Law 18,657

- Directed primarily at foreign funds of foreign institutional investors.

(Continued)

- Requires contract to be signed with the Republic of Chile.
- Requires authorization from the Superintendency of Securities and Insurances.
- Requires authorization from the Foreign Investment Committee.
- Restricts capital repatriation for five years.
- Imposes no restrictions on profit/capital gains remittances.
- Assesses remittance tax rate at a rate of 10 percent.
- Mandates a minimum total investment of U.S.$1 million, to be invested in: stocks of listed companies, securities issued by the State or Central Bank, registered bonds, commercial paper, bank securities, and a limited percentage of unlisted companies.
- Requires appointment of a local administrator.
- Imposes the following diversification rules:

  1. No more than 10 percent invested in securities of the same issuer.
  2. Cannot hold more than 5 percent of an issuer's capital.
  3. At the end of the first year, at least 20 percent must be invested in equities.
  4. At the end of the third year, at least 60 percent must be invested in equities.
  5. No more than 10 percent may be invested in closed corporations.

Foreign Investor Approval: For foreign investors entering Chile through either Decree Law 600 or F.I.F. Law 18,657, in order to sign a contract with the Republic of Chile, investors must first have their application to the Foreign Investment Committee (FIC) approved. The FIC application should include the following information:

- Amount to be invested
- Type of investment
- Copy of balance sheet
- Documents evidencing incorporation
- Power of attorney to the legal representative

In addition to the above, investors using F.I.F. Law 18,657

are required to provide the following documents to the Superintendency of Securities and Insurances:

- Articles or documents evidencing incorporation
- Corporate bylaws
- Certificate of incumbency
- Copy of local representative agreement

Most foreign investors fund their local cash accounts in large increments for the following reasons:

- Each funds transfer must be registered with the Central Bank.
- The withholding period for capital applies to each transfer of resources.
- Foreign investors must maintain, monitor, and fulfill the diversification requirements detailed in F.I.F. Law 18,657.

Foreign Ownership Ceilings: Foreign ownership of television stations, newspaper publishers, and other media companies is restricted. In addition, Foreign Investment Fund Law 18,657 forbids a total of more than 25 percent foreign investment in any one company.

There is a 10 percent limit for a single portfolio investing in any single issue, except those issued by the government or central bank. The limit is stricter with voting shares, of which a single portfolio cannot hold more than 5 percent.

Foreign Exchange Restrictions: All foreign exchange must be registered with the Central Bank.

Repatriation of Sale Proceeds and Income: No restrictions apply to repatriation of income or realized capital gains. However, repatriation of principal is restricted to one year if the investor entered the Chilean market through D.L. 600, or for five years if the investor entered through F.I.F. Law 18,657.

Taxes: For all investment funds or portfolios established under the auspices of Law 18,657, a flat rate of 10 percent withholding on the entire portfolio's income is assessed at the time of repatriation, regardless of the source of the income

(Continued)

(i.e., capital gains, dividends, or interest). A higher overall rate of 35 to 49 percent is assessed against all investment funds or portfolios established under the Decree Law 600.

There is an 18 percent value-added tax imposed on all service fees.

Securities Lending: There is no active securities lending market in Chile.

SOURCE: The Bank of New York

open the polls to a democratic presidential election on December 14, 1989. Chile's right-wing parties hoped to use the ballot to sustain continued military rule, via the election of Hernan Buchi. But the 70-year-old Aylwin won, with the united backing of 17 centrist and leftist parties, now called the concertacion.

Buchi, as Pinochet's finance minister, had masterminded Chile's economic boom of the 1980s. However, political analysts attributed Aylwin's victory largely to assurances that he would not alter the economic policies that had nurtured Chile's remarkable recovery.

Aylwin chose young, well-educated contemporary thinkers to run the economy. Foxley, who holds degrees from Harvard and the University of Wisconsin, was named finance minister; and Andres Velasco, with degrees from Columbia and Yale, became his chief of staff. Carlos Ominami, who had been a research associate in France, was named economics minister. Aylwin's single term ends in 1994.

Pinochet will continue to head the military until his scheduled retirement in 1998, when he will be 80. In late 1992, Pinochet warned that his army was "a sleeping lion" that could be aroused from its slumber if provoked too far. He had been provoked by the indictment of his former chief of secret police, retired general Manuel Contreras, for the 1976 murder of Letelier in Washington.

The skillful balancing act that has kept the army in slumber and maintained the stability of the ruling multiparty coalition has been seen as evidence of President Aylwin's political acumen.

Criticism from friend and foe alike could be a signal that Aylwin is doing a good, even-handed job. Both business leaders and political opponents have charged that his administration's "statist" proclivities endanger the economy's growth potential. His associates in the ruling coalition of center–left parties call for more government spending to remedy the "social debt" left by 17 years of military rule.

"The peaceful reconstruction of Chile has been possible, despite the confrontational nature of a 17-year authoritarian interregnum," says Edgardo Beeninger, Chile's minister secretary general of the presidency, "because the capitalism-versus-socialism dilemma that polarized Chilean politics no longer exists."

The Economy

Apparently seeing the pitfalls of statism, Pinochet and his advisers decided that the cure for their country's ills was integration of their national economy into the world economy. The administrations of both Pinochet and Aylwin have met this goal by creating a free market, attractive to international traders and investors.

Pinochet immediately nullified most of Allende's price controls and other restrictions on private businesses, and returned or paid retroactively for some of the nationalized enterprises. In response, major international banks reopened lines of credit to Chile. The resulting loans, together with rising world copper prices, sparked rapid economic growth in the late 1970s. That recovery, enhanced by disciplined fiscal policy, brought inflation down from its 1975 peak of 505 percent to less than 40 percent by decade's end.

A setback in 1982 was the result of a severe domestic recession caused by a combination of events, including the cutoff of foreign funds and the collapse of world copper prices. Remarkably, the inflation rate continued to inch down throughout this crucial period. By 1985 fiscal balance had been restored, and the economy resumed its advancement.

International trade was liberalized in 1985 by reducing tariffs to a highly competitive, uniform 11 percent, and by eliminating nontariff barriers. Other state-owned enterprises were sold off, which, along with easier investment rules, helped to lure foreign investors.

Looking ahead, Salomon Brothers expects that economic growth will likely be fueled by rising consumer demand. As a result, sectors such as construction, electric power, home-building products, and consumer products should fare well.

Natural Challenges and Opportunities

To know Chile's economic potential is to know its topography, which covers 302,778 square miles—the hard way. The country's name derives from an Indian word meaning "land's end," which describes the country's narrow stretch of 2600 miles southward along the Pacific coast, to the very tip of South America. No point is more than 150 miles wide. Chile's great north–south length, the lofty Andes Mountains sprawled along its eastern borders with Argentina and Bolivia, the pounding Pacific Ocean, the cold, shore-hugging Peru Current, the southern wetlands...all produce the many climates that accommodate, if not dictate, economic and social diversity.

The Desert North. The barren north, about one-third of the country's total length, is a high-altitude territory predominated by the Atacama Desert. It provides Chile's greatest natural asset, its copper mines. They contain at least 20 percent of the world's reserves, making Chile the leading copper producer of the western hemisphere. While copper still accounts for some 45 percent of exports, compared with nearly 80 percent in the 1970s, Chile is showing progress in diversifying and expanding foreign sales to make the economy less sensitive to world copper prices.

Middle Chile. The midsection of Chile, which contains Santiago and Valparaiso, features mild winters and warm, dry summers. It is home to more than two-thirds of the population, along with most offices of the national government, its many agencies, and many major financial and business institutions.

South Chile. Many of Chile's agricultural and forest products come from the rain-drenched south. Its forests are extensive, and export of wood products with higher value-added content, such as newsprint, have been rising. Export of all forestry products has been increasing an average 18 percent annually since 1986, totaling $1.1 billion in 1992.

Pinochet's agricultural policies, emphasizing modernization and efficiency, succeeded in expanding fruit and vegetable exports, which have increased 16 percent annually since 1986, to $1.2 billion in 1992. Topping the list are grapes, apples, and kiwis. Being south of the equator, Chile's growing season is winter in the United States, where residents welcome fresh-picked "out of season" fruits and vegetables.

Wine exports have been increasing at an average annual rate

of 46 percent to a total of more than $125 million in 1992, with the potential for continued extraordinary growth. In 1992, the *Financial Times* reported that Chile overtook Germany as the third largest wine exporter to the United States, after France and Italy. Chile's extremely long coastline makes it a natural for ocean-based industry. In 1992, Chile became the world's largest processor of fishmeal for export as fertilizer and animal feed, with sales exceeding $500 million. New aquacultural technologies have been rewarding in their application to seaweed "farming," which yields some 200,000 metric tons a year. Chilean agar, a gelatin, is extracted from the seaweed for sale to domestic and foreign food processors and other users.

Chile is also rich in iron, molybdenum, gold, and lithium. Coal production has been increasing, though profitability remains elusive. There was optimism about a large natural gas project launched in 1992. With oil reserves nearly depleted, Chile is dependent on imports for domestic needs.

Manufactured goods account for about 20 percent of Chile's GDP, or more than $6 billion, and reflect its natural attributes. The major industries are food processing, chemicals, metal working, pulp and paper, and textiles. By and large, they survived the shift to open markets and the removal of trade protection.

Privatization

Privatization, begun in 1974 by Pinochet, was in two stages, according to Hernan Somerville, former director of the Central Bank of Chile. The first stage—probably inspired by Pinochet's desire to recapture the favor and investment capital of alienated foreigners—returned many of the 600 foreign-owned companies Allende had expropriated to their former owners. Companies that weren't returned were sold to Chilean nationals.

The second phase, beginning in 1985, privatized properties the state had owned for years, such as those in energy, telecommunications, insurance, and transportation. They were offered to foreign as well as domestic investors. Among the sales were: Endesa, Chile's largest electric power company; 75 percent of Lan-Chile, an airline; Entel, a long-distance telephone company, and Compania de Telefonos de Chile (CTC), Chile's largest telephone company.

By 1992, 25 percent of Chile's GDP was government-controlled, down from 40 percent in 1974. The largest of the remaining 50 state-owned companies were the National Copper Company (Codelco) and the National Oil Refinery (Enap), and neither was expected to be sold.

A primary benefit of privatization was reduction of foreign debt with sales proceeds. Additional objectives offered by Somerville: To improve the economy's long-term efficiency; to broadly diversify corporate ownership; to reinforce the role and scope of pension funds by providing attractive investments; to provide the central government with the revenues to implement social programs.

A big boost to privatization was the debt-to-equity program, which allowed foreign investors to buy discounted Chilean foreign debt and trade it at par value for equity in state-owned companies. By mid-1992, debt-to-equity conversions totaled $3.6 billion. Because this move also raised the value of Chilean debt instruments in the secondary market, it reduced the role of conversions in privatizations.

Various Chilean nationals were also encouraged to participate in privatizations through employee stock purchase plans. Pension funds have also been investing in the shares of privatized companies.

The Aylwin administration slowed privatization, expressing concern about its possible utilization as a vehicle to create monopolies. But sources said privatization was expected to continue in the energy sector, perhaps involving major hydroelectric and related projects, as well as in the port and cargo transportation sectors.

Pensions

In 1981, Chile privatized its social security system, creating a defined-contribution program. Under the compulsory savings plan, 10 percent of each employee's earnings goes into the privately run Asociacion de Fondo Pensiones (AFP), which operates like a family of mutual funds and provides an individual account for each worker. In 1993, the aggregate value of employees' pension funds totaled approximately $14 billion.

In 1989 the funds were permitted to invest 30 percent of assets in Chilean equities, up from 5 percent. That boost helped to carry the domestic stock market to extraordinary heights. With the maximum allowable investment, the pension funds could account for 15 percent of the market's total capitalization.

As part of the effort to offset large inflows of foreign capital, the government authorized funds to invest up to 1.5 percent of assets abroad, and that cap will eventually climb to 5 percent. Even with the cap limited to 1.5 percent, the funds could invest more than $200 million in foreign equities.

In addition, a reform proposed in January 1993 would permit AFPs and insurance companies to purchase up to 70 percent of shares of all publicly traded Chilean firms (up from 1 percent of 43 specifically chosen large companies). It would also permit investment in a wider range of bonds.

Seeking to create new capital pools and to enhance their retirement systems, several other Latin American countries—including Colombia, Mexico, Peru, and Venezuela—have studied Chile's pension system, with an eye toward revising their own versions.

Foreign Debt Reduction

Chile has worked diligently since the mid-1980s to reduce its foreign debt. Like Colombia, Chile did not need a Brady restructuring plan, putting them a cut above the other major Latin American countries.

At year-end 1991, Chile's foreign debt, including loans from the International Monetary Fund, totaled $17.4 billion. Reductions since 1985 have totaled $10.9 billion, including some $3.6 billion in debt equity swaps, prepayments of private sector debts, and write-off of some corporate obligations. Major influences in the reduction of the debt burden have been a strong GDP and export growth. Merchandise exports accounted for 30 percent of GDP in 1992, twice the 1970 level.

Declines in foreign debt, combined with gains in export income, have "markedly improved Chile's debt profile in recent years," wrote Suhas L. Ketkar, economist with the First Boston Corporation, in October 1992. "The debt-to-exports, the interest-payments-to-exports, and the debt-service ratio all have fallen significantly, to return Chile to international creditworthiness of investment grade. Only the debt-to-GDP ratio of 55.4 percent in 1991 remains somewhat higher than desirable." In 1992, the ratio dropped to nearly 46 percent, and First Boston projects that it will fall to 43 percent in 1993.

Trade Agreements and Foreign Exchange

While actively pursuing bilateral trade agreements, Chile has been on the front lines in its drive for free trade throughout the western hemisphere.

A free trade agreement was signed with Mexico in 1991, and another was signed with Venezuela in 1993. It has a complementary agreement with Argentina. The pact with Venezuela will lower customs duties on bilateral trade to zero by 1999. Chile chose not to join Argentina, Brazil, Paraguay, and Uruguay in the Mercosur free-trade block, purportedly out of fear that to do so would be to link it to unstable economies.

In response to pressure for an agreement with the United States, President George Bush, on a visit in 1990, said Chile would be the first country in line, after the North American Free Trade Agreement with Canada and Mexico had been concluded. Chile expects a U.S. trade agreement to attract investment as well as trade.

In 1992, Chile changed its method of valuing its currency, previously pegged to the U.S. dollar; it is now linked to a basket of currencies of which the U.S. dollar has a 50 percent weighting. The market's exchange rate would be allowed to vary within a range of 10 percent, up or down, of the bank's official rate.

Work Force

There are 4.8 million workers in Chile, and the unemployment rate in 1992 was less than 6 percent. However there is a wide discrepancy in incomes, and, as noted earlier, the wages of most workers are low and poverty is rampant. Per capita GDP in 1991 was $2200.

Low-wage and industrious workers are an attraction for foreign business and industrial investors. As of 1993 the minimum wage was $25 a week, and a skilled industrial employee earned about $60. However, weekly incomes of $250 and sometimes more are not uncommon for copper mine workers in northern Chile.

Education

The Chilean literacy rate is about 96 percent, among the highest in Latin America. Eight years of primary education is compulsory. There are more than two million children in primary schools and some 750,000 in secondary schools. About 250,000 students attend the 20 universities, 12 of which were established in the 1980s. University autonomy, which had been taken away by Pinochet in 1973, was fully restored by 1990.

The Stock Market

The confidence of investors has been reflected in Chile's stock market. Although in the January to June 4, 1993 period, the Chilean market fell 8.4 percent in U.S. dollar terms, according to the IFC, it had posted gains in each of the prior 8 years. In its stellar year of 1986, it roared ahead by 134.4 percent in dollars, according to the IFC's index. The Chilean stock market reflects key components of the economy, where commodity-related industries, such as mining and forest products, have prominent places, along with electric utilities and telecommunications.

Until 1985, when Chile's stock market began its climb to international stardom, it traveled a troubled road. By 1940, 48 years after the first stock exchange was established, the securities market was a reasonably well-developed operation. However, imposition of interest rate ceilings in an inflationary economy slowed market activity to a crawl. It went into complete collapse in 1970, with Allende's nationalization of banks and many industries.

When Pinochet seized power in 1973 he imposed economic reforms that got the country moving. And the stock market followed; trading and prices moved apace, and continued bullish until 1981, when soaring interest rates lured investors to banks. They began drifting back to stocks a few years later, after interest rates had calmed and the severe economic recession of 1982 had faded from memory. By 1985, the market had resumed its climb.

The Exchanges

Chile's first stock exchange, the Bolsa de Corredores, was founded in Valparaiso in 1892. The next year the Santiago Stock Exchange—the Bolsa de Comercio—was established, and it soon overtook Valparaiso. A third exchange was subsequently formed, but Santiago remains the largest and busiest, handling the majority of trades.

An electronic exchange formed in 1989 utilizes computer screens. Modeled after NASDAQ system in the United States, it accommodates 8 percent of Chile's equity trading. A central depository was recently cleared for establishment and is expected to be up and running by 1994.

Forty-two brokerage firms operate on the Santiago Stock Exchange. Four kinds of instruments are traded besides equities, they are fixed-rate securities, short-term securities, futures, and currencies. The Santiago exchange also offers trading in stock index futures (the IPSA index). In 1993, it expected to launch trading of some options on shares and additional futures offerings.

In Chile, as in many other developing countries, much of the corporate stock is held or controlled by influential families and their associates. This explains, at least in part, why there consistently has been an intense concentration of market value and activity.

Though 245 companies were listed in 1992, 10 accounted for much of the market's $29.6 billion capitalization. They were: Endesa, Copec, Telefonos, Cartones, Enersis (the holding group that owns Chilectra), Vapores, Cervezas, Chilectra, Minera, and CCT, according to G. T. Management in San Francisco.

According to Salomon Brothers, the 10 largest market sectors, and their shares of market cap, were: Electric power (30 percent); Telecom (13 percent); Petrochemicals (11 percent); pension fund (7 percent); paper & pulp (6 percent); food & beverages

(8 percent); transportation (4 percent); construction (3 percent); banking (3 percent); and tobacco (3 percent).

Two indexes are used to track the Chilean stock market: the IGPA, a general index, and the IPSA, a selective index that charts the 40 most traded stocks.

Trading through Chilean Brokers

When dealing with a local broker, settlement of cash transactions usually is on the second business day after the trade, or by arrangement. There is no centralized settlement system, but a system is in the planning stages at present. A seller signs a stock transfer form that his broker takes to the buyer's broker for the buyer's signature. The transfer then is sent to the company for registration, which must take place within five business days of receipt.

Both stock exchange and brokerage commissions are paid. The exchange's commission ranges from 0.5 down to 0.04 percent, depending on the size and the nature of the transaction. Brokerage commissions are negotiable, generally scaling down from a maximum of 1 percent for individual investors to about 0.35 percent for large institutional trades. A value-added tax of 18 percent applies to both the stock exchange and brokerage commissions.

Market Information and Investor Protection

The major exchanges have daily, weekly, monthly, quarterly and annual publications. There is daily stock market coverage on international wire services, and regular publication of price-earnings ratios and yields.

International brokers and analysts, and some Chilean brokers, offer market commentaries and company reports in English. Consolidated audited annual accounts and quarterly statements must be provided by public companies.

The accounting standards of the public companies were rated as "good" by IFC. Market operations are overseen by Chile's Stocks and Securities Superintendency.

Foreign Investors

Nonresident foreign investors must abide by required registration procedures to ensure their repatriation rights. Investment income may be freely repatriated at any time, but capital may be removed only after it has been invested in Chile for a year, for investors who entered the Chilian market under decree law 600. Those entering under F.I.F. law 18,657 cannot repatriate their capital for five years.

Funds

Individual investors unable to invest directly in the Chilean stock market could consider purchase of shares in country or regional funds. Among the Chilean country funds listed in the 1992-93 edition of *The Wilson Directory of Emerging Market Funds* are these:

Funds	Market
Chile Fund Inc.	NYSE
Genesis Chile Fund Inc.	London
GT Chile Growth Fund	London
Five Arrows Chile Fund	London

According to Bankers Trust Company, at the end of 1992, three Chilean companies had ADR programs: Compania Cervecerias Unidas, Compania de Telefonos de Chile, and Distribuidora Chilectra Metropolitana.

7
Colombia

As Colombia has liberalized rules for foreign investors, increasing amounts of money have streamed into its stock market, seeking to share the fruits of its steadily expanding economy.

Market capitalization on Colombia's three Bolsas nearly quadrupled in the two years through 1992, according to the IFC. Year-end total value climbed from $1.4 billion in 1990 to $3.9 billion in 1991. In 1992, according to the IFC Price Index, Colombia's stock market was the world's best performer, posting advances of 36.1 percent in U.S. dollar terms. The market ranked third in the previous year, with gains of 173.9 percent in price and 48.4 percent in total return.

Colombia's main attraction was its steady, uninterrupted growth in gross domestic product for more than 20 years. It has had the highest performance in the region, achieving an average annual real growth rate of 4.2 percent in 1989, according to the U.S. Chamber of Commerce, with a reported accumulated real gain in GDP of 43 percent. Advances have continued into the 1990s, with inflation-adjusted GDP gains of 4.1 percent in 1990, 2.3 percent in mildly recessionary 1991, and 3.6 percent in 1992, to $48.5 billion. It has never had to restructure its foreign debt. It has no hyperinflation, the fiscal deficit is under control, and growth has been steady.

"Colombia has well earned its international reputation for prudent economic management," wrote Laurie MacNamara in the March 23, 1992, issue of the U.S. Commerce Department's *Business America*. "Sustained economic growth during the 1980s came through conservative fiscal policies, a sustained commitment to export diversification, and reasonable international debt contraction." In the 1980s, Colombia's average annual inflation rate was 24 percent, while the rest of Latin America staggered under an average 400 percent a year rate.

To open up the Colombian markets and encourage international participation, the government introduced a number of economic reforms: tariff reductions and other steps to free foreign trade; virtual decontrol of foreign exchange; tax structure revision; modernization of the capital market; and opening of the stock market to foreign investors. In addition, a slow but steady program of privatization of state-owned enterprises generated capital, stimulated private sector competition, and expanded the securities markets.

External economic factors are among Colombia's greatest strengths. They include a positive trade balance in excess of $2 billion, current account surpluses, and total 1992 foreign debt of US$16.5 billion.

A main priority of the central bank is to continue to reduce inflation, which Baring Securities predicts will be about 22 percent for 1993. The government's goal is to bring inflation down to 16.1 percent by 1995. GDP growth is expected to rise to 5.5 percent the same year.

While the inflation rate of 25 to 30 percent remains a concern, it has been stable during the past 15 years. Persistent problems, however, include 1992 unemployment of 11 percent, and a large portion of Colombia's nearly 33 million people living in poverty: per capita income in 1991 was $1300.

The 80 percent of Colombia's nearly 33 million people that live in the cities provides most of the country's 14 million workers. A major problem is lack of education. While five years of primary school education is compulsory, only 77 percent of the children enter school, and only 28 percent of them complete the five-year program. The U.S. State Department puts the Colombia literacy rate at 80 percent, some seven percentage points below the Colombian government's estimate.

Although Colombia has gained ground in its years-long struggle against the illegal drug trade, narcotics-related terrorism and guerrilla warfare, internal dangers and negative world image still persist. However "Colombia's reputation as a drug producer is not discouraging foreign interest," said Terence Mahony, then with Baring America Asset Management, Boston, to the *Financial Times* in late 1991. Investors, he said, are prepared to look more at the fundamentals, pointing to the country's economic growth, lack of hyperinflation, and well-managed companies.

Natural resources and geographic advantages contribute significantly to Colombia's economy. The 440,831 square miles that make Colombia the fourth largest country in the region are nestled in the mountainous northwest corner of South America, providing trade access both to the Atlantic—by way of the Caribbean Sea—and the Pacific. A diversified climate allows cattle ranching and the cultivation of coffee and other profitable crops. Petroleum, natural gas, iron, coal, emeralds, and other minerals add to its riches.

Government and Politics

Colombia has been a democratic republic since the adoption in 1886 of a constitution that established a centralized national government dominated by a strong President. While the Liberal and Social Conservative parties continue as major influences, the political spectrum expanded in the 1980s to include other voices, mainly from the left.

In 1990, the Liberals retained power with the election of economist Cesar Gaviria Trujillo, who previously had served as finance minister under Virgilio Barco Vargas, his predecessor, to a four-year term as President.

He immediately reversed Barco's hard-line strategy toward the narcoterrorists and took a more diplomatic path to end the violence, offering concessions to drug traffickers and their major narcoterrorist forces. He also put forth a series of decrees in 1990 that allowed cartel leaders to plead guilty to only one crime. That put a damper on U.S. efforts to extradite leading drug traffickers such as Pablo Escobar Gaviria (no relation to the President).

Several key drug traffickers, including Escobar, surrendered,

COLOMBIA

Currency: Colombian Peso (COP)

Stock Exchange: There are three stock exchanges in Colombia, located in Bogota, Medellin, and Cali (De Occidente). Equity trading is most active on the Medellin Stock Exchange, but overall volume is highest in Bogota and it is expected to become the dominant exchange in the future. There is a substantial OTC market, which is manifest in the fact that 70 percent of all debt securities trading volume occurs off the exchange.

Indexes: There are no major market indexes.

Types of Securities: Government securities, bankers acceptances, certificates of deposit, corporate bonds, municipal bonds, commercial paper.

Regulatory Body/Stock Exchange Supervision: The primary regulatory bodies are the Superintendencia De Valores (SDV) and the Superintendencia Bancaria (SB). The SDV oversees the capital markets and the SB oversees the banks and other financial intermediaries.

Depository: There is no central depository for equity and nongovernmental securities. Recently, a depository for securities issued by the Central Bank (Banco De La Republica) was established, although it is not yet widely used.

Settlement Information

Equities:

- T + 2 (but can be negotiated up to T + 5).
- Physical delivery only.
- Receive/deliver versus payment available.
- Same-day turnaround trades are not possible.

Fixed:

- TD or T + 1 for certificates of deposit.

- Book entry (Central Bank-issued securities only) or physical (all others)
- Receive/deliver versus payment available (against cashier's check only)
- Same-day turnaround trades are not possible.

Taxes:

- The tax reform legislation (Article 18-1) which became effective on 1/1/93, exempted all foreign portfolio investment funds from capital gains taxes.
- Providing taxes have been paid at the corporate level, all dividend income is tax-exempt.
- Interest income is subject to a 30 percent tax that is withheld by the local administrator.
- Capital gains taxes are still subject to the 12 percent withholding tax at the time of repatriation.
- There is a stamp duty of 0.5 percent.
- There is a 14 percent VAT tax on the purchase of all currencies.

Restrictions:

- Law #78 (established in 1989) and Regulation #49 (established in 1991) are the National Planning Departments General guidelines for all investment in Colombia. These laws have been expanded and detailed through the issuance of legislation establishing Resolutions 51 and 52 (in 1991) and Resolution 53/92 in (1992).
- All foreign investors are subject to the minimum investment periods.
- All foreign investors are forbidden from holding more than 5 percent of any one company's stock (or 10 percent if it is a primary issue).
- All foreign investors are subject to limitations on holdings of convertible bonds and any investments in the money markets.
- The current regulations require all foreign investors to obtain prior approval of the Superintendency of Securities and Insurances and the registration of all capital invested with the Central Bank.

(Continued)

- A prior approval is required for any investments in the following industries: toxic waste, public service, communications, and all industries relating to national security.
- The repatriation of income is limited to 100 percent of total capital invested and all capital gains.
- All foreign investors are required to appoint a legal adviser and a local administrator, through whom all applications and registrations are filed with the appropriate regulators and authorities.
- There are no limits on foreign exchange, although the market can become thin periodically throughout the day, causing a decree of illiquidity. The local administrator is responsible for:
  1. Registering with Central Bank
  2. Reporting to the Superintendency of Securities
  3. Monitoring ongoing compliance with local regulations
  4. Paying taxes on behalf of the fund
  5. Preparing financial statements for the fund
- The legal representative is responsible for:
  1. Obtaining Power of Attorney to represent the investor
  2. Drafting the administration agreement
  3. Submitting documentation from the investor evidencing its investment track record, official tax status, and that it is regulated in its home market.
- There are different methods of filing for investment approval, each with varying requirements and anticipated time frames for approval.

Securities Lending: None available at present.

SOURCE: The Bank of New York

but they continued to conduct business from prison. Escobar "escaped" in 1992, and the government reportedly was negotiating for his re-surrender. The violence has abated, but it has not ceased.

An article in *Current History* in 1992 (a journal covering events from a historical perspective) described cocaine as the shaping force in Andean politics and economics for the 1990s. Colombia's drug war has been an effort to tame narcoterrorism, not control the drug flow.

Colombia's drug kings and rebels "have killed hundreds, and ruined the most beautiful country in the world," said billionaire Julio Mario Santo Domingo III, chairman of the industrial complex that includes Bavaria, S.A., the monopoly beer-brewing empire that accounts for approximately 8.5 percent of the Colombian stock market's capitalization as of year-end 1992. Six companies in his empire are publicly traded (Bavaria, Avianca, Promigas, Banco Commercial, Colseguros, Cementos del Caribe).

In July 1991, in response to popular pressure, Colombia adopted a new constitution. One of its goals was to incorporate opposing forces into the political process and produce a more participatory and pluralist democracy. One of the early acts was to hold elections for governors (which until then had been appointed by the President). Four guerrilla groups—the Alianza Democratica/M-19 (the Democratic Alliance), the Popular Liberation Army (EPL), the Revolutionary Workers' Party (PRT) and Quintin Lame—disbanded, lay down their arms, and became political parties.

Gaviria's four-year term ends in 1994, and he cannot seek re-election. Though his Liberal Party retained its strong hold on the government in 1991, M-19 shows strong promise as a third party, winning 2 governorships, 9 seats in the Senate, and 15 seats in the Chamber of Deputies.

In 1993, a new agency, The National Tax and Customs Administration, was created to take over functions previously performed by three agencies. Its purpose is to centralize tax, import duty, and exchange rate controls. Baring Securities surmises this consolidation will reduce tax evasions, estimated at U.S.$1 billion a year.

The Economy

The largest sectors of the Colombian economy are agriculture, manufacturing, and financial services with the communications and building products the two sectors growing the quickest. Coffee makes up 20 to 25 percent of legal export earnings and is mainly in the private sector.

President Gaviria accelerated the pace of a trade liberalization program that the Barco administration had begun in 1990. The objective of the two-stage five-year program, known as *Apertura,* (economic opening) was to internationalize Colombia's economy by exposing domestic industry to foreign competition and revising government regulation of exports and foreign investment.

Among Apertura's major directives were the elimination of import licensing requirements; reduction of tariffs and import surcharges (with the goal of reducing the number of tariff levels to four by 1993); and liberalizing the financial, investment, exchange rate, and tax regimes.

At this writing, the reforms were well on their way. Only 3 percent of product categories are now subject to import licensing, down from 61 percent in 1990. Import licenses are still a requirement for products that could pose a national security risk, such as explosives and drug-related chemicals.

In 1991, tariffs were consolidated into three levels: 0 percent for primary goods and capital goods produced outside of Colombia; 5 percent for the same categories produced in Colombia; and 15 percent for all final consumer goods. The import surcharge was dropped from 10 percent to 5 percent.

Ports and railroads are being privatized, according to U.S. State Department dispatch.

In 1992, two oil fields were discovered in Casanare State that are thought to contain 2 billion barrels. It would be the largest find in the Americas since the Prudhoe Bay discovery, and could not only potentially displace coffee as Colombia's main legal export, but also propel Colombia into the club of major Latin American oil exports (with Mexico and Venezuela), according to *The New York Times.* However, capitalizing on this find may be difficult, as two guerrilla groups, the Revolutionary Armed

Forces of Colombia and the National Liberation Army, make their bases in Casanare.

Foreign Investment

Resolution 52, adopted in December 1991, allowed foreign investors to purchase up to 100 percent of the shares of locally listed companies, according to the IFC, eliminating the prior 10 percent cap. It also abolished the requirement that investment funds must remain in the country for at least a year.

Among other revisions applicable to foreign investors was the elimination of restrictions on remittance by foreign companies of their annual profits on Colombian interests, and full repatriation of all net profits.

Tax Reform

Under Apertura, the economic ministry reduced direct tax rates applicable to domestic and foreign companies. In 1986, the income tax base was broadened to make taxation more equitable, and double taxation of corporate profits was eliminated in the hope of stimulating capital investment.

To finance the fight against rebels and narcoterrorists, a "war tax" was enacted in 1991. It was imposed mainly on high-income individuals and oil and mining companies, which are primary targets of terrorism. The *Financial Times* estimates the 1992 cost of terrorism to the Colombian economy at 0.7 percent of GDP, or $3.4 billion.

Privatization

State-owned operations in the financial, manufacturing, telecommunications, and electric power sectors have been privatized, but the process might best be described as moving at "deliberate speed." Capel observed that the fairly modest plans "seem to be inconsistent with the degree of progress in other areas of liberalization in the country."

Sales of state-owned banks gained speed after the government's 1991 decision to assume past obligations of institutions being privatized. The government's dissolution of Colpuertos, which controlled the ports, accommodated their sale to private interests. Railroads also were being privatized.

Foreign Trade

Trade liberalization began under Barco and was continued under Graviria. Colombia has a natural advantage in having ports on both the Atlantic and Pacific oceans. Its major export partners are the United States, Germany, the Netherlands, and Japan, and its major import partners are the United States, Venezuela, Japan, Germany, and France.

To Gulfstream Global's Thomas Tull, one of Colombia's appealing economic aspects is its increasingly diverse export base. "Nontraditional exports are growing at a faster rate than traditional exports, such as coffee, petroleum, and coal," he says, "and that increasing diversity is steadily reducing Colombia's vulnerability to sharp moves in world prices of its leading traditional exports, such as coffee."

Nontraditional exports include agricultural products other than coffee; fishing products; manufactured goods, and minerals other than petroleum and coal. Based on data from Colombia's Central Bank, $3.7 billion in nontraditional exports in 1991 accounted for 48 percent of total exports of $7.6 billion. In 1990, nontraditionals brought in $2.6 billion, or 36 percent of total export revenue of $7.1 billion.

Though emerald sales comprise less than 5 percent of Colombia's total sales, in 1991, it sold $136 million in emeralds on the world market, fulfilling 60 percent of demand. Thomas Tull believes Colombia has the potential to become the emerald capital of the world.

Trade Agreements

Colombia participates in the United States-sponsored Andean Trade Initiative, a 10-year program legislated into existence by the Andean Trade Preference Act (ATPA). It's part of the war on drug production and export. Patterned after the Caribbean Basin Recovery Act of 1983, its objectives are:

- To promote economic development through private sector initiative in the four Andean countries of Bolivia, Colombia, Ecuador, and Peru,
- To encourage alternatives to coca cultivation and production by offering broader access to the U.S. market, and
- To stimulate investment in nontraditional sectors and diversify the Andean countries' export bases.

The chief advantage to participating countries is expanded duty-free entry into the United States for the duration of the program.

Colombia also is a member of the Andean Free Trade Area (AFTA), with Venezuela, Ecuador, Peru, and Bolivia, established in 1991 and put into effect January 1, 1992. Its intragroup trade is subject to uniform external tariffs of 5 to 20 percent, liberalized intraregional trade rules, and elimination of all subsidies to ensure a level playing field.

NAFTA is a source of concern to Venezuela and Colombian business executives. The two signed a pact with Mexico in 1991 for a gradual reduction of tariffs along Andean Pact lines. Colombia and Venezuela also have a separate free trade agreement, and Colombia entered an agreement with Ecuador and Bolivia in October 1992.

The Stock Market

Colombia's burgeoning economy had been tantalizing international investors for years, but it wasn't until the 1990s that meaningful participation in the still developing stock market became possible.

This market rose only modestly in 1992, reflecting a very difficult year for Colombia's economy due to severe power rationing, low coffee prices, and guerilla attacks on the oil and mining industries. The IFC reported a 36.1 percent increase, in U.S. dollar terms, for Colombia's market in 1992—compared with the spike of 173.9 percent logged for 1991.

The prognosis for Colombia's economy continues favorable, however. GDP growth in 1992 was 3.3 percent exceeding all estimates, and both the government and independent sources are forecasting an economic growth for 1993 in excess of 4 percent.

Liberalization of the rules for foreign investors include:

- Allowing free, at-will entry and exit of dividends, gains, and capital;

- Permitting foreign purchase of up to 100 percent of the shares of domestically listed companies (except defense, national security, and the processing, scrapping, and disposing of toxic wastes not produced in Colombia); and

- Allowing country funds to participate in domestic markets.

Legal procedures remain, according to the National Planning Department. To invest in Colombian stocks, foreigners first must obtain authorization to invest from the National Securities Commission, at which time they may transfer capital and invest through a designated financial intermediary, who also acts as their legal representative in Colombia. Finally, the investments must be registered at the foreign investment office of the Central Bank.

Colombia expanded the stock market by taking a leaf from Chile's book and establishing privately managed pension funds, which were authorized to devote portions of their assets to equities. Their increasing presence in the stock market, along with newly authorized country funds, added the institutional investment dimension needed to stimulate trading activity.

The Exchanges

Colombia has three exchanges. The oldest and largest, the Bogota Stock Exchange (Bolsa de Bogota), founded in 1928, accounts for more than half of total stock value traded.

The next most active, the Medellin Stock Exchange, was established by brokerage firms in 1961. In 1983, with the increase in industrial development in southwestern Colombia, business and brokerage firms formed the Bolsa De Occidente, in Cali, which is the smallest of the three.

About 70 brokerage firms operate in Colombia, a few of them active on all three exchanges. Trading is conducted under the traditional "open outcry" procedure, which the National

Planning Department said was gradually being displaced by electronic systems. As of 1993, all fixed-income paper trading on the Bogota and Medellin exchanges was being conducted electronically.

The National Securities Commission sets brokerage transaction fees, which are based on the size of the trade and are not flexible.

The stocks of 80 companies are traded on the exchanges, according to the IFC. Total market capitalization was $5.7 billion in 1992 and the 10 most active stocks represented 52.1 percent of the $203 million in value traded in 1991.

Individual Foreign Investors

Individuals could consider purchase of shares in a Colombian single-country or regional fund. As of 1993, Wilson Emerging Market Funds Research Inc. reported that there was one open-ended fund domiciled in Luxembourg: Colombian Investment Co. SICAV.

8
Mexico

Gains in Mexico's stock market reflect a decade of stern but successful measures that have rejuvenated the once ailing Latin American nation.

Thanks in large part to the leadership of President Carlos Salinas de Gortari, and his immediate predecessor, Manuel de la Madrid Hurtado, Mexico has been unshackled from its ruinous debt burdens, hyperinflation, and protectionist policies, and has established a new course of free-market economics. Inflation has tumbled and economic growth, although modest by some developing countries' standards, appears to be sustainable at about a real 3 percent rate. And the expected advent of the North American Free Trade Agreement (NAFTA) will provide continuing fuel for Mexico's economy, many believe.

The investment community has cheered the country's economic advances. In 1991, the IFC Price Index for Mexico vaulted 102.4 percent in U.S. dollar terms and in 1992, rose 20 percent in dollar terms, marking the fifth straight year of gains. Experts foresee more advances over time as the benefits of NAFTA—expected to take effect in 1994—filter through the economy. In 1993, GDP growth is being projected at about 2 percent, and inflation will be in the 9 percent range.

However, deep-rooted domestic problems must be addressed by a government seeking to join the ranks of the socially and economically developed nations: an inadequate educational system, widespread poverty, pollution, insufficient water supplies, and infrastructural deficiencies. But experts say progress already has been made. For example, grappling with infrastructural problems, the government in 1989 inaugurated a program to allow the private sector, for a period, to operate concessions on and maintain highways as a way to upgrade the quality of these roads; a similar plan for ports and airports is expected.

Government and Politics

With 761,604 square miles of territory, Mexico is the third largest nation in Latin America after Brazil and Argentina. As of the 1990 census, Mexico has a population of 88.3 million and a per capita annual income of $3458. Nearly half its population—40 million—live in poverty. Though literacy, at 87 percent, is high, the average Mexican has only a 6th grade education, and only 3 percent of its people have college degrees.

Mexico's government still combines democratic and dictatorial elements. Political expression is permitted, and a full spectrum of political parties is represented in the legislature, but the same party—the Institutional Revolutionary Party (PRI)—has controlled the government for more than half a century, and it has used the centralized presidency to perpetuate its control. Even today, the PRI's presidential candidate is virtually assured of election, and no other party has gained significant national status since 1929. Opposition parties exist but are fragmented and divided. A mere 1.5 percent of the national vote gives a party at least six seats, ensuring a large number of small parties represented in the chamber of deputies.

In the 1982 and 1988 elections, the PRI responded to Mexico's economic crisis by nominating professional administrators rather than career politicians. That gave the presidency in 1982 to Miguel de la Madrid Hurtado, whose policies unfortunately raised unemployment and drastically cut the living standard of middle-class and poorer Mexicans. The 40-year-old Carlos Salinas de Gortari, who holds a doctorate in economics, politics, and government from Harvard, was de la Madrid's successor. As de la Madrid's budget minister, Salinas had been the chief architect of the stringent economic policies of the mid-1980s.

Though the PRI-controlled electoral commission declared Salinas the winner with 50 percent of the ballots in a three-way race, the vote count was assailed by charges of massive fraud.

Salinas toughed out the fierce opposition confronting him when he took office in December 1988, convinced that his only course was to advance the economic reforms of his predecessor.

President Salinas's term ends in 1994. Though the PRI's challengers have become somewhat more influential, once again the next president is widely expected to be the ruling party's choice.

The Economy

Economic resurrection began when Mexico came under the leadership of a professional administration with the savvy, courage, and power base to make hard, unpopular decisions. When de la Madrid took charge in December 1982, he attacked the economic problems in a way that his predecessors would not have considered. His objective was to open the economy to the rest of the world. He proposed programs that he believed would bring stability and direction, and help to ease, if not eradicate, Mexico's chronic economic ills. Among the problems: $100 billion in defaulted foreign debt, double-digit unemployment, runaway inflation, rampant corruption, and poor foreign relations because of long-time protectionist policies.

De la Madrid faced a daunting task. Protectionist policies trace back to 1917, the year Mexico created a new constitution following a chaotic period after the Mexican Revolution. For the next six decades, Mexico's successive governments embraced economic policies of protectionism, nationalization of industries, and land reform that focused on nationalizing huge privately owned tracts, and distributing small plots (called ejidos) to poor peasants.

As far back as 1942, Mexico began borrowing from the World Bank and from private North American and European banks to finance its economic and industrial development.

Huge new oil fields opened to production in the 1970s, after prices had climbed to record levels in the wake of the OPEC oil shock, and Mexico escalated its borrowing during that decade to finance industrialization projects. Based on the substantial oil income Mexico and its creditors apparently thought would never end, the government borrowed heavily from foreign banks at high interest rates, and used oil income to subsidize services for the poor.

MEXICO

Currency: New Mexico peso (MXN)

Stock Exchange: There is only one stock exchange in Mexico, located in Mexico City. The Mexican Stock Exchange (La Bolsa Mexicana De Valores S. A. De C.V.) is charged with facilitating operations for the buying and selling of securities.

Indexes: The Mexican Stock Exchange Equities Index has been published since 1980. Trading volumes, which are reviewed every two months, dictate the companies included in the index and their respective weightings. As of the close of business on July 31, 1992, the index was comprised of 40 issues (34 companies). Telmex, Cifra, and Cemex accounted for the largest weightings as of that date.

Types of Securities

Equities: Foreign investors are allowed to purchase the following issues: B, C, and L shares and A shares that are registered in the Neutral Trust.

Fixed Income: Development bonds, petro bonds, adjustment bonds, treasury bonds, bankers acceptances, commercial paper, promissory notes, treasury bills, repurchase agreements.

Regulatory Body/Stock Exchange Supervision: The Stock Exchange is supervised by The Treasury and Public Credit Board and the Commision Nacional de Valores (CNV). The National Securities Commission (CNV) was established in 1946 and is loosely modeled after the U.S. Securities and Exchange Commission. The CNV is responsible for regulating and inspecting the stock exchange and brokerage houses, and for investigating any violations of stock market laws. The Treasury and Public Credit Board, in conjunction with the CNV, determines and establishes the policies and standards that guide and supervise the stock market.

The Mexican securities industry is regulated by the Securities Market Law, which was enacted in 1975. In addition to providing a regulatory structure for the industry, the law sets standards for brokers and empowers the CNV and Treasury Board to regulate the activities of various participants in the marketplace. Both the CNV and the Treasury Board oversee the issuance and trading (both primary auctions and secondary market) of all government securities.

The Banco De Mexico is solely responsible for establishing and regulating Mexico's monetary policy. It also monitors the activity of all domestic and foreign banking institutions.

Depository: There are two depositories in Mexico. S.D. INDEVAL S.A de C.V. was founded in 1978 and was privatized in 1987. It is the sole depository for equities, bankers' acceptances, and commercial paper. Banco De Mexico (the Central Bank) is the sole auction and clearinghouse and book entry depository for all government fixed-income securities.

Settlement Information

Equities:

- T + 2.
- Mainly book entry.
- Receive/deliver versus payment available.
- Same-day turnaround trades are possible.

Fixed:

- TD or T + 1.
- Book entry only.
- Receive/deliver versus payment available.
- Same-day turnaround trades are possible.

Taxes:

- Mexico has no reciprocal tax treaties.
- Taxes are withheld at source by the issuers.

(Continued)

- There is a 15 percent tax rate on interest on petrobonds, commercial paper, and bankers' acceptances.
- Capital gains on all government securities and corporate bonds are exempt from taxes. There is also no capital gains tax on equities.
- The interest on corporate bonds is taxed at a rate of 15 percent.
- There is no registration or exchange fee, no stamp duty, no ad valorem tax, nor are there any tax reclamations.

Tax exemptions are not allowed under any circumstances.

A tax reduction on commercial paper interest is available to certain eligible foreign pension plans that qualify and are registered with the Mexican Ministry of Finance and Public Credit.

Investment funds comprised of pension assets and nonpension assets are eligible for a partial exemption. The investment fund's tax exemption will be determined by the ratio of pension assets to the total of the investment fund. In January and July of each year, investment funds must provide the Ministry with a certificate issued by a first-level independent accounting firm indicating the participation percentage for the past six months (to be applied to the subsequent six months). All eligible pension and investment funds names are published on a monthly basis in the Federal Official Gazette of Mexico.

Restrictions for Foreign Investors: Collectively, foreigners can hold only up to 49 percent of any one company's B shares. Foreigners can buy C and L shares that have no voting rights but can only buy those A shares that are registered with the Neutral Trust.

Foreign Exchange: Until recently, foreign investors were not permitted to maintain cash accounts or balances in Mexican pesos. Previously, all income and sales proceeds had to be converted from Mexican pesos on a same-day-value basis. Foreign investors will not be allowed to maintain individual cash accounts exclusively in connection with securities transactions and their accompanying foreign exchange contracts.

Securities Lending: A regulation to permit securities lending and borrowing in the Mexican market was approved in 1991. However, until the fiscal treatment of the transactions is classified, there is little likelihood of substantial foreign participation.

SOURCES: The Bank of New York and Investment Placement Group, La Jolla, Calf.

The worldwide recession of 1982 sent oil prices plummeting and interest rates, already high, even higher. That was the year Mexico, which could no longer pay the interest on its $100 billion foreign debt, first went into default. Though bad loans were plaguing much of the emerging world, Mexico's level of debt threatened to unhinge the world's economy by collapsing the banks that had loaned to it.

It was in this pessimistic climate that Miguel de la Madrid Hurtado was elected president in 1982.

To show that de la Madrid was in earnest about opening the economy and reversing the protectionist policies of the prior 40 years, he had Mexico sign the General Agreement on Tariffs and Trade (GATT) in 1986. Tariffs were cut from 100 to 20 percent on average. Foreign investment was opened by permitting specific companies including Admiral, Chrysler, Ford, General Electric, General Foods, IBM, Monsanto, and General Motors to own 100 percent of their Mexican subsidiaries. Exports of manufactured goods increased, lessening Mexico's dependence on oil exports. Oil's share of exports dropped from 78 percent in 1981 to 35 percent in 1988. The government privatized 40 percent of its owned corporations.

However, these economic policies, designed by budget director (and future president) Carlos Salinas de Gortari, were causing severely painful side effects among Mexico's poor. By 1987 inflation had climbed to 159.2 percent, halving the purchasing power of the average Mexican's income from what had been in 1980. Subsidization of food, housing, and health had also been reduced, further squeezing an already tight situation.

The Salinas Strategy

As President, Carlos Salinas de Gortari was convinced that his only course was to broaden and accelerate the economic reforms he had initiated under de la Madrid. He knew that foreign capital and expertise were essential if Mexican industry was to become internationally competitive. After taking office, he reduced average tariff rates to 12 percent and eliminated import permits for many products. Salinas promulgated the Plan Nacional de Desarrollo 1989–1994 (National Development Plan), designed to actively promote foreign investment and to bring down inflation and achieve economic growth of 6.0 percent by 1995. By 1989, inflation had dropped to 20 percent, and by year-end 1992, it had contracted to 12 percent.

Salinas also encouraged international investment in Mexican companies. In 1982, in the wake of its default, the Mexican government had nationalized its banks, increasing government ownership to more than 60 percent of Mexico's economic enterprises. in 1989 and 1990, Salinas reduced government ownership by half. In addition he gave the government the power to waive or increase restrictions on foreign investment on a case-by-case basis, grant or deny import licenses, and manipulate incentives, tariffs, and price controls.

Government approval was no longer required for 100 percent direct foreign investment of up to $100 million. While larger investments required approval, they were allowed if the government didn't respond within 45 days. Areas previously prohibited or sharply restricted to foreign investment were opened.

Among the foreign companies that now have a stake in Mexico's industrial base are Wal-Mart, which entered a 50-50 joint venture with Cifra, Mexico's largest retailer, and Corning, with a $300 million alliance with glass manufacturer Vitro to sell tableware in Mexico and the United States. Firms that have established factories in Mexico include Kohler, Compaq Computer, Lotus Development, and Microsoft. Franchisers, too, have proliferated, such as McDonald's, Pizza Hut, and Baskin-Robbins. However, railways and all aspects of the petroleum industry remain closed to foreign investment.

In 1992 the *ejido* collective farms created in the 1930s were reprivatized, and ownership was transferred to the *ejidatarios* (farmers). They now have real property rights—they can sell or rent the land, or associate with farming businesses, which will permit private companies to invest in rural land. This opens up the possibility of joint ventures between food processors, *ejidatarios*, and banks supplying credit for investment.

In late November 1992, a plan to improve investment access and competitive conditions for foreigners was introduced. Many of the measures are designed to bring Mexican law into compliance with the requirements to be imposed by NAFTA.

The most important proposal, which was sent to Congress in

1993, will replace the 1973 foreign investment law liberalizing foreign investment policy and give clearer and more comprehensible guidelines. However, it is not expected to change investment restrictions for foreigners. In addition the revised Law of Competition (to replace the old 1934 antimonopoly law) will combat monopolistic behavior and unfair trading practices, and should give direct foreign investors (mainly multinational corporations) greater long-term comfort with the investment climate.

Trade Agreements

In 1990, President Salinas concluded that Mexico's logical trading partners were its northern and southern neighbors, and has since sought to enhance trading throughout the Western hemisphere. A free trade agreement was signed with Chile in 1991, a trilateral free-trade agreement with Colombia and Venezuela is scheduled to be signed by the end of 1993 and implemented in April 1994, and talks were continuing for an agreement covering Central America and the Caribbean.

Salinas' biggest accomplishment to date has been the negotiation of the North American Free Trade Agreement (NAFTA) with the United States and Canada, which was signed in December 1992. Canada's House of Commons approved it in May 1993. NAFTA is expected to take effect in early 1994 if approved by each country's legislature.

NAFTA would create a Free Trade Area encompassing all of North America, a market of 370 million consumers and with $6 trillion in total annual output. Freer trade would result from the elimination of tariff and nontariff barriers among signers. NAFTA would remove trade barriers in agriculture, manufacturing, and services and minimize investment restrictions for foreigners while protecting intellectual property rights. Environmental concerns would also be addressed. (A complete description of NAFTA is in the Appendix.)

If put into force, NAFTA is expected to add up to 2 percentage points annually to Mexico's real GDP growth rate. It would also tighten Mexico's links to the United States and Canada and diminish the chances of Mexico reversing its current economic course.

Foreign Debt Reduction

In 1986, the International Monetary Fund (IMF) and major U.S. and Swiss banks granted large new loans on favorable terms in order to prevent Mexico's economic collapse. There was fear that Mexico's continuing inability to service its foreign debt could cause an international financial crisis. Yet relief was only temporary, as Mexico could not meet even the most minimal debt-service requirements.

In 1989, the United States believed the answer to Mexico's continued economic woes lay in the Brady plan, named for then U.S. Secretary of the Treasury, Nicholas F. Brady. The Brady plan allowed roughly a 10 percent reduction in the principal of Mexico's external debt and a 20 percent reduction of the interest due in 1990. In turn, Mexico was required to take steps to reduce inflation, open its economy further to foreign investment, and follow IMF guidelines.

Mexico was the first Latin American country to restructure its debt under this plan. The deal reduced its net payments to creditors by $4 billion a year through 1994, and reduced loan balances by $10 billion. To help guarantee the new loans, the World Bank and the IMF agreed to provide Mexico with up to $3.9 billion of new money.

To comply with the Brady Plan, President Salinas implemented in 1989 Pacto para la Estabilidad y el Crecimiento Economico known familiarly as "Pacto," among the Mexican government, the trade unions, and private employers. Its aim was to lower inflation and interest rates. In October 1992, Pacto was renewed. Now known as PECE (Pact for Stability, Competitiveness, and Employment); it restricts government spending, limits rises in gasoline and electricity prices to less than 10 percent a year and minimum wage hikes to 7 percent, "with the private sector's commitment to absorb the cost increases without affecting the prices of goods and services," the IFC reports.

Mexico has used privatization, among other programs, to increase foreign investment, bolster markets, and retire debt. Salinas accelerated the privatization process that de la Madrid had begun. Proceeds from the privatization of more than 200 companies between 1989 and 1992 totalled $20.7 billion. Among the major privatizations were Telmex, the phone company;

Mexicana and Aeromexico, the airlines; and several sugar mills, supermarkets, and chemical companies. The privatization program was expected to be wrapped up in 1993 with the selling of 37 more state-owned organizations.

In 1992, Mexico changed its social security laws and approved the creation of a private pension system structurally derived from the Chilean model. Employers pay 2 percent of employee salaries into personal pension funds administered by the commercial banks, and 5 percent of salary into a personal housing fund administered by Infonavit, Mexico's housing agency. It is designed to run alongside the existing pay-as-you-go social security system.

In 1992, the widening of the flotation band around the exchange rate for the peso allayed fears of a currency devaluation. New bands allowed a decline of 40 centavos per day against the U.S. dollar, compared with the previous 20 centavos. Beginning in January, the currency became the "new peso" as three zeros were removed; the conversion rate was 1000 old pesos to 1 new one.

On the negative side, Mexico's continuing trade deficit— which was about $20.6 billion in 1992—will certainly pose an economic problem if not reduced in the near term. In the early 1990s, foreigners buying pesos for investment in Mexico kept the currency from tumbling. "Part of Mexico's negative balance of trade is due to the purchase of capital goods to build and upgrade factories to enhance competitiveness," explains David Marshall, a vice president with the brokerage firm of Inverlat International in New York. "We hope this will be a short-term problem. Assuming Mexico can turn into an export-oriented country, the trade deficit is not now a problem. But if Mexico has not solved its trade deficit problem within a few years, it will then face difficult economic times," he predicts.

The Stock Market

The country's only stock exchange, Bolsa Mexicana de Valores (BMV), was established in 1894 and is located in Mexico City. It is by far the largest in Latin America as measured by market capitalization.

The Mexican Securities Commission (MSC) monitors registration of new issues, sets disclosure and reporting standards, and oversees brokers and stock exchange operations.

Since 1982, participation and activity have exploded in Mexico's stock market. Trading volume at the end of 1991 was nearly 41 times higher than its level a decade earlier. And except for 1984, the market's capitalization advanced each year, rising from $3 billion in 1983 to $139 billion at the end of 1992, according to the IFC.

In late 1992, the CNV granted permission for the Mexican Bolsa to launch a second-tier small cap stock exchange, which will function as part of the Bolsa yet is considered akin to the over-the-counter market in the United States. This board will be known as the Mercado Accionario Intermedio, and it will give small to medium-sized companies that fail to meet the guidelines for listing on the main exchange access to the Mexican (and therefore international) capital markets.

However, Mexico does not have forward trading or a derivatives market. Although investors in a 1992 survey of emerging markets by Kleiman International rated Mexico's the best emerging market in terms of operational efficiency and regulatory oversight, the market also manifests such "emerging" characteristics as limited liquidity and sharp gyrations, as witnessed in 1992. In addition, the market is not yet a good proxy of the Mexican economy, with market value at year-end 1992 only 42 percent of its GDP.

Foreign investment, which had already been on the rise, intensified with the 1990 share issuances by Telefonos de Mexico (Telmex), the telephone company. As of December 1992, 67.2 percent of the market's capitalization was accounted for by the issues of only eight companies: Telmex (29.2 percent); Banacci (7.7 percent); Cifra (6.3 percent); Televisa (5.8 percent); Gears (5.0 percent); Group Financiero Bancomer (3.2 percent); and Cementos Mexicanos (Cemex) (5.4 percent) and Ttolmex (3.2 percent). Telmex is widely considered a proxy for the Mexican market.

Foreigners' participation has been encouraged in Mexico's market, either indirectly through one of the country mutual funds or through Depository Receipts or directly on the BMV. In 1989, the Nacional Financiera, the government's financing agency that regulates the securities market, created the Neutral

Fund to enable foreign nationals to invest in stocks of Mexican companies.

Mexican companies issue four kinds of shares: A, B, C, and L (for limited) shares. Foreigners can acquire C and L shares, but they carry no voting rights. Foreigners can buy only those A shares (except those issued by banks and financial holdings) registered in the Neutral Trust, and that do not carry voting rights. Instead, the trust exercises voting rights according to the wishes of the majority of shareholders. Foreigners can collectively hold up to a 49 percent stake in any one company's B shares, which do carry voting rights. Experts say A shares comprise the largest portion of issuances, followed by B shares.

Trading Practices

Trade settlements take place on the second business day. The S.D. Indeval (Institute for Deposit of Securities) serves as a clearinghouse and depository for all securities, except Government issues, traded in Mexico, eliminating the need for physical transfer of certificates.

Brokerage commissions range from 1.7 to 1 percent for trades by individual investors. Institutional investors pay a flat 0.85 percent commission. A value-added tax of 10 percent does not apply to foreign investors. There is no capital gains tax. All trades must be executed through a Mexican broker/dealer or the Mexican Stock Exchange. Otherwise, the purchase or sale is subject to a 20 percent withholding tax on the gross amount.

Nonresident foreign investors can remit funds in or out of Mexico without penalty, and no taxes are imposed on investment interest, dividends, or capital gains.

Foreigners wishing to invest in Mexican securities directly can acquire Depositary Receipts through their domestic brokers, or buy shares directly on the Mexican Stock Exchange either through a securities firm registered to do business in Mexico or directly through a Mexican brokerage firm. Bankers Trust Company reports that as of December 1992 there were 44 Mexican depositary receipt programs. (See Fig. 8-1.) As of 1993, Wilson Emerging Market Funds Research counted 233 mutual funds for Mexico, of which all but 13 are intended for domestic investors. Three closed-end funds include the unlisted Mexican Horizons Investment Company Ltd., as well as two listed on the New York Stock Exchange: the Mexico Equity & Income Fund Inc. and the Mexico Fund Inc.

Strategically, investors' shorter-term market plays may center on the capitalizing on opportunities from lowering interest rates, while longer-term plays are expected to emanate from such developments as the advent of NAFTA. Among the anticipated NAFTA beneficiaries are the food, retailing, automotive-related, construction, financial services, and telecommunications industries.

Already a number of Mexican companies have formed joint ventures with U.S. organizations, among them Cifra and Wal-Mart, to capitalize on lowered tariff barriers for cheaper sourcing of goods, among other advantages. Strong, competitive banks should also gain from expanded demand for trade financing.

David Marshall suggests looking for the healthiest companies within sectors, which he calls "survivors of free trade." The strongest companies should not only withstand the international competition that NAFTA will bring but also capitalize on the enhanced export opportunities from it. Companies Marshall expects to do well in the food/beverage industry after NAFTA include: Fomento Economico Mexicano, which holds about 50 percent of the domestic Mexican beer market, and is likely to substantially boost its small amount of exporting; Maseca, a tortilla maker whose products are likely to be in demand on the export market; and Grupo Herdez, another food processor that is likely to exploit opportunities after NAFTA, he believes.

In addition to NAFTA, lower interest rates in Mexico should bolster consumer spending and construction projects, enhancing the appeal of companies in those sectors. Two companies likely to benefit from the housing demand, says Marshall, are Internacional de Ceramica, a producer of ceramic goods, and Cemex, a large cement company based in Monterrey, Mexico. In addition Empresas ICA Sociedad Controlador, considered a leader in road construction, is expected to benefit in part from the sharply increased cross-border traffic anticipated after NAFTA's passage.

CUSIP	Security name	SEDOL	Exchange	Receipt settles	Symbol	Ratio FGN=ADR	Type	Country
008065104	AEROVIAS de MEXICO S.A. de C.V		PRTL	U.S.		10=1	SP-PLACEMENT	MEXICO
022069207	ALTOS HORNOS DE MEXICO SA		OTC	U.S.	ADEMY	1=1	UNSPONSORED	MEXICO
037488103	APASCO, SA de CV (SERIES A)		OTC	U.S.		5=1	SP-EQUITY	MEXICO
037488202	APASCO, SA de CV (SERIES B)		OTC	U.S.		5=1	SP-EQUITY	MEXICO
151290202	CEMEX S.A. B SHARES		OTC	U.S.		2=1	SP-EQUITY	MEXICO
151290301	CEMEX S.A. A SHARES		PRTL	U.S.		2=1	SP-PLACEMENT	MEXICO
171785207	CIFRA SA DE CV		OTC	U.S.	CFRAY	1=1	UNSPONSORED	MEXICO
21238A107	CONTROLADOR COMMERCIAL MEXICAN		OTC	U.S.		10=1	SP-EQUITY	MEXICO
219874203	CORPORACION MEXICANA DE AVIACON		OTC	U.S.		5=1	SP-EQUITY	MEXICO
219870300	CORP. INDUSTRIAL SANLUIS SERIES A-1		OTC	U.S.		10=1	SP-EQUITY	MEXICO
219870409	CORP. INDUSTRIAL SANLUIS A-2		OTC	U.S.		10=1	SP-EQUITY	MEXICO
003823962	EL PUERTO DE LIVERPOOL, S.A. DE C.V.			NON-U.S.		20=1	SP-EQUITY	MEXICO
291578102	EMPAQUES PONDEROSA (144A)		PRTL	U.S.		4=1	SP-PLACEMENT	MEXICO
292448107	EMPRESAS ICA-SOCIEDAD CONTROLADOR		NYSE	U.S.	ICA	1=1	SP-EQUITY	MEXICO
268910205	EPN SA DE CV		OTC	U.S.		10=1	SP EQUITY	MEXICO
344418207	FOMENTO ECONOMICO MEX.144A (GDR)			GLOBALLY		1=1	SP-PLACEMENT	MEXICO
400485108	GRUPO CARSO (144A) GDR			GLOBALLY		2=1	SP-PLACEMENT	MEXICO
P4949K104	GRUPO FINANCIERO BANCOMER (GDR)			NON-U.S.		20=1	SP-EQUITY	MEXICO
400486106	GRUPO FINANCIERO BANCOMER (144A)		PRTL	U.S.		20=1	SP-PLACEMENT	MEXICO
400487203	GRUPO GIGANTE S.A. (144A) GDR			GLOBALLY		10=1	SP-PLACEMENT	MEXICO
400488102	GRUPO INDUSTRIAL MASECA (SERIES A)		OTC	U.S.		10=1	SP-EQUITY	MEXICO
400488201	GRUPO INDUSTRIAL MASECA (SERIES B)		OTC	U.S.		10=1	SP-EQUITY	MEXICO
40048K105	GRUPO MEXICANO DE VIDEO		PRTL	U.S.		10=1	SP-PLACEMENT	MEXICO
400489100	GRUPO POSADAS S.A. DE C.V. (144A)			GLOBALLY		20=1	SP-PLACEMENT	MEXICO
400490207	GRUPO SIDEK PLC		OTC	U.S.		2=1	SP-EQUITY	MEXICO
400492104	GRUPO SITUR S.A. DE C.V. (144A)		PRTL	U.S.		10=1	SP-PLACEMENT	MEXICO
400493201	GRUPO SYNKRO, SA DE C.V		OTC	U.S.		1=1	SP-EQUITY	MEXICO

CUSIP	Security name	SEDOL	Exchange	Receipt settles	Symbol	Ratio FGN=ADR	Type	Country
003505227	GRUPO TELEVISA, S.A. DE C.V. (GDR)			NON-U.S.		2=1	SP-EQUITY	MEXICO
40049J107	GRUPO TELEVISA SA DE C.V. (144A)		PRTL	U.S.		2=1	SP-PLACEMENT	MEXICO
400494100	GRUPO VIDEO VISA S.A. de C.V.			GLOBALLY		20=1	SP-PLACEMENT	MEXICO
449496207	IEM SA		OTC	U.S.	HEMYEY	1=1	UNSPONSORED	MEXICO
458847209	INTERNACIONAL DE CERAMICA B SHARES		OTC	U.S.		5=1	SP-EQUITY	MEXICO
458847308	INTERNACIONAL DE CERAMICA S.A. "C"		PRTL	U.S.		5=1	SP-PLACEMENT	MEXICO
55267NAA9	MEXICO CITY-TOLUCA TOLL ROAD144A G			GLOBALLY		1=1	SP-PLACEMENT	MEXICO
732438304	PONDEROSA INDUSTRIAL, S.A. DE C.V		OTC	U.S.		1=1	SP-EQUITY	MEXICO
P8546P119	SEARS ROEBUBK DE MEXICO SA CV (GDR)			NON-U.S.		2=1	SP-EQUITY	MEXICO
81240K105	SEARS ROEBUCK DE MEXICO SA CV (144A)		PRTL	U.S.		2=1	SP-PLACEMENT	MEXICO
879403400	TELEFONOS DE MEXICO SA DE C.V.		NSDQ	U.S.	TFONY	1=1	UNSPONSORED	MEXICO
879403780	TELEFONOS de MEXICO SERIES "L"	2881612	NYSE	U.S.	TMX	20=1	SP-EQUITY	MEXICO
889557203	TOLMEX S.A. DE C.V.	2896122	OTC	U.S.		10=1	SP-EQUITY	MEXICO
893868208	TRANSPORTACION MARITIMA MEXICANA			GLOBALLY		1=1	SP-EQUITY	MEXICO
893868307	TRANSPORTACION MARITIMA MEX. (A SHS)			GLOBALLY	TMM	1=1	SP-EQUITY	MEXICO
898592506	TUBOS DE ACERO DE MEXICO SA		AMEX	U.S.	TTAM	1=1	SP-EQUITY	MEXICO
928502301	VITRO SOCIEDAD ANONIMA		NYSE	U.S.	VTO	3=1	SP-EQUITY	MEXICO

Figure 8-1. Listing of depositary receipts in Mexico. (*Source: Bankers Trust Company, January 1993.*)

9
Venezuela

With a gross domestic product of more than $55 billion in 1992, Venezuela, Latin America's oldest civilian democracy, would seem to have all the ingredients for economic success. But its political environment will have to improve for the economy to start moving in the right direction.

The events of 1992 cast a pall over Venezuela. Two failed coup attempts—one in February and one in November—and the attendant violence elicited discontent, fear, anger, and economic disruption in the population. In May 1993, political turbulence culminated with the resignation of President Carlos Andres Perez on charges of allegedly misusing $17 billion in government monies. He was the first President to be removed from office since Venezuela became a democracy in 1958.

There was cheering for the downfall of the unpopular system. However, The New York Times reported in late May 1993 that "some business people worried about the political stability of Venezuela, which has the hemisphere's largest oil reserves."

The early front-runner for the next presidential election, Oswaldo Alvarez Paz of the Social Christian Party, is an economic reformer whose stated objectives are: to build a strong free market economy; increase exports; and end corruption. He had been nominated to be his party's standard bearer on its April 25th presidential primary. The next day, the stock market jumped 11 percent.

But no matter who wins the December 1993 election, "virtually all the candidates represent a new generation, as compared to the old guard (Perez is 70 years old)," says Thomas Tull of Gulfstream Global Investors.

Can Venezuela solve the thorny problems that had created so much social unrest? One persistent problem, inflation, continues at a high rate. According to Paul D. Bodin, director of Carlsen & Co., a brokerage firm in Caracas, "The main factors in the failure to bring down inflation in '92 were the strength of aggregate demand, real wage growth in a number of sectors, and an expansion of the public-sector deficit." Inflation also roars along: In January 1993, J. P. Morgan reported that Venezuela's CPI rose nearly 32 percent in 1992, about one point more than in 1991 but about 3.5 points less than had been expected.

In 1992, high interest rates also kept investors at bay. According to J. P. Morgan, the nominal commercial bank lending rates as of May 1993 were reported at over 60 percent, or over 20 percent in real terms. According to the IFC Price Index, the Venezuelan market fell 42.7 percent (in U.S. dollar terms) in 1992, compared with a gain of 43.7 percent for 1991, but quite a drop from 1990, the first full year of serious foreign participation, when it topped the charts with price and total return up 587.8 percent and 603.2 percent, respectively.

Real GDP grew by 7.3 percent in 1992, about three percentage points less than in 1991's 10.4 percent. J. P. Morgan noted that the slowdown "was entirely due to a two percentage point drop in the oil sector—nonoil real GDP grew by 9.5 percent." Unemployment also fell to 7.2 percent in the second half of 1992. Growth was strongest in manufacturing (up 12 percent), commerce (17 percent), and construction (17 percent), the latter suggesting that investment growth was also strong. Among the productive nonoil sectors, the main laggard was agriculture, which rose by only 2.4 percent.

The Morgan data led to a cautious prognosis for Venezuela's near-term economic prospects: The rapid GDP growth of the past two years notwithstanding, J. P. Morgan has projected a much slower rate of growth for 1993—about 3.5 percent real growth for both total and nonoil GDP.

Government and Politics

Venezuela, a federal republic, has traveled a winding and often bumpy road since 1957, with periods of oppressive despotic rule, economic protectionism, recessions, and civil and social unrest.

Its population is 20 million, and with 352,145 square miles of territory, is Latin America's fifth largest country. Its coastline is 1244 miles on the Caribbean Sea, and it is bordered by Colombia, Brazil, and Guyana. It is the world's fifth-largest producer of oil, which accounts for 80 percent of its export revenue. Agriculture and minerals also contribute to its GDP.

In 1988, when Perez was elected to a five-year term as President, he was confronted with enormous problems. Per capita income about $2000, its currency, the Bolivar, was grossly overvalued, inflation was 40 percent, interest rates were 9 percent on deposits and 13 percent on loans, and the fiscal deficit was 9 percent of GDP. Most of these problems had come about during Perez's first term as President, from 1974 to 1979. Then, he had nationalized Venezuela's oil industry, and did all he could to replace imports by local products. "In theory, he advocated Latin American integration and third-world solidarity. In practice he cut off his country from the world," *The Economist* said in an August 1991 article.

Venezuela's heavy dependence on oil, and that commodity's whipsawing gyrations, created debt service and repayment problems in the 1980s. Though Perez was not constitutionally allowed to succeed himself, he won an unprecedented second term a decade later. He presented a different political persona when he took office in February 1989.

Upon taking office, he imposed a series of radical reforms designed to increase the efficiency and competitiveness of Venezuelan enterprises, reduce dependence on oil exports, and enhance Venezuela's image among domestic and foreign investors. He took the Bolivar's exchange rate off its fixed peg and converted it to a floating rate. He abolished price controls, undid ceiling and floor controls on interest rates, tightened controls on public spending, and allowed public sector prices to rise substantially. He also cut food and fuel subsidies. Almost within days, these austerity policies touched off bloody riots in Caracas that left some 300 people dead.

VENEZUELA

Currency: Venezuelan Bolivar (VEB)

Stock Exchange: The two stock exchanges are the Caracas Stock Exchange (CSE) with 90 percent of all stock market volume and the Maracaibo Stock Exchange (MSE) with the remaining 10 percent.

Types of Securities: Equities and Treasury bills.

Regulatory Body/Stock Exchange Supervision: Stock market activity is supervised by the National Securities Commission (Comision Nacional De Valores—CNV). The Superintendency of Foreign Investment (SIEX) is responsible for regulating all foreign investment. The banking industry is regulated by the Superintendency of Banks of the Central Bank of Venezuela.

Depository: At present, there is no depository in Venezuela.

Settlement Information

Equities:

- T + 1 (often delayed until T + 4 or 5)
- Physical delivery only
- Since April 1991, the procedure for trade settlements has required the certification or "blocking" of shares by the transfer agent prior to settlement. The purpose of the certification was to serve as the issuer's guarantee that, according to official registration records, the selling party owned the shares and they were available for delivery. This certification was in the form of a stamp affixed to the *traspaso* by the transfer agent.
- In addition to the requirement that the selling agent sign the traspaso, local transfer agents had been requiring the subcustodian to sign the registration release box of the traspaso prior to its certification or stamping. This procedure thus implied transfer of ownership prior to settlement.

1. On T + 1, brokers will present the traspaso to the sub-custodian for its signature requesting blocking only. Since client instructions are rarely available at this time, subcustodians are often forced to authorize the blocking without a prematching against instructions.
2. The broker will then deliver the traspaso to the transfer agent for blocking.
3. On the day before settlement date, the broker will return to the subcustodian with the certified traspaso and a check. At this point, the subcustodian will be able to match the trade information with the client instruction. If matched, the subcustodian will sign the traspaso authorizing the reregistration of the shares and release it to the broker. The check will be held overnight.
4. On settlement date, the broker will present the completed traspaso to the stock exchange for final settlement and collect payment from his counterparty. Simultaneously, the agent will deposit the broker's check. Actual proceeds will be available two days later after the check clears.

Likewise on a receive versus payment, the subcustodian will not issue a check to the broker until it has received and reviewed the certified traspaso, the broker's invoice, and a stock liquidation receipt, issued by the exchange.

Treasury Bills: Treasury bills are bearer instruments, and they are traded and settled in two different ways.

The first method is when the bills are offered in the primary market each Wednesday via closed-envelope auction at the Central Bank. To settle these trades, the Central Bank debits the purchaser's cash account that Friday (T + 2) and issues him an invoice for the bills. On the following Tuesday (T + 4) the certificates are received by the subcustodian and vaulted.

The second method is via the over-the-counter market where Treasury bills are actively traded. These trades are settled via the physical exchange of certificates versus a check at the subcustodian's counter. As with equities, fixed-income settlements normally occur on T + 5. Settlements of Treasury bills are much less problematic than equity settlements.

(Continued)

Taxes: As of 9/91, nonresident investors are exempt from withholding tax on dividends (previously 20 percent) and on interest income. The capital gains tax is 20 percent on gains of over 2MM Bolivars (with no deductible) or 30 percent on gains of less than 2MM Bolivars (with a 200M Bolivars deductible). Capital gains taxes on SAICA company investments (i.e., any company that is more than 50 percent publicly owned) are exempt until 8/31/93 if they are reinvested into another SAICA company.

Restrictions for Foreign Investors: In January of 1990, Venezuela amended its Foreign Investment Law by establishing Decree Law 727 which allows for direct foreign participation in its stock markets. Decree Law 727 eliminated the need for prior approval for foreign investment, allowed for the free repatriation of the proceeds, and eased most of the foreign ownership restrictions facing foreign investors.

Although Decree Law 727 allows foreign investment in Venezuela, all foreign investments still must be reported to the Superintendency of Foreign Investment (SIEX). This reporting is the responsibility of the registrar.

Foreign investors are prohibited from owning shares in certain industries such as oil and gas companies. Additionally, foreign ownership of Venezuelan banks and financial institutions is currently limited to 19.9 percent.

Securities Lending: While securities lending is not specifically prohibited by law, it is rarely practiced.

SOURCE: The Bank of New York

Like other Latin American heads of state, Perez knew free trade and open markets were the way to economic recovery. "Economic necessity, in the form of the IMF and the World Bank, pushed him along," *The Economist* concluded. "When he came to power, Venezuela was in a tight corner: To pay its debt (much of it incurred during his previous term in office) the country had at the end of 1988 just $3 billion in cash reserves, a current deficit of $4.7 billion, and a budget deficit of 9.3 percent of gross domestic product."

Though the people remained restive, Perez's many reforms began to show their effect. The GDP, which had dropped 7.8 percent in 1989, reversed its slide, gaining 5.7 percent in 1990, 9.2 percent in 1991, and 4.5 percent in 1992.

However, in early 1993, voters in several regions sent Perez a message of discontent by spurring his Democratic Action party, in favor of his chief opposition, the Social Christian Party (COPEI). Of the 22 state governors, 11 were from COPEI. Perez's forced resignation from office in May 1993 came nine months before his term of office would have ended. Immediately after Perez's resignation, Senator Octavio Lepage was sworn in as acting President, but opposition parties called for his removal. In June, Senator Ramon Jose Velasquez, 76, became the interim President to fill out Perez's term until elections could be held in December.

Alvarez Paz, the leading presidential candidate as of June 1993, is a lawyer and the governor of Zulia, Venezuela's key oil state. He won national popularity when he held out against armed rebel forces surrounding his home during the February 4 coup attempt last year.

As the COPEI candidate, Alvarez will run against the Causa R candidate Andre Velasquez, the 39-year-old governor of the state of Bolivar, and against the AD candidate, Claude Fermin, the 43-year-old former mayor of Caracas. Fermin's chances of getting elected have been dampened by Perez's unpopularity.

Why was Perez unpopular? According to an article by David Asman in *The Wall Street Journal*, "Venezuela's enormous income from the nation's $13 billion-a-year oil industry led to some of the most egregious examples of public corruption in the hemisphere. After Perez nationalized the oil industry in

1976, government revenues grew. But a severe currency devaluation in 1983 and years of greater than 30 percent inflation have lowered the purchasing power of the average citizen tremendously."

The Economy

Many of the gyrations of Venezuela's economy through the 1960s and 1970s occurred because of its dependence on oil. As the world's fifth largest oil producer, Venezuela's petroleum riches must dominate any evaluation of its national economy. Revenues from oil production have accounted for 70 percent of total government revenues over the last few years. It has the largest reserves outside the Persian Gulf, and is the second largest supplier of oil to the United States.

In 1990, oil exports accounted for 23 percent of its GDP and 80 percent of its total export revenues. In 1991, agriculture contributed 6 percent through coffee, cacao, cattle and hides; industry about 17 percent.

When Perez returned to office in 1989, he knew that maintaining the heavy oil-supported subsidies would be impossible, given the low price of oil. He immediately began instituting economic reforms that included eliminating most price controls, ending interest rate control, and imposing a more prudent fiscal policy to reduce the budget deficit. Subsequent phases focused on liberalizing trade to encourage foreign competition and enhance Venezuela's international economic role, easing foreign investment restrictions, and privatizing some of the many state-owned businesses.

Perez's reforms have had some effect. Though oil still dominated, other exports about doubled in volume, climbing above the 10 percent level of 1987 and earlier, accounting typically for about 20 percent of total export revenue.

Foreign Trade

Venezuela's major trading partners are the United States (64 percent), Germany, Brazil, Japan, Canada, France, Sweden, and

Italy. Exports were reported by J. P. Morgan at $14.9 billion in 1992, up from $14.1 billion in 1991. Imports in 1992 totaled $12.1 billion, up from $10.1 billion in 1991.

To encourage foreign trade as a precursor to joining the General Agreement on Tariffs and Trade (GATT), the Perez administration reduced tariffs in several waves to a range of 5 to 20 percent, depending on the product category, for an average levy of about 10 percent. It also abolished import licensing requirements.

Trade Agreements

Venezuela joined GATT in 1990. With Bolivia, Colombia, Ecuador, and Peru, Venezuela founded the Andean Free Trade Zone in 1991. Its objective was to stimulate trade within the group by liberalizing intraregional trade rules and assuring competitiveness by eliminating subsidies. A separate agreement was also signed with Colombia in 1992, and an agreement with Chile inked in April 1993.

Membership in the Caribbean Economic Community (Caricom) became more likely for Venezuela with the signing of a trade agreement that will open its market to duty-free imports from members of the community. Venezuela will allow one-way preferential access to its market for imports from the 13 Caricom countries. Tariffs will be reduced gradually over five years until a duty-free entry has been agreed to for the imports.

Privatization

In 1990, the Venezuela government owned some 250 enterprises, which accounted for about 30 percent of GDP. As part of its economic reform program, the Perez government embarked on a privatization program that included: the state airline VIASA, several banks, and some major hotels. Moreover, in 1991, some $1.9 billion was realized from the sale of 51 percent of Compania Anonima Nacional Telefonos de Venezuela (CANTV), the telephone monopoly.

The former Perez government had planned to privatize more

than 100 enterprises by year-end 1993. Under Carlos Hernandez Delfino, president of the Venezuelan Investment Fund, in charge of privatization, the program had been expected to include the sale of three electricity generation and distribution companies: Enelbar, Enelven, and Enelco. Sale of the Planta Centro thermal-power-generation plant had also been planned.

The national oil company, Petroleos de Venezuela S. A. (PDVSA), has only been authorized to enter into joint ventures. It is not expected to be privatized any time soon. However, given its ambitious $4 billion expansion program through 1996, the company has been welcoming some foreign participation to help finance expansion. In 1992, "for the first time since the oil industry was nationalized in 1976, Venezuela signed agreements with foreign companies to produce oil," *The New York Times* reported in July 1993.

Tax Reform

Progress on the Perez government's tax reforms had been slow, and to some observers, insufficient. Venezuela reduced its corporate tax rate to 30 percent, from 50 percent; eliminated the tax on stock dividends; and simplified the income tax system.

In mid-1993, the Venezuelan Congress had still not acted on the government's tax package (the national value-added tax and a business assets tax proposed in 1991), which experts felt could help produce a manageable public sector deficit with an inflation rate of less than 30 percent and a deficit of over 6 percent of GDP with inflation easily pushing 40 percent. With Perez now out, it is unlikely these measures will soon be passed.

The 1987 tax on foreign income, put into place to protect Venezuela from foreign investing, was abolished in 1989.

Foreign Debt

Venezuela's external debt was $31.5 billion in 1991, according to the Central Bank, down from more than $38 billion eight years earlier. Capel characterized Venezuela's debt problems as "minor compared to those of many other Latin American economies."

Venezuela, which had never missed an interest payment on its foreign debt, entered into a Brady Plan agreement in December 1990. The restructuring of its commercial bank debt "sharply cut the debt servicing burden by lowering applicable interest rates and by stretching out maturities," First Boston's Suhas Ketkar said. "While Venezuela's debt to GDP ratio exceeds the comparable ratios in other major Latin American countries, its other measures of creditworthiness are far better than those for Argentina, Brazil, and Mexico."

The Stock Market

Foreign investment in Venezuela's stock market became possible in 1990, with enactment of an amendment to its Foreign Investment Law. Its main provisions:

- Remove the prior-approval requirement for foreign investment. However, all nonresident investments must be reported to the Superintendency of Foreign Investment. Such reporting is the registrars' responsibility.
- Enable the establishment of brokerage firms.
- Permit free repatriation of investment proceeds.
- Reduce most ownership restrictions facing foreign investors.

However, it's still a heavily restricted market. Nonresidents are prohibited from owning any shares in certain industries, such as oil and gas companies, and ownership of Venezuelan banks and financial institutions is limited to a total of 19.9 percent of holdings by all foreign investors.

The Exchanges

More than 90 percent of the transactions in this volatile and thinly traded market take place on the Caracas Stock Exchange (CSE), a private company founded in 1947. A second market, the Maracaibo Stock Exchange (Mercado de Valores de Maracaibo C.A., or Maracaibo Bolsa), was formed in 1986; 54 brokers work at the exchanges.

Trading is by open outcry, with no electronic system in place.

Trades settle by mutual agreement on T+1 to T+20, but frequently on T+5. Because of the large number of delayed trades, the Bank of New York occasionally advises its clients to exercise their right under Exchange Rules 90 and 91 to cancel trades 48 hours after the contractual or scheduled settlement date. There is no central depository or clearing agency in Venezuela. The Caracas exchange was said to be studying the feasibility of establishing one.

At the end of 1992, the stocks of the 66 companies listed on the exchanges had a total capitalization of $7.6 billion, according to IFC, and the 10 largest companies comprise roughly 70 percent of that capitalization. In its *Emerging Stock Market Factbook* for 1993, the IFC rates Venezuela's market as having "adequate" account standards.

The Caracas Stock Exchange publishes an annual bulletin that provides comprehensive data. The investment banking firms of J. P. Morgan and James Capel & Co. had research coverage for a number of years, and other securities firms recently instituted research coverage, including Bear Starns and Baring Securities.

Market Update

Trading in Caracas had slipped to very low volume, Daily average volume was in the $5 to $8 million range in 1992–1993, compared with an average $38.5 million a day in 1991, and about $100 million a day during the more bullish period of 1990.

But Venezuela's market hit bottom on March 17, 1993, which represented a 57 percent sell-off from its peak of February 1992, says Tull of Gulfstream Global Investors. Between March 17 and June 21, the Caracas Stock Exchange Index climbed about 20 percent, reports Tull, a Dallas-based manager who has 6 percent of his Latin American portfolio in Venezuela.

In early 1993, Bodin of Carlsen & Co. cited a few companies that were trading below their par value, including: Sudantex de Venezuela, a well-managed, well-diversified textile company; Veneseta, a holding company of Sudantex; Venepal, a well-managed paper company with continued strong export potential; and CANTV, the Venezuelan telephone company.

Salomon Brothers has pointed to construction-based stocks such as Vencemos, a large cement company with 48 percent of local market share, as well as Ceramica Carabobo, which manufactures tiles, refractories, and earthenware, and Madosa, a company with a strong position in household appliances.

Investment Options

According to Bankers Trust, nine depositary receipts programs had been created by Venezuelan companies by the end of 1992. Those issuing them in the United States: B.I.L. Sivensa (144A warrants), Ceramica Carabobo, Corimon, Mantex, and Siderurgica Venezolana Sivensa.

10
Hungary

Hungary took its first hesitant steps toward a market economy in 1968 and made quiet progress for 20 years. So it was poised to move forward rapidly once Mikhail Gorbachev started to loosen the Soviet Union's grip on the bloc known as the Council for Mutual Economic Assistance, or Comecon.

Hungary bowed out of the Warsaw Pact in 1990. Thereafter, the movement toward a market-driven economy chugged ahead in earnest. According to Montgomery Asset Management, "Hungary has undertaken the fastest privatization in the history of the world. However, most of the easy privatizations—particularly in the consumer goods area —have already been accomplished. Hotels, banks, and utilities are next to be privatized and are expected to be more difficult."

A five-year plan for economic reform began in March 1991. In 1992 the recovery hit some unavoidable snags. Trade was squeezed by dissolution of the U.S.S.R. and East Germany, two former major markets. A summer drought damaged Hungary's agricultural production by 15 percent. Exports continued to rise by about 12 percent in 1992, but the combination of continuing recession and unfavorable weather caused GDP to contract 8 percent in 1991 and 7.5 percent in 1992, increasing the deficit and causing the IMF to suspend loans to Hungary.

The other impediment to progress was the Bankruptcy Act, which took effect in April 1992. This law was intended to discourage many companies from assuming excessive debt. Instead about 3000 to 4000 firms in arrears on income and social security taxes took the opportunity to bail out by declaring bankruptcy. In this climate, privatization slowed.

Personal savings rose to 15 percent of income in 1992, but savings are being hoarded by skittish families. This will slow the pace of full recovery in industrial production. Public consumption, too, is limited by a large budget deficit and declining profitability of the banking sector, 90 percent of which is still state-owned.

Reuters reported that 25 percent of Hungary's citizens lived below the poverty line by year-end 1992. Unemployment, at 8.3 percent in 1991, had risen to 11 percent, or 700,000 people, by September 1992. A rise to 17 percent or higher was predicted for 1993.

Under Communist rule, all Hungarian workers were required to contribute to social welfare funds. But the value of these funds has fluctuated until there is now only a chasm of deficit left to meet unemployment and pension obligations.

But considering the turmoil in Eastern Europe, Hungary is remarkably stable. The governing party of Prime Minister Jozsef Antall, the Hungarian Democratic Forum (HDF), has a freely elected majority in the National Assembly. Thus far Antall has prevailed over challenges from Istvan Csurka, the dissident leader of the HDF's right wing. The ethnic tensions that have riven the rest of the region, especially the former Czechoslovakia and Yugoslavia, have not torn at Hungary.

In 1991 and 1992 the private sector accounted for 30 to 35 percent of the GDP. Third-quarter 1992 foreign investment of $4.5 billion accounted for 60 percent of the total investment in private companies. More than 50 percent of the foreign money that went to Eastern Europe went to Hungary, and Montgomery Asset Management believes that "some political backlash on foreign ownership is inevitable."

Inflation fell to 23 percent in 1992, from 35 percent in 1991. Removal of price-control mechanisms and subsidies, and the staged devaluation of the currency unit, the Forint, accounted for the upward leap of inflation in 1991. Wages were capped at 28 percent to prevent a wage explosion.

Privatization revenue for 1992 was about US$80 million. Hungary is still in the running to become the first former

Communist nation to make the transition from Marxist to market economy.

Government and Politics

Hungary, known to its citizens as Magyarorszag, has been a presence in the Danube valley region since the 9th century. Its borders today encompass 35,919 square miles in the center of the valley. The population is 10.6 million, more than 90 percent of whom are ethnic Magyars. Almost one-fifth of the population is over 60 years of age.

The present republic functions under the 1989 version of its constitution. Its parliament has one house with 386 members, and representation is proportionally determined. The government is freely elected by popular vote.

Hungary has about 10 major political parties. Three of these parties make up the Parliament's ruling coalition: the Hungarian Democratic Forum (the majority party), the Independent Smallholders Party (revived from the pre-Communist era), and the Christian Democratic People's Party. The next elections are scheduled for March 1994.

The education system, which is still under state control, is excellent: Literacy levels stand at 92 percent, and nearly 95 percent of children continue to the secondary school level; 20 percent enroll in academic schools, 35 percent in technical–vocational schools, and 44 percent in three-year apprentice schools. Over 9 percent of the 18–22 age group attends universities, professionals schools, or technical colleges.

History

Hungary functioned under a feudal system from the eleventh century, when it was established as an independent kingdom, through 1918, when the Hapsburg-ruled Austro-Hungarian Empire dissolved in the wake of World War I.

The Treaty of Trianon, which portioned out the Dual Monarchy after World War I, parceled one-third of Hungary's ancestral lands to Romania, Czechoslovakia, the former

HUNGARY

Currency: Hungarian Forint (HUF).

Stock Exchanges: The Budapest Stock Exchange (BSE) was reestablished on June 21, 1990, after a closed period of 40 years. Both equity and bonds trade on the exchange. 10 percent of the total volume is on the BSE, while the remaining 90 percent occurs on the unregulated OTC market.

Indexes: There are no major market indexes in Hungary.

Types of Securities: Equity, corporate and government bonds, Treasury bills, and bank-issued certificates of deposit.

Regulatory Body/Stock Exchange Supervision: The National Bank of Hungary (NBH) is responsible for the monitoring and regulating of all capital inflows and outflows. The State Securities Supervisory Board is responsible for regulating the securities markets. Trading in Hungary is regulated by the following three laws.

- No. XXIV Act of 1988, on Investments of Foreigners in Hungary.
- Law VI of 1988, on Business Societies, Associations, Companies, and Ventures.
- Act VI of 1990, on Securities Trading and the Stock Exchange.

Depository: The BSE operates its own depository, which holds all exchange-traded securities during settlement. The exchange has custody of its members' assets and for all exchange-executed trades. All stock exchange members must maintain a cash account at the National Bank of Hungary for the purpose of settling trades against payment.

Settlement Information

Equities:

- T + 5 (cash), T + 3 (securities).
- Physical delivery only.
- Receive/deliver versus payment available.

- Same-day turnaround trades are not possible for BSE-executed trades. They are possible for OTC trades, but are discouraged due to market inefficiencies.

Fixed Income: Foreign participation is not permitted.

Taxes:

- There is no withholding tax on dividends and interest.
- There is no capital gains tax imposed on investors from countries that have treaties with Hungary.

Restrictions for Foreign Investors:

- Foreign investors are permitted to purchase only registered shares.
- Foreign investors must pay for all trades in hard currency.
- Foreign investors must register all hard currency security purchases with the Central Corporation of Banking Company (CCBC), to ensure that they will by able to repatriate the proceeds when said shares are sold.
- Foreign investors must advise the NBH of all dividends or interest that is converted to hard currency.

Securities Lending: Securities lending is prohibited by law in Hungary.

SOURCE: The Bank of New York

Yugoslavia, and Austria. This division disrupted Hungary's economy by severing it from much of its market for agriculture and industrial products, and from most sources of raw materials and energy.

By 1944, Hungary had the second highest per capita income in Eastern Europe (after Czechoslovakia). That same year it was occupied by the Nazis. World War II destroyed much of Hungary's industrial plant and transportation infrastructure.

Postwar efforts to rebuild under a Democratic government were subverted by Soviet-supported Communists, who seized power in 1948 and consolidated in 1949. The central government took over management of the economy, removed production incentives, collectivized agriculture and industry, and established Comecon, an economic sphere centered on the Soviet Union.

By 1950 a plan for boosting heavy industry had been launched, experienced managers had been purged, and the Soviet Union had installed itself as the Eastern bloc's major trading partner, absorbing 25 percent of Hungary's exports.

Soviet troops crushed the 1956 uprising, which had aimed to free some sectors of the economy. State monopoly control was reinstated, and Janos Kadar was installed as prime minister, a post he held until 1988.

A small dose of relief came in 1968, when declining growth rates prompted slightly more autonomy for state enterprises in investment and production, economic incentives, and more competitive prices. The economy was also opened to foreign trade and credit.

By the early 1980s, Hungary's economy was the most liberal in the Soviet bloc. Among the reforms instituted then were income and turnover taxes, cuts in subsidies, a competitive banking system, the privatization of state-owned enterprises, and encouragement of foreign investment. By 1986 the private sector was contributing 7 percent to the GDP.

In 1987, Hungary introduced a two-tier banking system, separating central banking and commercial banking functions. A year later, national per capita income reached the equivalent of $8760, moving Hungary into the category of medium-developed countries.

Gorbachev's deliberate loosening of the Soviet grip prompted Hungary to install a new leader, Karoly Grosz, who promised more political participation and more market-oriented economic reforms. After the Berlin Wall came down in 1989, Hungary made provisions for free, multiparty elections and abolished the Communists' political prerogatives.

Local government was decentralized, with commissioners appointed by the President to oversee operations. The commissioners have a measure of financial and policymaking autonomy.

Elections for parliament and President were held in March and April 1990. The HDF won 165 of the 386 seats, but low turnout for the presidential election rendered it invalid. In August 1990, the parliament elected former political prisoner Arpad Goncz to a five-year term as President.

The Economy

Up from Communism

Hungary's transition to democratic governance has been relatively smooth. The United States and other wealthy countries have devised aid programs to stabilize the currency, promote investment, and provide management and technical advice.

Far more difficult has been Hungary's transition to a productive, competitive market economy. The $21 billion debt, shortages of capital and expertise, and antiquated industrial facilities and infrastructure cannot be fixed overnight.

As Soviet dominance receded, Hungary's international political and economic links expanded. In 1990 it was the first Eastern European country to receive full membership in the Council of Europe, the main consultative association of European democracies. In 1991 it negotiated a trade agreement with the European Community (EC) that could bring it EC membership by the year 2000. An income tax and a value-added tax were introduced, while business taxes were reduced and reformed.

In 1990, at the end of Communism, mining, manufacturing, and agriculture were the two major components of GDP. Exports to Comecon countries dropped to 24 percent and imports to 18 percent, and exports to EC countries rose to 28 percent.

By 1991, exports to Comecon countries were less than 20 percent, and Hungary's most prominent trading partners were Germany, Austria, and Italy. Trade was no longer based on rubles, moving instead to a basis in international prices of convertible currencies. This move "dollarized" Soviet oil exports, tripling Hungary's energy bill and increasing its debt.

Economic changes continued in 1992 with new rules to govern insurance, banking, and telecommunications as private industries, and to encourage privatization through employee stock-ownership plans. Exports were up, and Hungary actually had a trade surplus.

But by year-end 1992 about 25 percent of the citizenry was living below the poverty line—casualties of the massive bankruptcy declarations triggered by the Bankruptcy Act.

Parliament considered bills that would establish a financial structure for private pension funds. Also under consideration was creation of a coupon system for ownership in state firms, similar to the voucher system in Poland and the Czech and Slovak republics.

The coupons would be 10-year notes with interest rates of 40 to 50 percent of the Hungarian National Bank's base rate, and would permit buyers to purchase shares of state companies that haven't yet been privatized. Unlike Poland's system, where each citizen over 18 gets vouchers for free, Hungarians would have to purchase the coupons. However, they would be made available at 1 to 2 percent of par value.

The social security deficit for 1992 was approximately US$4 million, and the deficit for the entire budget was about US$20 million. The 1993 budget imposed a 6 percent value-added tax on staple foods and most other zero-rated products.

Hungary is aiming for full convertibility of the Forint by 1993–1994. More than 90 percent of the prices were free of central control by 1992. Price liberalization is essential to reducing inflation. As of May 1992, subsidized goods accounted for only 4 percent of consumer spending.

Controlling the budget deficit will be a challenge for the government. Savings are up, but savers, according to *The Economist*, are mostly families nervous about the economy and intent on financial security.

Six commercial ports were scheduled for construction on the Danube, which should help spur international trade. In late 1992, Hungary signed a trade accord with Poland and the former Czechoslovakia. In early 1993, it signed a trade agreement with the newly independent republic of Kazakhstan.

Dealing with Debt

In 1972, the formation of joint ventures with Western working capital was permitted. Hungary began to build debt in 1973. By 1982 it was $11 billion, and by 1987 it was more than 300 percent of hard currency exports, a level comparable to that of several Latin American countries.

Since 1990 the number of both short-term and long-term bank loans has declined, and the share of official credit and bonds has risen. In May 1992 bonds were $5.5 billion, or 25 percent, of total debt.

Hungary's $22 billion debt could place it in a vulnerable position regarding foreign assistance. IMF suspended Hungary from its loan program because its 1992 deficit was 7.5 percent of GDP. EC membership is also conditional on progression to a market economy.

Hungary is still committed to servicing debt without a Brady-type plan, in order to preserve and enhance access to international capital markets. The Antall government is opposed to renegotiating Hungary's debt.

Hungary ended 1991 with a current account surplus of $267 million, following a 1990 surplus of US$156 million. Debt service commitments in 1992 totaled US$3.8 billion, about 28 percent of anticipated export income.

Privatization

Legislation was adopted in 1989 and 1990 to ensure the orderly transformation of approximately 2000 state enterprises into corporate form and ultimately into private hands. The SPA was created in 1990 to supervise the process.

There are three types of privatization: those led by the SPA, those brought about by a simplified enterprise-initiated procedure, and those resulting from the initiative of domestic and foreign investors.

In 1991, the privatization program was decentralized. Managers now have more ability to privatize their own enterprises. They can select external advisers from an approved list, and more privatization proceeds can go to the enterprise.

In 1991, 9 out of 10 privatizations were to foreigners, and 85 percent of funds came from foreign investors. In 1992, 60 percent of the funds for privatization came from foreigners. As of April 1992, 10 percent of state-owned assets were fully privatized and 20 percent partially privatized. The government aimed at privatizing half the state-owned enterprises in 1993-94.

In 1993, Hungary expected to put up telecommunications companies, public utilities for natural gas and electricity, and banks for privatization.

In January 1992 the SPA announced proposals to plough privatization proceeds back into three funds, to allow quicker and safer investments, and to remove much of the political and business risk involved in takeovers. One fund would help restructure state enterprises; another would temper unemployment resulting from privatization; and the third would provide guarantees against liabilities such as environmental damage.

In 1992, Privatization Minister Tamas Szabo in essence privatized the privatization program, by permitting a list of 130 consultants to take responsibility for selling about 278 midsize state companies. Credit Suisse First Boston won the mandate to advise the government on a privatization strategy for the banking sector.

The Markets

The Investment Funds Act of 1991 established the legal framework for investment funds and provides safeguards for their clients. Foreigners have been major investors on the exchanges and in Hungarian shares traded on the Vienna market.

The bond market, in existence since 1983, continues to thrive, offering primarily government short-term (two- to four-year), fixed-income paper. Interest rates of 13 percent on one-month government paper and 17 to 18 percent on longer-term paper is down substantially from over 30 percent in 1991. Nevertheless, it has been spurring demand for fixed-income instruments, according to Balazs Bathory, a trader for Creditanstalt Securities in Budapest.

In 1992, Budapest's stock market had an uninspiring year in local currency terms. The Budapest Stock Exchange Index fell 1.5 percent, a 17.6 percentage point recovery from its 19.1 percent tumble in 1991. (However, according to the IFC, Hungary's market in 1992 fell 11.4 percent in U.S. dollar terms.) In a report published in January 1993, Suzanne D. Patrick & Company, New York, noted that the index's nearly flat performance in local currency in 1992 masked a considerably worse across-the-board performance of all listed stocks, since the prices of shares that were not part of the index had deteriorated over time. The average performance of all listed stocks fell from a negative 12.8 percent in 1991 to a negative 22.8 percent in 1992 in local currency terms, the report stated.

In 1992, according to Suzanne D. Patrick & Company, only three stocks or less than 15 percent of all listed equities, had posted gains, as compared with either their initial offering price or their 1992 price performance. These three stocks averaged 36.9 percent returns before dividends. In comparison, the year before, nearly 50 percent of the listed stocks on the Budapest Stock Exchange (BSE) had posted gains, which averaged 12.2 percent for that group.

The Stock Exchange

The Budapest Stock Exchange was founded in 1864 as the Budapest Commodity and Stock Exchange. It flourished until 1948, when the Communists shut it down. The reemergence began in 1983 with the establishment of an unregulated bond market. In the next five years, 350 bonds were issued.

In 1990, the Act on Securities and the Stock Exchange established a legal framework, setting the conditions of public offering and trading and creating an independent self-regulatory group, the Stock Exchange Commission. The Budapest Stock Exchange (BSE) reopened in June 1990 with the listing of one stock, the former state-owned travel agency, Ibusz. According to Suzanne Patrick, an equities analyst specializing in stocks listed on the Budapest and Warsaw Exchanges, the meteoric rise of Ibusz's stock price caused subsequently listed stocks to be overvalued. After a quarter passed in which no new stocks were listed on the Budapest exchange, five new listings occurred between November and December 1990. In 1991 there were 14 new listings, but in 1992 listing activity dwindled to three companies, with two of these listings taking place in December. Trading volume in 1991 amounted to $160 million, and market capitalization totaled $518 million. In 1992, trading volume shrank to $76 million, while market capitalization rose to $582 million.

The shares offered are either bearer or registered, with foreign buyers restricted to the registered category. The BSE operates its own depository to hold securities during the registration process, which takes 3 to 14 days, and to maintain custody of assets for trades through the exchange. No tax is applied to registration. Trades are settled on the fifth business day.

Hungarian shares must be traded on the BSE before being listed on a foreign exchange. Membership is open only to foreign and local companies whose sole activity is dealing in securities. Foreign-owned companies can also become members, but their firms must be incorporated in Hungary. As of January 1, 1993, banks can operate only through single-purpose subsidiaries.

The EC gave the BSE money to invest in a computerized trading floor, expected to be in place in 1993.

Brokerage fees vary from 0.5 to 2 percent, depending on the size of the trade. Commissions on large deals are negotiable, and small deals may have a minimum fee. By early 1993 the most active brokers were: CA Brokers Ltd.; Kulturvest Investment Ltd.; Girozentrale Investment Ltd.; and Lupis Brokerhaz Ltd. Austrian, Swiss, American, and Japanese brokers also participate. There is limited but expanding securities reporting, and research in Hungarian, German, and

English languages. Besides brokers' reports, Reuters provides a daily market report, a listing of new issues, and securities prices.

Foreign Investors

In 1992, the National Bank of Hungary established conditions under which nonresidents can buy units in open-end and closed-end investment funds. Nonresidents can purchase registered investment units or closed-end real estate funds and open-end and closed-end funds, provided these funds are invested in equities only. Nonresidents may obtain up to 20 percent of the total units in investment funds with Forint-denominated bonds, including government bonds.

Foreigners have the right to reinvest the income earned into any other security or convert it to foreign currency. Remittance of foreign currency is performed via the investor's custodian bank, which maintains a local currency Central Corporation of Banking Companies (CCBC) account with the National Bank of Hungary. The CCBC imposes a 3 percent fee.

The Foreign Investment Act of 1988 provides full protection for foreign investors against a company's nationalization, and allows profits, dividends, and capital to be remitted overseas. Hungary has signed bilateral investment protection treaties with most West European countries, and is a member of the International Center for Settlement of Investment Disputes and the Multilateral Investment Guarantee Agency.

The environment for foreign investors is liberal. There is no withholding tax on dividends or interest and no capital-gains tax on investors from countries that have treaties with Hungary. Hungary has concluded tax treaties to eliminate or reduce withholding taxes with 20 countries, including the major EC nations and the United States.

Proceeds from trading can be transferred into hard currency only if it can be proven that shares were purchased in hard currency. Dividends can be converted into hard currency only if the National Bank of Hungary has first been consulted.

Foreigners can be majority owners of any Hungarian enterprise, without special permission. The only restriction on foreign ownership is that non-Hungarians may own bearer shares for no longer than three months, which allows time for conversion to registered shares. Hungary also permits foreign-currency bank accounts.

Investments to Consider

Some good areas for direct investment mentioned early in 1993 by Balazs Bathory and Gabor Sitanyi of Creditanstalt in Budapest include insurance, hotel development, telecoms, car production, and pharmaceuticals.

Parliament approved an insurance bill in 1992, to remedy the shortage of good life and accident insurance companies in Hungary. Two Hungarian companies, both state-owned, are State Insurance Co. and Providential. Austrian firms such as Merkur have been selling insurance policies under the counter in Hungary, and want to go legal.

Hotel development is worth considering, because Hungary is one of the most attractive locales in Eastern Europe for foreign tourists. Many hotels have been constructed in Budapest in recent years. The biggest one—Corvinus, owned by a Geneva company, Danubius—was introduced on the stock exchange in December 1992.

In 1991, Hungary's net tourism surplus was US$550 million, reflecting an 8.5 percent increase in the number of visitors. Arrivals from Eastern Europe and the Soviet Union dropped sharply, while those from North America, Western Europe, and East Asia rose significantly.

Hungary was approved to hold the World Expo in Budapest in 1996, conditioned on its following the timetable of the Bureau International de Expositions. Between 10 and 12 million visitors may come, and it is estimated that the equivalent of US$11 billion will be required to improve transportation, telecommunications, and infrastructure for the Expo.

Entering 1993, the most heavily traded equities on the Budapest exchange were: Fotex, Ibusz, Dunaholding, Skala-Coop, Styl, and Konzum. Fotex, the most active, also has an American depositary receipt that trades over the counter in the United States.

In the second quarter of 1992, Suzanne D. Patrick & Company was recommending exclusively garment manufacturer Styl, which Patrick called the most modern garment manufacturer in Central Europe. With a substantial export component principally to high-end German labels, and growing sales even in a depressed domestic market, the company is expected to post 7.4 percent earnings growth between 1993 and 1996. The company's stock was trading well below 10 times earnings, which is a 30 percent discount to the average price-earnings ratio on the Budapest Stock Exchange, according to Patrick.

Another sector worth watching is telecommunications. Hungary entered 1993 with only 9 telephone lines per 100 people, compared with 49 per 100 in the United States. It can take up to 12 years to have an order filled for a new phone. By the turn of the century, Hungary hopes to have one of Europe's most advanced telecommunications systems.

The Hungarian Telecommunications Company plans to increase investments in equipment over the next three years to a total of $1.5 billion. US West started to build a cellular network in Hungary, in partnership with the government, in 1991. An accounting code for all Hungarian companies was drafted in the early 1990s by Price Waterhouse.

Some industries to watch in the future, according to Balasz Bathory of Creditanstalt Budapest, are pharmaceuticals and computers. Somewhere not to look? Heavy industry. "It's all bankrupt," says Bathory.

A publicly listed fund is the closed-end Hungarian Investment Company that trades on the London Stock Exchange.

11
Poland

Poland deserves a closer look. Its political and economic land-scape is still littered with problems left over from decades of Communist rule, yet several points indicate strength. The government of Poland, like most Eastern European governments, is slowly gaining confidence that the economy will work just fine—if officialdom gets out of the way.

Along with many neighbors in Eastern Europe, Poland is determined to reorient its economic focus Westward. In 1991, the European Community took in 56 percent of Poland's exports, up from 32 percent in 1989. The share exported to former members of the Soviet-dominated Council on Mutual Economic Cooperation (Comecon) dropped to 17 from 35 percent. Trade with former Comecon republics began to revive in 1992.

Inflation is shrinking from 1990's peak of 586 percent, but is still high. Poland's Central Statistical Office reported inflation of 44.3 percent in 1992, down from 60 percent in 1991. For 1993, Morgan Guaranty Trust Company predicted a drop to 34.4 percent. Creeping devaluation of the zloty as well as the budget deficit have fanned inflation.

Real GDP climbed about 1 percent in 1992, the first positive result in four years. In 1993, GDP was expected to grow by about 2 percent.

Unemployment has climbed due to dissolution of state-owned companies. In 1992, 350,000 Poles lost their jobs, increasing joblessness to 14 percent or 2.5 million. Wages fell an aver-

age 9 percent in 1992, according to Central Planning Office estimates, while pensions lost 6 percent of real value. Per capita
monthly income in late 1992 was the equivalent of US$227.

But the private sector share of the economy is rising. In 1992,
it reached 50 percent. Since 1989, 7.5 million small and midsize
businesses have been established, which employ 56 percent of
the population.

Like Hungary, Poland is an associate member of the EC and
intends to seek full membership. Some observers predict this
achievement in the first decade of the next century. Poland has
accepted a plan to adjust the legal system to EC standards.
Priority will be given to laws regulating the economy, such as
customer duties, financial services, trade, industry, protection of
copyright, and the environment.

Government and Politics

Poland today comprises 120,000 square miles, roughly the size
of New Mexico. The population of 38 million contains 98 percent ethnic Poles. The northern border is the Baltic Sea, and its
neighbors include Germany and the former Czechoslovakia. In
its pocket of Europe, Poland is the only area that provides a
potentially significant domestic market.

Under Communism, the political system consisted of a one-
house parliament (Sejm), with infrequent meetings and members appointed by the Party, and no presidency.

Martial law was imposed on 1981 and lifted in July 1983. This
status remained until 1988, when worker strikes again rocked
Poland. In March 1989, Communist rulers completed talks with
representatives of the opposition, and the Solidarity trade union
was relegalized. Elections in June 1989 marked the end of
Communist domination. The Polish United Workers Party dissolved itself and formed a smaller socialist party. The Sejm
remained as the parliamentary body. The first free election was
held in October 1991.

The political freedom in Poland is as much a curse as a blessing, as the country is rife with dissension. Entering 1993, 11
major parties were represented in the Polish parliament. Over

30 political parties vied for seats, and only 42.5 percent of the eligible population voted. No party received more than 12 percent of the vote. Continual infighting among officials brings stagnation, resignations, and the need for new coalitions.

Prime Minister Hanna Suchocka, a former professor of law, was elected in the summer of 1992. While her coalition government appeared to be off to a healthy start, with successful resolution of strikes in mining and manufacturing in August 1992, it nonetheless suffered a one-vote parliamentary defeat on May 28, 1993. As of this writing Suchocka remained as caretaker prime minister ahead of the September 19 elections. But so many competing parties could result in further infighting.

History

Poland dates its founding to 966, when its ruler accepted Roman Catholic Christianity, placing Poland within the orbit of Western culture. The union of Poland and Lithuania extended the Polish border far to the east in 1569. Internal weakness and pressure from neighboring states caused the Polish kingdom to vanish from the map in the late 18th century, due to partitioning by Russia, Austria, and Prussia.

After World War I, Poland was back on the map. In that reincarnation, one-third of the population was made up of Germans, Ukrainians, and Jews. Nazi Germany's attack of Poland in 1939 triggered World War II.

Following 1945, Poland's boundaries were restructured. It lost the eastern territories it had prior to eighteenth-century partitioning but gained in the west, where there were rich resources of minerals. The mix was good for development of the economy, but Poland suffered shortages of the labor and equipment needed to rebuild.

The Soviet Union which assumed control of Poland soon after the war's end, nationalized all natural resources and most factories. Attempts to collectivize farms were abandoned in response to riots in the city of Poznan. Private hands retained control of 80 percent of cultivated lands.

More riots broke out in 1970, when national price increases

POLAND

Currency: Polish zloty (PLZ).

Stock Exchanges: The Warsaw Stock Exchange (W.S.E.) commenced operations in 1991. Additionally, there is an active OTC market that trades in most securities.

Indexes: The main market index is the Warsaw Stock Exchange (Warszawski Indeks Gieldowy, Wig). It is considered to be an indicator of the average price change of exchange-traded securities.

Types of Securities: Equities, warrants, corporate bonds, government securities

Regulatory Body/Stock Exchange Supervision: The primary government regulatory authority is the Polish Securities Commission (PSC). Although the stock exchange is self-regulating, it is supervised by the PSC. The PSC also supervises the National Depository of Securities, the banks, and brokerage houses.

Depository: The National Depository of Securities (NDS) is the central depository. The NDS is managed by the stock exchange.

Settlement Information

Equities:

- T + 2.
- Book entry (exchange-traded) and physical delivery (OTC-traded) available.
- Receive/deliver versus payment available.
- Same-day turnaround trades are not possible.

Fixed Income:

- T + 2.
- Book entry (exchange-traded) and physical delivery (OTC-traded) available.

- Receive/deliver versus payment available.
- Same-day turnaround trades are not possible.

Taxes: A 30 percent withholding tax is charged on dividends and interest, unless reduced pursuant to an applicable tax treaty.

Restrictions for Foreign Investors:

- All investment using hard currency funding must be processed through a duly licensed Polish bank.
- The repatriation of interest requires a special foreign exchange permit issued by the National Bank of Poland and the Ministry of Finance.
- Foreign investors require specific permission to invest in the management of sea ports, dealings in real estate, defense industry companies, and the financial sector.

Securities Lending: Securities lending is not currently available in Poland.

SOURCE: The Bank of New York.

were attempted. This scenario was rerun in 1976, when another attempt to raise prices brought riots followed by arrests. Opposition crystallized into public action organizations, which were limited by dependency on Western support.

Attempts were made to increase prices region by region. But strikes began in the mid-1980s. Membership in the Solidarity strike committee, led by Lech Walesa, grew to over 10 million, or about 25 percent of the population.

In June 1981 the United Workers Party held a congress to establish rules for competitive election and rotation of leadership. New leaders came to power in October, but only weeks later martial law was declared on December 13. Banks were closed, so Poland could not meet its debt service. Western sanctions imposed under U.S. leadership limited trade and cut off loans and talks of loan rescheduling.

The Economy

Up from Communism

Poland's economy changed completely during the Communist period. Agricultural production had never met Poland's needs, contributing to a foreign trade deficit. Large-scale industrialization and reconstruction began in 1949. Farm output increased from 1950 through the 1970s, particularly in grain and potatoes. However, government attempts to reform the farmers led to agricultural decline by 1980.

By the end of the Communist era in 1989, 56 percent of GNP came from manufacturing, mining, and power production, and less than 15 percent from agriculture. More than half of Poland's exports to members of the Comecon trading bloc was in machinery, fuel, and energy. The Soviet Union was a customer for coal, pharmaceutical products, and electronic components.

The emphasis on heavy industry hurt the environment and caused shortages in housing and consumer goods. Poland went from an exporter to an importer of grain, needed to feed pigs slaughtered for export. Other exports included textiles, chemicals, clothing, footwear, ships, and other transportation equipment.

Although the United Workers Party at its height had over 3 million card-carrying members, support for the Communists was never strong.

In January 1990, a crash program was launched to promote Western investment, make the Polish zloty convertible with Western hard currencies, end government subsidies, and reduce the national debt. The effects: real incomes declined by over 50 percent; inflation the first month was 80 percent; and shortages continued. In addition, 400,000 lost their jobs and many more were furloughed without pay. By June 1990, 90 percent of prices were freed.

In 1991, state-owned enterprises underwent a structural crisis: Privatization was slower than expected. Tax revenue fell short of expectations, and expenditures moved steeply upward, partly due to the unemployed status of 12.7 percent of the labor force.

But by mid-1992, the Suchocka government began to move toward a market-oriented economy. Emergency budget proposals included a 10 percent cut in real pensions and social service payments, a hike in the top bracket of income tax rates, a 10 percent increase in sales taxes, and a temporary 10 percent tax surcharge on many imports.

There was parliamentary resistance to the austerity policies. For example the Sejm rejected the pension cut proposal in October 1992. The government commercialized the national insurance system and decentralized responsibility for welfare benefits.

But the need for change is evident. A November 1992 report from S.J. Rundt & Associates notes that metallurgy and engineering are down, "having been traumatized by the collapse of the Comecon market. Weapons, for example, made up 40 percent of Poland's industrial output four years ago. Now it's just 18 percent, and it's shrinking."

Plans are afoot to restructure the coal and steel industries, cutting production and employment over the next decade. According to reports, Poland also won Solidarity backing for a plan to force restructuring of state unions that wouldn't take these steps voluntarily.

Key factors in Poland's recovery are the growth of exports, gains in productivity, and a mild upturn in investment activity.

Mariusz Kolecki, area manager for Poland with Creditanstalt in Vienna, spells out some challenges facing the Polish economy: the performance of the German economy, as Poland depends on Germany more than it did on Russia; the threat of inflation; compliance with the Mass Privatization Program; and development of the capital market. Experts say Poland will also have to resolve the problem of widespread tax evasion that has caused a sharp fall in tax income. The government is moving forward with new tax measures: a hike in sales tax was one move; and in July, a value-added (VAT) tax was scheduled to take effect.

Debt Forgiveness

Negotiations with the IMF raised the debt ceiling as a percentage of GDP to 8 percent for 1992, and cut it to 5 percent from 6 percent for 1993, enabling Poland to receive a $660 million standby loan from the IMF.

Debt stood at $44.9 billion, or 7.5 percent of GDP, in 1992, down slightly from $48.4 billion, or 8 percent of GDP, in 1991.

In January 1993, Poland announced its intention to cut debt service payments on a $1.1 billion loan extended as a revolving trade facility in 1983. This is on top of a halt in the servicing of its commercial debt in March 1992.

Trade

For 1992, Poland had a trade surplus of $512 million and in 1993 the surplus was "set to grow by nearly $300 million," according to Morgan Guaranty Trust Co.

Polish authorities have faced unexpectedly high social costs during the transition to a market economy, according to the *Financial Times*. As a result they opted to reinstate economic protections in early 1992, including new duties, wider import licensing, and consideration of an import levy system to protect agriculture.

A 20 percent average duty now exists for a wide range of food imports. Customs duties were raised for a range of products in January 1992. Trucks and motor vehicles were hiked to 35 percent from 15 percent, but components could still be imported duty-free; electrical equipment was raised to 20 percent; food and textiles to a range of 25 to 35 percent; and luxury goods to 45 percent.

A trade agreement was signed in August 1992 to keep energy supplies coming from Russia in exchange for food from Poland.

Privatization

Privatization is a crucial component of Poland's conversion to a free market economy. In October 1992, Suchocka and her cabinet presented a new set of initiatives to representatives of the labor union to spur the privatization program. Management and workers in state enterprises (except the 600 in the mass privatization program) would have three months from enactment to choose a privatization strategy: public sale of shares, sale to a strategic foreign or domestic investor, partial transfer of ownership to management of workers, or sale of a controlling interest to an institutional or bank investor. Bankruptcy procedures could be initiated against insolvent firms that do not present viable privatization plans.

The program has been gaining steam. As of mid-1993, about one-quarter of Poland's 8500 state enterprises had already been privatized. And in April 1993, Poland's parliament approved a modified, but long-awaited mass privatization plan. The program calls for transferring ownership of 600 state and municipally owned enterprises to designated National Investment Funds. According to the *Financial Times*, "shares in the NIFs, tradeable over-the-counter to start with and subsequently to be quoted on the Warsaw Stock Exchange, will be distributed to the population for a small registration fee, equivalent to $20, or 10 percent of an average month's salary."

Fund managers will be appointed by a state selection committee. By late 1993, this body "will choose from a growing list of foreign and domestic fund managers who have expressed interest in managing the funds," said the *Financial Times*. The task of the fund managers, it said, "is to convert the enterprises in their portfolios into profitable investments."

The new funds are due to be launched at the start of 1994.

The Stock Exchange

The Warsaw Stock Exchange reopened in 1991 after a 50-year hiatus. At the end of 1992, the market's capitalization stood at $22.5 million, more than double its level in 1991. The market's cap ballooned further in 1993— reportedly to a peak of about $800 million—during an April and May bull run. Investors cheered several developments: approval of the mass privatization program as well as approval of a $660 million standby loan from the IMF, a slight fall in interest rates, and generally, a rising tide of foreigners' investments. But after rocketing 175 percent between April and May, the market retreated after the fall of the Suchocka-led government rekindled political uncertainty.

In 1992, the Warsaw Stock Exchange advanced 6.9 percent in local currency terms, representing a 20 percentage point gain over 1991's performance. (However, Poland's market in U.S. dollar terms fell 21.5 percent in 1992, according to the IFC.) In local currency terms, 1992 brought a considerable improvement in the number of stocks trading in positive territory—a tribute to the quality of new listings, holds Suzanne Patrick of the investment research firm of Suzanne D. Patrick & Company, New York. Whereas in 1991 only two stocks (or one-fourth of all listed equities) ended higher on the year, by the end of 1992 seven stocks had gained over their new issue price, while five stocks had advanced over their 1991 performances alone, she reports.

Both domestic and foreign investors can buy and sell shares on the exchange. Trades must be executed through a Warsaw-based brokerage firm, since companies listed on the Warsaw exchange do not trade elsewhere and telephone lines inside the exchange are restricted to Warsaw. Trades must be transacted in the Polish currency, the zloty.

Foreign Investors

Most direct foreign investment, entering 1993, had come from large multinational corporations: About 67 companies from around the world, including AT&T, RJR-Nabisco, International Paper, Fiat, Ikea, Levi Strauss, Coca-Cola, Asea Brown Boveri, and PepsiCo, have put money into Polish firms.

However the investments have been private placements, and little or no equity has been issued. And only in 1992 did Poland's laws change to permit foreign entities to issue and purchase debt on the domestic capital or corporate market.

The Law on Joint Ventures of June 1991 introduced favorable conditions for foreign businesses. A foreign investor may participate directly as a shareholder in privatizing or ownership transformation of state enterprises and municipal property.

Other possibilities are setting up joint venture companies with the participation of foreign capital and establishing companies with complete foreign ownership (a limited-liability company requires minimum founding capital of about US$3000, while a joint stock company requires about US$77,000).

A license from the Ministry of Ownership Transformations is needed if a joint venture is involved in managing seaports or airports, wholesale trade in imported consumer goods, rendering legal services, trade in property, or direct manufacturing for military purposes. Investors also need special governmental approval to invest in the financial sector, including in banks, brokerage houses, insurance companies investment funds, or casinos.

Investments to Like

For portfolio investors, some areas in Poland that might be good investments in the coming years: telecommunications, road construction, and automobile construction. Jack Brzezinski of Creditanstalt in Vienna speaks of plans that are still in the idea stage for a highway that would run from Berlin through Warsaw to Moscow.

Poland, like the rest of Eastern Europe, has strong infrastructural needs in telecommunications. Poland passed legislation splitting its national telephone operation into six regional companies, and may eventually privatize some of them.

Britain's Cable and Wireless is building a digital network in the port of Gdansk, in exchange for a license to operate a telephone system for 25 years, and France Telecom and Ameritech won the Polish nationwide license in an auction. In return they must make cash donations toward the cost of updating Poland's wire-based network, a direct competitor, and reimburse the government for the cost of administering the auction.

Many stocks listed in Warsaw are those of established companies with strong export markets and national franchises. The stocks Creditanstalt's Kolecki considers blue chips are: Wedel, a confectioner 67 percent owned by PepsiCo that manufactures the most popular chocolates in Poland; Elektrim, a trading company that deals in electrical equipment and provides technical services to Polish companies; the breweries Okocim and Zywiec; and the construction company Mostostal. The top three in market cap are Zywiec, Wedel, and Elektrim.

Suzanne Patrick likes Prochnik, a coat manufacturer, Zywiec, and Exbud, a construction company. Exbud has a long-standing export business base, is independent from domestic consumer trends, and has internationally audited financial records. In late 1992, Exbud was also trading at a discount to book of 50 percent, and has a high dividend payout rate.

Prochnik and Zywiec are both in the midst of modernization programs, which Patrick believes will be very favorable to long-term earnings progression. Both are also trading at 20 to 30 percent discounts to the average P/E ratios of the Warsaw Stock Exchange.

Even though Poland is a vodka-drinking company, beer consumption is increasing. For an investment, Kolecki also likes the brewery Zywiec. Says Kolecki, "Breweries will always do well—beer consumption doesn't change much with economic conditions." Patrick rates Okocim a "hold"; she recommends purchasing shares if any further offering should have prices below about US$6 per share.

Wedel and Elektrim are the two cheapest, with P/E ratios of 2 and 2.5, respectively.

A not-so-hot stock is Swarzedz, according to Suzanne Patrick in *The Wall Street Transcript*, as it is in furniture production, a market that takes a while to develop. Irena and Krosno, glass manufacturers, might also be problematic.

The paper industry also bears watching by foreign investors. Eight paper mills are due to be privatized before year-end 1994.

12
Portugal

For most of this century, the Portuguese government has willingly, consistently, and almost enthusiastically painted its economy into Europe's geopolitical corner. Ruinous colonial policies and guerrilla wars, repressive, quasi-isolationist governments, minimal infrastructure spending and stubborn backing of low-wage industries and inefficient agriculture had all hampered the Portuguese economy. These elements did not, however, diminish the expectations and spirit of the Portuguese. In the past five years economic and social changes have come rapidly and dramatically. As Luis Vaz Pinto of Baring Securities observes, "The Portuguese economy underwent a remarkable transformation during the late 1980s and [is] rapidly becoming a full-fledged member of the [EC] community...[its] main strength coming from investment and export growth rather than consumption."

A tumultuous celebration marked the night of President Anibal Cavaco Silva's first national victory in 1987. The Portuguese middle class jammed the streets of Lisbon, boisterously (but peacefully) celebrating a victory that, to them, meant change for the better after a period of Marxist and then socialist governments. The means for realizing these expectations may come through Portugal's growing stock market, continuance of the privatization process and restructuring, as well as other mechanisms for distributing wealth to the middle class. Whereas the ancient prince Henry the Navigator looked west and south across the oceans for Portugal's future, today's Portuguese navigate east and north to the European Community.

The government has a broad-based mandate to integrate Portugal's economy into the rest of Europe in time for the European Monetary Union (EMU). Since joining the EC in 1985, Portugal has benefited enormously. In 1992, 2 percent of its GDP came in the form EC grants and subsidies. Other inflows of capital equaling 10 percent of its GDP have followed these subsidies and grants. This partially explains the electorate's increasing acceptance of its slightly-to-right-of-center-government. It also explains why the Portuguese seem willing to exchange austerity today for expected gains tomorrow.

Gains have already been significant. *Emerging Markets Analyst* (EMA), a publication of The Bank Credit Analyst, points out that Portugal's 1993 budget deficit has been trimmed to 4 percent of GDP, compared with its hopes to achieve a target of 3 percent by 1997. Inflation has already dropped from 35 percent to single digits over an 18-month period. Looking ahead, inflation and industry restructuring will remain "the two major economic policy issues facing the Portuguese government," says the EMA.

Portugal is likely to meet the 0.6 debt-to-GDP ratio this year. While Portugal held the EC's presidency during the first half of 1992, its currency the escudo joined the European Rate Mechanism (ERM) with a wide intervention band of 6 percent (which will narrow to 2.5 percent by 1995). Portugal is thus limited to defending its currency by fiscal and monetary policy, not by government fiat.

The Economy

Fiscal and Monetary Policy

To develop a more modern state and economy, the government has had to make some tough fiscal and monetary policy decisions. Infrastructure investments to rebuild an old and outdated transport system and utility network, and to retrain the labor force, have accounted for nearly 18 percent of Portuguese governmental expenditures. Thus, it is not hard to understand why deficits have soared in the late '80s and early '90s.

To comply with EC standards, budget deficits had to drop.

Luis Vaz Pinto of Baring Securities commented that "this government wants to reduce the budget deficit to 4 percent of 1993 GDP and 3 percent in 1994," higher than the Quantum 2 plan submitted to the EC. However, the excess is due largely to a shift in fiscal years. Still enthusiastic, Vaz Pinto goes on, "The 1992 budget was the first step in the right direction," saying that this budget incorporated tax reforms limiting private consumption growth. This has reduced pressure on the public debt market, freeing more capital for equity investments.

High deficits overheated the Portuguese economy, fueling inflation. Interest payments in 1992 forced the budget into the red. In an attempt to check inflation with monetary policy, the government kept the pressure on the money supply and boosted interest rates to high levels. But as government borrowing falls, interest rates—which have now been dropping—should decline further and reduce budgetary interest expense.

Inflation, which historically had run in the 8 to 10 percent range, shot up dramatically in 1988 and peaked at just under 35 percent during the summer of 1990. Since that peak it has fallen steadily, and seems to have returned to its pre-1988 zone of between 8 and 10 percent. The decline was due in part to the relatively high interest rates that attracted foreign capital to Portugal.

Competitive wage rates have also had an impact. The two devaluations of the Spanish peseta, one in November 1992 and one in May 1993, forced the Portuguese government's hand in three respects. First, it reduced the rampant currency speculation in the escudo caused by its close association with devalued peseta. Second, the Portuguese government had to keep comparative wage parity with Spain, one of Portugal's leading trade partners (over 15 percent of exports). And third, it had to remain a viable destination for direct investment by Spanish companies relocating basic industries. The close linkage of the two economies forced Portugal to follow Spain's lead, but it was clear that the latest devaluation was done reluctantly, and that given Spain's recent instability, Portugal's economy might be unhooking at last.

PORTUGAL

Currency: Portuguese escudo (PTE).

Stock Exchanges: There are two stock exchanges, the Lisbon Stock Exchange (LSE) and the Oporto Stock Exchange (OSE), as well as an OTC market. The LSE commands the majority of the total trade volume.

Indexes: There are no major market indexes in Portugal.

Types of Securities: Equities (bearer and registered), government and corporate fixed-income securities, as well as convertible securities and warrants.

Regulatory Body/Stock Exchange Supervision: The Banco De Portugal (Central Bank) regulates and supervises the inflow/outflow of all currency. The Comissao De Mercado De Valores Mobiliarios (CMVM) regulates, supervises, and administers the Portuguese capital markets.

Depository: The Central De Valores Mobilarios (Central), established in 1991, is the depository for all fungible bearer shares and bonds. All other securities are held in bearer form.

Settlement Information

Equities:

- T + 3 (T + 4 in practical terms).
- Physical or book entry (fungible bearer shares only).
- Receive versus payment available, but deliver versus payment is not.
- Same-day turnaround trades are possible for securities quoted on the continuous market, or by combining an OTC trade with an exchange trade, but are not common practice.

Fixed Income:

- T + 3 (T + 4 in practical terms).
- Physical or book entry (fungible bearer shares only).

- Receive versus payment available, but delivery vs. payment is not.
- Same-day turnaround trades are possible for securities quoted on the continuous market, or by combining on OTC trade with an exchange trade, but are not common practice.

Taxes:

- Dividends are taxed at an effective rate of 15 percent.
- There is no capital gains tax on long-term share holdings.
- There is a stamp duty on OTC trades.
- There is a stock exchange tax for all trades from 0.04 to 0.50 per MIL, depending on the security.
- There is also a 0.05 percent stock exchange tax for all trades executed off the exchanges.
- Foreign investors whose home countries have double taxation treaties with Portugal can reclaim applicable taxes withheld at source.

Restrictions for Foreign Investors:

- All foreign investors must open a local cash account, to be used for capital market transactions only.
- Overdrafts are forbidden for foreign investors.
- Cash loans are forbidden for foreign investors.
- Central bank approval is required for foreign investor participation in primary market transactions.
- There are no government regulations setting foreign ownership limits, but companies are allowed to impose specific limits under certain conditions.

Securities Lending: Legislation for securities lending has been enacted, but guidelines and regulations have not been issued as of yet.

SOURCE: The Bank of New York and other sources.

Privatization

For Portugal, privatization will mean selling off, in the next decade, over 60 wholly state-owned companies and hundreds of lesser stakes in other businesses. The privatization sword has two edges. First, the Portuguese treasury receives the proceeds and applies 80 percent to reducing the public debt. Second, privatization will by definition increase market capitalization, since more of the country's capital stock will become available through the market. Portuguese privatization has had its shares of scandals and setbacks, but the outlook is positive. In 1989, during the first privatization phase, over 210,000 investors soaked up nearly $2.5 billion in assets. The *Financial Times* reported in November 1991 that the state stood ready to "have sold more than double the equity on offer...if demand could have been satisfied."

However, the Portuguese state seems to be following a rather deliberate and simple privatization strategy (see Table 12-1): To maintain political advantage and individual expectations, first privatize companies in domestic, nonstrategic sectors; second, privatize those companies that control the flow of international commerce. In the first two years the entire brewery sector, by the third year a significant portion of the banking sector, and by the fourth year, the insurance sector were privatized. In the fourth year (1992), the government offered all domestic freight truckers. In the fifth year, the plan offered small portions of the national airline, oil companies, and steel and cement producers. Whether the government fully privatizes these industries will no doubt become a point of considerable debate in Portugal.

Foreign Direct Investment

Major equity capital comes into Portugal through direct investment, especially when encouraged through EC incentives. During 1991, the OECD reported that investment into Portugal was more than $2 billion or 3.5 percent of gross domestic product (GDP) and nearly 13 percent of all investment. Though foreign direct investment comes in large bite sizes, the local multiplier will spread the benefits around to many Portuguese firms.

Table 12-1. Privatizations

Company	Industry	1989	1990	1991	1992	1993	Total %
TAP	Airline					49	49
BESCL	Banking			40	60		100
BFB	Banking			80	20		100
BPA	Banking		33		20	20	73
BPSM	Banking				100		100
BTA	Banking	49	31			16	96
CPP	Banking				100		100
SFP	Banking			100			100
UBP	Banking					61	61
Centralcer	Brewery		100				100
Unicer	Brewery	49	51				100
Cimpor	Cement						0
CMP	Cement					100	100
Secil	Cement					80	80
Alianca	Insurance	49		51			100
Bonanca	Insurance			60	15		75
Cosec	Insurance					40	40
Imperio	Insurance				100		100
Mundial Confianca	Insurance				100		100
Tranquilidade	Insurance	49	51				100
Diario Noticias	Media			100			100
Petrogal	Oil				25	25	50
Portline	Shipping			80			80
Siderurgia	Steel					90	90
RN Algarve	Transport				100		100
RN Duoro/ Minho	Transport				100		100
Rodocargo	Transport				100		100
Socarmar	Transport				55		55
Transporta	Transport				100		100

SOURCE: Lehman Brothers

Portugal's competitive advantage in the industrial sector is its low-wage workers. In fact, it has the lowest wage costs in the EC and thus affords a more cost-efficient manufacturing platform than many Eastern European countries. However, it remains to be seen whether Germany, Europe's economic powerhouse, will turn more often to its eastern neighbors for low-wage production.

Since 1989, Portugal has received about $5.4 billion in EC financial assistance. The money goes primarily for infrastructure projects. However, in Portugal a significant portion of the money helps Portugal to make the transition from an economy based on low-wage industrial and agricultural sectors to one with higher value-added products. This is an important transition, since higher wages will create a higher standard of living, which in turn will greatly influence the performance of domestic firms.

For example, a joint venture between Ford and Volkswagen to build a major assembly plant in Setubal will contribute an investment of $2.8 billion. Other automobile-related manufacturing has followed. GM is building an electronic ignition plant, Ford an audio plant, and Valmet (Finland) a tractor factory. All of these facilities have received various construction incentives, from 36 to 52 percent of construction costs. Other industries also are active. Pepsi is rumored to be building a snack food plant and is planning to open fast-food restaurants. The French insurance company, UAP, gained control of a major Portuguese insurer. With this type of investing comes mainstream management practices and experience. However, the price Portugal pays will be a contraction in its textile and shoe industries, as wage rates increase and workers move to higher value-added jobs.

Portugal is also actively seeking to enhance and upgrade its image as an inexpensive vacation destination with good food and wine, beautiful beaches, accommodating people, and low-priced souvenirs. In fact tourism is Portugal's largest industry, and it accounts for a sizable portion of the 55 percent of Portuguese GDP in the service sector. However, since the warm-water beaches are limited to the Algarve and space is limited, the Portuguese government wants to change the focus in the tourism industry. The current objective now is to attract higher-end tourism through better facilities and more upscale attractions such golf courses. This will bring the tourism industry into direct competition with those in France, Italy, and Spain. To accomplish this goal, the Portuguese may have to turn to foreign developers and operators and encourage direct investment.

Foreign Financial and Strategic Investors

Officials in Lisbon have had major concerns about foreign purchases of stocks in its recently privatized companies. Foreign control is, *de jure*, forbidden, and only in certain cases has foreign ownership percentages been permitted to rise as high as 35 percent. However, driven by the need to receive better prices, the government has accommodated foreign interests. For example, the French insurance group UAP gained control over Alianca Seguradora even while a limit of 30 percent foreign ownership was in effect. UAP used the soon-to-become common ploy of reaching an understanding with a Portuguese insurance company in which the foreign investor held a minority position. The Portuguese government basically winked at the arrangement. This attitude on the part of Portuguese officials reflects their understanding of the EC and the practical difficulty of retaining Portuguese control in an open market. Thinking along these lines will more than likely dominate the coming Portuguese political discussions.

The Stock Market

Although somewhat sluggish at this writing, the Portuguese stock market may become pivotal in the regeneration of the Portuguese economy and the maintenance of the middle class's high expectations.

The Bolsa de Valores de Lisboa (Lisbon Stock Exchange), established in 1901, and the Bolsa de Valores do Oporto (the Oporto Stock Exchange), founded in 1891, have been electronically linked since 1990. The market is heavily dominated by banking stocks, which comprise some 50 percent of the market.

Equity investing is new to Portugal. Domestic insurance companies, by regulation, can allocate only 15 percent of their port-folios to equities. And consider that the newly organized and quickly growing ($900 million) domestic mutual fund industry allocates only 25 percent to equities.

The owners of much of Portugal's private capital have invested in either agriculture, closely held businesses, or high-yield government debt. As a result the stock market may not gain much momentum soon from domestic investors. "There's practically no activity in the Portuguese stock market, making it very illiquid," says Jose Garcia of Salomon Brothers. "In case some problem arose, it would be very hard to get out." But with so many liquid and interesting markets in Western Europe, it is unlikely that investors will look at the Portuguese stock market over the near term. However, some analysts have a more posi-tive outlook. Douglas Dooley of J. P. Morgan points out that "the Portuguese stock market has evolved a lot over the last couple of years. The market was small and had exchange con-trols that kept foreigners out." He adds, "Now that's changing."

In 1986 the government opened the market to foreign investors, and it jumped nearly 500 percent pre-Crash (October 1987). Thin trading made prices soar, and thin trading brought it plummeting just as quickly, as foreign investors sought to exit the market post-Crash. Since then the market, in terms of per-formance, has bobbled along with very little interest on the part of foreign or local investors. Part of this is owing to investors' skittish outlook on thinly traded markets. As Douglas Dooley notes "It's hard to get out once you're in—at a good price."

In 1992, the IFC's Price Index for the $9.2 billion Portugal market tumbled 22.6 percent in U.S. dollar terms, as the market reflected fears—later realized—of a currency devaluation. Other factors included the weakness in Europe's economy, which is important to a country like Portugal where exports account for more than 35 percent of the economy, and where real interest rates are high (about 15 percent).

High interest rates meant that the bond market, on a govern-ment-backed, risk-free basis, significantly outperformed the equity market. Concern over Portuguese inflation and possible devaluation of the escudo, and more interest in other nation's stock markets, have also inhibited performance. The growing mutual fund industry, which has developed balanced special equity funds, may reduce trading risks for many individual investors. The Portuguese mutual fund industry has grown from 5 funds in 1985 to over 100 today.

Changes are under way that will increase the market's capitalization and trading level. In 1992, the government initiated a string of stock market incentives for companies and investors alike. For individual investors, the government proposed tax savings on up to 20 percent of equity investments.

Depending on size and liquidity, both public and private securities trade on three market tiers. The first tier, or "Official Market" trades Portugal's 40 relatively liquid blue-chip companies and public debt on the CATS system. Smaller companies are quoted twice daily. The second and third tiers, or the "Unofficial Market," are characterized by less liquid issues. The second tier trades equities of small companies and bonds issued by public and private entities guaranteed by the Portuguese state. Prices are quoted when trading exists. The third tier is similar to an unquoted market, where brokers must sponsor listed companies. For securities not listed on the stock exchange, brokers and financial institutions trade these issues outside the exchange.

The stock market has benefited from several operational improvements. First, the Sapateiro law, enacted in 1991, increased the equity market's viability by improving liquidity and transparency. Second, a new Securities Market Commission began to supervise and regulate the Portuguese securities markets. The third brought the electronic linking of the Lisbon and Oporto stock exchanges, and by April 1991 a continuous CATS system similar to Madrid's was up and running. This has increased the efficiency of the two markets and has fostered added financial cooperation between the northern industrial areas and the central government in the south. Fourth, the Sapateiro law created a Central Securities Depository to facilitate clearing and settlement through the book-entry method.

A board of governors oversees the Lisbon market. Each member represents one of the following interest areas: the Minister of Finance, stockbrokers, financial institutions, and listed companies. Each has a representative on the board. Portugal has about

20 brokerage firms, of which less than a half-dozen undertake formal research that they make available to foreign investors. The Minister of Finance has influence over board decisions. In particular the minister appoints stockbrokers, and only Portuguese citizens with specific skills can become stockbrokers.

Lehman Brothers, Baring Securities, and others suggest that foreign investors in Portuguese equities might take a value-oriented approach and limit themselves to relatively liquid issues. Based on continued infrastructure development—fed by EC funding—and strong personal income growth, both look to engineering, construction, and retail as robust sectors. Early in 1993 the stock of Soares da Costa, the largest construction company, was "still looking attractive for the long term," said Josephine Jimenez of Montgomery Asset Management, in San Francisco.

Analysts foresee rebounding in earnings-per-share growth, low price-earnings ratios, and a favorable position for Portugal's economy. Hastened by the financial deregulation of late 1992, interest rates should decline further, giving a boost to share prices even as they aid corporate earnings. Reducing inflation will also stabilize the business environment. But investment timing will be critical, since Portugal's future will trail European macroeconomic events more than many other European countries'.

Wilson Emerging Market Funds Research lists five closed-end funds for Portugal. The three trading on the London Stock Exchange are: the Oporto Growth Fund Ltd., the Portugal Fund Limited, and the Portuguese Investment Fund Limited. In addition the Capital Portugal Fund trades on the Lisbon Stock Exchange, and the Portugal Fund Inc. is listed on the New York Stock Exchange.

The ADR of Banco Comercial Portugues trades on the New York Stock Exchange.

13

Greece

The Economy

Investors in Greek companies took a beating in 1992, when their stocks fell 33.3 percent. Clearly, the Athens stock exchange was an "awful market" in 1992, says Koenraad Foulon, a vice president with Capital Research International in London.

Summing up a woeful year, a January 29, 1993, article in the *Financial Times* noted that only 2 small investment companies joined the bourse in 1992, compared with 17 entrants in 1991. A recession in Europe, high real interest rates, and the government austerity program in Greece slammed the values of stocks on the Athens exchange.

The market rallied in January 1993 in response to news that Greece was going to get $16 billion in its second EC package for infrastructure development. But it remained unclear when an improvement in fundamental economic problems would allow for sustained market gains.

From the *Financial Times:*

> [A]s the government's economic stabilization program entered its third year, inflation is forecast to decline faster, dropping to 9 percent by the end of the year. A fall in interest rates, currently standing at about 27 percent is also expected, gathering speed after the summer. The real test for the market this year [1993] will come when the government launches a series of privatizations through the stock market.

In early 1993, Greece seemed saddled with too many problems to make a quick recovery. It appears that "tough times" will remain for the foreseeable future, said Vincenzina Santoro, an economist with Morgan Guaranty Trust Co. in New York. Whatever improvements may emerge for the Greek economy and business climate, they will be shadowed by the cloud of recession gripping Western Europe. Greek businessmen and politicians cannot expect much economic help at home either, particularly with problems in the consumer sector caused by an increased tax burden.

A budget plan calls for a 25 percent nominal increase in revenues and a 12 percent increase in real terms. Greece is raising the withholding tax on interest payments to 15 from 10 percent. Also going up: the value-added tax, which will apply to more items, and gasoline and diesel taxes.

Greeks can expect to pay more taxes because of improved collection measures, including more tax audits. Its government is getting coached on tax collection by the United States Internal Revenue Service and by the International Monetary Fund. This is necessary, as Greek business and personal taxes for 1992 were only 6.1 percent of GDP. By comparison, American businesses and individuals pay 13.3 percent of the U.S. GDP, and Italians pay even more—14 percent of their GDP.

The Greek government needs collection pointers because tax evasion is endemic. Still, more taxes means less net revenue for Greek business and individuals—and that could have a negative impact on private spending.

Greeks can't expect to make up those tax losses on increased salaries. Public sector wages in 1993 were expected to be limited to an 8 percent increase, well below the expected inflation rate. Yet tax increases are needed, say Greek politicians, to cover the government's heavy interest payments and normal spending.

Even so, it is questionable whether the Greek government will receive the increases in revenues it is expecting. Since Greece is heading for an election, it is unlikely that politicians will be willing to reduce government spending.

Much like the U.S. government, the Greek government can't curb its public borrowing enough to solve massive debt problems. Politicians made little progress in reducing borrowing in

1991. While they did some debt reduction in 1992, analysts following Greece say far less was done than what is needed to get the economy humming.

Greece is not reaching European Community targets for reduced borrowing. Total outstanding debt is now about 85 percent of GDP. Much of that deficit can be traced to spending while the Greek Socialist party held the purse strings, and the more conservative New Democracy government now in power is having a hard time tackling that inherited deficit.

In 1991 and 1992, interest payments on the national debt absorbed a large part of the Greek economy's financial resources. High interest rates have made borrowing difficult for many Greek business enterprises. Banks frequently charge 32 percent interest on short-term commercial loans.

In 1980, the Greek public sector borrowed about 3.9 percent of GDP. In the 1990s, it borrows about 15 percent of GDP annually.

To contain national borrowing, the government launched a privatization program that is far from meeting its self-declared goals. Investment by foreigners helps the drive for privatization, but the Western European recession has reduced the flow of these funds.

The Greek government is always in the market for money. Restrictions on Greek banks forced them to invest 30 percent of their deposits in government Treasury bills through July 1992, and 20 percent through July 1993, when this practice was abolished. T-bills yielded low returns for the banks, taking a toll on the national economy.

The European Community is not pleased with Greece's public sector borrowing and its inability—at least until some signs of relief surfaced in 1993—to slow the pace. The oversize and underproductive public sector is a primary villain in the persistent problem of low productivity. The Greek education system is also partly to blame, for not offering a curriculum aimed at producing an efficient work force.

As long as government borrowing outpaces revenues, inflation will continue to run rampant in Greece. Businesses are finding it a difficult challenge to devise longer-term investment strategies. Greece has the highest inflation rate in the EC, at 14.5 percent.

GREECE

Currency: Greek drachma (GRD).

Stock Exchanges: Athens Stock Exchange (ASE).

Indexes: No major market index.

Types of Securities: Equities, government bonds, corporate bonds.

Regulatory Body/Stock Exchange Supervision: Central Bank of Greece.

Depository: Use of the Athens Central Depository (CD) is mandatory for registered securities and optional for bearer securities. The depository uses a physical clearance and custody process.

Settlement Information

Equities:

- T + 2 (bearer) T + 2/T + 5 (registered buys/sales).
- Physical only (either at depository or subcustodian).
- Receive/deliver versus payment available.
- Same-day turnaround trades are not possible.

Fixed Income:

- T + 2.
- Physical only.
- Receive/deliver versus payment available.
- Same-day turnaround trades are not possible.

Taxes:

- Dividends on bearer shares have a base tax rate of 45 percent.
- Dividends on registered shares have a base tax rate of 42 percent.
- Government bonds are tax-exempt.
- Corporate bonds are tax-exempt if they are linked to investment programs issued before 1/1/91.

- Corporate bonds are taxed at 10 percent if they are linked to investment programs issued after 1/1/91.
- All other corporate bonds are taxed at 10 percent.
- There is no capital gains tax or stamp duty.

Restrictions for Foreign Investors: There are no foreign ownership limits.

Securities Lending: Not available at present.

SOURCE: The Bank of New York

Despite some recent progress on the inflation front, investment analysts wonder if the current government won't reinflate the economy to ensure its reelection in April 1994.

"Is it reasonable to expect that this government will go along with their austerity program, or will they change and reinflate the economy in the hopes that they, the New Democracy Party, can win the elections?" asked economist Santoro. The conflict in Yugoslavia cut off Greece from some of its traditional export routes into European Community countries but new routes through Bulgaria and Romania have been created.

Greece also faces problems in Albania. Albania has a minority population of 400,000 Greeks. If a civil war in Albania were to break out, the Greek government could be drawn into a conflict.

Yet despite the persistence of many problems, economists and stock analysts agree that Greece is making strides toward reviving the economy via significant structural changes. New policies include cuts in real wages for public sector employees, increases in real interest rates and public tariffs, privatization of ailing national companies, liberalization of banking laws, and incentives to foster investment.

Greece wants to lower inflation to below 10 percent, from its recent high of almost 22 percent in 1990. It is also trying to reduce public sector borrowing to 3 percent of GDP, from 19.5 percent in 1990.

Greek politicians say they want new investments for restructuring and modernizing industry, new programs for professional training and retraining of workers, and new environmental protection programs.

Privatization

In 1991, the Greek parliament passed a law aimed at speeding the pace of privatization. Efforts are under way, with the help of foreign consultants, to sell off 49 percent of the Organization of Hellenic Telecommunications; Olympic Airways; and Hellenic Organizations of Tourism, which includes hotels, ski resorts, casinos, national oil refineries, national banks, and insurance companies. These privatization projects are scheduled to be completed by year-end 1993.

In spring 1992, Greece signed a provisional contract for the sale of Heracles General Cement Co., one of Europe's largest cement companies.

"Macroeconomics of Greece are improving" Koenraad Foulon of Capital Research International has said. "Inflation is now at 14.4 percent, coming down from 17 percent. The underlying inflation is 11.5 percent, and we can easily expect 9.5 percent [inflation for 1993]."

Progress on inflation happened while Greece was imposing tax increases. "I think we can expect to see further improvement in the inflation rate," said Santoro of Morgan Guaranty Trust. "I doubt that we will see it in double digits again. The Greek government is planning on single-digit inflation by 1994. But I think the most likely result will be somewhere between 10 percent and 13 percent. I haven't decided what the most likely result is going to be," said Santoro.

Generous pensions for public sector employees are also beginning to fall in real terms. The number of years of employment necessary to qualify for a pension has been increased, and the retirement age has been raised from 33 to 58 for women and from 43 to 60 for men. Employee contribution rates to those pensions are also being raised modestly.

Infrastructure spending is up about 30 percent, an investment that will help the country in the longer term. In early 1993, one analyst was optimistic:

> I think people underestimate that the budget deficit is improving substantially. You don't see it immediately in the figures, because Greece had a budget deficit of 8.1 percent for 1992 and we expect a budget deficit of 7.9 percent for 1993.
>
> But for the first time in many years, Greece has a primary surplus of 2 percent in 1992 and it will most likely have a 5 percent primary surplus in 1993.
>
> Budget deficit figures are still high, as Greece still carries the heavy weight of the interest payments. But if you exclude those payments, instead of a deficit, there is a primary surplus. So you see, there is underlying improvement.

Enrique Sarcento of Schroder Investment Management expected that "the broader economic picture will not improve dramatically until the end of 1993." He believes that investors in the Greek stock market should focus on "defensive sectors," including companies involved in infrastructure development.

With elections coming in 1994, will Greece continue to keep inflation low? Santoro thinks that

> Perhaps it is more logical to take the optimistic view and say these conservative politicians are doing a good job.
>
> They have a reasonable chance of going to the electorate and saying, "Look, sure we have made it hard for everybody, but you got solid results, and Greece now enjoys the respect of the international community."

Greece has made startling progress in wage negotiations for the public sector. Wages went up 4 percent in January 1993 and were set to go up another 4 percent in June. By U.S. standards those are big increases, but in Greece they are lower than the current inflation rate. Wages will probably go only a little higher for the private sector than for the public sector.

Greece got additional help in 1993 from the European Community, which increased the amount of development funds coming from the EC Special Cohesion fund. Early in 1993, Greece's finance minister was setting priorities for projects, emphasizing infrastructure and industrial development. By limiting the number of projects, less money will be wasted on possible inefficiencies and incompletions.

Infrastructure improvements are likely to include an expressway in the north and some railways. Stocks that could benefit from these priorities include companies in the construction, transportation, engineering, and finance sectors.

The Stock Exchange

According to the IFC, as of December 1992, there were 129 listed companies on the Athens stock exchange. Market capitalization was US$9.489 billion in U.S. dollar terms. After strong gains in 1989 and 1990, the Greek stock market fell 21.8 percent in 1991, and 33.2 percent in 1992. In the period between January and June 4, 1993, the market advanced 3.3 percent in dollars, according to the IFC.

Primary market activities have been low. For example, there were 14 new listings in 1991, compared with 28 new issues in 1990. In mid-year 1992, the open outcry system used on the Athens floor was replaced by automated trading.

Foreign investors account for about 20 percent of daily transactions. Common stock comprises the bulk of market listings.

Stocks to Watch

According to Koenraad Foulon, corporate earnings in 1993 should be lower than in the year before as the effects of economic stagnation in Europe and the crisis in Bosnia take their toll.

However, investors can still find value in the market. Among the perceived attractive buys is Hellenic Bottling Co., the dominant force in the soft drink market with 70 percent saturation. Hellenic Bottling owns the franchise to bottle and distribute Coca-Cola in Greece, and also offers several of its own brands.

Consumption of soft drinks is expected to increase 6 to 8 percent a year in Greece. Hellenic Bottling has acquired a Coca-Cola bottler in Northern Ireland, and has formed a joint venture in Bulgaria for the bottling and distribution of Coke.

Infrastructure improvements could benefit Michaniki, the dominant construction company in Greece. Its major projects include Athens Metro, the Gulf of Corinth bridge, Athens airport, the Acheloos river diversion, and extensive Greek highway projects.

A company planning major expansion is Nikas, a producer of meat products such as salami and bacon. It has 20 percent of the market for meat products in the entire country and 60 percent in the metropolis of Athens. The processed meat market in Greece is almost virgin territory.

Some Greek companies that are small in size are excellently managed, according to Foulon:

> You have attractive, appealing companies, but they are all those with very small market capitalization. I am talking about $200 to $300 million, and some $500 million. They are not big, but they are interesting. I have visited these companies very often, and it is incredible how well they are run.

Investment Options

As an alternative to direct stock investing in Greece, Wilson Emerging Market Funds Research lists two closed-end funds:

the Greece Fund Ltd., trading on the London stock exchange, and the Greek Progress Fund SA, trading on the Athens exchange.

Another option in the Greek market is investment in American depositary receipts. Entering 1993, Bankers Trust Co. reported three available ADRs for this purpose: Globe Group SA, John Boutari & Son Wines & Spirits Co., and John Boutari & Son Wines & Spirits PR. All trade over the counter.

14
Turkey

The Economy

Abruptly reversing 1992's poor performance, the Turkish stock market roared in 1993, soaring 82.3 percent in U.S. dollar terms by June 4, according to the IFC.

Economic growth—albeit in an inflationary environment—seemed to be back on track. Interest rates were easing, and in early 1993, a new vehicle was launched to help bolster Turkey's capital markets. As Koenraad Foulon, a vice president of Capital Research International in London describes, "the government passed legislation giving tax incentives to institutions such as banks and insurance companies to invest in so-called 'type A' funds, which are mutual funds created by banks that must have 25 percent of their assets invested in equities. Earnings would be taxed at no more than 15 percent," which was less than half of the normal tax rate that they would have faced.

Institutions grabbed at the opportunity, taking money out of Treasury bills and reallocating it to the type A funds. The development helped ignite the stock market that had plunged 54.8 percent in dollar terms in 1992 and 44.1 percent in 1991.

In 1993, the market advanced further for a time after the June selection of Tansu Ciller, a free marketeer, as Turkey's new Prime Minister.

At the heart of Turkey's attractiveness, however, is its robust economy. Over the past decade, this country at the juncture of Europe and Asia had been increasingly liberalizing its economy. The result was high economic growth—the highest in the OECD before the 1991 slowdown. In 1992's revival, real GDP grew 5.9 percent. And growth was expected to be at least 5 percent in 1993.

But although 1993's events generally seemed favorable for this country whose economy had suffered from the Persian Gulf War, some big problems still loomed.

Most importantly, Turkey needs to resolve its public sector spending problem. To illustrate the magnitude of that problem, the public sector borrowing requirement was 11 percent of GNP in 1992, down from 14.4 percent the year before. Although in 1993, it should ease further to about 9 percent, many feel the level is still too burdensome. For example, Morgan Guaranty Trust Company reports that, as a percent of GNP, the average public sector borrowing requirement between 1986 and 1990 was a lesser 7.8 percent.

In the late 1980s, borrowing climbed in step with a move by Turkey to raise the economic growth rate. This accelerated spending, especially by the public sector. The budget deficit climbed, as did the money supply and inflation, although a new stabilization program debuted in January, 1992.

Trying to Lick Inflation

But many agree that, to slay the deficit/inflation dragon, Turkey must attack some key problems, chief among them its need to expand privatization, and also to bolster its inadequate tax collection system.

With a new government installed in mid-1993, it remained unclear how much could be accomplished short term. An assessment at mid-year seemed to show a mixed picture. David Maslin of Morgan Guaranty Trust wrote in June 1993: "Efforts to meet the overall PSBR (public sector borrowing requirement) target of 9 percent of GNP in 1993 focus on higher tax collections to boost consolidated budget revenues to 28.1 percent GNP, up from 23.2 percent in 1992. Privatization revenues are planned to bring in $1.5 billion—1.2 percent of GNP, or triple the 1992 outcome. Overall expenditures, however, are to rise to 32.4 percent of GNP from 28.8 percent last year, due mainly to higher spending on health care and education."

Many believe that Turkey's most pressing requirement is the unloading—privatization—of the state sector. "The scope is vast," Morgan Guaranty illustrates. "There are approximately 200 State Economic Enterprises (SEEs), more than half of which are majority-owned by the government. SEEs account for 90 percent of Turkey's energy production, 75 percent of its mining output, 33 percent of manufacturing, 58 percent of transportation, 100 percent of telecommunications, and about 25 percent of financial services."

While the privatization of big state enterprises, such as telecommunications, is expected to cause some economic pain, some analysts believe that Prime Minister Ciller—previously Turkey's economy minister—will speed the program.

Improving Tax Collection

Improved tax collection is another pressing need. The underground economy, for example, has taken its toll. As one analyst put it, "you just have to walk around Istanbul's Grand Bazaar to see what a black economy is."

But here, too, measures are being taken. Even as the government tries to put a lid on public sector wage increases, new tax measures taking effect in 1993 include: imposing a minimum 23 percent tax rate on companies, including banks, under administrative authority provided by existing investment tax incentive legislation." And, pending at mid-year, was legislation to cut the nominal tax rate but scrap many exemptions," reported Morgan Guaranty.

Moreover, among other moves, items covered under the value-added (VAT) tax would be expanded, and the government would be widening its tax net by opening more tax offices in the country, several analysts reported.

Economic Gains

Turkey's economy has generally responded well to liberalization programs. Since the 1980s, the opening of the economy has

TURKEY

Currency: Turkish Lira (TRL).

Stock Exchanges: The Istanbul Stock Exchange (ISE) was established in 1986.

Indexes: There is no major index in Turkey.

Types of Securities: Equity (common or preferred), corporate and government bonds, money market instruments.

Regulatory Body/Stock Exchange Supervision: The capital Markets Board, established in 1982, regulates the securities markets.

Depository: There is a depository run by Vakibank that is owned by stock exchange members. Access is limited to exchange members and it does not provide corporate action information. It is not widely used at present.

Settlement Information

Equities:

- T + 1.
- Physical delivery only.
- Receive/deliver versus payment available.
- Same-day turnaround trades are possible.

Fixed Income:

- Trade date (secondary market, government bonds), T + 7 (primary market, government bonds).
- Physical delivery only.
- Receive/deliver versus payment available.
- Same-day turnaround trades are possible on a negotiated basis.

Taxes:

- There is no withholding tax on dividend and government bond interest.
- There is no capital gains tax.

- All banking service fees and charges (including custody bills and FX fees) are subject to a 5 percent transaction tax.
- There is no stamp duty tax.

Restrictions for Foreign Investors:

- There are no foreign exchange restrictions (but inflow/out-flows over US$50,000 must be reported to the Central Bank).

- There are no foreign ownership limits, but government approval it required if a foreign investor is gaining control of a company.

Securities Lending: Does not yet exist in Turkey.

SOURCE: The Bank of New York

encouraged entrepreneurship, and generally, the rise of a middle class. While exports—as well as imports—have been rising, domestic demand from the fast-growing population feeds Turkey's economic growth. Economic momentum is necessary since Turkey's population is growing at 2.1 percent annually.

Before the liberalizations of the 1980s, "Turkey's economy was in the hands of four big families and the state sector," recalls Foulon of Capital Research. "Over the past decade, there has been a fantastic growth of the middle class." The policies of former President Turgut Ozal, who died in office in April 1993, helped fuel "an entrepreneurial spirit in the country."

A run-down on Turkey's recent economic history: GNP climbed at an average annual rate of 6.4 percent during the First Plan period between 1963–1967; it advanced 6.7 percent during the Second Plan from 1968–1972; 7.2 percent during the Third Plan (1973–1977), slightly above 2 percent during the Fourth Plan (1979–1983); and just over 6 percent during the Fifth Plan from 1984–1987. For the Sixth Plan running from 1990–1994, projections cite an average annual growth of 7 percent.

On the trade front, Turkey is seen as being well situated to expand opportunities in Europe, when that region's economies improve, as well as to the Middle East and republics of the former Soviet Union. Although it is expected to take some years before Turkey is admitted to the European Community (EC), it has already been lowering its customs tariffs on goods from the EC. According to the *Financial Times*, "By the end of 1995, Turkey should have lifted all import restrictions on EC goods and adopted the Community's common external tariffs."

Recent History

Turkey traces civilian rule back only to 1973.

When it was the center of the Ottoman Empire, it stretched at the height of its power, from the Persian Gulf to Morocco and into Europe.

Modern Turkey traces to 1922, when a district army officer, Mustafa Kemal, and his forces, abolished the sultanate. Kemal named himself Turkey's first President in October 1923.

Using his powers, Kemal began to modernize Turkey. At the time, 10 percent of the population could read. Kemal abolished the Islamic religious courts and religious instruction in schools, and he also replaced use of Arabic lettering with the Latin alphabet. In appreciation for his various contributions, this revered leader became known as Kemal Ataturk, the father of the Turks.

By 1946, Turkey had ended its one-party political era. In 1950, it held its first free elections.

The new democracy was overthrown by a military coup in May 1960. Four months later, the freely elected Democratic Party was dissolved. The new army rulers established a bicameral legislature, a senate and a national assembly packed with supporters of the military.

Civilian rule, in its current incarnation, returned in 1973. Although the population is predominantly of the same religion—Moslem—Turkey remains a secular state.

Political problems include Turkey's need to resolve its conflict with Kurdish separatists. Furthermore, the crisis in Bosnia has caused great concern among Turks, who regard Moslem Bosnians as ethnic relatives.

The government led by Tansu Ciller is expected to continue Turkey's pro-Western bent. Her selection as Prime Minister came after Suleyman Demirel moved from Prime Minister to President after Ozal's death. The choice of Ciller (Turkey's first female Prime Minister) was evidently applauded both inside and outside of Turkey; according to reports, Istanbuls's stock market jumped 10.5 percent on the news.

The Stock Market

The Istanbul Stock Exchange, in its current form, was founded in 1986. Eighty years earlier, during the Ottoman Empire, the so-called "Imperial Securities Exchange" was created in Istanbul, largely to trade sovereign bonds issued by the Sultan to finance the Crimean War against Russia. Given the vast extent of the Ottoman Empire, this exchange quickly became one of the most active financial centers in Europe, exchange officials say.

However, the exchange's growth was halted by the outbreak of the Balkan War, and subsequently, World War I. Very little happened until the economy was opened to market factors in 1980. From then on, liberalization moves provided the impetus to create an emerging market in turkey.

At the end of 1992, according to the IFC, Turkey's market had a capitalization of $9.931 billion and 145 listed shares.

There are no restrictions on shares that foreigners can buy. However, purchase and/or possession of more than 10 percent of the equity of a company must be reported to the Treasury.

According to Istanbul Stock Exchange officials, since stocks are of bearer type, there is no reliable breakdown of stock ownership. But estimates put the individual ownership at about 30 percent, while the institutional investors and fund managers account for the rest of the transactions. Foreigners are believed to be mostly institutional, and, on a typical day, they represent only a fraction of the trading volume, about 2 or 3 percent.

Trading is conducted on the Big Board. Open outcry is not used. Each stock has a panel reserved for transactions. The board is divided into columns like members' initials, buy and/or sell, and the quantity. Members' floor traders enter their prices on the board, and a transaction is concluded when the price is crossed out with a felt-tipped pen by the other party. While actual trading has been manual, post-trade functions have been automated. Full automation is expected to take place by early 1994.

The Istanbul exchange has opened a new market for rights coupons, which trade on a special board. Block trading and special orders are also conducted on different boards. At present, the exchange does not offer trading in stock futures, forwards, or options. However, the exchange reports that "the infrastructure to introduce such markets has been completed, and once the relocation to a new building is completed, it is assumed that more emphasis and consideration will be given to operating such sophisticated markets."

What to Buy

Capital Research's Foulon generally recommends exploring companies that enjoy strong domestic demand, that have ample cash flow that can be used to finance internal capital expenditures. "There are quite a few of these," he maintains. And although the market soared in early 1993, valuations at mid-1993 still looked reasonable. Overall, corporate profits were expected to average 20 percent growth in real terms in 1993, he said.

A fast-growing holding company, the Koch Group, reportedly has had the highest market value of all Turkish companies, the equivalent of $870 million in 1991. Another company to consider is Ege Biracilik, a brewery based in Istanbul. An increase in beer consumption is tied to the rising tourist business as well as increasing local demand. Ege is a dominant brand in Turkey, and the company boasts a good distribution system.

Given Turkey's high inflation, an investment in the stock of a supermarket company has advantages, since grocery prices can be altered quickly, as soon as overnight, if necessary. In this category, some analysts have recommended Migros.

For investors who prefer not to buy stocks directly on the Istanbul market, Wilson Emerging Market Funds Research Inc. lists two funds for international investors, Turkey Trust plc, which trades on the London Stock Exchange, and the Turkish Investment Fund Inc., on the New York Stock Exchange.

According to Bankers Trust Company, Turkey's Net Holdings Inc. has an ADR that trades over the counter.

15
South Korea

Midway through 1992, the mood of South Koreans was grim. The stock market was in the doldrums, the trade balance had been in deficit, many small- and medium-sized companies were going bankrupt, and overall economic growth, while still robust, stood well below the double-digit rates of 1986–88. "People were very pessimistic," recalls John Lee, portfolio manager of the Korea Fund managed by Scudder Stevens & Clark in New York, who visited Korea in the summer of 1992. "In extreme cases, people would say things like: 'This is the end of the world.'"

By year's end, attitudes had brightened. Even the stock market stood 48 percent above its mid-year low, following an easing of interest rates and a massive support program by the Korean government. The general attitude was that Korea was coming to grips with critical problems, including its newfound uncompetitiveness in trade. Robust economic growth was expected to recur by 1994. And more successes seem to be in store for this small East Asian land. Having grown from a largely agricultural nation into one of the Four Tigers of Asia, South Korea is today the No. 1 Asian candidate to join the Organization of Economic Cooperation and Development (OECD), now comprising 24 developed countries.

Korea's successes have brought it new challenges and opportunities. Shedding its dictatorial past, South Korea held democratic elections in 1987. In December 1992, the country elected Kim Young Sam as its first nonmilitary President in three decades. Kim, who won on a platform of "Reform Amid

Stability," captured 42 percent of the vote. A former dissident, Kim had joined with the ruling Democratic Liberal Party two years earlier. The pragmatic leader is expected to pursue a moderate pace of changes and reforms, in keeping with Koreans' preference for stability.

When they had less enfranchisement in the past, Koreans had taken to the streets for demonstrations to demand political and economic changes. In 1987, a wave of demonstrations "virtually brought down the government of authoritarian president Chun Doo Hwan, forcing the military to accept democratic elections," reported the *Far Eastern Economic Review*. Although democracy has been unsettling in the short term, it has brought attention to social welfare issues such as housing construction and improved transportation, and encouraged the government to throw more support toward smaller businesses.

Economically, this country of 43 million people is undergoing a dramatic refocusing as it grapples with its status as an "almost developed" nation. Aided by its educated, disciplined, and motivated work force, Korea built a dynamic economy based on mass production of goods for export. But in time Korea's economic successes caught up with it amid a—previously—strengthening currency and clamors for higher wages. Salaries shot up 15 to 18 percent annually between 1988 and 1991. GNP per capita income stood at $7014 in 1991—more than double its level in 1987. The level was expected to reach about $8400 in 1993.

Increasingly uncompetitive against lower-wage countries, including those of Southeast Asia, Korea has charted a new course by shifting production of more basic goods to lower-wage countries, while emphasizing higher technology and value-added production at home.

Financial deregulation is expected to extend the supply of credit available to strategic sectors. Small- and medium-sized companies will be particularly targeted for stimuli as the government seeks to encourage innovation and competitiveness. Speaking in New York in January 1993, Cha Dong-Se, president of the Lucky-Goldstar Economic Research Institute in Seoul, Korea, said that Korea's new government "is poised to embark on working out measures to invigorate the economy that has been losing steam." The "New Economic Initiatives" include several points: a "drastic" reduction in government regulations concerning private business activities; stabilizing costs, such as interest rates and wages, to encourage facility and R&D investments; strengthening support for small- and medium-sized companies that are "facing severe difficulties, particularly with raising funds"; bolstering domestic financial institutions through mergers and acquisitions and increases in capital; implementing a second-phase deregulation of interest rates; and requiring everyone to use their real name in financial transactions. The latter would not only enhance the government's ability to collect taxes but also make political parties "more accountable for their funding and spending," he said. For small business, among other things, the government had already raised the size of the state-run Credit Guarantee Fund, which provides credit to smaller companies, Cha said.

In terms of specific programs, the government had already been identifying key sectors of the economy that should be encouraged. In high technology, they included factory automation, high-definition television, aerospace, and semiconductors. Experts say the latter would not include the highest levels of technology, such as biotech and semiconductor manufacturing equipment—areas that would pit it against strong competition from Japan and the United States. Given the trade deficit in telecommunications, the government, which has long had a powerful influence on the economy, is also encouraging more domestic production of telecommunications products. According to the *Far Eastern Economic Review,* South Korea's government is urging private industry "to spend at least 5 percent of sales on research and development, and to pool resources in high-tech projects such as liquid crystal display technology. The government will allow firms to amortize 90 percent of high-tech investments in one year beginning in 1993, and plans to spend $1.3 billion on the promotion of science and technology."

Where domestic capabilities won't suffice, the government is wooing foreigners to set up shop in Korea and/or engage in cooperative deals. Hopefully, that will result in transfers of technological capability from foreigners to Koreans. To attract the desired outsiders, the government has agreed to ease restrictions on foreign investments and foreign trade and to provide

SOUTH KOREA

Currency: Korean won (KRW).

Stock Exchanges: The Korea Stock Exchange (KSE) is located in Seoul. There is also an over-the-counter market that trades the stocks of 47 companies.

Instruments: Equities (bearer and registered), convertible bonds, allotment letters, zero coupon bonds, floating and fixed-rate notes, money market instruments.

Index: The Korea Composite Stock Price Index (KCSPI) is the main index in Korea.

Regulatory Body/Stock Exchange Supervision: The Korea Securities and Exchange Commission makes decisions on major issues relating to new issuances and market trading.

Depository: The Korea Securities Settlement Corporation (KSSC), established in 1974, is the central clearinghouse and depository for all securities. Its use is mandatory for brokers but optional for banks.

Settlement Information

Equities:

- T + 2.
- Book entry of physical settlement.
- Receive/deliver versus payment available.
- Same-day turnarounds are possible, but uncommon.

Fixed Income: Same as Equities.

Taxes:

- The withholding tax on dividends and interest generally ranges from 10 to 20 percent.
- Taxation treaties mean that many foreign investors do not have to pay a capital gains tax.

Restrictions for Foreign Investors:

- All foreign investors must obtain an Investment Registration Card (IRC) and Investor Identification Number.
- All foreign investors must appoint a standing proxy to legally represent them in Korea.
- All foreign investors must appoint a foreign exchange bank (usually their subcustodian).
- Foreign investors cannot purchase fixed income securities.
- All foreign investors must deposit 40 percent of the purchase price of securities being bought in advance, unless an exemption is obtained.
- Total foreign investment in most individual companies is limited to 10 percent (of aggregate value) or 3 percent per individual investor.
- Foreign investors cannot trade on margin or overdraw their cash accounts.

Securities Lending: Not presently permitted in Korea, but being evaluated by the Central Bank.

SOURCES: The Bank of New York, The Korea Stock Exchange, and other sources.

more protections on intellectual property. However, this hasn't yet happened to the extent foreigners had hoped. A *Wall Street Journal* article in May 1993 cites that land acquisition has been simplified and intellectual property is better protected, but foreign direct investors are pulling out their assets, or bypassing Korea entirely, and investing in China.

To Andrew Kim, president of Sit/Kim International Investment Associates Inc., in New York, "medium-tech [should be] the target market for Korea." In his view, Korea's forte will be in middle-level industry, mass-producing goods such as automobiles, trucks, and memory chip semiconductors. In these arenas, he feels the country can best utilize its existing mass manufacturing and marketing skills.

Moving Offshore

Internationally, the need to find new markets has become patently obvious. Not only has competition eroded export opportunities for basic goods, but exporting in general has been limited by sluggishness in the developed world. As a result, Korea has been mining for new business opportunities while shifting production to lower-wage countries. According to the *Far Eastern Economic Review,* the number of Korean companies "investing abroad in 1991 rose to 52, up 21 percent from the previous year." As of mid-year 1992, overseas foreign investments totaled $4.1 billion.

In 1992, South Korea's government normalized diplomatic relations with both the People's Republic of China (PRC) and with Vietnam—moves that will enhance economic opportunities for Korean companies. According to Young J. Zoh, president and chief investment officer of The Clemente Korea Emerging Growth Fund Inc., New York, Korea's Pohang Iron & Steel (POSCO) has already been a major beneficiary of new ties with Vietnam. In a joint venture with the Vietnamese government, POSCO's construction subsidiary built a steel manufacturing plant in Vietnam, and set up a joint venture with that country to build a highway between Ho Chi Minh City and Haiphong. Even before the embassies had put out their rugs, China ranked as Korea's fourth-largest trading partner—after the United States, Japan, and

Germany. By the mid-1990s, the PRC was expected to bump past Germany to become Korea's third-largest trading partner.

Just days before South Korea and China formalized relations, it was reported that the two countries had, in a first-of-its-kind deal between the two nations, agreed to set up an industrial complex for South Korean companies in Tianjin, China. Under the plan, Korean companies would obtain rights to 130,000 square meters in Tianjin for 50 years. The state-operated Korea Land Development Corporation would manage the construction of an industrial complex slated for completion by year-end 1994.

This new and warming relationship between China and South Korea wasn't good news in Pyongyang, the capital of North Korea. With the former Soviet Union broken up by the course of history, Pyongyang's list of reliable allies was becoming frighteningly short.

For economically ailing North Korea, the need to reunite with the South has become even more urgent; but for South Korea, roadblocks still exist. Beyond military considerations—including North Korea's activities in nuclear development—the major concern lies in paying for unification. Estimates have unification costing South Korea $200 billion or even more. Given the obstacles, political union is unlikely to occur before the late 1990s, and is already being preceded by closer economic and social ties.

Economically, South Korea sees a variety of benefits to be gained from ties to the North. These include tapping into the northern neighbor's natural resources, such as timber, water, and minerals, as well as its pool of cheap labor. Friendlier relations with North Korea would mean that Seoul could also trim defense spending, which in 1991 totaled $10.4 billion, or 4.5 percent of GNP.

At the end of 1991, both sides inked a nonaggression pact, which, according to the *Far Eastern Economic Review,* was "the first legal framework through which political and economic exchanges could take place." Among many other items, the pact set up military, political, and economic commissions to pursue specific issues of integration. In 1988 the two Koreas began trading with each other, usually through a third country. Although initially trade levels were small, they're expected to grow to $1.8 billion in coming years.

On the commercial side, Kim Woo Choong, chairman of the Daewoo Group, emerged as South Korea's leading businessman and unofficial envoy to help develop business liaisons between North and South Korea. North Korea is interested in promoting light industrial production in designated areas. In Nampo, North Korea, the government wishes to create a manufacturing complex for light industry. In the closing quarter of 1992 a delegation, reportedly formed by Daewoo and including South Korean government officials as well as representatives of some other Korean companies, visited the Nampo site to study the plan.

Kim Woo Choong had become lead businessman after Chung Ju Yung, the founder of Hyundai Heavy Industries, fell out of favor with South Korea's ruling party. Although Chung had pioneered business ties with North Korea, he antagonized South Korea's political leaders by running for president in 1992 as an opposition candidate. (Kim had considered, but discarded, a bid for the presidency.) Chung has now been put on trial for illegally diverting profits from Hyundai to finance his failed bid. With the advent of a new South Korean president, it remains to be seen whether Daewoo's Kim will remain lead businessman to develop economic dialogues with North Korea. Early in 1992, political/economic dealings between North and South Korea were "frozen," reports Andrew Kim of Sit/Kim International. "There [was] nothing going on."

Chaebols

Hyundai and Daewoo are among the most prominent Korean industrial conglomerates, known as *chaebols,* which form the backbone of the economy. *Chaebols* are large family-controlled businesses that typically have a number of publicly owned subsidiaries. They were established in the 1960s by then President Park Chung Hee, who had come to power following a 1961 military coup. Wishing to legitimize his government, President Park decided to launch an exporting drive that would bolster the economy. To carry out the plan, he needed strong companies.

Chaebols were built up with the help of government-subsidized credit. Expanded into many-armed octopuses of business, today's chaebols often have as many as 30 or 40 companies in their group. Their advantages include "effective management," economies of scale that "allow them to attract better personnel. They can also afford R&D crucial to developing high value-added products, and they have the capacity to market abroad which many smaller firms lack," according to David I. Steinberg, professor of Korean studies at Georgetown University.

Chaebols have successfully lived up to President Park's designs, both economically and militarily. For instance, Steinberg pointed out that in 1987, the top ten chaebols accounted for 40 percent of all bank credit in South Korea, 30 percent of value-added in manufacturing, and two thirds of the value of all of the country's exports. Militarily, the chaebols have been crucial to the country's defense. According to Steinberg, starting in the 1970s, chaebols provided South Korea with the weaponry it sought after the United States backed away from fighting land wars in Asia.

But the relationship between government and chaebols is changing. While the two parties still need each other, rising tension was illustrated in 1992 by the fact that Chung took on the government, the first time that had happened. According to Steinberg, one major area of public concern about chaebols centers on the "large income discrepancy between chaebol leadership and workers at large," even while the government has put pressure on labor to keep wages down.

To make chaebols less of a political target "one answer may be for them to increase their degree of public ownership," Steinberg points out. Meanwhile, chaebols are under pressure from the government to slim down. They have been asked to sell unnecessary businesses, including real estate holdings, and to narrow their business focus to three core areas that could qualify for special financial consideration from the government. They are also being discouraged from continuing to subsidize unprofitable businesses within their group.

Some cooperation already has been seen. Samsung has found reasons for separating two companies, Chonju Paper Manufacturing Company (now known as Hansol Paper) and Shinsegae Department Store, from the group. According to Zoh of the Clemente Korea Emerging Growth Fund, Daewoo's chairman announced the intention to dissolve the Daewoo Group by divestment. While that process should take some time, an unconfirmed market "rumor is that Daewoo Heavy Industries would be the first entity to be divested," Zoh reported. As a general rule, he believes divestment of chaebol entities would enhance their operational efficiencies and productivity.

Investment Climate

Characteristically, Korean companies are highly leveraged. When the economy is booming and vital signs, such as inflation, are under control, indebtedness isn't a problem. But in the early 1990s, the economy wasn't in top shape. Interest rates rose—before later falling back—and the economy softened, even though many companies were in the throes of a capital spending boom. Manufacturers' profits became squeezed. Indeed, in 1992, the IFC reported a record number of corporate bankruptcies, and GNP growth of 4.7 percent (a 12-year low), down from 8.4 percent in 1991.

But there was light at the end of the tunnel. By the end of 1992, 3-year corporate bond yields had fallen to 13.5 percent from about 19 percent at the beginning of the year. In March 1993, rates were down to 11 percent. According to the IFC, the government's economic stabilization program "to cool an overheated economy with surging inflation and property prices...seems to have succeeded." Real GDP is projected to grow 6 percent in 1993, and inflation to climb 5 percent.

The Korean economy appears to be gaining steam again. Signs of improvement in the trade deficit have surfaced, and expectations abounded that the trade balance would emerge into the black by 1994, or 1995 at the latest. In 1992 the IFC reported that "although hampered by sluggish economies in OECD countries, Korea's exports were boosted 6.6 percent to $76.6 billion, mostly due to other emerging Asian countries, including China. In 1993, Baring Securities expects to reach $82.4 billion, a 7.6 percent rise. Wage hikes fell from 16 percent in 1991 to just below 10 percent—meaning that productivity increases had surpassed wage inflation.

The Stock Market

Although Korea's stock market languished in the early 1990s, there were reasons to be optimistic for the future. A number of analysts predicted that investors would focus more on Korea's economic strengths once the uncertainty preceding the 1992 presidential election had past. In second-quarter 1993, Barry Gillman of the money management firm of PCM International Inc., Short Hills, New Jersey, rated Korea "the top of the Asian emerging markets" in attractiveness. Among the factors he cited were favorable price-earnings ratios of 15.2 in 1992, down from 17.3 in 1991, and price-to-cashflow ratios on stocks. The P/E ratio is expected to drop to 13.1 at year-end 1993.

The market itself had a capitalization of $107.4 billion as of December 1992 and 688 listed companies, according to the IFC. Established in 1956 and located in Seoul, the Korea Stock Exchange (KSE) is the country's only exchange. According to the KSE, 99 percent of the transactions on the exchange are executed by the Stock Market Automated Trading System, leaving a few issues to be executed manually on the trading floor. As of the end of November 1992, 83.2 percent of total turnover came from individual investors, 14.5 percent from institutions, and 2.4 percent from foreigners, the exchange said. Among listings, finance has been the dominant sector.

In 1992, the 10 most actively traded stocks were, in order: Daewoo, KEPCO, Bank of Seoul, Dongsu Securities, Commercial Bank, Daewoo Heavy Industries, Lucky Securities, Goldstar, Daewoo Electronics, and Daishin Securities. The Korea Securities Settlement Corporation, a subsidiary of the Korea Stock Exchange (KSE), acts as the clearing agent of the KSE and as the central depositary for share certificates. A book-entry system is used for clearing securities transactions, and in 1987 an over-the-counter market was established.

Since the early 1980s, the market has gradually become more international. Although highly automated and operationally efficient, the market still greatly restricts foreign investment. Korea's stock market first opened to direct foreign investments on January 3, 1992. Before then, foreign portfolio investors commonly could buy only convertible bonds and/or funds and trusts that invest in the Korean stock market.

As of January 1992, the Korean government allowed foreigners to buy up to 10 percent of a Korean company's outstanding shares, with a maximum holding of 3 percent per investor. Many foreign investors were unimpressed with this skimpy "opening," which coincided with a then bear market that had endured since 1989. Indeed, even after a market rally in the second half of 1992, the IFC price index for the Korean market climbed 3.5 percent in U.S. dollar terms for 1992.

In 1992, foreign investors were not rushing into Korea. According to the IFC, as of November 1992 net foreign investment in Korea totaled $1.53 billion, with the largest amounts coming from British investors ($570 million) and Americans ($390 million). "Including other direct holdings, such as offshore funds, total foreign ownership of Korean-listed companies amounted to less than 4 percent of the total listed shares," the IFC reported.

Administrative requirements provided formidable obstacles, especially when the market first opened to direct foreign investment. To buy shares directly, foreigners have had to apply to Korea's Securities Supervisory Board to obtain an identification card. When the market first opened, only individual investors and corporate entities were eligible for an ID, thereby effectively leaving out foreign governments, pension funds, limited partnerships, and unit trusts.

Every ID holder also needs to appoint a standing proxy to provide such custodial services as collecting dividends and handling corporate actions. Korea's arrangement proved particularly difficult for foreign investors because, when the market first opened, only licensed Korean securities companies were allowed to be standing proxies, a rule that violates some U.S. investment regulations.

During 1992, the Korean government modified some of these investment complications. Among the changes, it allowed banks to serve as standing proxies, and it expanded the list of qualified investors to include foreign governments, pension funds, limited partnerships, and unit trusts.

In another liberalization move, Korea's Ministry of Finance (MOF) approved investments by foreigners in the Korea Electric Power Corporation (KEPCO) and in Pohang Iron & Steel

Company Limited (POSCO), the market's two largest capitalized shares. Foreigners could begin investing in POSCO in October 1992 and in KEPCO in November. Non-Koreans as a group could buy up to 8 percent of the shares of these companies, while individual investors would be limited to 1 percent stakes.

Moreover, the MOF decreed that some companies could apply to have their ceiling on foreign investments lifted to 25 percent of shares. As of July 1992, companies eligible to apply were joint ventures and those that had issued securities under the Overseas Securities Issuance Regulations, such as convertible bonds. Although most companies retained a 10 percent limit on foreigners' investments, rumors abounded that Korea would lift this limit to at least 15 percent, between 1994 and 1995. The government reportedly has plans to consider raising the 10 percent foreign ownership ceiling on Korean stocks. Foreigners were snatching up a select group of high-growth, small- to medium-sized companies whose stocks had low price earnings ratios. As of August 1992, Daewoo Securities reported that 27 issues had already hit their 10 percent cap on foreign investment and were thus trading over the counter among foreigners. While the price premium on these shares then averaged about 10 to 15 percent above that paid by domestic investors, the premium for the particularly popular stock of Korea Mobile Telecommunications Corporation stood at about 40 percent.

Funds provide an alternative to buying stocks directly in 1993. Wilson Emerging Market Fund Research listed 905 funds for Korea, of which 42 were available to international investors. Closed-end funds trading on the London Stock Exchange include: the Clemente Korea Emerging Growth Fund, the Daehan Korea Trust, the Drayton Korea Trust, the First Korea Smaller Companies Fund, the Korea Asia Fund Limited, Korea Emerging Companies Trust (1), Korea Liberalization Fund Limited, Korea–Europe Fund Limited, and the Schroder Korea Fund plc. The Korea Fund Inc. trades on the New York Stock Exchange, as does the Korean Investment Fund Inc.

Depositary receipts provide another investment option. According to Bankers Trust Co., as of December 1992 the four ADR choices were: Samsung Co. Ltd. (common shares),

Samsung Co. Ltd., (144A), Samsung Electronics Co. Ltd. (common shares), and Samsung Electronics Co. Ltd. (preferred shares). KIA Motors issued global depositary receipts. Other GDRs, according to Clemente's Zoh: Hyundai Motors and Hansoi Paper.

Renewed Optimism for the Stock Market

After peaking in 1989, the Korean stock market fell into a long slumber for a variety of reasons, including higher interest rates, economic slowing, and political uncertainty prior to the late 1992 presidential election. With money market rates relatively high, many individual Korean investors chose those investments over companies' shares. In August 1992, as the market stood more than 50 percent below its 1989 peak, the Korean government stepped in with massive support. According to Young J. Zoh of the Clemente Korea Emerging Growth Fund, it was the government's strongest market intervention to date.

To provide financial assistance, the Ministry of Finance announced that it would require institutional investors to inject 3.9 trillion won (about $4.9 billion) into the bourse. Specifically, the MOF said that banks would have to buy stocks worth 1.5 trillion won for trust accounts over the next six months; insurance companies would have to purchase 0.7 trillion won of stocks over the next six months; 20 pension funds would be required to invest 1.2 trillion won in stocks over the coming year; and 500 billion won would be added to the existing Stock Market Stabilization Fund. In the latter case, funds would come from newly converted and established securities houses, which would have to commit 140 billion won to the fund, and from companies that would provide 360 billion won, coming from some of the proceeds of rights offerings and public stock offerings in the coming year. Illustrating the government's commitment to the program, among other moves it also suspended for one year investigations into the sources of cash for stock investments.

In the short term, the moves put a floor on the droopy stock market that ended 3.5 percent higher in dollar terms, according to the IFC. And longer term, a number of investors saw reasons to be optimistic, since Korea's economic and market fundamentals were expected to improve. Zoh of the Clemente Korea Emerging Growth Fund sees "excellent long-term prospects for the market," as it benefits from such fundamental factors as lowered interest rates and signs of improvement in both the trade deficit and in inflation.

Mr. Zoh also points to favorable technical market factors. "The Korean market goes through ten-year cycles and five-year minicycles," he says. "The technical charts show the Korean market headed for a rally starting in 1993."

Some attractive sectors, according to Zoh, are electronics and construction. Electrical and electronic machinery companies should benefit from the incentives the government will be providing to key industries, while construction should gain from participation in domestic infrastructural projects such as the planned bullet train between Seoul and Pusan. The expected construction of a natural gas pipeline from Siberia through North Korea and into South Korea will present more opportunities for companies with a focus on civil engineering, such as Hyundai Engineering & Construction. Residential builders, such as Woosung Construction, should gain from a lifting at the end of December 1992 of a 1992 restriction on permits for residential building. Opportunities in China, and eventually North Korea, bode well for prominent companies such as POSCO, with its construction subsidiary. In Korea, excitement in the telecommunications area should be stirred in 1993, when additional mobile telecommunications carriers are expected to be selected. Until now Korea Mobile Telecom has been the sole carrier.

In electronics, Zoh points to Korea Computer, a leading producer of computer terminals used in banks, and Taeil Media Company, the world's second largest manufacturer of magnetic heads. Taeil Media has been seizing opportunities, both to cut costs and fortify its position. In Harbin, China, the company makes disk drive parts at low cost. To keep abreast, the company acquired the U.S firm of National Micronetics Incorporated to provide research and new materials for magnetic heads for computer disk drives. Zoh sees Taeil Media as well positioned to produce high-quality as well as competitively priced products.

Peregrine recommends investing in banks and securities companies such as Daewoo Securities, Korea First Bank, and Shinhan Bank.

The Korean people's determination, hard work, and laudable achievements make their country an attractive locale for investors, but the market is a tough one to penetrate. Yet even with its problems, Barry Gillman of PCM believes that Korea's market is "worth the trouble."

16
Taiwan

In 1949, the backwater island of Taiwan became home and refuge for Chinese nationalists fleeing from communist control of mainland China. Today, Taiwan is an economic powerhouse.

The island's transformation is all the more impressive considering the myriad obstacles its people faced. Diplomatically shunned by many countries that recognize the government of mainland China—the People's Republic of China, or PRC—and, until recently in a state of civil war with the PRC, life was tense on Taiwan. Until recent years, nationalists on the island vowed to reclaim power on mainland China, and animosity burned brightly between nationalist and communist.

David Peng, with Aetna Investment Management, Asia Pacific Limited, in Hong Kong, recalls many manifestations of political tension while growing up on Taiwan. On two offshore islands claimed by Taiwan, Quemoy and Ma-tsu, loudspeakers blasted propaganda at the nearby mainland, which reciprocated with its own verbal missives. Each semester there were air raid drills in school, and teenagers from the China (Taiwanese) Youth Corps would visit the schools to drum in anticommunist messages through songs, dances—and even show lurid photographs of atrocities on the mainland.

But times have changed on Taiwan. Social and political rigidity have eased as Taiwan developed its own strong economy and political self-confidence. Martial law was lifted in 1987. Opposition political parties have been legalized and allowed to compete with the ruling Kuomintang party (which originated as the nationalists from China). There are fewer social constraints, and ever-expanding socioeconomic contacts with the PRC have created a freer, less authoritarian atmosphere on the island. Liberalizations have also helped to open Taiwan to the opportunities of the 1990s.

As another sign of political progress, Taiwan, in December 1992, voted in its first fully democratically elected legislature. But that election did not ease the political uncertainty, since opinions differ on the thorny, fundamental issue of Taiwan's proper relationship to mainland China. Views on the island range from a desire for political unification to formal independence. Attitudes toward China have contributed to a splintering within the Kuomintang Party (KMT). Generally, the more liberal Taiwanese-born faction within the KMT prefers to coexist with the mainland, while continuing to develop Taiwan's own potential; the conservative old guard fears antagonizing the mainland and looks forward to unification. Lee Tenghui, who became Taiwan's first native-born President in 1988, has been moving to solidify support for the Taiwanese-born camp.

But the Taiwan–mainland China political status and relationship will likely remain murky for some time. In 1991, President Lee declared an end to the "period of communist rebellion" on mainland China, effectively terminating over 40 years of civil war with the PRC. However, actual reunification with mainland China remains years away because of the political gulf in attitudes between the two sides.

China seems to view this island as a province of the PRC, but indicates that it would allow Taiwan to maintain its own economic "system." Taiwan rejects the idea of political rule by communists, instead holding to a "one country, two governments" formula for reunification.

Given the differences in views, Edwin A. Winckler, research associate at Columbia University's East Asian Institute, sees no imminent signs of unification. "Eventually there will be some political reformulation, but one that will bear no resemblance to the formulas now being proposed," he says. Before Taiwan politically united with China it would want to see "how the patterns of relations between the two sides" evolve. That means the reality of unification "isn't worth talking about for another 15 years," he believes.

However, businesses haven't been waiting for unification. In early 1993, indirect investments by Taiwanese companies in China were estimated at $6 billion, and by March 1993, the PRC represented the single largest destination for outbound Taiwan capital. Given the ban on direct investment, Taiwanese wishing to make direct investments in China use a backdoor route. As a common strategy, a company sets up a subsidiary operation in a locale such as Hong Kong or Singapore, from whence it moves into China. (But even companies investing in China through a third country are restricted as to size and type of investment.) In the fourth quarter of 1992, Taiwan eased its restrictions, allowing small- and medium-sized enterprises to bring up to US$1 million to the mainland through third-country financial institutions.

As Taiwan strives for greater productivity, China will provide an important advantage, especially as competing nations try to tighten links with other former or current socialist/communist countries such North Korea and Vietnam. Among China's attractions are its abundance of cheap labor and natural resources and, eventually, greater access to a huge domestic market.

While companies in many countries have been seeking to tap into this opportunity, the Taiwanese "see China as their birthright," observes Peter Kurz, Baring Securities' chief representative on Taiwan. As an advantage over foreign competitors, the Taiwanese speak the same dialect as the Chinese of the PRC's Fujian province, just across the Strait of Taiwan; and, the Taiwanese maintain many pre-1949 personal and family ties with Chinese mainlanders.

One vision for Taiwan sees it as part of a South China economic triangle that would envelop Hong Kong's 6 million people, the 110 to 120 million in fast-growing South China, and Taiwan's population of just over 20 million. Such an arrangement would create "a very powerful" bloc, says Jeff L. T. Lee, head of trust banking at the Union Bank of Switzerland in Taipei. "We see this as the most important development in Asia outside of Japan."

TAIWAN

Currency: New Taiwan (NT) dollar.

Stock Exchanges: The Taiwan Stock Exchange Corporation (TSEC).

Indexes: The Taiwan Stock Exchange Index is the most widely used.

Types of Securities: Equities (preferred and common), government and corporate bonds, money market instruments and debentures.

Regulatory Body/Stock Exchange Supervision: The Securities and Exchange Commission (SEC) governs and regulates the securities markets.

Depository: The Taiwan Securities Central Depository (TSCD) is the central depository and clearinghouse.

Settlement Information

Equities:

- T + 1.
- Physical or book entry (majority of securities).
- Receive/deliver versus payment is available.
- Same-day turnaround trades are prohibited by law.

Fixed Income:

- Trade date.
- Physical delivery only.
- Receive/deliver versus payment available.
- Same-day turnaround trades are prohibited by law.

Taxes:

- There is no capital gains tax.
- Dividends are subject to a 20 percent withholding tax.
- A stock transfer tax of 0.3 percent of the transaction value is paid by the seller.

Restrictions for Foreign Investors:

- There is a 5 percent foreign investment limit on holdings of any one company's stock.
- Total foreign ownership of a company cannot exceed 10 percent.
- The total foreign investment quota is US$5 billion, and the investment ceiling per foreign institutional investor is US$100 million. Applications to exceed the $100 million limit will be reviewed on a case-by-case basis. Foreign institutional investors can purchase unlisted, open-ended unit trusts without regard to foreign ownership limits.

Securities Lending: Currently prohibited by law.

SOURCES: The Bank of New York and Citibank N.A.

The Economy

New Economic Opportunities

Exporting, which originally spawned Taiwan's "economic miracle," will remain vital to its economy and to an expected economic pickup in 1993. Taiwan's 1992 trade surplus was $9.5 billion compared with $13.3 billion in 1991. The overall economy—whose GDP growth slowed to 6.1 percent in 1992, from 7.3 percent the year before—is expected to regain some momentum in 1993, helped by an anticipated rise in exports. Estimates for 1993 GDP growth are in the neighborhood of 6.8 percent. Exports should benefit from a decline in value of the New Taiwan dollar (NT dollar) from its all-time high against the U.S. dollar in mid-1992, as well as anticipated growth in the U.S. economy—long a key market for Taiwan. Over the next few years, many analysts believe Taiwan can maintain real annual economic growth of at least 6 to 7 percent. But exporting will slowly but surely lose some ground to expansion of the financial industry, consumer spending, and massive investments in infrastructure.

Rising costs at home will continue to drive more low-end manufacturing to countries that pay lower wages. According to Baring Securities, Taiwan surpassed Japan in 1990 as the leading source of direct foreign investments in Malaysia. In 1991, Taiwan was the second largest direct foreign investor in Thailand, after Japan.

At home, value-added production and increasing emphasis on technology are being encouraged. As far back as 1980, the Hsinchu Industrial Park, 60 miles from the capital city of Taipei was established for scientific and technological research and development. Designed to bring in 200 high-tech companies and a work force of 74,000, its ostensible aim was to improve Taiwan's ability to export goods, and it has already made a remarkable difference in Taiwan's high-tech economy, according to S.G. Warburg Co.

For many companies, however, value-added production has very practical and immediate business applications. A textile company, for example, would produce high-quality fabric in Taiwan, ship it to China—for labor-intensive assembly work such as dyeing, finishing, and clothing making—then return the finished product to Taiwan for reexport.

In infrastructure development, Taiwan has embarked on a massive Six Year National Development Plan that runs from fiscal 1991 to 1996. Originally targeted for $300 million, the program has reportedly been scaled back somewhat, and most projects aren't expected to be finished within the target period. Nonetheless, the lengthy list of designated projects includes highways; urban mass-transit systems; new ports; an airport at Taichung; sewage treatment; housing; and much more.

Taiwan should get a powerful economic boost from the enormous spending on infrastructure. "The Directorate-General of Budget, Accounting and Statistics officially projects that the national development plans to add three to four percentage points to GDP per year over the target period" although some projects have been slow to leave the starting gate, says Thomas Brizendine, assistant manager of the international department of Polaris Securities Company Limited in Taipei. To pay for the program, the government has been issuing short- and medium-term debt instruments. Although Taiwan had $82.5 billion in foreign exchange reserves as of February 1993, that theoretically could be spent on infrastructure or other business development, experts say. The reserves are ultimately meant as financial protection. For example, Taiwan could use the money to pay for necessities or even military equipment if it faced a perilous dispute with the PRC. The 1994 budget allots 22.8 percent—the largest share—to defense.

Beefed-Up Financial Sector

The highly educated and motivated Taiwanese have enjoyed an increasingly rising standard of living. From $50 per year in 1950, Taiwan's per capita income climbed to $10,215 in 1992. Extremely low unemployment has been at well under 2 percent since 1989. Rising wealth, however, has spawned a nagging inflation problem that the central bank has combated, beginning in 1989, with tightened monetary policy.

The authorities were also attempting to check what had become a speculative bubble in the stock and property markets in the late 1980s. Taiwan was swimming in cash from rapid growth in the money supply, a high savings rate, and a huge trade surplus. Excess cash began to chase stocks and real estate, in part because people had few other attractive places to park their money.

Seeing the need and recognizing the value of becoming a sophisticated financial center, the government has taken numerous steps, particularly since 1988, to liberalize and beef up the financial sector.

In a December 1991 report for The Asia Society in New York, Professor Hungmao Tien of the University of Wisconsin cited a "number of policy initiatives aimed at internationalizing and liberalizing [Taiwan's] economy and finances. Existing restrictions on import tariffs, foreign banks, and insurance companies, transactions in gold and foreign currencies, and exchange rates have been modified or removed."

He pointed out that "the Finance Ministry authorized 15 new [private] commercial banks. The government has taken steps to privatize three major state-controlled banks. Communication facilities for improving international finance transactions and trade are modernizing. One goal is to turn Taipei into a major international center of finance in the Asia Pacific region."

In 1993, experts say additional economic liberalizations, including reduced tariffs, are expected, as Taiwan seeks to become a signatory to the General Agreement on Tariffs and Trade (GATT).

Casino-esque Stock Market

Established in 1961, Taiwan's stock market features computerized trading and settlements. Its automated trading operations are said to be the world's best. As of year-end 1992, the capitalization stood at a sizable $101.12 billion, according to the IFC, and there were 256 listed stocks. In 1992, the 10 most actively traded stocks on the Taiwan Stock Exchange, in order were: Hualon Corp., Tay Feng Tire, Chia Hsin Flour, Chung Shing Textile, China Development, China Steel, Pacific

Construction, Kwong Fong Industries, Reward Wool, and Yue Loong Motor.

Although the market is operationally sophisticated, it has traditionally been casino-esque in nature, and in the past was not seen as any backbone of the economy. Although trends are said to be changing, Taiwan's stock prices have moved on rumors, news events, ramping by big-time speculators and technical analysis. The market has attracted largely domestic Taiwanese investors, and foreigners' participation has been limited. It wasn't until 1983 that foreign portfolio investment was allowed in Taiwan through investment funds. When the market opened to direct stock investing by foreigners in the beginning of 1991, rules were still restrictive: non-Taiwanese investors (banks, insurance companies, and fund managers) can hold only 10 percent or less of all outstanding shares of a company, and each foreign investor can hold no more than 5 percent of any listed company's issues. These investors must meet qualifications on specific asset and capital minimums, as well as length of experience requirements. As of the beginning of 1993, Taiwanese individual investors accounted for 96 percent of trading value, while foreigners comprised about one-quarter of 1 percent.

To enhance market depth and stability, the government is encouraging more market participation by institutional investors. In 1992, Taiwan's Securities and Exchange Commission formally approved 11 new securities investment trust companies, each of which would be able to raise funds of between $4 to $5 billion New Taiwan (NT) dollars from domestic investors. Much of that money was expected to be invested in the stock market.

In 1992, Taiwan expanded foreigners' ability to participate in its market. Among the moves, it eased its remittance policy on capital gains, permitting them to be repatriated freely at any time after three months instead of the previous one-year restriction. Taiwan also broadened allowable participation by foreign institutions. The list was expanded to include the world's 1000 largest foreign banks; insurance firms with 5 years' business experience; fund managers with minimum assets of $300 million and 3 years' business experience, reports the IFC.

In early 1993, the Central Bank of China also doubled to $100 million the allowable limit that a foreign institutional investor can bring to the Taiwan stock market. In addition, the lid on total foreign stock investment was to be raised to $5 billion from the previous $2.5 billion cap.

Other liberalizations have been forthcoming. In 1992, for example, the government gave its blessing to trading of foreign commodities and financial futures in Taiwan, beginning in 1993. The country is also expected to create a domestic futures exchange market.

But for foreign investors, a number of deterrents still exist, Among them: continued concern about market volatility and speculation and even problems related to the tight T-plus-one settlement time for trades. On the bright side, brokers say that trades never fail since, if they did, the Taiwanese broker would lose his license for three years. But T-plus-one settlements cause headaches for foreign investors, especially in distant time zones, since they make it difficult for foreigners to ask their local custodian for funds in time to settle the trade, explains Mark Tajima, a consultant with Emerging Markets Consulting Group International.

Ways around the problem are far from ideal. In one complex solution, an investor could give power of attorney to a local Taiwanese broker to authorize a local subcustodian agent to handle the settlement. But in so doing, the investor, his money manager, and his global custodian are all cut out of the transaction, meaning that the investor loses much control over his account. As another option, if a local broker settled the trade using his own money, he would charge interest on the loan.

With its sharp peaks and deep troughs, market volatility has been another source of concern to many foreigners. In the late 1980s, bullish investors, awash in cash, drove the market to its pinnacle, as the local index surpassed 12,000 in March 1990. But the market subsequently plunged over the next two-and-a-half years, leaving the index at 3377 at the end of 1992 before rebounding slightly in 1993.

Besides its volatility, the market is also known for ramping—where cash-rich speculators pour money into a stock. "Big hand" speculators have been known to operate with up to $1 billion. But by 1992, even those players began to be fright-

ened off by reports of a government crackdown in illegal activities. In September 1992, the market was jolted by what the IFC
called "the largest-ever insider trading scandal, which resulted
in a total of NT$9 billion (US$360 million) in defaulted stock
payments." According to a report in the *Asia Business Journal,*
"textile tycoon Oung Ta-ming was sentenced to three-and-one-
half years in prison for his role in a US$22 million stock scandal,
and major (market) player Lei Po-lung was detained that
September for questioning about NT$9 billion of payment
defaults."

The scandal may not have long-range implications for the
people involved. For instance, Thomas Brizendine of Polaris
Securities reports that, while his conviction was on appeal,
Oung Ta-ming in late 1992 was elected to Taiwan's legislature.
But government actions to improve the market should have positive long-range effects. Many believe that the crackdown on
illegal dealings, along with the government's programs to
attract more institutional participation, will limit the kind of
excesses seen in the past.

How to Play the Market

Meanwhile, in 1993, many investors began warming to Taiwan's
market. Investors cited then-attractive valuations, improved
economic fundamentals, and opportunities to address China
plays through this market, instead of, or along with other markets, such as Hong Kong's. From January through June 4, 1993,
Taiwan's market rebounded with a gain of 31 percent in U.S.
dollar terms, according to the IFC's global price index.

For foreigners, investment funds are still the easiest way to
play the Taiwan stock market, especially if they're making only
a relatively small allocation. Four of the better-known funds
available to foreigners include: the closed-end Taiwan Fund Inc.
and the ROC Taiwan Fund, both of which trade on the New
York Stock Exchange; and the open-end Taipei Fund and
Formosa Fund.

Through funds, investors skirt the investment requirements
and limitations and the machinations of a volatile market.
Danny Chan, president and chief executive officer of the

International Investment Trust Co. Ltd. in Taipei, investment advisor to the ROC Taiwan Fund, illustrates the disadvantage foreign investors have already faced in Taiwan. Between the market's opening to direct foreign investments in January 1991 and August 1992, "none of the offshore investors managed to outperform funds managed locally in Taiwan," he reports.

American depositary receipts are available for Asia Cement Corporation (144A) and China Steel Corporation (144A). China Steel Corporation also has a non-U.S. depositary receipt program, according to Bankers Trust Co.

Foreigners interested in direct stock investments are frequently urged to diversify their portfolio by picking a cross section of stocks and are also encouraged to pursue broad economic themes. Possibilities include overall economic development, investing in China, infrastructural development, consumer spending, and technological developments. More and more listed companies are expected to qualify as "China plays," either because they've made direct investments in the PRC or because they service customers doing business with the PRC. Some of the better-known companies now considered "China plays" are: Great Wall Enterprise; Cheng Shin Rubber Industrial; President Enterprises; and Wei Chuan Food—whose PRC investments reportedly include a baby-cereal plant in Beijing, an MSG plant in Gueilin, and a milk powder plant in Shanghai.

As 1992 drew to an end, many experts were unclear as to whether investments in the PRC could eventually enhance the earnings of Taiwan companies. Many of these investments had been in the range of a modest $1 to $5 million; by late 1992, the biggest legal investment was believed to have been made by Cheng Shin Rubber Industrial, with its $20 million stake in a bicycle tire plant in Xiamen, China. Commonly, production in China would be meant for export, although some foreign companies can get approval to sell certain products locally.

To capture opportunities in consumer spending and infrastructural development, Chan of IIT likes President Enterprises in the food industry and Far Eastern Department Stores in retailing. Both companies are the largest in their industries in Taiwan, and should have "steady profit growth in the face of increasing consumer spending," he says.

Although infrastructural development is a hot topic in Taiwan, Kurz of Baring Securities thinks that "it's a bit more difficult to find good infrastructure plays than good China plays."

While construction, including cement, would be an obvious choice, Kurz points out that the earnings potential of many listed construction companies is restrained by exposure to the residential and office building area, both of which have become overbuilt. Cement companies also have their drawbacks, since "the Taiwanese are fairly high-cost producers, cheaper imports could make up for any shortfall in supply," he holds. One company Kurz does recommend is Hua Eng Wire & Cable, whose attractions include its 50 percent share in the optical fibers market.

Some might wonder if Taiwan's market—with its increasing focus on China plays—will be overshadowed in time by growth in China's stock markets. But Mr. Kurz thinks not. In his view "there will always be a separate Taiwan market representing a separate country." Although opportunities will be found on the Shenzhen and Shanghai markets, Taiwan's market is "more advanced, freer, and it's undergone reformation." Thus, compared with China's fledgling markets, Taiwan's "is more mature and more of an institution," he holds. The market "represents Taiwan's companies and their exposure to China."

Political separation from the PRC has a positive effect on Taiwan. Even if political/economic upheavals again roil the PRC, Taiwan could continue to rely on its own economy and not be dragged down by China. In contrast, Hong Kong, after returning to China in mid-1997, "would feel the full brunt of disruptions in China," Kurz maintains. To Kurz, the Taiwan advantage is that it can capitalize on opportunities in China and elsewhere while still enjoying "downside protection" from upheavals in the PRC.

17

The Republic of Indonesia

Blessed with a range of natural resources and a huge domestic market of about 185 million people and political stability, the former Dutch colony of Indonesia has attracted foreign investment and posted strong economic growth.

Under the stable (though strong-handed) rule of President Suharto for more than 25 years, Indonesia has successfully diversified and liberalized its traditionally protected economy. However, it remains unclear which economic course he plans to take. Experts say the country is unsure whether it can (or should) become a leader in high technology, or if it should emphasize industries with lower technological requirements.

Indonesia's economy was historically rooted in agricultural and natural resources development. But after its economy was jolted by an early 1980s dive in commodity prices, diversification and private sector development were seen as the solutions.

So far, Indonesia's progress has been impressive. In a speech given in New York in early 1993, J. Soedradjat Djiwandono, Indonesia's vice minister of trade at the time, pointed to a number of achievements that underlie "the soundness of our development strategy." He cited: exports in 1992 that reached $32 billion, nearly double the level of five years earlier; non-oil exports accounted for 69 percent of total exports, up from 44 percent in

1986; foreign and private banks accounted for more than half of all deposits, "and the private sector share of credit extended has increased by almost 50 percent." In addition, he reported that listed firms on Indonesia's main stock exchange in Jakarta had jumped to more than 150 from 24 in 1987, while the market's capitalization ballooned to $12 billion from $72 million during the five years through 1992. GDP growth had averaged "well over 6 percent per year during each of the past three years," he reported.

Investment incentives, coupled with Indonesia's natural attractions, including its natural resources and abundance of cheap labor, attracted direct foreign investment—most heavily from Japan. Its 185 million population places it fourth in the world. Low labor costs are illustrated by the fact that Indonesia's GNP per capita stood at $615 in 1991. The country is Southeast Asia's largest oil exporter and the world's largest liquefied natural gas exporter, as well as the world's second largest producer of rubber, tin, and palm oil. But although commodities remain important, nonoil manufacturing "has become the single most important source of growth" in Indonesia, said Djiwandono. Between 1987 and 1991, Indonesia's manufactured goods more than trebled in value, accounting for more than 80 percent of nonoil exports in each of the past four consecutive years, the official reported.

Starting in the 1980s, direct foreign investment was wooed more aggressively as a source of private monies. Although Indonesia had had an investment law since 1967, a barrage of new liberalizations were initiated in the middle 1980s—starting with tax law changes. Foreign direct investment soared. Approvals of direct foreign investment leapt from $800 million in 1986 to $10.2 billion in 1992. In 1993, Baring Securities projected that Indonesia's foreign investment would grow to 4.8 percent of GDP, compared with an estimated 4.4 percent in 1992.

Even before embarking on 1980s liberalizations, Indonesia solicited input and ideas from abroad. Since 1975, the investment firms of Lazard Frères et Cie, Lehman Brothers, and S.G. Warburg & Co. Ltd., acting in concert, have been financial advisors to Indonesia's government, primarily concerning commercial financing. In addition, for many years Indonesia has sent bright students abroad for economic education. This has created the so-called "Berkeley mafia"—a sobriquet for those high-level governmental officials who have attended the University of California at Berkeley and other Western institutions, and returned home with a desire to promote greater free market programs. In March 1993, investor concern was aroused as some of the foreign-trained economists were replaced in President Suharto's cabinet at the start of his sixth term. But in a May report, Baring Securities was confident that "there will not be any drastic changes in the current (economic) policy, and all modifications will be implemented in a gradual manner."

Recent Economic Challenges

Among the problems of the early 1990s were initially rising inflation that spurred a tightening of monetary policy and higher interest rates, a current account deficit, and high levels of debt. Some of these problems have been reduced—interest rates have dropped to 14.3 percent from the high of 20.2 percent for the SBI (Indonesia's treasury bill) in 1991. Inflation rises in 1990 and 1991 shrank to 7.6 percent in 1992. Baring Securities projects that the current account deficit of $3.8 billion in 1992 will fall to $3.2 billion in 1993.

Bank lending rates have dropped, from 27 percent to 22 percent as of March 1993. But the industry is facing a rising tide of bad loans as well as the need to meet tightened capital adequacy ratios. According to the IFC, banks have been required to attain a capital adequacy ratio of 7 percent by March 1993, and 8 percent by December.

Indonesia's public and private medium-and-long-term external debt climbed from $57.2 billion at the end of 1990 to an estimated $63.5 billion at the end of 1991. The debt–service ratio has been relatively stable, falling from 33 percent in 1990 to 32 percent in 1991, and remaining there for 1992. It is expected to drop to 31 percent in 1993. Improvement is expected to continue, as the debt–service ratio is expected to fall to 25.8 percent by 1995 and to around 20 percent by the year 2000.

INDONESIA

Currency: Indonesian rupiah (IDR).

Stock Exchanges: There are two stock exchanges, the Jakarta Stock Exchange (JSE)—main exchange—and the Surabaya Stock Exchange (SSE).

Indexes: The Jakarta Composite Index (JCI) is the main index in Indonesia.

Types of Securities: The "regular" market has four types of instruments: shares, rights, corporate bonds, and convertible bonds.

Regulatory Body/Stock Exchange Supervision: The Capital Market Supervisory Agency (BAPEPAM) and the Ministry of Finance regulate the stock market.

Depository: A central clearinghouse, called PT Kliring Deposit Efek Indonesia, is expected to become fully operational by the end of 1994.

Settlement Information

Equities:

- T + 4.
- Physical settlement only.
- Receive/deliver versus payment available.
- Same-day turnaround trades are not possible.

Fixed Income: Not applicable.

Taxes:

- Dividends are subject to a 20 percent withholding at the source. Residents of tax treaty countries, among them France, Germany, Japan, and India, are taxed at 15 percent. Tax treaties with a number of other countries are now being negotiated or are expected to be discussed in the future.
- A capital gains tax is being considered.
- The JSE charges a 1000 IDR stamp duty per contract.
- A 0.1 percent stock exchange clearing fee is levied by the JSE.

Restrictions for Foreign Investors: There is a 49 percent ownership limit on the shares of most listed companies, although this restriction may soon be lifted.

Securities Lending: Not yet available.

SOURCES: The Bank of New York and the Jakarta Stock Exchange.

Indonesia has not had to reschedule debt payments with creditors since 1965. In 1992, Standard & Poor's Corp., a New York-based credit rating agency, for the first time rated Indonesia's debt, assigning it an investment grade rating of BBB−.

In his budget message for 1993–94, Suharto noted that, in 1993, the country would complete both its current five-year economic development plan, called REPELITA V, as well as its first 25-year Long-Term Development program. As the nation looked ahead to its Second Long-Term Development program, Suharto said it needed to focus on several key areas: infrastructural development; human resources development through education and training; the need for technological enhancements; the generation of funding sources for development; and the continuation and intensification of "institutional reformation," including all "all state apparatuses and institutions."

But to some observers, his most dramatic message concerned the specific issue of oil subsidies. "The government has come to the conclusion that they must be abolished," he said. "In other words, the selling price of fuel oils must be raised." The president pointed to today's high energy consumption and noted that "by the end of the century, we may become a net importer of oil." Before the 1993 election, Suharto had already removed the oil subsidies. Oil prices rose, and tariffs were hiked for transport and electricity. Crosby Securities felt these moves were positive, as it would allow Indonesia to conserve resources and prevent wastage. Fuel prices rose 27 percent, electricity 15 percent, and transportation costs 10 percent.

Politics

President Suharto is widely applauded for his economic initiatives. Holding his current position since 1967, Suharto is credited with resurrecting the economy from the ruins left by his predecessor, President Sukarno, who was driven from power after a failed coup in 1965. Suharto's so-called New Order created policies that redirected the country toward economic growth. Over the years President Suharto has been "regarded as the best thing to happen to Indonesian economic development," points out

Julian Mayo, assistant director of Thornton Management Ltd. in London. Although he's had "hands in everything, you could say the same thing about leaders in a lot of other countries."

President Suharto has been head of state for more than 25 years. In 1993 the septuagenarian was, as expected, reelected to his sixth five-year term. The year before, the ruling Golkar (it stands for Golongan Karya) party he heads had won the parliamentary elections with 68 percent of the votes—although that was down from 73 percent in 1987. Suharto's international stature increased in 1992, as Indonesia assumed the chairmanship of the 108-nation Non-Aligned Movement.

On the bright side, political stability has allowed Indonesia to focus on pressing economic/developmental issues. But government, big business, and the military still hold wide influence, and the Suharto family over the years has amassed wide national influence and power. Freedom of speech is restrained, and corruption is said to be rampant. The November 1991 massacre on the island of Dili, East Timor, where between 50 and 100 unarmed civilian protestors were gunned down by Indonesian troops, illustrates the extent to which authoritarianism can be carried. Although 10 members of the security forces were subsequently prosecuted and two generals in charge of East Timor province dismissed, Indonesia reportedly also cracked down on the protestors. In a September 1992 editorial, *The New York Times* said that "Jakarta continues to keep East Timor off limits to the foreign press, so that the world's attention will not focus on the punitive sentences (nine years to life) handed down against demonstrators at the November incident."

Traditionally, business and government have had cozy links. In the private sector, big business groups, often owned by the minority ethnic Chinese, form the cornerstone of Indonesia's economy. Companies in the group make up an important part of the stock market.

The three biggest groups are the Salim Group, the Astra Group, and Sinar Mas. Illustrating the size and power of Indonesia's conglomerates, the biggest of them embrace at least 100 to 200 companies, while the smaller ones include 25 to 30 companies, experts say. These executives "are well connected with high-ranking government officials, including the First Family," observes one money manager. The business groups wield influence over the obtaining of the licenses and other concessions needed to do business in Indonesia.

Although the conglomerates have made contributions to job creation among other things, they've also been criticized for the wealth they've brought to a few families—while many people remain poor. The managerial prowess of the conglomerates has also come under more scrutiny in the aftermath of the 1992 Astra episode. Late that year, control of the Astra group changed from the founders, the Soeryadjaya family, to a consortium of investors led by Prayogo Pangestu, a noted Indonesian businessman. This occurred following the collapse of Bank Summa, in which the Soeryadjaya family had been financially involved. It remains to be seen how much restructuring of the Astra group will become necessary.

The First Family's Business Dealings

President Suharto's own family also has its tentacles in Indonesian business. Some examples from a 1990 report by Crosby Research: "the President's second son, Bambang, heads the Bimantara Group, which has a wide variety of business activities, including those in agriculture, electronics, financial services, petrochemicals, transportation, and telecommunications. Bambang's younger brother, "Tommy" Suharto, runs the Humpuss Group, which has dealings in air and sea transportation, petrochemicals, energy, and agriculture. The President's cousin, Sudwikatmono, is connected with the Salim business group, the largest in Indonesia, while the President's half-brother has shareholdings in quite a number of companies."

The First Family's business dealings were detailed in the April 30, 1992, issue of the *Far Eastern Economic Review* (*FEER*), which according to the *Review* was banned from street sales in Indonesia. One facet of the account concerned "Tommy" Suharto's activities in the clove business. In late 1990, Tommy was awarded a monopoly on the sale of cloves used in cigarettes. The idea was to form a cooperative that would bolster participants' ability to compete in the cloves business. Tommy, according to the *FEER*, "promised to double the price of cloves paid to farmers...and would finance the monopoly by quadrupling the price of cloves sold to cigarette makers." On the instruction of the President, Tommy even got subsidized credits from the central bank. But before long Tommy reported to the parliament that the monopoly "was effectively bankrupt." Flooded with "the equivalent of more than two years' of clove stocks," it "could not pay its debts. He suggested to legislators that the best solution to the problem was to have clove farmers burn half their crops."

Theories abound as to why President Suharto has risked undermining his good works by allowing his family such free rein. Some hypothesize that the children's ventures keep a check on the Chinese influence in business. Others theorize that the Suharto family feels entitled to privileges because of the President's successes at national development. In a generally favorable June 1992 article, *The Asian Wall Street Journal* nevertheless wrote that "though Mr. Suharto has removed many trade monopolies, he has allowed new ones to be set up, often to the benefit of relatives. The expanding business activities of his six children are a source of much resentment, causing an erosion of support for the president among educated Indonesians."

"It's a patronage society," acknowledges Wayne J. Forrest, executive director of the American Indonesian Chamber of Commerce in New York. "It has to have been, to build stability." Indonesians hope the West will "understand their form of democracy (and business practices), because Indonesians think it's right for them....They have a cultural predilection for calm, and believe that their own people are not yet mature enough" to make the best political and economic choices for the nation.

The Stock Market

In 1912, the colonialist Dutch introduced capital market operations to Indonesia, and the markets remained open until World War II. Throughout the pre-war years, Indonesia had three stock exchanges: Jakarta's which opened in 1912, and those in Surabaya and Semarang, which debuted in 1924. Although the

Indonesian government reopened Jakarta's stock exchange in 1952, the market remained dormant for many years. In 1976 a presidential decree established the Capital Market Executive Agency (BAPEPAM) under the Ministry of Finance. BAPEPAM was responsible for supervising and running the stock exchange. In the 1987–88 period, the government issued a series of deregulation packages, reforms, and policy adjustments, with the intent of spurring development of the capital market. Reforms, including permission for foreigners to buy stock directly in the market, initially triggered a market boom in listings and in share prices. But market activity overwhelmed Indonesia's ability to cope with it, and numerous problems came to light. Many investors began to complain about an array of market problems ranging from inadequate supervision to a lack of ample or reliable information about listed companies.

In 1991, a new Capital Market Supervisory Agency (also with the acronym BAPEPAM) was created as a supervisory body for the capital market, while the Jakarta Stock Exchange Inc. (JSE) was established as a private firm owned by member brokers. In April 1992 privatization of the Jakarta Stock Exchange, called the PT Bursa Efek Jakarta, was completed.

Today there are two private stock exchanges, the dominant JSE in Jakarta and the Surabaya Stock Exchange in Surabaya, Indonesia's second largest city. The Bursa Parallel, created in 1987, is a small over-the-counter market in Jakarta. Although trading is still performed manually, the JSE will become fully automated in 1994 when the exchange moves to a new building, the exchange reports.

The JSE has three types of markets, the regular market, the non-regular market, and the cash market. Regular trading, for shares, rights, and corporate and convertible bonds, is based on an auction system performed continuously during trading hours. The nonregular market handles block sales, crossing, the foreign boards, and odd-lot trading. Brokers who fail to deliver securities on a T-plus-four basis have to buy the missing securities from the cash market and are not allowed to handle additional "regular market" transactions before the failed trade is settled. At the end of 1992, Indonesia's market cap stood at $12 billion, double the level of one year earlier, and there were 155 listed shares.

While the limitation is expected to be raised, foreigners can now buy up to 49 percent of the shares of listed companies. Once that level has been reached, foreigners can purchase those stocks only from other foreigners, and the transactions are logged on a separate "foreign board." According to the JSE, as of December 1992 foreigners owned about 49 percent of the shares available to them.

In 1992, the 10 most actively traded stocks on the Jakarta Stock Exchange were, in order: Astra International, Bank Bali, Indocement Tunggal Prakarsa, Indah Kiat Paper & Pulp, Bank Internasional Indonesia, Kalbe Farma, Japfa Comfeed, Inti Indorayon Utama, HM Sampoerna, and Indorama Synthetics.

Starting in mid-1990, Indonesia's market went through a two-and-a-half-year trough. In 1992, the IFC's Price Index for Indonesia rose 0.9 percent in U.S. dollar terms, after a 43 percent drop the year before. Bearishness emerged in the face of tightened money supply, disappointing corporate results, and such other concerns as market supervision and regulations. Among the distressing developments was news of a huge foreign exchange trading loss in 1990 by Bank Duta. Initial euphoria after the late 1980s market reforms gave way—which undermined confidence in the banking system. Also, Bentoel, a large cigarette maker, defaulted on its debt in 1991; and the Mantrust conglomerate needed to reschedule its debt.

Cases of bad corporate reporting also proved troubling. For example, "Argo Pantes reported one set of earnings when listing on the stock market, and, within six weeks gave new figures that were 65 percent below the original ones," says Julian Mayo of Thornton Management. Such cases suggest inadequate market regulation. "Authorities simply weren't prepared for the burst of activity that took place, and couldn't keep track of everything going on, " he said.

In response to the problems, new moves and regulations sought to upgrade the market's professionalism, among them the separation of the JSE's management from that of BAPEPAM. The government also wishes to bolster funds available for long-term investment in the capital market. To that end, new rules for pension funds, which took effect in April 1993, are expected eventually to expand Indonesia's pool of institutional assets.

In addition, a privatization program is expected to gain steam eventually, further expanding the supply of available equities. According to the Indonesian government, "over 50 state enterprises, including 5 state commercial banks and the national airline Garuda, have been identified for eventual privatization."

In the first five months of 1993 (through June 4), the IFC's global price index for Indonesia was up 32.2 percent in U.S. dollar terms. And at least some market participants have been encouraged about the market's long-range prospects. Abigail Rotheroe, senior investment manager of the closed-end Java Fund managed by Wardley Investment Services in Hong Kong, sees the market doubling in size over the period from about 1995 to 1997. "Well into the future," Dennis Lim, research manager of Templeton Worldwide in Singapore, can foresee Indonesia's market becoming the third largest in Asia, after, eventually, China's and Japan's markets.

But in the meantime he sees "quite a lot of room for improvement in this market." At mid-year 1992, Lim, whose firm manages the closed-end Indonesia Development Fund, observed that "information on corporate actions (including dividends, rights issues, and bonus issues) are difficult to obtain on a timely basis, accounting standards are lax, and reporting and disclosure requirements are not adequate.

"But the biggest problem," in his view, concerns the issue of foreign versus locally held shares. According to Lim, once shares reach their 49 percent limit on foreign ownership and begin trading only among other foreigners, their price premiums can run as high as 50 to 60 percent above the listed price paid by domestic investors. To try to capitalize on the situation, some companies prefer to list only a small portion of their issued capital. They wait to list more stock until the price is at a premium among foreigners. Companies use this approach as a way to obtain higher prices for their stock, he reports.

In the early 1990s, the bulk of stock market trading came from foreign investors. But a variety of factors, including tax law changes, were expected to encourage local market participation—by those who can afford to in this relatively poor country—once interest rates have declined sharply.

What to Buy

What shares should investors buy? While some experts maintain that smaller companies portent higher growth opportunities, foreigners often choose the larger companies' stock for liquidity reasons. Typically, foreigners are said to focus on the 10 to 20 largest-capitalized stocks.

Crosby sees three additional sources of growth for Indonesia: higher tourism spending, emergence of a larger middle class, and easing of monetary policy. Consumption patterns have shifted to nonfood and miscellaneous items, which means that with economic growth, the middle class will buy consumer durables such as cellular phones, motorcycles, and other higher-valued goods.

As its recommended strategy, Baring Securities suggested in a May 1992 report that investors selectively pick individual shares. Baring illustrated that, during a late 1991/early 1992 market advance, some high fliers jumped over 60 percent in price. They included the stock price of Duta Anggada Realty, which leapt 102 percent; Indorayon, which climbed 87 percent; Semen Gresik, which advanced 74.1 percent; and Tigaraksa Satria, up 73.3 percent. "Additionally, the diverse range of betas for 47 analyzed companies has further supported our view that a highly selective approach—compared with a sectoral approach used for developed markets—is needed in Indonesia," the firm said. In Indonesia, "companies within the same sector may trade on very different ratings for a protracted period of time."

In January 1993, in the category of larger companies, Baring was recommending only overweight positions in the agribusiness and pulp and paper sectors, citing in particular the stocks of Japfa Comfeed and Charoen Pokphand in agribusiness and Indorayon and Tjiwi Kimia in pulp and paper. Although the consumer and banking sectors were among those that Baring recommended for a "neutral portfolio weighting," companies recommended for an overweight position in the consumer sector were Gudang Garam, Kalbe Farma, Modern Photo, Mayora Indah, and Tigaraksa Satria, while in banking, overweighted positions were recommended for the stocks of Bank Bali, Bank Internasional Indonesia, and Lippo Bank.

As alternatives to direct stock investing, Wilson Emerging Market Funds Research in 1993 listed 25 country funds for Indonesia, most of which are domiciled abroad. Closed-end funds include the Indonesia Fund Inc. and the Jakarta Growth Fund Inc., which trade on the New York Stock Exchange; the Batavia Fund, the EFM Java Trust plc, the Indonesia Equity Fund Ltd., the Jakarta Fund (Cayman) Ltd., the JF Indonesia Fund Inc., and the SHK Indonesia Fund Ltd., which are listed on the London Stock Exchange.

According to Bankers Trust Company, P.T. Inti Indorayon Utama was the only Indonesian company for which an American Depositary Receipt was available as of December 1992.

18
Malaysia

Malaysia, a multiracial Southeast Asian nation of 18.5 million, is a country with big plans. By the year 2020 the country, which is still in its industrializing stage, aims to qualify as an economically developed nation. To get there, the country has mapped out 5- and 10-year programs to steer economic growth and to help ensure that the economy averages 7 percent growth each year.

"Vision 2020," as the long-range program is known, aims to enhance the well-being of all Malaysians while helping to broaden and upgrade the once agriculturally dependent economy.

In the wake of the 1980s downturn in commodities prices, Malaysia recognized that it needed a broader economic foundation. The country began aggressively to court private, including foreign, investment, which resulted in a spurt in manufacturing. That sector is today the nation's engine of growth. Overall, development has put a fire under Malaysia's economy, which jumped ahead nearly 9 percent a year between 1988 and 1991. Even with the slowdown in 1992, real GDP grew 8 percent in 1992 versus 8.8 percent the year before and 9.8 percent in 1990. As spillover effects, this economy has brought a multitude of new shopping malls and in Malaysia's capital of Kuala Lumpur, sleek new buildings that grace the city's skyline.

Officials hope that strong economic growth will filter through all sectors of society, ultimately correcting long-standing racial woes. In 1969, resentment between Chinese Malaysians, who control much of Malaysian business, and poorer native Malays (*bumiputeras*), who comprise 55 percent of Malaysia's population, exploded into riots.

The government had initially used economic policies to try to elevate the lot of the *bumiputera* (a word that translates as "prince of the soil"). Malaysia's 20-year New Economic Policy (NEP) of 1971 ordained that the native *bumiputeras'* share of corporate ownership should increase to 30 percent by 1990, with 40 percent going to other Malaysians and 30 percent to foreigners. But the *bumiputeras* never achieved 30 percent corporate ownership during the NEP.

After that program, the successor National Development Policy (NDP) adopted in 1991, omitted corporate ownership quotas for native peoples. Instead of ethnic quotas, the government now sees strong growth—especially in the private sector—as beneficial to all.

The Economy

Since the 1980s, Malaysia has looked to the private sector to be the country's main engine of growth. To achieve its long-range goals, the government seeks accelerated industrialization, value-added production, higher technological capability, and the use of more local content in production.

Already, overall manufacturing comprises more than one-quarter of Malaysia's GDP. According to the current Sixth Malaysia Plan, which runs from 1991 to 1995, manufacturing is targeted to grow 11.5 percent a year to reach one-third of GDP by 1995.

Small- to medium-sized businesses are being encouraged as important contributors to the overall goals. That sector is seen as providing local sources of parts needed in manufacturing—thus limiting the need to import them—and as conduits, facilitating the transfer of technology from the major foreign producers to Malaysian organizations.

Policies to woo direct foreign investment have already paid off handsomely. According to Crosby Securities, total foreign investment in Malaysia stood at M$17.7 billion in 1992, to comprise an estimated 12.5 percent of its GDP that year.

Industries being targeted for investment by the Malaysian Industrial Development Authority (MIDA) include: rubber products, palm oil, timber, electronics, industrial machinery, chemical and petrochemicals, nonferrous metals, nonmetallic mineral products, textiles, and transportation equipment. Favorable tax treatment is awarded on a case-by-case basis. Among other criteria, favored projects would generally provide value-added components to manufacturing, and the production process would entail higher technology and lower labor requirements, given the country's tight labor market.

The government's contributions entail offering incentives to foreign direct investors, enhancing education and technical training, pursuing infrastructural projects, and continuing with the privatization program. In education, the government is encouraging home-grown science and managerial capability. Private businesses are being offered financial incentives to provide education and technical training, while state-run technical schools and universities are more heavily emphasizing or upgrading technical instruction.

According to the *Far Eastern Economic Review,* infrastructure spending in the Sixth Malaysia Plan is budgeted for M$104 billion. M$19 billion of that is targeted for completion of projects already under way. Not included is spending on a second international airport, to be completed before Malaysia hosts the Commonwealth Games in 1998. In addition the government is attempting to grapple with the tight labor market by allowing in more foreign workers.

But economic challenges abound. As a long-term issue, Malaysia's economy remains influenced by forces outside of its control, including the possibility of increased trade protectionism as well as the vagaries of commodities prices. In the shorter term, efforts to shift the economy and maintain robust growth have taken their toll. Most notably, red-hot growth in the early 1990s gave way to rising inflation, even as the trade balance suffered amid rising imports of capital goods.

By 1989, the country's balance of payments had soured amid the weight of hefty imports, particularly of capital goods by Malaysia's rapidly expanding manufacturing sector. In 1991, the current account deficit worsened to US$4.6 billion, or 9.6 per-

MALAYSIA

Currency: Malaysia Ringgit.

Stock Exchanges: Kuala Lumpur Stock Exchange (KLSE).

Instruments: Equities (ordinary and preferred), bonds, debentures, warrants.

Index: The KLSE composite.

Regulatory Body/Stock Exchange Supervision: The Securities Commission.

Depository: The Malaysian Central Depository (CDS) is being phased in on a stock-by-stock (counter-by-counter) basis. Trading practices will not be affected. Until the CDS is completely phased in, there will be a dual system (i.e., CDS and existing system).

Settlement Information

Equities:

- T + 7 (ready basis), T + 3 (cash market).
- Physical only (at present).
- Receive versus payment available, but not deliver versus payment.
- Same-day turnaround trades are not possible.

Fixed:

- T+3.
- Physical only (at present).
- Receive versus payment available, but not deliver versus payment.
- Same-day turnaround trades are not possible.

Taxes:

- Dividends are taxed at a rate of 34 percent, withheld at source.
- Capital gains are not taxed.

- A stamp duty is charged at three points: on the contract note, where buyer/seller each pay M$1.00 for each M$1000 of the transaction value; on the transfer document, where the buyer pays M$3.00 for each M$1000 of the transaction value; and on the share certificate, where the buyer pays M$2.00 for every certificate registered.

Restrictions for Foreign Investors: Foreigners may normally own up to 30 percent of a company, although exceptions exist for higher limits. Foreigners acquiring 15 percent or more, or a M$5 million or more stake, must obtain approval of the Foreign Investment Committee.

Securities Lending: Prohibited by law in Malaysia.

SOURCE: The Bank of New York

cent of GDP, from $1.7 billion the year before, reports Baring Securities. But by 1992, inflation and trade problems appeared to be ameliorating. Inflation was forecast to ease in 1993, even as the trade picture brightened.

According to Baring, consumer prices in Malaysia climbed 4.7 percent in 1992, compared with 4.3 percent in 1991 and 3.1 percent in 1990. In 1991, Malaysia's central bank tightened monetary policy, which contributed to 1992's slowed pace of economic growth and attracted speculative capital, but the central bank has since eased.

The government's 1993 budget found widespread support. As the *Financial Times* described, "While the budget made reductions in some areas of government expenditure in an effort to control inflation and make further inroads into the current account deficit, business (and the stock market) was heartened by corporate and income tax cuts." Among other things, the corporate tax rate was trimmed to 34 from 35 percent; the development tax was abolished and income tax rates sliced by one to two percentage points. However, as the IFC reported, the government also proposed a tax similar to the VAT, as well as applying higher excise duties and a 5 percent levy on areas not yet taxed, such as telecommunications. The budget also called for higher contributions by employers and employees to compulsory savings.

Rapid industrialization has put a strain on Malaysia's existing power capacity, according to Crosby Securities research. The problem is not as bad as that in the Philippines, which suffers frequent brownouts, but there are emerging power shortages, with more frequent blackouts during peak periods. Thus, evidence of infrastructure insufficiency could deter foreign investing.

Colorful Politician

Politically, the dynamic Prime Minister Dr. Mahathir Mohamad has carved a name for himself on the world stage, championing third world issues while helping to stoke the red-hot economy at home. First elected prime minister in 1981, he heads the recently reconstituted United Malay Organization (known as

UMNO Baru or New UMNO), which has headed each coalition government since Malaysia's 1957 independence from Britain. There are four parties in the coalition, including the Malaysian Chinese Association (MCA) and the Malaysian Indian Congress (MIC). UMNO represents the ethnic Malays.

The government, established in 1963, is a constitutional monarchy. The king is elected every five years by the nine sultans who make up the Conference of Rulers, who select one of their number. Malaysia's Parliament, which is constituted broadly on the lines of Britain's Westminster system, consists of a Senate and a House of Representatives.

The Prime Minister is drawn from the Parliament members of the party in the majority in the House of Representatives.

To many observers, Malaysia is an authoritarian state, with a planned economy and controlled press. Dr. Mahathir, a surgeon by training, is the country's first prime minister to be educated in Malaysia. A champion of developing countries, he's known as being opposed to developed countries trying to dictate to the third world. No fan of decadent western values, he'd also like Malaysia to replicate the successes and practices of hard-working East Asian countries such as Japan. But in the past he has also criticized laziness in his own country. As Professor Kit Machado of California State University, Northridge, has written, the prime minister has had a "long-standing concern with what he regards as serious defects in Malay values and behavior."

These views, according to Machado, surfaced in Mahathir's 1970 book, *The Malay Dilemma*. Mahathir asserted that rural Malays lacked sufficient individual enterprise, independence, initiative, pride in work or competitive ability. "He stressed that effecting changes in *bumiputera* values and behavior were essential to national development," Machado reported in the book *The Evolving Pacific Basin in the Global Political Economy: Domestic and International Linkages* (Clark, C. and Chan, S. eds).

In mid-1993, question marks surrounded who would ultimately succeed 68-year-old Mahathir, and whether his outspoken style would endure. According to the *Financial Times*, in November 1993, UMNO is scheduled to hold elections for party posts. While Mahathir is expected to retain the party's leadership, a pre-election battle has been brewing among contenders for the number two post that presumably would lead to becoming prime minister.

In the meantime, Mahathir and his government have been grappling with delicate political/economic/social issues both at home and abroad. On the international front, the prime minister has been a cheerleader for trade opportunities, especially in his own backyard and among developing countries generally; he's also bristled at the formation of perceived trade blocs in the developed world. He fears these could impinge on Malaysia's vital ability to export. A controversial plan furthered by Malaysia called the East Asia Economic Group (the term "group" was later softened to "caucus") reportedly miffed leaders of neighboring Asian countries, who hadn't been consulted before it was announced. It would consist of the six Asian countries plus Japan, China, South Korea, Taiwan, and Hong Kong. It worried the United States and the European Community, who saw it as an exclusionary trading bloc, yet the Malaysian Trade Office sees it as a forum for countries to discuss issues of common interest, and enable them to speak as a unified bloc, much as the GATT or G7 countries do. South Korea recently affirmed its willingness to participate.

Malaysia is also actively participating in the creation of the ASEAN (Association of South East Asian Nations) Free Trade Area, known as AFTA. (Besides Malaysia, the other members of AFTA are Thailand, Indonesia, Singapore, Brunei, and the Philippines.) The pact will involve a market of over 330 million people and a total GDP of US$310 billion. It calls for establishing a free trade area by the year 2008. The first step is lowering tariffs among participants to between 0 and 5 percent over 15 years. Malaysia, whose tariffs averaged around 20 percent in 1992, is one of the early nations scheduled to lower its tariffs. The rest will lower their tariffs between now and 1996, with the Philippines dropping theirs last. As of this writing, Malaysia had already cut import duties on 600 items.

The Religious Factor

Islam is Malaysia's predominant religion. While the country is generally secular, and provides freedom of religion, an extremist

Islamic faction nonetheless is in power in one of Malaysia's 13 states. The task has been to limit the influence of the extremist sector, which could undermine economic programs, while still acknowledging the importance of Islam in Malaysia. A Muslim himself, Mahathir has been trying to "contain those zealots who would like to impose Islamic law on everybody," says Machado of California State University. As Rudner of Carleton University explains, the extremist faction prefers a closed society. The sector "opposes science, technology, and secularism."

Thus far, Malaysia's strong economy has kept enthusiasm for the extremist view in check. But sources report that the prime minister also helps to contain the situation partly by supporting/attending Islamic functions at home. Moreover, he often sides with Islamic countries on international issues.

The Stock Market

Development of Malaysia's capital markets is seen as important to the country's overall progress. Such development got under way in 1930, when the Singapore Stockbrokers' Association was formed. At the time, Singapore was still a Malaysian state. In 1960, the Malayan Stock Brokers' Association was reorganized to form the Malayan Stock Exchange. In 1964 the name was changed to the Stock Exchange of Malaysia and Singapore. In 1973 it became the Kuala Lumpur Stock Exchange Berhad, which was incorporated under the Companies Act of 1965, and on December 27, 1976, it became the Kuala Lumpur Stock Exchange. Malaysia also has a Bumiputera Stock Exchange located in Kuala Lumpur.

The Kuala Lumpur Stock Exchange (KLSE) had a market capitalization of US$94 billion and 366 listed companies at the end of 1992. However, in a 1992 to 1997 five-year plan, the stock exchange is targeting market capitalization to grow to M$350 billion. Naturally, "the way to get there," according to Nik Mohamed Din, executive chairman of the KLSE, "is to get more good companies listed. These include privatizations of government-controlled organizations as well as private companies." Nik would also like to see "more foreigners in the market, to increase the weighted average of share prices."

Larger stocks are listed on a main board, while smaller shares are listed on a second board. Companies seeking a listing on the main board must have made an average pretax profit of not less than M$4 million per year for three of the past five years, while a pretax profit of M$2 million per year must have been posted within that time frame. Companies wishing to list on the second board must have averaged pretax profits of no less than M$2 million per year for the past three years, and have earned at least M$1 million in pretax profits for one year during one of the past three years, according to a report by the Ministry of Finance.

Recent market developments include: the planned debut of a Kuala Lumpur Options and Financial Futures Exchange, slated to open in 1994; the opening of a central depository system for the KLSE in 1992—at which time the market would also become fully automated; and the creation of a Securities Commission in 1993 to regulate the capital markets.

Until January, 1990 the KLSE operated jointly with the Stock Exchange of Singapore (SES). Before the split, many international fund managers preferred to buy Malaysian shares in Singapore, where they considered the brokers to be more experienced. After the markets separated, all Malaysian company listings were removed from the SES. But a new over-the-counter market in Singapore, the CLOB (Central Limit Order Book) International, listed 133 actively traded Malaysian stocks as well as a few other foreign issues. Despite the existence of the CLOB, trading on the KLSE continued to climb. Today, brokers say that trading of Malaysian shares in Malaysia is heavier than in Singapore. That trend should become even more pronounced, experts believe, after the KLSE's system is fully scripless, by 1994 or 1995.

Although two stocks—Malaysia Telekom and Tenaga Nasional, the electric utility—together account for 40 percent of the market's index, the range of sectors represented on the market is relatively wide. These sectors include: manufacturing, banking and finance, property, hotels, plantations, textiles, shipping, packaging, oil, beverages, and gaming, among other areas. "Plantation and tin stocks are investment opportunities not readily available elsewhere in the world," points out Crosby Research Ltd., citing Malaysia's exceptional breadth of choices in the region. In comparison, "Hong Kong enjoys a preponderance of property, banking, and manufacturing stocks....Thailand's bourse is heavily slanted toward banking, construction, and manufacturing....the Philippines offers "a limited choice outside of oil and mining stocks, while in Singapore, property, banks, and shipyards comprise the bulk of opportunities," and Indonesia's market remains small, says Crosby Research.

While some experts disagree, Crosby also cites Malaysia's accounting standards and corporate disclosure. "Malaysia has basically adopted British accounting standards," the firm explains. "Companies are required to" divulge "more information on their accounts than all other countries in the immediate region, with the only exception of Singapore." That city-state "essentially [employs] the same standards as Malaysia," says the firm.

Barred from Some IPOs

According to some estimates, foreigners comprise roughly 25 percent of investments on the exchange. Malaysia sets a 30 percent limit on foreign ownership of shares, although exceptions exist for higher limits. Generally foreigners are prohibited from buying shares of IPOs, except in the cases of specifically designated government privatization. The 1992 Tenaga IPO, then the largest flotation of issues on the KLSE, was the first to allow foreigners to buy in.

Prices of new issues are generally set low for the benefit of local investors, particularly *bumiputeras*. Once listed, the price of the newly listed stocks typically jumps, thus eliminating foreigners from participating in this important profit opportunity. Foreigners, naturally, are not thrilled. As Eric J. Ritter, vice president of W. I. Carr (America) Ltd. in New York, puts it, "If I could have access to more primary market issues, I could get more overall foreign participation in the market."

Other complaints about the market include: relatively high dividend taxes and commissions, the barrage of rights issuances that has hit the market, and the fact that, as Kleiman International Consultants Inc. puts it, "few large share blocs outside of privatization launches are available."

Caution Light

The market's performance lately has been reasonably strong. After falling 13.1 percent in U.S. dollar terms in 1990, the IFC's Price Index for Malaysia gained 9.4 percent in 1991, followed by a hefty 24.6 percent rise in dollar terms in 1992 as a peak in interest rates helped to power that rally. For the first 5 months in 1993 (to June 4), the market advanced 19.6 percent in dollar terms, according to the IFC's global price index for Malaysia.

When it comes to stock picking, investors are cautioned about companies in which the government exerts influence. Typically, these involve several larger organizations, including the Renong conglomerate, Malaysian International Shipping Corporation, or Malaysian Airline System, among others, several brokers said. Government influence can affect profits; for example, if companies with government contracts have to provide low cost services, or if their rates get cut by government decree. Moreover, fearful of antagonizing the government, some companies that depend on government contracts may avoid declaring too much profit.

To eschew such problems, some brokers recommend selected smaller capitalization stocks—a sector that's also promising in its own right. As Crosby Research points out, smaller Malaysian shares have outperformed larger stocks "over almost all time periods." Some brokers also caution about commodities stocks. To Ritter of W. I. Carr, "It's better to stay away from this sector" where earnings can be whipsawed by gyrations in world market prices. "In the long run it makes sense" anyway to eschew commodities, he says, because "the manufacturing sector has taken over as the engine of Malaysian growth."

As attractive sectors, Glenn Lee, a director of Crosby Securities in New York, touts banking and finance, which should benefit from strong loan demand and, in the finance area, increased securitization of corporate debt; the construction and manufacturing sectors, which should gain from Malaysia's robust growth and the government's programs; and gaming, especially Resorts World, the only company licensed to operate a casino in Malaysia, Lee says. S. G. Warburg also likes gaming stocks and banks, and mentions Malaysian Industrial Development Finance as a stock to look at.

With so much going for the overall economy, the Malaysian market seems destined to benefit. The market lost some steam in the early 1990s, partly as higher interest rates drained liquidity and as previously high-flying corporate earnings descended back to earth. But as interest rates ebb, analysts, including Lee, expect a favorable reaction from investors. For his part, Mr. Lee recommends a slight overweighting of Malaysia's market for long-term investors—those looking out through the end of 1994. He believes they should target 22 percent of a regional Asian portfolio for the Malaysian market, compared with a regional market capitalization weighting of 21.1 percent, he said.

Crosby's Lee recommends overweighting Asia as a whole, and giving a slight edge to Malaysia. Why is Malaysia so favored? In addition to the decline in interest rates, the country generally enjoys generally strong economic growth. "These factors bode well for both the long and short term," Lee holds.

For those not wishing to buy shares directly, Wilson Emerging Markets Funds Research in 1993 listed 17 Malaysian country funds for international investors. Six of the closed-end country funds are listed on the London Stock Exchange. They are: Aetna Malaysian Growth Fund, Genesis Malaysia Maju Fund, Malaysia Capital Fund Limited, Malaysia Equity Fund Limited, Malaysia Select Fund Limited, and Malaysia Emerging Companies Fund Limited. The Malaysia Fund Inc. trades on the New York Stock Exchange.

As of December 1992, Bankers Trust Company reported that 15 Malaysian companies had issued American Depositary Receipts. They are: Bandar Raya Developments Berhad, Berjaya Corporation (Malaysia) Berhad, Boustead Holdings Berhad, Genting Berhad, Inter-Pacific Industrial Group Berhad, Kesang Corporation Berhad, Kuala Lumpur Kepong Berhad, Lion Land Berhad, Malayan Credit Ltd., Malayan United Industries Berhad, Perlis Plantation Berhad, Resorts World BHD, Selangor Properties Berhad, Sime Darby Berhad, Supreme Corporation Berhad.

19

The Philippines

It is ironic that the Philippine stock market should have bounded ahead in 1991, amid a raft of bad news. That year, economic growth declined as the country grappled with a debt crisis, austerity measures, political tumult, the aftermath of 1990 mud slides, and an earthquake. For the first time in six centuries, 1991 also brought the disastrous volcanic eruption of Mt. Pinatubo. But instead of being psychologically buried under molten lava, the Philippine stock market leapt 56.8 percent in U.S. dollar terms according to the IFC Price Index, outperforming all other Asian markets. In 1992, the market gained another 17.2 percent, according to the IFC.

The year 1992 brought some good news to the Philippines. Highlights included the peaceful election of a new president, additional economic liberalizations, a sharp drop in the inflation rate—nearly 18 percent at the end of 1991 to 9.0 percent one year later—lower interest rates, favorable debt arrangements, and a new oil discovery that could aid the Philippine's future prospects.

But although the economy has been improving somewhat, impediments to growth, especially the severe energy shortage, remain for now.

The Philippines, an archipelago of 7100 islands on the Pacific Rim, has been one of the poor sisters of Asia. During the 1970s and 1980s, as other regional countries vied for foreign investments and new export markets, the Philippines clung to its traditional nationalism and protectionism. As a result, potential investment opportunities went elsewhere. Ferdinand Marcos, who ruled from 1965 until his 1986 ouster, was seen as having pillaged the nation with his cronyist capitalism. According to some sources, President Marcos amassed over $10 billion on an official salary of $5000. Even as he parceled out opportunities to his close friends, many other Filipinos' income levels shrank; overall poverty remained rampant. Even today, the Philippine elite controls much of the economy, while the poor continue to endure severe living conditions. To take one example, outside of Manila, the country's capital, a shantytown has sprung up around "Smokey Mountain," a huge garbage dump where poor people can gain access to food scraps.

In November 1991, the London-based magazine *The Banker* captured the Philippines' plight:

> Back in the 1950s and 1960s, the Philippines was second only to Japan as an economic power in the region. Nowadays, it ranks alongside the basket cases of Laos, Vietnam, and Cambodia, and suffers the indignity of being on the borderline for help from the International Development Association—the World Bank's soft-loan arm that provides concessionary finance at low rates to countries with (annual) per capita incomes of $700 and below. The Philippines, with a per capita income of $731 as of 1991, is already hovering around that mark.

The 1980s brought the first flickers of change. In 1983, the nation was already beset by debt and trade problems heavily linked to the 1979 oil price shock, when Senator Benigno Aquino returning to his homeland from the U.S., was assassinated. The event triggered a massive flight of capital, worsening the country's financial problems. A debt crisis ensued. Some three years later, when the Marcos regime had finally collapsed after a fraudulent election, the arrival of President Corazon Aquino ushered in "people power." But a new era had yet to dawn. Conflicts from the political left and right ultimately weakened her presidency, and coup attempts were frequent.

Aquino accomplished very little until her last year as president. But in that important final year, she did set the stage for a new economic era by undertaking economic liberalizations and reforms that her successor, General Fidel V. Ramos, could carry forward.

The Advent of Ramos

In May 1992, Ramos, a former chief of staff and defense secretary in the Aquino administration, won the presidency by a modest 24 percent plurality. He had been Aquino's preferred candidate, and her endorsement had helped to secure him the victory. Seen as pro-business, President Ramos' victory initially cheered the stock market. In addition, "Ramos is lucky because a large portion of the program he's now pursuing was already adopted" under Aquino, pointed out Professor Carl Lande of the University of Kansas in 1992. The "protectionist mindset had already been dropped, and the country is now committed to an export-oriented industrialization strategy," he held.

Overall poor economic management, especially in the Marcos years, left the Philippines with a heavy debt burden. Today the country owes $30 billion in foreign debt, with a total debt bill of some $45 billion. One of Aquino's accomplishments was to create an Economic Stabilization Program that aimed at trimming fiscal and public sector deficits. The budget deficit was to be capped, public expenditures were to be cut, and revenue-enhancing measures to be taken. To control inflation, money supply was to be kept in check. The Aquino administration also passed the 1991 Foreign Investment Law, which allows up to 100 percent foreign ownership in companies not on the so-called negative list.

Upon his arrival at Malacañang Palace—the presidential residence—President Ramos endorsed a continuation of the Economic Stabilization Program and shortly thereafter announced the total elimination of all regulations governing foreign exchange restrictions in the Philippines, ending over 40 years of currency controls.

In mid-1992, *The Philippine Star* newspaper reported that "a new six-year economic development plan envisages further trade and investment liberalization and will underscore the role of the private sector in reviving the economy." The new plan, covering 1993 to 1998, would have the private sector propel economic growth, while the "government...would promote a competitive exchange rate policy and a liberalized trade and investment climate," the newspaper said.

PHILIPPINES

Currency: Philippine peso (PHP).

Stock Exchanges: The two stock exchanges, the Manila Stock Exchange and the Makati Stock Exchange, have merged into a single Philippine Stock Exchange. Full unification is expected in late 1993.

Index: The Manila Composite Index (comprised of 27 stocks).

Types of Securities: Common A shares only owned by Filipinos, B shares owned by Filipinos or foreigners, preferred shares, and government bonds.

Regulatory Body/Stock Exchange Supervision: The Central Bank of the Philippines, the Board of Investments, and the Securities and Exchange Commission regulate and monitor the securities markets and foreign investment.

Depository: There are no depositories in the Philippines.

Settlement Information

Equities:

- T + 4.
- Physical settlement only.
- Receive/deliver versus payment available.
- Same-day turnaround trades are not possible.

Fixed Income:

- Negotiated settlement.
- Physical settlement only.
- Receive/deliver versus payment available.
- Same-day turnaround trades are not possible.

Taxes:

- Dividends and interest are taxed at a rate of 35 percent, withheld at the source. *Exceptions*: Trusts and individuals pay 30 percent. Hong Kong incorporated companies pay 15 percent. Residents of any of the 20 countries that have double tax treaties with the Philippines can reduce the tax rate by filing proof of residency with their local agents.

- Stock dividends are exempt from tax.
- There is no capital gains tax.
- There is a 0.25 percent transaction tax paid by the seller.
- There is a stamp duty of PHP0.50 per PHP200, par value.
- A transfer fee of PHP49.50 per stock certificate is charged by the transfer agent.

Restrictions for Foreign Investors:

- Foreigners may own up to 100 percent of a Philippine company, except for those in industries on the foreign investment negative list. Included on the list are defense-related companies and manufacturers and distributors of dangerous drugs.
- Foreigners cannot buy A shares.

Securities Lending: Not available at present. Lending does occur as an accommodation between brokers.

SOURCE: The Bank of New York

According to some press reports, the Ramos administration is targeting to have direct foreign investments reach $1.5 to $2 billion a year by the 1995 to 1997 period. The largest inflows are expected to come from Asia, including Japan and Taiwan. But evidently, they aren't yet rushing in. Between January and December 1992, foreign direct investments recorded with the central bank fell to $328 million compared with $415 million during the same period in 1991. According to a J. P. Morgan report, "The decline is attributed to the widespread recession in industrial countries and continuing problems with the Philippine power sector. Nevertheless, the investment trend viewed on a monthly basis shows a strong pickup during the May to October period" versus January to April. Although real GDP has recently been stagnant, with growth flat in 1992, Baring Securities has projected 2 percent GDP growth in 1993 and 4.3 percent in 1994.

Among its attractions for investors, the Philippines boasts an ample supply of well-educated people whose English language skills are widely considered the best in Asia. Wages are also low, and the population of about 62 million people could eventually provide an attractive consumer market. But crime has been a problem. Despite the creation of the Presidential Anti-Crime Commission, the rash of kidnappings, especially of Chinese Filipinos, increased during 1992. It was feared that unless this problem was eradicated, foreign business executives might become increasingly wary of the Philippines.

After the hair-raising coup attempts during the Aquino administration, given the corruption before it, foreign investors remain concerned about Philippine political stability. An optimistic Ray Jovanovich, senior investment manager of the Manila Fund, maintains that "Ramos is aware of this, and he'll exercise a great deal of authority and control. He's disciplined and adept." A graduate of West Point military academy in the United States, Ramos "helped overthrow Marcos and defended Aquino through seven coup attempts. His days start between 5 and 5:30 in the morning, and he's appointed able technocrats to carry out economic programs," says Jovanovich, who points to Finance Secretary Ramon del Rosario as well as Jose Cuisia, the central bank governor. "These people," he says, "are focused policymakers who come from the private sector."

Other Challenges

The complete closing of the two huge U.S. military bases, Clark and Subic, in the Philippines meant a substantial job loss for Filipinos and weakened ties with the U.S. But although the Clark base was effectively destroyed by Mt. Pinatubo's eruption, Subic is undergoing conversion to commercial use, especially for ship repairing. According to the San Francisco–based Montgomery Asset Management, "With interest ranging from ship-repair firms, such as the Keppel Philippine Shipyards and Sembawang Shipyards, Ltd., to industrialists, a lot of energy is being dedicated to the project in hopes of turning Subic Bay into a major commercial port."

These days, the Philippines' main problem is a lack of adequate infrastructure, including telecommunications, transportation, and above all electrical power. Electrical brownouts can last from four to eight hours and sometimes much longer in some buildings, severely disrupting business schedules and deterring many companies' willingness to expand. By year-end 1992, many companies had acquired their own power generators—a development that Ray Farris, an economist with Crosby Research in Hong Kong, dubs a "band-aid" and a "tremendous waste of resources for a country that has severe capital shortages."

At least some blame the problem on governmental neglect. In 1992, Crosby Research wrote that "the product of the government's failure to implement its power development schemes of the last five years is that generating capacity has grown only 1 percent in total while demand has grown at an average rate of almost 8 percent per annum since 1987. The thermal plants that account for some 55 percent of the Philippines installed capacity are old and poorly maintained, resulting in a 70 percent reliability ratio at best which frequently falls below this under the strain of prolonged peak operating conditions. Hydroelectric facilities, 32 percent of installed capability, are highly vulnerable to drought."

Soon after its coming, the Ramos administration zeroed in on the problem. Among other steps, a host of new power projects were approved and the creation of a new Energy Department was announced. Construction of seven new power facilities, which together should produce about 800 megawatts of electricity is in progress. Many believe that as all these new facilities come on-stream the country's power crisis will recede. In the meantime, Crosby Research believes brownouts and other symptoms of power shortages will continue into 1994, with relief not coming until 1995.

Oil Finds

In 1992, a new oil discovery in the Philippines threw a lifeline to the feeble economy. Early reports hold that the Malampaya fields may contain about 370 million barrels of recoverable reserves of oil, making Malampaya one of the world's major oil and gas finds in recent years. According to Philippine Asia Equity Securities Inc., Malampaya, now being explored, has yielded one viable test well. It could be put into production by 1995 and tapped for full production by 1998. Taken together, Malampaya, along with the West Linapacan field, which is now producing 13,800 barrels of oil per day, and the Octon field, which is also expected to be in production by 1994, could account for at least 40 percent of the country's daily oil needs by early 1995, says Philippine Asia Equity.

Debt Reduction

In the early 1990s, the Philippines seemed to be successfully digging out of the financial mire. Through 1992, interest rates on the 91-day T-bill had fallen by nearly 700 basis points as inflation cooled. The government was also levying some additional tax increases to allow it to increase expenditures while, hopefully, remaining within its economic stabilization targets. Traditionally tax collection has been a significant problem in this country of rampant tax evasion.

More exciting, however, has been the headway made in denting the debt problem and securing new financial aid. In July 1992 the country restructured $4.5 billion in commercial debt, a package that, over a five-year period, saves the Philippines $1.8

billion in debt service payments—and will yield as much as $3 billion in cash flow over the next 6 years. These monies can be rechanneled into economic growth, Farris of Crosby Research points out. In addition, the deal paved the way for the Philippines to reenter the voluntary debt markets in 1993—the first time in a decade.

The new arrangement means that debt servicing will come to 15.7 percent of total exports, compared with 38.1 percent at the peak in 1987, says Farris. "It's a significant improvement. By itself, the debt restructuring won't create a boom. But it's part of a reform process that releases growth constraints in the economy," he says.

Between the eased debt problems and the opportune oil discovery, the Philippines seem finally to be gaining some advantages. But the critical test will remain its ability to attract manufacturing, export products, and essentially, to act more like its successful brethren in the Pacific. Says Eric Sandlund, managing director of Tyndall International Asia Limited, in Hong Kong, "Oil is just icing on the cake." As its main meal, "the Philippines has to come through with adequate economic liberalizations, privatizations, and other moves to make it easier for foreigners to participate in that economy." In his opinion, "there's no reason that the Philippines can't enjoy export opportunities that other countries have had." But for now, the oil play is something "I can't invest in. I'll wait until that really happens. For now, I have to invest in what I know is doable."

The Stock Market

The Philippine stock market began with the Manila Stock Exchange in 1927, which was joined by the Makati Exchange in 1963. The market had a 1992 capitalization of about $13.8 billion, according to the IFC. As of the end of the year, there were 170 listed companies, but only about 10 of these are considered highly attractive to foreign investors. Five stocks, those of Ayala Corp., Philippine Long Distance Telephone Co., Philippine National Bank, San Miguel Corp., and Manila Electric, dominate the market and comprise roughly 55 percent of market capitalization.

Some market improvements are in the works. In 1992, the country's two rival stock exchanges, the Manila and the Makati, agreed to merge their operations into a new Philippine Stock Exchange (PSE). According to Baring Securities, the intent was to create a computerized system so that all trades will be executed from a central board, thus eliminating the open outcry system. The result is expected to produce a more transparent market, and one with greater liquidity as participants focus on one exchange instead of two.

Full unification of the two exchanges is expected to occur in late 1993. Among the changes from the markets' unification, as reported by the U.S.–Philippine Business Committee: removing arbitrage opportunities; simplifying listings procedures; cutting operating costs; and releasing a $200 million loan from the Asian Development Bank and another $500,000 from the U.S. Agency for International Development to help train the Philippines' Securities and Exchange Commission (SEC) and exchange personnel.

Besides prospects for market improvements, other attractions for the Philippines market include the reporting requirements in which listed companies provide monthly earnings updates to the Philippine SEC, and the fact that repatriation of profits was greatly streamlined with the lifting of foreign exchange controls.

Nonetheless the small market, dominated by local investors, remains volatile and speculative. On the bright side, recent rules have greatly liberalized what foreigners can do in the Philippine market. Foreigners can now own up to 100 percent of a Philippine company except for those in industries on the foreign investment negative list, which include companies in the defense industry and producers and distributors of dangerous drugs.

To ensure trading liquidity, investors are usually cautioned to buy shares in the largest 10 to 20 companies. But some money managers believe that even four or five stocks will give adequate exposure. Among the most oft-mentioned shares: those of San Miguel Corporation, which is in the beverages, food, and packaging industries, and accounts for 4 percent of the Philippine GDP; the Philippine Long Distance Telephone Company (PLTC);

the Philippine National Bank; Ayala Land Inc.; and the Manila Electric Company, which is primarily a distributor of electricity from the government to the private sector. "Those would be the first-tier stocks. A notch below that would be companies such as Robinson's Land Corporation in the property area," says Francisco S. Rodrigo, portfolio manager of the First Philippine Fund managed by Clemente Capital Inc. in New York.

Gradually, more companies are expected to list their shares. As of May 1992, 11 major companies had already been privatized, according to Baring Securities. And as of this writing, several more major organizations are still awaiting privatization. Newly listed in January 1992, Manila Electric's stock price vaulted 140 percent during 1992, while the price of International Container, which listed in May 1992, tripled in value over the rest of the year, reports Homer Perez of Philippine Asia Equity.

In 1992 the market initially rallied strongly, only to fall back partly amid disappointing earnings reports and general concern about the economy and power outages. But by 1993, Perez of Philippine Asia Equity saw market sentiment improving, amid signs that the government was taking steps to ameliorate the power problem. Looking ahead, he believes that economic improvement in the Philippines could benefit such consumer companies as the San Miguel food conglomerate, as well as interest-rate–sensitive businesses that could benefit from the lower interest rates. In the latter case, Perez suggests companies linked to the auto industry, ranging from those who make auto loans to tire manufacturers. Crosby Securities believes the sectors that will benefit most from an economic recovery are manufacturing, agriculture, and construction.

Josephine Jimenez of Montgomery Asset Management reports that, among the attractions of the large blue chips, Manila Electric was expected to post 33 percent real earnings growth in 1993, while Philippine Long Distance could expect to log 15 to 20 percent annual growth in the volume of installed telephone lines. And, now in a position to reap benefits from major capacity expansion, San Miguel's nominal earnings could grow 24 percent in 1993, Jimenez holds.

Jimenez also believes that tourism will become increasingly important in the Philippines. Real estate companies already engaging in tourism-related development projects are: Ayala Land, Ayala Corp., and Kuok Philippine Properties. Moreover, foreseeing more vessels sailing the Pacific, particularly with the growing economic importance of China, Jimenez believes the Philippines is geographically and economically positioned to benefit from the trend. The two dominant players in ship repair, she says, are Keppel Philippine Shipyards and Cebo Shipyards & Engineering Co.

For those not wishing to invest directly in the Philippines market, Wilson Emerging Market Funds Research in 1993 listed 10 country funds for international investors in the Philippines, all of which are domiciled abroad. Among the six closed-end funds, the First Philippine Investment Trust plc, the JF Philippine Fund Inc., and the Manila Fund (Cayman) Limited, are listed on the London Stock Exchange, while the First Philippine Fund Inc. is listed on the New York Stock Exchange.

Bankers Trust Company reports that, as of December 1992, four Philippine companies had issued depositary receipts. Those with ADRs are: Ayala Corp., the Philodrill Corp. and San Miguel Corp., while Manila Electric's is a global depositary receipt.

20
Thailand

The year 1992 was a turning point for Thailand. Ironically, the bloody May crackdown on pro-democracy protestors in Bangkok led to strengthened democratic institutions and a further loosening of the military's political/economic grip.

The military's long reign of influence had already been waning before the May 1992 massacre. A growing middle class and an increasingly strong and internationally linked economy had undermined the need for a heavy military presence. The bloodbath of mid-May 1992 was the culmination of what had been peaceful demonstrations against the elevation to prime minister of General Suchinda Kraprayoon, who had not been an elected member of parliament. Protestors instead wanted to see democratic principles followed.

After Thailand's king intervened, Suchinda resigned and then-businessman Anand Panyarachun accepted the post as interim prime minister. New elections held in September brought Chuan Leekpai to power as head of a pro-democracy coalition government. It appears that democracy is finally putting down strong roots in this country that, over the previous six decades, had seen more coups than democratic elections.

By 1992, the military was in economic and political retreat. As *The New York Times* reported in August 1992, besides meddling in politics, Thai military commanders had also "enmeshed themselves in, and often mismanaged, state-owned corporations. Their influence over large public works contracts has led to allegations of corruption." The advent of the Anand caretaker government brought new checks on military power. Among the changes were: the removal of General Issarapong Noonpakdi as chairman of the Telephone Authority of Thailand, the ouster of Air Marshall Anan Kalinta as chairman of the communications authority, and the replacement of Air Chief Marshall Kaset Rojananil as chairman of Thai Airways International.

Years ago, the military's influence was recognized as useful in helping the country fend off Communism and in giving support to fledgling businesses. Military officers serving on corporate boards could, among other things, help companies to secure lucrative contracts. But by the late 1980s and early 1990s, many companies no longer needed that kind of support. In fact, the military's May 1992 crackdown temporarily cast a cloud over the country and disrupted its economy. Fortunately, the economic impact proved to be milder than had been feared. For 1992, Thailand's real GDP growth rose 7.5 percent, which was lower than the previous year's 8.2 percent rise but slightly higher than forecasted after the May massacre.

The crackdown encouraged a slowing of investment activity. In 1991, total investment advanced 4.9 percent in 1992, after a 13.2 percent gain the year before. But on the bright side, inflation fell to 4.1 percent in 1992, from 5.7 percent the year before. And the current account deficit shrank to $6.7 billion in 1992, from $7.6 billion in 1991.

Initially, the military crackdown sparked a selloff in stocks. On May 19, 1992, the Stock Exchange of Thailand (SET) index lost 8.9 percent of its value—making it the steepest one-day loss in the SET's history. But the downturn was short-lived. For the year 1992, the IFC Price Index for Thailand actually gained 35.9 percent in U.S. dollars terms, ranking it as the second best performer after Colombia among the markets in the IFC Composite Index.

The market's performance reflected the underlying booming economy, where GDP growth has averaged about 7.3 percent over the last 10 years, with the figure climbing as high as 13.2 percent in 1988, followed by 12.3 percent the following year. Thailand's real GDP growth between 1986–1990 averaged an impressive 9.9 percent. The stellar performance has been largely due to the nation's aggressive efforts to court investment and expand its once agriculturally dependent economy. As the country wooed foreigners with tax incentives and other attractions, net direct foreign investment leapt from $183 million in 1987 to an annual high of $2.3 billion in 1990, according to Baring Securities. In 1992 and in 1993, the level was expected to be $1.6 billion, the firm reported. Although the single largest amount has come from Japan, in 1991 Taiwan was the second largest source, followed by the United States, Baring reported.

The Economy

Economic Attractions

Besides its relatively cheap labor force, Thailand boasts such other attractions as its conservative and staunchly independent central bank, an entrepreneurial spirit and respect for private business among the Thai people, and culturally, the tolerant nature of the people that contributes to their trainability and attractiveness as workers. Unlike its Southeast Asian neighbors, Thailand was never colonized. (The word *thai* means "free.") Moreover, with its strong agricultural base, Thailand has also escaped the starvation that has influenced behavior in other lands. These factors have contributed to the country's receptivity to new ideas and to foreign participation in the economy.

In Thailand, entrepreneurship caught on in the 1930s, when the government could no longer afford a large bureaucracy. Explains Graham Catterwell, Crosby Research Ltd.'s Bangkok representative: Historically Thailand's elite sector of population was woven into the bureaucracy and worked for the King. In the early 1930s, after that bureaucracy had swelled beyond the government's ability to afford it, a large number of layoffs occurred. The elite then started to enter or form businesses. Chinese immigrants were major contributors to Thailand's business development. Many had become well integrated into the society and had married indigenous Thais.

The result has been the creation of a more integrated, harmonious society than exists even today in, for example, Malaysia.

THAILAND

Currency: Thai baht (THB).

Stock Exchanges: The Stock Exchange of Thailand (SET) is divided into two boards, the Local (main) Board and the Foreign Board.

Indexes: The SET Index is the main index in Thailand.

Types of Securities: Equities (common and preferred), unit trusts, warrants, debentures (straight and convertible), government and convertible bonds.

Regulatory Body/Stock Exchange Supervision: There are four main regulatory agencies:

- The Ministry of Finance (MOF) regulates the SET and the overall securities industry.
- The Securities and Exchange Commission supervises financial institutions.
- The SET Board of Directors sets exchange policies and operating regulations.
- The Association of Members of the Securities Exchange establishes rules for member firms.

Depository: The Share Depository Centre (SDC) is a division of the SET. Its use is mandatory for both local and foreign investors. It has primarily been a depository for shares and warrants, although corporate bonds are being admitted for deposit starting in 1993.

Settlement Information

Equities:

- T + 3.
- Book entry only.
- Receive/deliver versus payment available.
- Same-day turnaround trades are possible.

Fixed Income:

- Negotiated settlement period.

- Physical delivery only.
- Receive/deliver versus payment available.
- Same-day turnaround trades are possible.

Taxes:

- There is a 15 percent capital gains tax for foreign institutional and corporate investors, but individual investors are exempt.
- There is a 10 percent withholding tax on dividends for foreign investors.
- Where they exist, taxation treaties can reduce the above tax liabilities (at source).

Restrictions for Foreign Investors:

- Total foreign ownership of any one company is generally limited to 49 percent of its capital, but can be further reduced by a company's own memorandum or articles of association. Foreign ownership of banks and finance companies is 25 percent.
- Foreign investors can buy "local shares," but they are not entitled to dividends, rights offerings, or proxy voting of them.

Securities Lending: Prohibited by law.

SOURCE: The Bank of New York

In that country, tensions still exist between the indigenous *bumiputera* and the Chinese community.

By the mid-1980s the Thai government, beset by debt and afflicted by the downturn in commodities prices, elected to take a new course: increase emphasis on manufacturing—especially export-oriented products—and (more recently) place greater emphasis on value-added production. In 1984, Thailand's currency, the baht, which was formerly pegged to the U.S. dollar, was devalued and pegged to a basket of currencies. In the mid-1980s, the country also initiated its drive to attract direct foreign investments.

The program to attract foreign investment has been highly successful—so much so that it has put a strain on the country's infrastructure and helped to fuel inflation. Many believe that the economic slowdown sparked by the Persian Gulf crisis brought a needed cooling to the economy. Thailand needed to allow its infrastructure—including roads, ports, telecommunications services, and the like—to catch up with economic development. In January 1992, a value-added tax of 7 percent was implemented.

A host of private and public infrastructural development projects are in the works. In addition, given the decline in foreign investment, the government is now using incentives to steer new investment toward the provinces and out of congested Bangkok.

Infrastructure Spending

The flood of direct foreign investments in recent years intensified the need for greater power production, as well as better transportation and communication facilities. While experts say that international telephone service has improved, better mass transit and other infrastructural improvements are needed, especially in Bangkok. Not including the private projects, the government has, in fact, targeted to spend $35 billion on infrastructure during the current seventh economic plan that runs from 1992 to 1996. That's reportedly about a 150 percent rise over infrastructural spending in the previous five-year plan. Of the total spending, transportation accounts for some $16.5 billion, while $6 billion is targeted for telecommunications, $11 billion for utilities, water works, and electricity projects, and the remainder for energy projects, according to Thienchai Charnchanayotin, head of Thai research for SBCI Finance Asia Ltd. in Bangkok.

While Thailand's national GDP per capita was $1916 in 1992, the income of Bangkok workers runs substantially higher. Growing incomes have brought a rise in consumer spending. In January 1992, disposable income got a further boost from reduced personal income taxes (corporate taxes dropped 30 percent as well), and in April 1992 salaries of workers in government and state-run enterprises rose 25 percent. According to Crosby Research, salaries of many lower-ranking workers in large private companies also rose substantially in 1992. In mid-1992, Tira Wannamethee, director, Barclays de Zoete Wedd (Asia) Ltd. in Bangkok, reported that although consumer spending has ebbed from its previous breakneck 12 to 15 percent growth level, it should continue to expand 5 to 6 percent a year, giving Thailand, with its population of more than 57 million, an edge over smaller Malaysia and poorer Indonesia.

Thailand should also benefit from its location as a gateway to Indochina. Crosby sees it as the center of a potential new growth region that encompasses Indochina (Laos, Cambodia, Vietnam), Burma, and the southern minority areas of China (Yunnan province). "Thailand will become a major source of direct and indirect investment flows, particularly to Laos and Cambodia," predicts Tira Wannamethee. Some investors in the 1988–89 first wave of investment into that region became "disillusioned," especially with the effect of the inadequate legal systems. Among other problems, Vietnam's government didn't recognize private property. Subsequent reforms triggered a second wave of investment interest, which is now taking place and allows investors to "go in under slightly better terms. And once [these countries] get their act together, you'll see a strong third wave," he predicts. It may take 5 to 10 years for Indochinese business links to contribute significantly to Thailand's economy. However, as a long-term view, he says that the "Bank of Thailand (the country's central bank) would like to promote Thailand as a regional financial center for Burma (Myanmar) and Indochina. Already, the baht is the most acceptable foreign currency in those countries." The firm of J. P. Morgan and others believe that, if the authorities continue to promote infrastructure development nationwide, rather than just in Bangkok, Thailand's long-term attractiveness will increase for investment and tourism.

Education, AIDS, and Other Problems

But Thailand is certainly not without its problems—ranging from political drama to such festering social woes as the limited educational attainment of much of the populace to the growing AIDS epidemic. Widespread prostitution has hastened the spread of AIDS (acquired immune deficiency syndrome) largely among the poorer sector. But statistics show that 500,000 to 600,000 Thais are currently infected with the AIDS virus, and by the end of the decade, four to five million will have contracted the disease from heterosexual contact alone. This will slow Thailand's ability to grow.

It remains unclear how much the government will spend on combating the AIDS problem; thus far, much of the effort has centered on prevention through education.

Thailand's weak level of educational attainment became a pronounced problem as foreign investment flooded in during the late 1980s. As of 1988, 63.1 percent of the work force had no more than a primary school education. The problem, experts say, is that rural people see little point in sending children to secondary school. A shortage of skilled labor—a problem for foreign investors—is reflected in the fact that, according to some accounts, Thailand has only 15 scientists and/or engineers per 10,000 population, compared with 122 in South Korea.

Both the government and business have been grappling with the problem. Among the steps taken thus far: extending compulsory education from six to nine years, and including more vocational training in the curriculum. Some companies have themselves provided training, sometimes in cooperation with universities. Among other moves, the government has also been campaigning to encourage expatriates, especially Thai scientists and physicians, to return home.

Thailand has also taken steps to shore up its savings pool, as the savings rate has been declining steadily since 1989. Notably, in 1992, Thailand's Ministry of Finance issued licenses creating seven new mutual fund companies, which were in addition to the existing Mutual Fund Company that had previously held a monopoly. By early 1993, the eight fund organizations had combined assets of $2.7 billion, and their assets were expected to keep growing rapidly as new products were offered. Catterwell of Crosby Research anticipates that "there will be a progressive growth in the size of domestic institutional monies."

The Stock Market

The Stock Exchange of Thailand (SET), located in Bangkok, has experienced a boom in size and trading volume in recent years. Launched in 1975, it began operations with only 14 quoted corporate and 2 government securities. As of 1992, according to the IFC, it had 305 listed companies and a market cap of $58.3 billion.

The market had gotten off to a slow and bumpy start, having been born in 1962 of a private initiative. Initially that market, called the Bangkok Stock Exchange Co. Ltd., had little volume and folded in the early 1970s. In the latter part of the 1960s, the government took a hand in planning a securities market. It hired Professor Sidney M. Robbins of Columbia University, a former chief economist with the U.S. Securities & Exchange Commission, to prepare what became a master plan for developing Thailand's capital markets. From there a task force was formed to put the plan into action. In May 1974, legislation established the new Securities Exchange of Thailand, which began in April 1975. The name was changed to the Stock Exchange of Thailand in January 1991.

In the early days, few companies wanted to list their shares because of the corporate disclosure requirements that listing entailed. Prior to the mid-1980s, officials say they had to beg companies to list their stock on the exchange. The trend changed as companies saw the equity markets as attractive sources of capital, and an alternative to borrowing.

Larger companies have been able to list on the SET through standard listing. Smaller firms can list through a category called "provincial" or "local." Among other qualifications, listed companies must have had a total net profit for the last three consecutive years of not less than 25 million baht. Listed companies provide quarterly balance sheets and income statements to the SET, annual reports, and an annual audited financial statement.

The "authorized" category, generally for smaller companies, was abolished in 1993 and replaced with a "provincial" category, for companies whose business is outside of the Bangkok region. Companies already in the authorized category were to be given three years to meet the standards of regular listing.

Almost all listed securities on the SET are common stocks. Four sectors—the banking, building and furnishing materials, finance and securities, and property development sectors— account for more than 60 percent of total market capitalization. At year-end 1992, the 10 largest stocks in market capitalization were: Bangkok Land, Bangkok Bank, Thai Airways International, Siam Cement, Thai Farmers Bank, Tanayong, Siam Commercial Bank, Krung Thai Bank, Land and House, and Bank of Ayudhya.

Foreign investment in the market began to catch on in 1986, with an improvement in the Thai economy. According to the SET, foreigners' portion of total transactions climbed to 14.4 percent in 1990, from 7.8 percent in 1986, but it dropped to 8.2 percent in 1991 amid political uncertainty following a military coup. As of December 30, 1992, foreigners' transactions accounted for 7.4 percent of the total.

Thailand's stock market is certainly not wide open to foreigners. Collectively, non-Thais generally can hold up to a maximum of only 49 percent of a Thai company's stock. That level can be further reduced by a company's own memorandum or articles of association, or laws governing business, such as the 25 percent limit for commercial banks and finance companies. A foreign board was created in September 1987 to distinguish trading in foreign shares from local shares (often at a considerable premium).

Thailand's market has a high trading turnover rate that in some months can exceed 20 percent of market capitalization, some experts report. Moreover, as is characteristic of an emerging market, stock prices historically have been volatile. A boom period from 1977 to 1978 boom came to a screeching halt following the late 1978 collapse of Raja Finance, a leading provider of margin financing to the stock market, whose stock had been a high flier. After the 1979–1981 trough, a subsequent slow recovery led to what the exchange calls a "second boom" starting in 1986 that was powered by economic recovery. In 1990, the Persian Gulf Crisis and higher interest rates drove the market 23.4 percent lower in U.S. dollar terms, according to the IFC Price Index. But starting in 1991 the market rebounded, climbing 17.0 percent that year and 35.9 percent in 1992 in dollar terms, according to the IFC index.

On the regulatory front, the mid-1992 creation of an independent Securities & Exchange Commission introduced an important strengthening of Thailand's securities markets. As Washington, D.C.–based Kleiman International Consultants describes, the SEC "has been created to police the primary and secondary markets—prone to instances of insider trading and listing discrepancies—leaving the exchange itself to focus on daily operations, which have been hard-pressed by skyrocketing volume."

The new SEC was quick to bare its teeth. In November 1992, the SEC filed a case against Song Watcharasriroj, known as Sia Song, and 11 associates, for allegedly manipulating the stock price of Bangkok Bank of Commerce and failing to disclose the extent of holdings in the bank. The market fell on that news, as well as on the government's urging of a curb on margin financing, amid a sense that the government was cracking down on speculation. According to the IFC, the government subsequently took several steps to boost market activity. These included setting up a fund of 5 billion baht to support the market. Brokers contributed to an additional pool of 10 billion baht.

How to Play the Market

Even after the market's 1992 gains, an enthusiastic Thienchai Charnchanayotin of SBCI Finance Asia Ltd. in Bangkok pointed to a price-earnings ratio of about 12 for 1993 earnings. "The market still looks cheap compared with others in the region," he said in February 1993. The 1992 estimated earnings per-share growth of 25 percent "should prove conservative, and 1993's earnings should climb by another 20 percent."

Most widely touted have been the banking and finance sectors, which were expected to produce handsome profits. Some analysts forecast 1993 earnings growth of 20 percent for banks, following their even stronger 1992 performance. In Thailand's robust economy, loan demand—the bulk of Thai banks' business—will continue strong. Economic development in the provinces bodes additional opportunity for banks—at least some of which have already been benefiting. Popular choices among stocks include Bangkok Bank, the country's largest and most profitable commercial bank, whose earnings climbed 33 percent in 1992 and were expected to gain another 15 to 20 percent in 1993. (As of October 1992, the stock of Bangkok Bank had a price-earnings ratio of 9.62, making it the cheapest of the Top 20 stocks on the SET. However, its stock was trading at a premium among foreign investors.)

In the finance sector, the top three houses in the underwriting business—Phatra Thanakit, Dhana Siam Finance and Securities, and Finance One—were all seen as well positioned to benefit from the growth in the capital markets. Not only could they benefit from brisk trading in the stock market but also from demand for underwriting; more and more companies seeking capital are expected to issue stock as an alternative to borrowing money from banks.

Experts debate whether companies in cement, wire, and other areas of infrastructure are attractive, given the overbuilding in the property area. However, some companies do seem likely to benefit from the spending on infrastructural development. Thienchai Charnchanayotin of SBCI points to Sino Thai Engineering and Construction, the second largest contractor in Thailand—and the largest listed one. "Although its stock has been trading at a considerable premium, it still looks good," he maintains.

Besides favoring banks, Graham Catterwell of Crosby Research stresses plays on growing domestic demand, such as marketing and distribution companies, and some manufacturers producing containers for toothpaste and hairspray. In the property sector, he emphasizes residential stand-alone semidetached and detached housing developers, such as Land & House and Quality House.

For investors who prefer not to buy shares directly in the Thai market, four companies have issued American Depositary Receipts. They are: Advanced Info Service Ltd., Asia Fiber Company Ltd., Charoen Pokphand Feedmill Co. Ltd., and Shinawatra Computer & Communications.

As of 1993, Wilson Emerging Market Funds Research listed 47 country funds for Thailand, of which 25 are available to international investors. Of the 25, 11 trade on the London Stock Exchange and 2, the Thai Capital Fund Inc. and the Thai Fund Inc., trade on the New York Stock Exchange.

21
India

Aboard a bus in Bombay in late 1991, Gautam Adhikari, then an associate editor of *The Times of India* (and now a consultant with the World Bank), overheard two middle-aged women discussing stocks. In earlier times, the conversation might have startled him. But by late 1991, amid a raft of economic reforms in once socialist-minded India, the stock market had rocketed. People from many walks of life were pouring money into shares. "Businessmen, airline stewardesses, housewives, and others—people I'd never expected to be interested in stocks—were discussing how they'd made money in the market," Adhikari recalls. Not everyone grasped what was going on. But according to Adhikari, "the better-informed knew that the economic changes were good for us."

At least many are hoping so. After decades of central economic planning and two centuries of British colonization, huge, ancient India is now steering a new course away from the central planning that had created a closed economy toward a more free-market system. Although gradual reforms had begun years earlier, the big economic about-face occurred in mid-1991, amid a balance-of-payments crisis. To secure aid amid a desperate shortage of cash, the country embraced radical reforms. These were inaugurated in the federal budget of fiscal 1991–92 and were pursued in subsequent years. As New Delhi blasted the ramparts of its fortress-like country, many cheered the new era by investing in shares. The future seemed bright—if tumultuous sociopolitical problems could be contained.

With more than 860 million people, India could become one of the next economic miracles. Its middle class alone is almost two-thirds the size of the population of the United States. India has ample natural resources. And among its vast, diverse people is a driving spirit that enabled the country in 1947 to demand and obtain independence, and to form a free, albeit fractious, democracy. While many of the nation's passions have long been directed toward the political scene—due to the long struggle for independence—the country possesses a pride in its heritage and development. Many people have lamented India's poverty and failure to keep pace with the developed world. And as the country sees the benefits of capitalism elsewhere in the world, it appears increasingly receptive to the idea of employing many of these ideas at home.

Since the 1950s, India's economy had been ensconced in regulations, licensing arrangements that created monopolies, and a huge state-owned industrial sector. Banking and other financial industries were government-run, especially since 1969, when major private banks were nationalized. Foreign direct investment was limited to a minority stake in a company, and until September 1992, foreigners were barred from investing in the Indian stock market except through approved investment funds. Despite structural hindrances and impediments on India's free-market economy, economic growth generally has been advancing. According to Baring Securities, the nation posted a compound annual economic growth rate of 5.5 percent for the period from 1985 to 1990, with the services sector registering the fastest growth.

However, the country's current account deteriorated starting in 1985. A key problem was the rise in overseas borrowings, producing higher interest and principal payments on debt. In 1990 the Persian Gulf War precipitated a hike in the cost of oil and petroleum imports, worsening the current account deficit, even as capital inflows fell and India's official reserves became depleted. The country faced a balance-of-payments crisis. Without help, India was going to have to default on its loans.

As the country turned to the International Monetary Fund (IMF) for emergency cash to pay its bills, it triggered a process that led to an economic overhaul.

India got immediate aid from the IMF's Contingency and Compensatory Finance Facility, followed by a structural adjustment loan. The World Bank stepped in, providing a $500 million loan for structural adjustments in December 1991. A year later, it provided another $500 million to help establish a fund to help support and retrain workers laid off when state enterprises are shut down. In mid-1993, the World Bank announced a $300 million loan to help India liberalize its trade and investments regime. India also annually gets about $3.5 billion from the World Bank mainly for project financing.

According to David Maslin, vice president and senior economist with Morgan Guaranty Trust Co. in New York, "India will remain heavily reliant on official sources of finance—requiring up to $3 to $4 billion annually—until access to commercial markets can be restored." India's total gross external debt reached some $79 billion at the end of 1992, up from $70 billion in 1990.

Financial Reforms

Aid to India came with strings attached. Lenders wanted drastic long- and short-term economic reforms, including a lifting of restrictions on private and foreign banks, substantial liberalization of the capital markets, an end to the system of licensing business and subsidizing exports, privatization of state-owned enterprises, and a fully convertible currency.

A number of measures have already been implemented. In 1992, India's currency, the rupee, was made partially convertible and was then fully floated in March 1993, even as additional liberalizations were promised; according to David Maslin, import licensing was removed for all but a small "negative" list of products; import tariffs have also been reduced. The plan, says Maslin, "is to bring India's tariff structure in line with international levels in three to four years," which means the top tariff will be 35 percent by the 1997–1998 budget.

Among other industrial reforms, the government, in 1992, outlined 34 priority areas in which investment proposals involving up to 51 percent foreign equity receive automatic approval within two weeks. (Up to 100 percent foreign ownership is pos-

INDIA

Currency: Indian rupee (INR).

Stock Exchanges: There are 22 stock exchanges. The 5 main exchanges are located in Bombay (65 percent of volume), Delhi, Calcutta, Ahmadabad, and Madras.

Indexes: The 3 main indexes are the BSE Sensitive Index, the National Stock Index, and the Economic Times Index.

Types of Securities: Equities—A and B shares, preference shares—debentures, corporate bonds, government bonds.

Regulatory Body/Stock Exchange Supervision: The Securities and Exchange Board of India (SEBI) regulates the securities market and foreign investment. The Reserve Bank of India (RBI) regulates all monetary policy and currency inflows/outflows.

Depository: The Stockholding Corporation of India is preparing a feasibility report on the establishment of a central depository.

Settlement Information

Equities:

- Fortnightly settlement account period, usually commencing on a Friday. Settlement of outstanding balances normally takes place on the first Thursday of the next account period.
- Physical settlement only.
- Receive/deliver against payment available on a very limited basis only, if the broker will fund the gap between the deliver-in and the pay-out or the pay-in and deliver-out dates.
- Same-day turnarounds are possible, provided that no short-selling takes place at any stage.

Taxes:

- Withholding tax on dividends and interest income is 20 percent.

- The short-term capital gains (holding period under 1 year) tax is 30 percent for nonresidents, while long-term capital gains are taxed at 10 percent for foreign institutional investors.
- The capital gains tax is 10 percent for offshore funds and GDRs.

Restrictions for Foreign Investors:

- All foreign institutional investors (FII) must apply to the SEBI and the RBI for approval to invest directly in India's markets.
- There is a 24 percent ceiling on the total holdings by all FIIs in a given company, while a single FII can own up to 5 percent of a company's paid-up capital.

Securities Lending: Not available at present.

SOURCE: The Bank of New York

sible for export-oriented companies, including those in export-processing zones.) The number of industries reserved for the public sector has been steadily reduced.

The budget for fiscal 1993–94 extended reforms. Among its moves were a reduction of the short-term capital gains tax rate for foreign investors to 30 percent, slicing the commercial lending rate to 17 percent from 18 percent, giving high-priority sectors such as power generation a 5-year tax holiday, and allotting more spending to agriculture, education development, and encouraging nonpublic investment in infrastructure, power, and hydrocarbons.

Other capital markets reforms of the early 1990s include: allowing direct stock investments by institutions, permitting private sector mutual funds to be established, and scrapping of the old bureaucratic Office of Controller of Capital Issues that regulated the issuances of stocks and debentures. This agency "used to dictate the price of new issues," explains Maslin. "Prices would usually be set" below market level, making them "low enough for poor people to buy. But that made them unattractive for issuers. Now, although companies still go through registration (on issues), there is no effort by the government to price the issue."

Outlook for Reforms

Reforms—especially if more are forthcoming—should continue to bolster the economy. Already in fiscal 1992–1993, real GDP growth was revised upward to about 4 percent, due to better than expected industrial and agricultural output and increased exports to now former Soviet Bloc countries. Estimates of GDP growth over the next five years run in the 5 to 6 percent range. Inflation has fallen from double-digit levels earlier in the decade. And as another positive sign, the government was committed to reducing the federal deficit to 5 percent of GDP in fiscal 1992–93, in line with IMF stipulations.

Budget-cutting—ranging from defense spending to industrial subsidies—has been widespread. In fiscal 1991–92, measures provided for revenue enhancements through higher taxes, including on corporations, and plans to privatize state-owned companies.

Politically testy issues have not been addressed head-on. For example, the government has been dragging its feet in such areas as banking reform, where powerful interests have a stake, and in dealing with financially sick state-owned industries. Morgan Guaranty's David Maslin reports that "some 58 deficit-ridden state companies constitute a serious drain on the budget." Some defunct state businesses are even still paying former employees, he says. These organizations will need to be restructured; some may need to be shut down.

In fact the government has proposed a gradual exit from unprofitable businesses, with compensation for laid-off workers provided by the establishment of a National Renewal Fund. In the early 1990s, privatization consisted of the government selling shares in some of its healthy enterprises to mutual funds. (However, India's largest petrochemical company was scheduled to become the first state enterprise to sell shares directly to the public as part of the government's plan to partially privatize major national industries.) According to the *Financial Times* newspaper, India plans to sell up to 49 percent of all state companies, with the government maintaining a controlling stake. In 1991, shares in 31 state companies were sold in the first phase of privatization. In the second phase that took place in October 1992, "the eight companies involved include some of India's best performing government-owned enterprises: the Steel Authority of India, Hindustan Petroleum Corporation (formerly Esso Eastern), Bharat Petroleum (earlier Burmah Shell), and the high-precision machine tools manufacturer, Hindustan Machine Tools."

Trade unions and left-wing groups have screamed at the prospect of closing badly performing state companies. In one example, the press reported that, in June 1992, some 15 million manual and white-collar workers went on strike in response to leftist union calls to denounce economic reforms. Their complaints included: the opening of the economy to multinationals, the reported intention to freeze wages, and the expected closure of ailing state companies. But although interest groups have wailed loudly, the majority of the public has supported the reform/restructuring process. The sense is that the process has already started to produce returns. Gautam Adhikari of the

World Bank sees "a surprisingly wide degree of support for the policies that have pushed reform." However in late 1992 and early 1993, such optimism was temporarily curbed by outbreaks of violence in the streets of India and resultant political tussles.

Government and Politics

As a multiparty democracy, India employs a British-style parliamentary system of government. Politics and economics have long been interwoven, since the long-dominant Congress party was born of the movement to oust colonialism. After India achieved independence in 1947, the country's first Prime Minister Jawaharlal Nehru established inward-looking social democratic programs and policies that tilted toward socialism. National "self-sufficiency" was a popular slogan.

The Congress party governed from 1947 to 1977 and from 1980 to 1989, and again regained control in mid-1991. Nehru held power from 1950 to 1964, when he died. Starting in 1966, his daughter Indira Gandhi served as India's third prime minister. Defeated in 1977, she regained the premiership in 1980, which she held until her assassination in 1984. Her son, Rajiv Gandhi, then became prime minister. Although his party was defeated in 1989, he ran again, and was expected to win in 1991 before he, too, was assassinated during a campaign rally near Madras.

After Gandhi's murder, his widow Sonia rejected the offer to head the Congress-I party, after which P.V. Narasimha Rao was chosen. In the 1991 election, although Congress-I won many more seats than any other party, its number of seats in parliament initially still fell short of the required number for a working majority. Rao's party has since garnered more support, and the party now has a slim, working majority in parliament.

Initially, many underestimated Rao. They believed that this seemingly quiet, unassuming career politician in his seventies would be a short-term prime minister. In fact, Rao surprised many with his vigor and his administrative ability. Thus far, out of necessity, his cause cèlébre has been economic reform on a grand scale. Although Rao wasn't the first Indian prime minister to consider sweeping economic changes—that distinction can be traced back to Mrs. Gandhi's second term in office, in the late 1970s—he, along with Finance Minister Manmohan Singh, among other supporters, has been the first to implement them.

He has done so with sensitivity to India's socioeconomic environment. Professor James Manor of the Institute of Development Studies, University of Sussex, in England, holds that "like European Social Democrats, Rao understands that market forces don't take care of everything. He understands that the state has to look after the poor and vulnerable. He doesn't believe in trickle-down economics."

To some observers, Rao seems likely to keep a close watch over the reform process. For instance, Manor anticipates that Prime Minister Rao will remain in power at least until late 1994 or early 1995, by which time the economic liberalizations should have spawned tangible benefits, following initial hardships. According to Manor, the prime minister is likely to call an election at a favorable time before his term ends in 1996, to help secure a victory for the Congress-I party.

In the meantime, the going will continue to be rough for Rao and his government. December 1992 brought the worst flare-up of communal violence since the partition of India in 1947. The destruction of the Babri mosque at Ayodhya by Hindu militants in December 1992, and the ensuing riots which took a heavy death toll, undermined public confidence in the government. Even as the right-wing Hindu Bharatiya Janata Party was openly challenging the government, it was thought that Human Resources Minister Arjun Singh—a member of the Congress-I Party—might stage an internal challenge to Rao's leadership. Seen as no fan of the economic reforms, Arjun Singh was expected to curtail that process if he came to power. But a responsive Rao flexed his muscle. Shaking up his cabinet in early 1993, he increased the number of ministers who were seen as likely to support him. Moreover, the government's budget for fiscal 1993–94, which came out in February 1993, forged ahead with additional economic reform plans—a strategy many thought was designed to bring national attention back to the economy and to demonstrate that the government was maintaining its grip.

The Economy

Business was severely shaken by the violence of December 1992. But after the Rao government weathered a rocky first half of 1993, confidence appeared to be returning. More and more investors seemed to agree with Professor Manor's view that the profit-making opportunity remains strong, in light of India's reforms and growth prospects.

In the short term, reforms will require difficult adjustments for companies used to a protectionist economy. As Baring Securities has described, "reforms will initially lead to increased competition, resulting in lower prices and margins for all companies in industries affected by the reforms. Eventually, restructuring will enable the strongest companies to achieve economies of scale and reduce costs."

Nonetheless, a devalued rupee has already been aiding export opportunities. An expected drop in corporate tax rates should further enhance profits. Vinod R. Sethi, vice president, Morgan Stanley Asset Management Inc. in New York, predicts an average 25 percent growth in corporate earnings over the five years through 1997.

"You'll see earnings consistently doing well over the next decade or two," says Sethi. "Supply-side bottlenecks historically chained the Indian economy. Between the loosening of those chains and the growth in incomes, there will be sustained growth over the next two decades," he says, noting that the already large middle class is growing by 7 percent annually.

Sethi also illustrates how lifting business restrictions can quickly produce benefits. He says that in the early 1980s it used to take about five years for an Indian consumer to obtain a motor scooter. At that time only two products were available. But three years after the sector was delicensed in 1986, India became the world's largest producer of motor scooters.

India's corporate sector has constituted only a small 15 percent of GDP. Rural agriculture remains the country's dominant employer. In the corporate arena, roughly 30 big, family-owned businesses have dominated, although entrepreneurs also have sprung up around them. Among the best-known names in family-controlled conglomerates: the Tatas in steel, edible oils, trucks and automobiles; the Birlas in textiles, autos, and cement; the Mafatlals, heavily into the textile industry; and the Ambanis, in petrochemicals and textiles.

What will happen to these organizations and to others as a result of reforms? Many are expected to need restructuring to help them in the new economic environment. Some may not succeed. But others have already responded to the opportunities presented by a growing economy. Tata Steel, Reliance Industries, Essar Gujarat, and the Birla-owned Grasim Industries were reported to be among the organizations with major expansion projects designed to enhance earnings.

In the meantime, Sethi of Morgan Stanley reports that new entrepreneurs have been grabbing market share from the dominant companies. In his view, "small- and medium-sized companies are likely to be best able to capitalize on the opportunities brought by reforms. These companies no longer have to obtain licenses and have influence in New Delhi." Not only will they have smaller payrolls than the big conglomerates, he points out, but they will also be likely to have newer plant and equipment.

The Stock Market

In India the financial press is widely read, and there are dozens of financial journals that publish information on equities. In the early 1990s the media certainly had plenty to write about. Not only did share prices skyrocket in 1991, amid euphoria about reforms, but they continued to soar in early 1992 as prices on the Bombay exchange—the leading exchange in India—more than doubled from January to April 1992 and peaked at 4500 in August of that year. Suddenly, news broke of the biggest securities scandal in India's history. That development triggered a freeze on the bank accounts and shareholdings of a major broker who was at the center of the fraud. Although stock prices plunged, and were again hit by the outbreak of religious violence, the market still closed just over 22 percent higher on the year in U.S. dollar terms, according to the IFC Price Index. The year before, the IFC Price Index for India gained 16.6 percent in dollar terms.

Gains had been triggered by euphoria over reforms, including expectations that foreigners would be allowed to buy shares directly in the market. But the early 1992 uptrend came to an end by May of that year. As the IFC describes, the downturn had initially been sparked by "rumors of imminent broker defaults and government intervention to halt the intense speculation, and secondly, by the revelation of the illegal funneling of funds allocated for investment in government debt securities into the stock market."

"Big Bull" stockbroker Harshad Mehta, founder of the Growmore Financial Services empire, was accused of being the ringleader in a scheme in which fraudulent bank receipts were used to finance stock purchases. These bank receipts represented transactions of Indian government bonds that had not yet settled. When the Reserve Bank of India, the central bank, noticed that there were many fewer bond trades to settle than bank receipts outstanding, it launched an investigation that spurred participants in the scam to dump their shares to try to avoid getting caught. According to a *Wall Street Journal* account, Mehta, who was arrested, had allegedly handled more than one-third of the funds and bonds missing in the $1.26 billion securities scandal. "He heads the list of 44 individuals and companies whose properties were seized by the Indian government between May 14 and July 2, 1992, because of their alleged involvement in the scandal." The imbroglio forced the Bombay exchange and most others to close for nearly five weeks. Some government officials as well as bankers were tied to the scandal.

Although the scandal marred the reputation of India's markets, it was expected to prod India to beef up market rules and operations.

The market itself is large and varied. India currently has 22 stock exchanges and an over-the-counter market. The Bombay exchange, with market cap of $65.1 billion, is the oldest in Asia as well as the largest in India. According to the IFC, the Indian market has over 6700 listed stocks, although experts say the effective universe is around 1200. About one-third of the market's capital is held by domestic institutional investors, while another third is held by management insiders and another third by individual investors.

In September 1992, the market opened to direct stock investing by foreigners. But a number of restrictions and limitations remain. For example, foreigners are restricted to a maximum 24 percent holding in the issued share capital of any one company, while each foreign institutional investor may hold no more than 5 percent of one company's issued stock. Foreign individual investors are not able to buy shares directly in India. Moreover, before investing, foreign institutional investors must apply to the Securities and Exchange Board of India (SEBI—the regulatory body for the capital markets) and to the Reserve Bank of India. Nominee companies with affiliates or subsidiary companies of a registrant foreign institutional investor are treated as separate entities and must register separately.

Taxes are another issue that the 1993–1994 budget took pains to ameliorate. Among the reforms was lowering the withholding tax on capital gains to 30 percent from 65 percent on investments held for less than one year. Stocks are divided into two categories: "A," which have an active market, and "B" for less actively traded stocks. In group A, stocks are traded over a 14-day account period, and the settlement can take another 2 to 3 weeks. Shares as well as cash are settled through a clearinghouse. The trading account period and settlement time frames for Group B shares are similar to those for Group A, but here only cash is settled through the clearinghouse.

Once a trade has finally been settled, the stock registration process can take up to another 10 weeks. Investors must register ownership of their stocks with the issuing company in order to qualify for bonuses, dividends and participation in rights issues.

Securities can be sold only in India. No short selling is permitted. Foreign institutional investors can appoint a SEBI-approved custodian bank to custody securities and confirm transactions.

Such complications and delays can be unnerving. "There's a lot to clarify before large institutions invest in India," says one Hong Kong–based market participant. Given the substantial differential in capital gains taxes between stocks held for more than, or less than, one year, investors need to understand when the holding period begins. "Do you count waiting periods when the shares you bought have actually been registered?" he asks. "If so, investors may have to hold shares longer than one year to avoid paying the higher capital gains tax."

Foreigners are expected to become increasingly enthusiastic about India's market after reforms take stronger root. And in fact, the stock market staged a strong rally in mid-1993, partly as concerns eased about political and social upheavals. By mid-year, press reports also cited growing investor interest in finding an attractive, large alternative emerging market to China's.

What to Buy

Sethi of Morgan Stanley points out that, with so many companies to choose from, investors aren't confined to India's largest 30 to 40 stocks. While the large cap stocks tend to track the overall market, according to Mr. Sethi investors should dig deeper, exploring a second tier of 200 to 300 shares with relatively low price-earnings multiples that stand a good chance of outperforming the larger-cap stocks. Morgan Stanley, manager of the closed-end Magnum Fund, sees the cement, finance, cotton and textiles, and automobile spare parts sectors as attractive.

Among the stocks Sethi recommends: the Housing Development Finance Corporation (HDFC), a company with the potential for strong growth over the next 10 years amid India's rising demand for housing and increasing incomes. HDFC has about an 80 percent market share in housing finance and covers 1600 cities and towns in India. In early 1993, Sethi reported that this stock "is available at a reasonable P/E ratio, currently about 14 times 1993's earnings.

"We also like Gujarat Ambuja, one of the most efficient cement producers in the world, with top-of-the-line management and a sound production and marketing strategy," said Sethi. For example, the company has tried to market cement as a branded product, not as a commodity. Founded in 1986, this relatively new company is already one of the dominant cement producers on India's west coast, even as its capacity is expected to jump 300 percent over the next five years, said Sethi.

Sethi also recommends a young textile company called Indo-rama Sytetics, a producer of high quality cotton and blended yarn, with "strong export markets," and Indian Seamless Tubes Ltd., one of what he said are 12 manufacturers in the world making seamless tubes that "have wide application in process industries." The company has posted 40-percent-plus annual earnings growth "for a long time," and should show growth of about 30 to 35 percent during the next three to five years, he said.

Investing in funds provides an option to direct stock investments. Wilson Emerging Market Funds Research in 1993 counted six India country funds for international investors, of which five are closed-end and are domiciled abroad. They are: the India Fund, which trades on the London Stock Exchange; the India Growth Fund Inc., listed on the New York Stock Exchange; the India Magnum Fund N.V., which trades on the Amsterdam Stock Exchange; and the private India Investment Fund Limited and the Second India Investment Fund Limited. Additional funds were also in planning.

According to the IFC, 1992 brought the first two global depositary receipt offerings by Indian companies: Reliance Industries and Grasim Industries.

22

Pakistan

In 1992, political and economic events roiled the Karachi Stock Exchange. Reversing course from a 160 percent surge in dollar terms the year before, the IFC Price Index for Karachi fell 20.5 percent and the returns index fell 18.4 percent in 1992. Investors had little to cheer about. After a heavy supply of new issues put pressure on the market, bearishness was reinforced by political upheavals and a disastrous flood in September.

Pakistan is certainly no stranger to tumult. This South Asian country of over 115 million people is what Professor John Adams of Boston's Northeastern University calls "rough, ready, and very frontierish." Created in 1947 from the partition of British India, Pakistan was designed to be a home for India's Muslims. (The country was ruled as a dominion until it was finally declared an Islamic republic in 1956.) Economic growth has been impressive. Although Pakistan "was poorer than India in 1950," entrepreneurship and industriousness helped to propel it past India, Adams says. GDP per capita in Pakistan was about $415 million in fiscal 1991–92.

But growing pains have been acute. Since becoming a nation, Pakistan has experienced some 25 years of quasi- or direct military rule. A wave of nationalizations in the 1970s under the late President Zulfikar Ali Bhutto was later followed by a swing back toward market economics. Crime, political instability, limited tax collection, and a thriving underground economy are features of life in Pakistan. As a carryover from the country's formulative period, the military remains a significant force in political/governmental affairs.

On the economic front, the country's GDP growth averaged about 6 percent over the 1980s. But by the latter part of the decade, economic problems had begun to mount for this long insular and bureaucratic country. As Baring Securities reports, amid increased governmental spending, a yawning federal budget deficit reached 8.5 percent of GDP in 1988. That forced "a macroeconomic stabilization and adjustment program under the guidance of the IMF to bring the deficit under control." Pakistan's current account deficit was ballooning, as red ink reached $2.8 billion in the fiscal year ended June 1992, data from Baring Securities show. In addition Pakistan's low domestic savings rate keeps a lid on the amount of financial resources the country can internally tap for development. Its narrow export base—highly reliant on cotton and rice—leaves it vulnerable to market vagaries.

In the 1990s, Pakistan set a new economic course—one that depended much more heavily on the private sector for growth and development.

Between November 1990 and September 1991, the government of then newly elected Prime Minister Nawaz Sharif unveiled a package of economic reforms, reforms aimed at deregulating and stimulating private business and bolstering the previously meager level of foreign investment. According to the Pakistani publication *Economic Review*, reforms are intended to increase national income by 7 percent, industrial production by 12 percent, and exports by 20 percent annually. "The emphasis will be on rural industrialization and the growth of infrastructure to facilitate economic development, and the strategy will consist of lifting all holds that impede private sector participation in making the country self-reliant, which is the government's central goal."

As described by Baring Securities, some of the key liberalizations and reforms include:

- Launching a major privatization program that includes 115 industrial units, 45 other state-owned organizations, and four banks

- Allowing foreigners to obtain 100 percent equity stakes in companies with no prior government approval, except in certain industries restricted for security or religious reasons

- Eliminating the need for government permission to remit dividends or divestments
- Allowing Pakistanis to have foreign currency accounts
- Granting tax holidays for new industries for three years in urban industrial estates, eight years in designated "backward" areas, and five years in other rural areas
- Establishing Special Industrial Zones that offer five-year tax holidays and various export incentives
- Abolishing licensing requirements for most goods
- Reducing the maximum tariff rate from 125 to about 90 percent, further reducing it to 50 percent by 1994, and dismantling some nontariff barriers
- Slashing customs duties on imported plant and machinery

Besides opening up commercial banking to the private sector, reforms also opened the door to allow foreigners to buy stock directly in Pakistan's market.

Cautious Outlook on Reforms

Although the economic reform program was initially applauded, sobering reality soon set in. Even before the Sharif government fell in July 1993, political battles had been intensifying. Moreover, in September 1992, a flood that killed more than 1000 people also damaged the cotton crop—a critical component of the economy, since Pakistan is a major cotton-producing and -exporting country.

All the while, questions were arising over the degree of, or handling of, reforms. To some observers, the twin goals of rapidly privatizing over 150 state-owned businesses at the same time that the government was trying to maximize revenues from these sales seemed overzealous and unrealistic. In addition, the need for further liberalizations seemed apparent. As Baring Securities had pointed out, even after proposed reductions in tariff rates, the rates would remain relatively high. And a "substantial portion of the industrial sector [would remain] subject

PAKISTAN

Currency: Pakistan rupee (PKR).

Stock Exchanges: There are three stock exchanges in Pakistan: The Karachi Stock Exchange (the main exchange), The Lahore Stock Exchange, The Islamabad Stock Exchange, plus the Over-the-Counter Market (OTC).

Indexes: The State Bank of Pakistan Index and the Karachi Stock Exchange Index.

Types of Securities: Equities, government bonds, commercial paper.

Regulatory Body/Stock Exchange Supervision: The Ministry of Finance's Corporate Law Authority, The Controller of Capital Issues, and the Central Board of Review regulate the securities markets and all foreign investment.

Depository: A central depository is scheduled to open by 1994.

Settlement Information

Equities:

- All trades executed between Sunday and Thursday settle on the following Monday.
- Physical delivery only.
- Receive/deliver versus payment available.
- Although possible, same-day turnaround trades are not common for international investors.

Fixed Income:

- Negotiated settlement period (very limited secondary market).
- Physical or book entry (mainly) at Central Bank.
- Receive/deliver versus payment available.

Taxes:

- There is no capital gains tax.

- For countries with tax treaties with Pakistan (including the U.K. and the U.S.), the tax rate for dividends is 15 percent. For countries without a tax treaty, the tax rate is 16.5 percent. Anyone receiving dividend income above PKR100,000 in any year—regardless of country of residence—will be taxed at 16.5 percent.

Restrictions for Foreign Investors:

- There are no foreign exchange controls or restrictions for foreign investors.
- There are no restrictions, reporting requirements, or limitations on investment.

Securities Lending: Does not yet exist in Pakistan.

SOURCE: The Bank of New York

to investment and import restrictions because of the government's domestic content or deletion policy."

Among other problems is the fiscal deficit, which Baring calls the main macroeconomic challenge facing Pakistan. Heavy defense spending as well as debt servicing contribute to the problem. As a portion of export earnings, Baring Securities said in a July 1992 report that debt servicing was expected to reach an estimated 25.6 percent in fiscal year 1993, while the military annually claims about 30 percent of total budget outlays. "Military expenditure continues to dominate the federal government's budget, at a time when external military assistance has declined," the firm said. "U.S. aid to its former 'front-line state' has been suspended since October 1990, following Pakistan's failure to comply with U.S. nuclear nonproliferation legislation under the Pressler Amendment. Even if the impasse is resolved, the United States is unlikely to resume the aid levels of the 1980s that made Pakistan the third largest recipient of U.S. aid," Baring maintained.

Pakistan's three-year economic stabilization program that runs through fiscal 1993–94, has included the following targets: 6 percent GDP growth, a 5.5 percent government deficit as a percentage of GDP, and a current account deficit of 2.5 percent of GDP. Given its difficulty with budget-cutting, the government has sought to boost revenues through the introduction of a range of new or higher taxes and improvement of tax collection from smaller businesses and the "informal economy." But, at least through the Sharif government's tenure, progress in widening the net had been slow.

In August 1993, caretaker Prime Minister Qureshi, who assumed that post after Sharif resigned in mid-1993, unveiled a number of initiatives designed to grapple with some of Pakistan's socioeconomic ills. According to the *Financial Times*, some key points in the economic portion of his program included: imposing taxes on "both the income and wealth of Pakistan's feudal landowners"; tightening control over the banking system and granting autonomy to the central bank; and speeding up the privatization program.

Among other steps, Qureshi also devalued the rupee by 9 percent. "Interest rates were raised by two percentage points" to encourage savings, "and a quick disbursing loan was sought frm the IMF [International Monetary Fund]," the *Financial Times* reported.

Social Ills

Crime, health care, illiteracy, and an inferior role assigned to women in this male-oriented society are among the social issues that need to be addressed. Improvements in infrastructure, including expansion of power supplies, communications facilities, and roads, are also needed. In the province of Sindh, home of Karachi, the nation's business capital, the crime wave became so intense in 1992 that the military was sent in to try to restore law and order. Although politics and ethnic strife have often been to blame for increasing violence, experts say hardened criminals have taken advantage of the situation to step up their illicit activities.

Among domestic woes is a reported overall 27 percent literacy rate. But the rate for women runs lower on average than that for men. While illiteracy is bolstered by the fact that Pakistan's sizable rural population is severely underemployed and has limited access to schooling, the end result is that the country falls short in its supply of well-educated people to employ. And with so many women unable to read and write, Pakistan runs the risk that many of its children will be similarly impaired.

In a 1991 report, the Asian Development Bank said that the government was devoting less than 10 percent of its current expenditure and 15 percent of its development expenditure to education, health, and population planning. "Unless a major increase in government spending in these three areas takes place, significant progress in dealing with these problems is not possible, and the long-term development prospects of the country will remain in jeopardy."

According to Baring Securities, a social action program was introduced in fiscal 1991 to boost investment in social services and human resources development. In addition, infrastructure was afforded "top priority" in the government's fiscal 1993 budget, with emphasis on the development of rails, roads, and ports, and significant participation by the private sector. But even so, the government's budgetary constraints limit what it can do. As a result, Baring Securities has reported that the government's spending aimed at addressing "severe social and economic gaps" has barely kept up with inflation.

Government and Politics

With its ethnic strains and periodic political upheavals, Pakistan's is a tumultuous society. The country is 97 percent Muslim, with about 78 percent of the population of the Sunni branch of that faith. Islamization of the society, articulated by then-President Zia in 1980, culminated with the 1991 passage of the Shariat laws, which follow the teachings of the Koran and the Sunnah. (Under Shariat law, western principles of interest do not apply, explains Montgomery Securities. Instead, depositors share in the profits of the bank.)

But Pakistan's politics have been tough and gritty. The system is parliamentary. The president and prime minister are each elected to five year terms, but in different years.

Historically, the military has played a central role in Pakistan. In 1958, eleven years after Pakistan was established, a coup brought General Marshall Mohamed Ayub Khan to power, which he held until he was forced to resign amid a 1969 coup. His successor, General Agha Muhammad Yahya Khan, called for the nation's first general elections, which ultimately resulted in a split of the vote between West and East Pakistan. A civil disobedience campaign in East Pakistan was followed by army intervention and eventual war with India. In the end, after Pakistan lost the war, East Pakistan became Bangladesh, a move that forced Yahya Khan to resign and transfer power to Zulfikar Ali Bhutto as President. Eventually, civil unrest led to President Bhutto's ouster in 1977.

General Zia, who became President in 1978, held power until he was killed in a 1988 plane crash that some believe was an act of sabotage. In March 1985, Mohamed Khan Junejo became Pakistan's first prime minister in eight years, but in 1988 Zia removed him from office. In 1988, in the first open election in more than a decade, Benazir Bhutto—daughter of the late

President Bhutto—became prime minister. But she was removed by Khan two years later on charges of corruption. Sharif was elected prime minister in 1990. In December 1988, President Ghulam Ishaq Khan, who had assumed power after Zia's death, was elected to a five-year term.

Sharif, an industrialist by professional background, was initially successful in promoting economic reform. But by 1992, his political strength and standing were eroded by political infighting. In April 1993, President Ishaq Khan dismissed the Sharif government over issues of constitutional powers and dissolved the National Assembly. Although in late May, the Supreme Court overturned those actions and restored Sharif as prime minister, both Ishaq Khan and Sharif resigned in July 1993 as, according to *The New York Times*, "Pakistan's increasingly restive army demanded an end to the standoff" between them. Moeen Qureshi, a former World Bank official, became caretaker prime minister until the October 1993 parliamentary elections. Wasim Sajjad, formerly chairman of the Senate, became acting President until the November 1993 presidential vote.

Companies and Sectors

Pakistan's economy is heavily agrarian. In the fiscal year ended 1991–92, agriculture accounted for 25.6 percent of GDP, while manufacturing's share totaled 17.6 percent, the wholesale and retail sector 16.5 percent, and all others much smaller amounts, reports Christine Myers, an investment manager with G.T. Management (Asia) Ltd., in Hong Kong. Pakistan's dominant industry is textiles. The Pakistani publication *Economic Review* reports that "cotton yarn and cloth production account for 66 percent of all large-scale manufacturing in the country." Over 50 percent of revenues derive from import tariffs.

The agricultural sector has been described as feudal, with wealthy landowning families enjoying political and economic clout and many other people tied to the land. However, the new taxes on landlords introduced by Moeen Qureshi's government in mid-1993 were widely seen as a bold step toward reducing this sector's influence, while expanding Pakistan's tax base.

In the corporate world, "much of the business traditionally has been in the hands of a few large companies," says Professor William Richter of Kansas State University. "At one point, the phrase often quoted was that "90 percent of Pakistani industrial wealth is in the hands of 22 families." Since the 1960s, however, that has broadened considerably. Although there still exists a cadre of important business families, an entrepreneurial sector of small businesses has also emerged, and with it, a growing middle class.

Trade Agreements

Pakistan is well poised to benefit from the increasing trade opportunities in the Central Asia region, comprised of over 300 million people. Since the breakup of the former Soviet Union, an Economic Cooperation Organization (ECO) has been formed in Central Asia, which includes Pakistan, six of the former Soviet states (Kazakhstan, Kyrgystan, Azerbaijan, Turkmenistan, Uzbekistan, and Tajikistan), Afghanistan, Iran, and Turkey.

The Stock Market

Pakistan's stock market includes three exchanges, the main market officially called the Karachi Stock Exchange (Guarantee) Limited (KSE), as well as the Lahore Stock Exchange (Guarantee) Limited and the Islamabad Stock Exchange (Guarantee) Limited. There is also an over-the-counter market.

The Karachi Stock Exchange, the oldest and largest, came into existence in 1947. It was later converted into a registered company, limited by guarantee, in 1949. Although as many as 90 members were enrolled at that time, hardly half a dozen of them were active as brokers. Initially, only five companies were listed. But the picture has changed. By the end of December 1992, the market's membership (including the 5 corporate members) had reached 200, with almost 140 active members trading in 628 listed companies. At the end of 1992, the market's capitalization was $8 billion, according to the IFC.

The 10 most actively traded stocks in 1992 were those of: First

Habib Bank Modaraba, First Hajvairy Modaraba, Trust Modaraba, Bank Commerce Al-Habib Limited, Bankers Equity Limited, Indus Bank Limited, Mehran Bank Limited, Union Bank Limited, and Dewan Salman Fibers Limited. Modarabas are closed-end fundlike investments, managed by the bank whose name it bears, that trades on an exchange.

Although a barrage of new listings has helped to expand Pakistan's market, liquidity remains limited. Many public companies are closely held, primarily by the controlling family. Further limiting liquidity, at least 10 percent of the capital issued to the general public must be offered to the National Investment Trust (NIT). The NIT is an open-ended mutual fund set up by the government that invests savings for small investors. As of mid-1992, the NIT owned 12 percent of the market's capitalization, according to Baring Securities.

The market's performance has been volatile of late. According to the IFC index, Pakistan's market fell 20.5 percent in U.S. dollar terms in 1992, after a 161.2 percent rise in 1991—the year it opened its market to foreign investment.

Besides liquidity constraints, other frequently lamented problems include insider trading, inadequate corporate reporting, and the time-consuming paperwork required to register shares with the issuing company. According to Baring Securities, stock registration takes at least 45 days and can drag out as long as 75 days.

So far, experts say, the bulk of foreign stock investment in Pakistan has come from Asia. By 1994, a depository is scheduled to open in Pakistan, which should ease some of the problems foreigners have had investing in that country.

As an investment strategy, Christine Myers of G. T. Management believes that investors in Pakistan need to "stick to market leaders" and, generally, the larger companies. Typically, Meyers says, these listings will have market capitalizations of more than $50 million, including Adamjee Insurance, the largest non-life insurance company in Pakistan, with its $57 million market capitalization, or ICI Pakistan (a subsidiary of Imperial Chemical Industries in the U.K.), the nation's top chemical manufacturer, which has a market capitalization of approximately $160 million.

Myers sees "tremendous value" in the Pakistan market, where, on the whole, stocks are "cheap relative to other markets where earnings are rising." But she recommends buying Pakistani shares on a bottom-up basis:

> You have to be careful of the companies you choose, because international accounting standards are not universally applied. We invest in companies that have been established for a number of years. These companies would also have accounts that have been audited by an international accounting firm, and a good performance track record as well as being exposed to sectors we like.

Besides Adamjee, some other oft-mentioned stocks include Pakland Cement Limited, which Baring Securities calls "one of Pakistan's most efficient cement producers" and which should benefit from expenditures for infrastructure; the Bank of Punjab (which operates only in the economically important province of Punjab), with its large and growing loan and deposit base; and Nishat Textile Mills Limited, the largest integrated textile firm in Pakistan, which has also been successful at exporting.

Investors who prefer not to buy shares directly in Pakistan can invest through funds. Wilson Emerging Market Funds Research lists 26 Pakistan country funds, of which all but 4 are domiciled in Pakistan. Others are: the unlisted Credit Lyonnais Pakistan Growth Fund, the open-end GT Karachi Fund listed on the Dublin Stock Exchange, the open-end, unlisted Pakistan Special Situations Fund, and the closed-end Pakistan Fund, listed on the Hong Kong Stock Exchange.

23
The People's Republic of China

In January 1992, Deng Xiaoping, paramount leader of the People's Republic of China (PRC), made a surprise visit to Southern China. Touring special enterprise zones earmarked for foreign investment, the patriarch—then 87 years old—walked the streets, talked with the people, and gazed at a landscape that had once been rice paddy fields and now gleamed with skyscrapers. He even visited the fledgling stock exchange in Shenzhen, a city bordering on Hong Kong.

By all accounts, he was highly impressed. Following this tour of his nation's south, Deng produced an official document championing the need for accelerated economic reforms. Although conservatives disagreed with the patriarch's ideas, their voices became increasingly muted over the year as more politically astute Chinese leaders leapt on the bandwagon, seeking a faster pace of reforms.

The Chinese Communist party turned up the heat on October 12, 1992, at the opening of its 14th national congress, the first since the 1989 crackdown. General Secretary Jiang Zemin's keynote speech lavished praise on Deng and outlined China's latest theory for grafting capitalism onto communism: the "socialist market economy."

As reported by United Press International, Mr. Jiang boasted: "We can truly say that we have started a new revolution, the objective of which is to fundamentally change the economic structure that has hampered the development of the productive forces." Jiang called for an economic growth rate of at least 8 to 9 percent, and said that the "socialist market economy" would accommodate at least some elements of capitalism.

There were ample reasons to set up tents in the reformist camp. Despite reforms to date, China, with its 1.2 billion people and 5000-year-old civilization, is today backward and impoverished by international standards. The country that long ago invented printing, the magnet, and gunpowder fell behind the world's pace of development over the past 200 years as wars, invaders, and inadequate leadership impeded its progress. In 1992, China's GDP per capita was only about $370, compared with about $15,900 in Hong Kong.

The advent of communist rule brought some improvements to China, along with some notoriously misguided, even destructive eras. The failed Great Leap Forward of the 1950s and the 1969 Cultural Revolution, featuring an attack on liberalism, were major setbacks to China's progress. Trauma arising from the Cultural Revolution and its aftermath afflicted the country for some 10 years. The period from 1966 until Chairman Mao's death in 1976 has become known as China's "lost decade."

The rise of Deng Xiaoping to supreme power ushered in an era of economic reforms. In 1978, the pragmatic Deng initiated the Open Door Policy on foreign trade and investment. He also implemented the Four Modernizations (in agriculture, industry, science and technology, and defense) that had been defined by the late premier Zhou Enlai.

As intended, reforms began to breath new life into China. Over the 1980–1990 period, real GNP advanced at about a 9 percent average annual rate, and the overall economy more than doubled. Farmers became relatively well off. Through reforms, they were allowed to make use of surplus land not needed for producing their quota of crops. Hundreds of foreign business ventures sprang up in designated special-enterprise zones and in "open" coastal cities and coastal areas that offered economic, including tax, incentives.

Reforms transformed Guangdong province in southern China into an economic powerhouse. With its proximity to Hong Kong, its access to ports, and other advantages, Guangdong became the home of three special-enterprise zones. This made it a draw for foreign business, especially from Hong Kong. Between 1981 and 1990, the province's average annual GNP ballooned 15.8 percent. During that period, the province registered "one of the [fastest] regional growth rates in the world," according to the brokerage firm of W. I. Carr (Far East) Limited in Hong Kong.

In 1991, Guangdong residents enjoyed the highest annual income level in China, according to W. I. Carr. The firm said that income in the province averaged $421, versus $415 in Shanghai and $376 in Beijing.

But reforms needed to be accelerated to provide more jobs and a better standard of living. The pool of workers is increasing, even as the state sector where an estimated one-third of enterprises are losing money, appears unable to accommodate more employees.

As General Secretary Jiang Zemin admitted in October 1992 at the opening of the Chinese Communist party's 14th national congress:

> At present the overstaffing, overlapping, and inefficiency of many party and government organizations cuts them off from the masses and so greatly hampers the efforts to change the way enterprises operate that there is no alternative to reform.

Layoffs are continuing in the state sector. At the same time, the income gap is widening between people in the coastal areas being developed and those in the poorer interior. As a result, many northern Chinese have migrated to Guangdong in search of jobs.

Political developments are also fueling the need for more reforms. Until recently, Chinese leadership seemed confident of its ability to control the public, as illustrated by the events of June 4, 1989. That spring, when pro-democracy sentiment rose up from a crowd gathered in Beijing's Tiananmen Square, Chinese hard-line leadership quashed it in what became the notorious June massacre. It was clear that Chinese leadership intended to brook no dissent.

But two years later the collapse of Communism in Eastern

CHINA—SHANGHAI

Currency: Renminbi.

Stock Exchanges: Shanghai Securities Exchange (SSE).

Indexes: The Shanghai Securities Exchange Index and the Jingan Index.

Types of Equities: A shares (for resident Chinese investors only), B shares (for foreign investors only).

Regulatory Body/Stock Exchange Supervision: The China Securities Regulatory Commission, the administrative arm of the Securities Commission of the State Council, plays an executive role in monitoring the markets.

Depository: All listed securities are operated in a scripless environment. Clearance and settlements are handled by the Shanghai Securities Central Clearing and Registration Corporation, a wholly owned unit of the Shanghai Securities Exchange.

Settlement Information

Equities:

- T + 3 for B shares.
- Scripless/book entry only.
- Receive/deliver versus payment not available for B share trading, since settlement is in U.S. dollars.
- Same-day turnaround trades are not possible.

Fixed Income: Not available to foreign investors.

Taxes:

- Capital gains taxes of 0 to 20 percent had not been charged to foreign investors as of mid-year 1993.
- Dividends are not taxed.
- Stamp duty: 0.30 percent of transaction value.
- Brokerage fee: 0.60 percent of transaction value for local brokers, negotiable for foreign brokers.

- Stock exchange levy: 0.05 percent of transaction value.
- Registration fee: 0.10 percent of par value (buyer and seller).
- Clearing fee:
  —under custodian bank: US$8 per transaction
  —not under custodian bank: US$4 per transaction
- Depository fee: US$20 per registration number.

Restrictions for Foreign Investors:

- Foreign investors cannot purchase "A" shares or other types of financial instruments other than B shares.
- Foreign investors must register their investment accounts separately at each exchange.
- B share investors holding more than 5 percent of the total issued shares of a listed company must report this information to the People's Bank of China.

Securities Lending: Not yet available.

SOURCE: The Bank of New York

Europe and the former Soviet Union posed a new and ominous threat to the leadership of China. As the rejection of Communism swept around the world, China's leaders needed to respond positively to keep the movement off their doorstep. The Deng faction chose aggressive economic reforms as a way to mollify the people while allowing the Communist party to retain power.

Continuing Reforms

Indeed, economic reforms have been continuing. The first phase of reforms, in the 1980s, was mainly intended to kick off the process. But although reforms stalled during 1988–91, amid economic austerity, they were resurrected in 1992 as reformers sought to accelerate activity in order to complete China's modernization.

In industrial development, Special Economic Zones (SEZs) were created in 1980 to attract foreign investment through low-tax treatment and other incentives. (The five SEZs are in Shenzhen, Shantou, Zhuhai, Hainan, and Xiamen.) In 1984, the concept was expanded to include tax-advantaged Economic and Technological Development Zones (ETDZs) for manufacturers in 14 cities along China's coast. In 1989, large areas of China's coast land became Open Coastal Economic Zones, whose tax treatment was halfway between that of SEZs and China's standard tax treatment, reports Stuart Valentine, a solicitor in the Hong Kong law firm of Clifford Chance. In 1990, Shanghai's Pudong development area was granted the status of an SEZ. Now China also has special zones for high-technology companies. "And the very latest is something called 'tourist zones,' which is a concept now being developed," says Valentine.

Among other reforms: the conversion of many more state-owned businesses, to enable them to sell their shares; trimming governmental bureaucracy; and the elimination of many sinecure posts. To enhance China's growing market economy, price controls on 593 items and materials were lifted in 1992 and about 90 percent of prices have now been liberalized. On the trade front, tariffs have been reduced to meet the requirements of joining the General Agreement on Tariffs and Trade. According to press reports, these and other reforms have sparked a surge of foreign investment.

Deng is credited as the chief architect of China's reform and modernization. During the first half of 1992 he was said to prefer at least 10 percent annual economic growth. Formal targets—originally 6 percent for 1991 and 1992—were adjusted downward to between 8 and 9 percent by the national congress in October. The concurrent 20-year plan through the year 2000 calls for an average 7 percent economic growth over the life of the plan. In 1992, China's red-hot economy grew 12 percent, and forecasts put 1993's growth at about 10 percent.

Many economists doubt that China can sustain a 12 percent annual growth level. However, quite a few analysts expect that an 8 percent level can be achieved. Even that pace would make a significant difference to China, whose economy is already ranked as the world's third largest.

But so far the PRC has not learned how to control its boom/bust economic cycles. During the 1980s, spurs in economic growth triggered inflation, forcing Beijing periodically to clamp down on credit conditions. Its heavy-handed measures (its monetary tools are limited) would send the economy spinning downward. After inflation soared in 1988, a three-year economic austerity program (1989–1991) successfully trimmed price escalation. But by 1992, inflation was again on the rise, reaching a broiling 15.7 percent annual rate in major cities in the first quarter of 1993. In May 1993 China responded by lifting interest rates, and as inflation persisted, raised them again that July as part of a package of anti-inflation measures. There had been concern that inflation might spill over to the consumer sector; conceivably, savings, estimated at more than $200 billion, could be redirected into purchases. But the inflationary problem was different in 1993. This time it was fueled by a capital spending boom, while consumer demand seemed to be under better control than in the 1987–1988 period when prices soared by more than 30 percent in some of the big cities.

Nicholas Kwan, senior economist with Merrill Lynch, Pierce, Fenner & Smith (Singapore) Private Limited, believes that inflation can now be checked, or at least postponed, because of China's improved output, especially outside of government

CHINA—SHENZHEN

Currency: Renminbi.

Stock Exchanges: Shenzhen Stock Exchange.

Index: The Shenzhen Index.

Types of Equities: A shares (for resident Chinese investors only), B shares (for foreign investors only).

Regulatory Body/Stock Exchange Supervision: The China Securities Regulatory Commission, the administrative arm of the Securities Commission of the State Council, plays an executive role in monitoring the markets.

Depository: All listed securities are operated in a scripless environment. Securities are deposited with the Shenzhen Securities Registration Company (SSRC). "A" shares can also be held in physical form.

Settlement Information

Equities:

- T + 3.
- Scripless/book entry only (although A shares can be rematerialized after settlement).
- Receive/deliver versus payment available (against Hong Kong dollars only for B shares).
- Same-day turnaround trades are not possible.

Fixed Income: Not available to foreign investors.

Taxes:

- Capital gains taxes of 0 to 20 percent had not been charged to foreign investors as of mid-year 1993.
- Dividends are taxed at a rate of 10 percent (for the portion exceeding the 1-year time deposit rate).
- Stamp duty: 0.30 percent of the transaction value.
- Brokerage fee: 0.50 percent of the transaction value for A shares and 0.70 percent of the transaction value for B shares.

- Stock exchange levy: 0.05 percent of transaction value.
- Registration fee: 0.30 percent of par value chargeable to the buyer only.
- Clearing fee: 0.10 percent of the value of each transaction.
- Depository fee: 0.15 percent of month-end portfolio value.

Restrictions for Foreign Investors:

- Foreign investors cannot purchase A shares or other types of financial instruments.
- Foreign investors must register their investment accounts separately at each exchange.
- Prior approval of the People's Bank of China must be obtained before any B shareholder can acquire more than 5 percent of the total shares of a listed company.

Securities Lending: Not yet available.

SOURCE: The Bank of New York

enterprises. "The nonstate sector is growing fast," he reports. "If China produces more goods to meet demand, price rises can be contained."

Kwan waxes optimistic with his own economic forecast for China. As his best odds, he gives China a 60 percent chance that it will manage "soft" economic landing in this cycle and average 7 to 8 percent economic growth over the next 8 to 10 years. He sees the country as having only a 30 to 35 percent chance of "running into another hard landing" and repeating its boom/bust cycles as in the past, and he foresees, at most, a 5 to 10 percent likelihood that the PRC will regress into internal economic and political chaos.

China's Companies

China's economy is split into three kinds of operations: the state, cooperative, and private sector. Although still comprising the bulk of the economy, the state sector has been one of China's problems that encourages reforms. This sector includes operations in heavy industry, raw materials, larger retailing operations, and, generally, areas of strategic importance. Although changes are in store, this sector has been weighed down by bureaucracy, excessive staffing, the need to provide a host of social services to its workers, and production focused on meeting production schedules rather than earning profits.

The nonstate sector has proved to be much more vibrant. Statistics show that industrial output of government enterprises in 1991 was 53 percent of the nation's total, down from approximately 75 percent in 1982. In 1991, the output of state enterprises climbed 8 percent, compared with 18 percent in collective enterprises, 24 percent in private businesses, and 54 percent in foreign-invested enterprises, according to *Taipan,* a publication of Agora Incorporated in Baltimore.

Foreigners have done business in China and often gained from it. Money manager Robert Lloyd George, chairman and CEO of Lloyd George Management in Hong Kong, tells of a friend in Hong Kong who set up a successful textile factory in

Shanghai. The arrangement stemmed from the fact that the friend's aunt had been left behind when the family escaped from the communists in 1949. Although her emigrant family had been sending her money, they decided by the late 1970s to establish a textile factory in Shanghai and put their aunt in charge of it.

Today, the factory makes about $10 million a year. Its successes are due to such factors as China's low wage scales, coupled with managerial expertise imported from Hong Kong. "But it was the family connection that originated the idea," Lloyd George points out.

Plexchem Asia Limited in Hong Kong—a distributor, trader, and producer of industrial commodities—has been doing business in the PRC since 1980. Its chairman and CEO Alan Frishman appreciates the lower cost of land rentals and labor costs in China. To illustrate these benefits, Frishman points out: "In Hong Kong, you're paying workers maybe $800 a month, compared with maybe one-tenth of that in China." Given the cost savings, he maintains that operating in the PRC not only "significantly improves companies' profitability but gives them a competitive edge."

Since 1979, foreigners have been able to participate in China's growing economy through direct investments. Entities open to direct foreign investment are: equity joint ventures; cooperative joint ventures; foreign-owned businesses, as well as processing and assembly agreements in which foreigners provide the raw materials that China processes for a fee; and compensation deals. In the latter case, foreigners provide services and/or technical training to the Chinese in exchange for finished products produced by the Chinese, according to Wardley Investment Services (Hong Kong) Limited.

In 1984, China took a significant step forward when a Communist party congress approved the concept of converting some enterprises into companies limited by shares, also known as joint stock companies. By the mid-1980s, converted companies began to sell shares to employees, other enterprises, and—to a limited extent—the Chinese public. This invariably led to the creation of stock trading and stock exchanges. Although trading had unofficially begun earlier, the Shanghai Securities

Exchange officially opened in December 1990, followed by the Shenzhen Stock Exchange in July 1991. In late 1991, China took the monumental step of allowing foreigners to buy shares in Chinese companies.

The opening of China's market stirred international attention. Foreigners were both curious and excited about this perceived long-term opportunity in this new emerging market. Clifford Chance's Stuart Valentine hailed the move as "the biggest development in China for foreign investors since 1979," when direct foreign investment became legal.

For Chinese companies, it provided access to a new source of foreign capital, one that in many cases would not have engaged in direct investing in China. So far the development has been confined in scope, since only a relatively small number of companies have issued stocks. Most organizations converted to "companies limited by shares." The only ones that can issue stock to the public have been state enterprises and equity joint-venture companies. As of mid-1992, according to Valentine, there were 3220 Chinese companies limited by shares (joint stock companies), compared with over 3.3 million Chinese collective enterprises and 37,000 foreign investment enterprises.

Under the new arrangement, foreigners would invest in a separate "B" class of stock, while only Chinese nationals would be permitted to buy "A" shares. "B" shares carry the same rights and obligations as "A" shares, but can be bought only by foreign investors.

In 1993, China created an additional class of stock to facilitate the direct listings of Chinese companies on foreign stock exchanges. Known as "H" shares (for Hong Kong), or "I" shares (for international), they carry the same rights and obligations as "A" shares and "B" shares, but they can only be traded on stock exchanges outside of China.

Companies issue B shares to gain foreign currency needed to finance capital investments in foreign technology and/or to help pay dividends to foreign investors, says David Whittall, an economic analyst with Baring Securities (Hong Kong) Limited.

Analysts say that companies approved for B share trading are among China's best. China Southern Glass, largest glass producer in Southeast Asia, was the first company to list "B" shares in Shenzhen. Its profits soared 144 percent in the company's fiscal year 1992, according to Baring Securities. Baring's David Whittall highlights the attractions of several other companies that were among the earliest issuers of B shares. For example, Shenzhen China Bicycles is the world's largest bike producer, with about a 30 percent world market share. As output and sales increased, Baring forecasted that the company's year-on-year profits would climb almost 54 percent in 1992, followed by expected gains of 39 percent in 1993 and about 30 percent in 1994.

Shenzhen Konka, another joint venture, is believed to be the largest manufacturer of television sets in China, Whittall notes. Shenzhen Properties & Resources Development benefits from having 30 percent of its land bank in booming downtown Shenzhen and the remainder in Fujian province, which is expected to attract increasing amounts of foreign investments, especially from Taiwan.

As is the case in every other country, companies in China have their problems. Shenzhen Konka, for example, exports most of its television production, which, according to Baring Securities, holds down profit margins because of strong competition in that market. Shanghai Vacuum Electronic Devices Company Limited, one of China's major producers of television components, was the very first company to issue B shares, which trade in Shanghai. "As might not be expected, it has heavy debt and excessive staffing, as well as marginal accounting practices," reports George Bergland, president of Amer-China Partners Limited. "Although its B shares were rapidly sold," at its initial offering, "buyers may have been thinking less of providing capital for a China enterprise than [finding] a place to make a quick turn on investments."

Risks

For investors, China presents a wide array of both attractions and risk. In the plus column: phenomenal economic growth, an enormous domestic market, low labor costs, a manufacturing base, and an enduring entrepreneurial spirit among its people.

On the face of it, the opportunity appears unsurpassed in the world.

But ample social, economic, and market risks loom in this communist-controlled land. China has been known for its political purges and rehabilitations, human rights violations, and repression of publicly expressed ideas. Although reformers emerged even more in control after the 1992 14th party congress, differences of opinion at the top are likely to continue. And it remains unclear what political agenda will emerge after the eventual death of Deng Xioping.

Among the economic and market-related worries: inflation, credit curbs, currency devaluation, and the quality of corporate accounting practices. In addition, investors also fear that impediments to trade—vital to much of China's private sector activity—could arise. As the prospectus for The China Fund Inc. points out, "revocation by the United States of China's most-favored nation trading status, which the U.S. Congress considers annually, could adversely affect the trade and economic development of China, and indirectly, the economy of Hong Kong."

From most investors' perspectives, China's stock markets are still too new, volatile, and small to attract sizable investments. Investors must also bear in mind that "China may require governmental approval for the repatriation of investment income, capital, or the proceeds of sales of securities by foreign investors. In addition, if there is a deterioration in China's balance of payments, or for other reasons, China may impose temporary restrictions on foreign capital remittances abroad," reports the prospectus for The China Fund.

Investors complain about China's perceived inadequate legal system and corporate rules, including accounting practices. At this point, while there are national guidelines, China has neither a comprehensive national law covering joint stock companies nor a comprehensive national securities law. Shanghai and Shenzhen have developed their own separate laws on local joint stock companies and their own regulations governing their markets.

In China, legal enforcement of existing laws is weak, and typically China creates detailed law as to the regulation of activities after those activities are already under way. Valentine of Clifford

Chance illustrates the time-lag effect of Chinese law. Although a Communist party meeting in late 1978 authorized foreign investment in China, no laws regulated equity joint ventures until the second half of 1979 or cooperative joint ventures until 1988. In the meantime, joint-venture contracts and loan agreements were signed, meaning that "the law was effectively written into the contracts." Laws involving securities have been evolving since 1984. But, since Shanghai had no company law until May 1992, and Shenzhen only created its law in March of the same year, prior investors in companies located there "wouldn't have known what kind of animal they were buying," points out Valentine. "There had been nothing to spell out what a 'joint stock company' was, other than rather obscure regulations on 'foreign-related companies' in the special Economic Zones and other basic local rules," says Valentine.

Management and accounting practices in the PRC have been structured around the needs of the mother country, not foreign investors. As previously mentioned, state enterprises have been socialist, not profit-oriented in structure. Workers had become accustomed to an "iron rice bowl" mentality that guaranteed employment.

The situation is better for the private sector. Although private businesses typically also provide at least some social services to employees, they enjoy greater freedom to set their own staffing levels. As Baring's Whittall describes, "in Shenzhen, managers can now determine what level of staffing allows them to operate profitably. They don't have to take on more people than they need."

Traditional Chinese accounting practices "have been quite different" from internationally accepted standards, says Matthew Harrison, senior manager with the accounting firm of Price Waterhouse in Hong Kong. Differences have tended to be more in the areas that require judgments by organizations, such as accounting for asset depreciation and taking provisions for unrecoverable debts. The quality of accounting practices has varied among organizations. While some companies have kept detailed books and records, other companies may have had gaps in their records and may not have used computerized systems.

But lately "there have been great advances in accounting practices in China," says Harrison. New accounting rules have been promulgated for joint-venture companies, wholly owned foreign enterprises, and for companies limited by shares. For example, experts report that as of July 1, 1993, all Chinese companies are being instructed to adopt new accounting practices that, although not generally accepted accounting principles (GAAP), would be understandable to Westerners.

The need to provide financial information in a form satisfactory to "B" share (or "H" or "I" share) investors in Chinese companies has been one of the main factors in promoting the introduction of international accounting concepts in China.

In foreign exchange, China's currency, the renminbi, remains nonconvertible, although that situation is expected to change at some point in the foreseeable future. For now, however, international portfolio investors must rely on the ability of the companies in which they invest to generate foreign exchange in order to pay dividends to holders of "B," "H," or "I" shares.

Some taxation issues have yet to be put to rest. At present, along with trading and brokerage-related fees, B share investors pay a stamp duty of 0.30 percent of the stock transaction's value. Although the government has not been collecting a capital gains tax on profits from securities trading, that situation could change, market experts point out.

Listings

China's market developments have been controlled. Companies allowed to list shares have had to fulfill a greater number of requirements when issuing B shares than A shares. In general, companies wishing to list B shares are expected to have an audit performed by international accountants before the initial public offering and produce a stable and adequate supply of foreign exchange to pay dividends. In Shenzhen, among a number of other rules, companies listing B shares must have a minimum return on capital of 10 percent in the year preceding the listing, and 8 percent over the two years prior to the year of the listing. In Shanghai, among other requirements, B share issuers must have been operating profitably for at least two consecutive years prior to the listing, reports Credit Lyonnais International Asset Management (HK) Limited.

Beijing has imposed a number of regulations aimed at creating orderly markets. The cornerstones are a ban on short-selling, meant to curb speculation, and the requirement that foreign investors must report stock holdings of over 5 percent in any one company.

Since the renminbi is not internationally convertible, B share trades take place in foreign currency. In Shenzhen, B shares are quoted and trades are settled in Hong Kong dollars. In Shanghai, B shares are quoted in U.S. dollars, and trades are settled in the same currency.

Settlement of B shares is "scripless" in both Shenzhen and Shanghai, eliminating the need for physical delivery. Cash and stock entries are processed in book-entry form, and trades are settled on the third business day after the trade occurs.

Thus far, Shanghai and Shenzhen are the only officially sanctioned exchanges for the trading of listed stocks. In the future, additional exchanges are expected, perhaps in the northern Chinese cities of Tianjin and Shenyang.

Even if more exchanges debut, it appears likely that the Shanghai exchange will ultimately become the premier market. The gateway to China's heartland, and home of more than 13 million people, the city of Shanghai is China's business and industrial capital. The market capitalization of its listed shares typically dwarfs those of Shenzhen.

Stock trading began in Shanghai in the 1890s, but the market was closed in 1949 as the Communists rose to power. Reopened officially in 1990, Shanghai was the first exchange to offer trading in B shares, starting in early 1992. But Shanghai was initially slower than Shenzhen to list additional B shares. Until mid-year 1992, Shanghai had only one B share listing. However, the advent of eight additional companies' B shares in mid-1992 (and many more A shares) helped to put a damper on prices. Those developments were followed by the mid-August riot in Shenzhen. Anger over news that the government had run out of applications to buy shares in 14 new stock offerings triggered an outbreak of violence. Official corruption was alleged.

The ugly incident triggered concern that the government might curtail stock market development—and possibly even shut them down. But some of those fears seemed to subside after the government, in September 1992, revealed plans to create a regulatory body independent from the central bank, which had been handling market supervision. Subsequently, a new Securities Commission of the State Council (SCSC) (cabinet) and its administrative arm, the China Securities Regulatory Commission, assumed responsibility for market regulation. While the SCSC formulates broad market regulations and strategies, the Regulatory Commission sets day-to-day policies.

But the rioting, the flood of new issues, and other political/economic/currency problems took their toll on the market in the second half of 1992. As of late January 1993, 4 out of the then-10 stocks trading in Shanghai were trading at below their new issue price, reports Oscar Wong, deputy managing director, G. T. Management (Asia) Ltd. in Hong Kong. Although all B share stocks in Shenzhen were then trading above their IPO (initial public offering) level, "many of the earlier listings were half or more below their peak" in price, says Wong. By late in the year, the price-earnings ratio for B shares had plunged from about 30 to 40 times earnings, at their peak in 1992, to as low as about 12 to 13 times 1992's earnings in Shanghai. In Shenzhen, the P/E ratio fell to a low of about 15, Wong said.

By late July 1993, the number of listed B shares had reached 29—17 in Shenzhen and 12 in Shanghai—according to Bruce Corben of Baring Securities. But since the market still seemed illiquid and risky, many foreign investors were still opting for "China concept" stocks trading in Hong Kong and elsewhere.

How to Invest

Today, international portfolio investors can play China through direct purchases of Chinese shares, through funds that invest in Chinese and/or other equities, and via the stocks of foreign companies that do significant business with and in China. In the fourth quarter of 1992, Brilliance China Automotive Holdings, a Bermuda-incorporated holding company for a Chinese minibus maker, listed on the New York Stock Exchange.

By mid-1993, two Chinese companies—Tsingtao Brewery and Shanghai Petrochemical Complex—had been approved to list on the Hong Kong Stock Exchange, and seven others were awaiting such approval. The other seven companies are: Yizheng Joint Corporation of Chemical Industries, Kunming Machine Tool Plant, Guangzhou Shipyard Plant, Ma An Shan Iron and Steel Company, Dongfang Electrical Machinery, Tianjin Bohai Chemical Industry Group Co., and Beijing Renmin Machinery General Plant. Selected by China's State Council, the nine companies are mostly heavy industrial businesses with earnings in foreign currency from exports.

For investors with strong stomachs, buying B shares is the "purest play" on China. But choices are certainly limited, and experts say that many of them change hands infrequently.

China funds provide an alternative to buying B shares directly. By the second quarter of 1993, there were 35 China mutual funds, with assets totaling about $1.1 billion, reports the newsletter *The Micropal Emerging Market Fund Monitor.* Employing different styles, a small number have been investing heavily in B shares, while the majority feature a mix of investments, including Chinese B shares or China-play stocks listed on foreign exchanges, particularly Hong Kong's. Some funds also make direct investments in Chinese companies. Three of the funds—The China Fund Inc., JF China Region Fund, and Greater China Fund—are listed on the New York Stock Exchange.

The China Fund Inc., managed by Wardley Investment Services (Hong Kong) Limited, was underwritten by Oppenheimer & Company Incorporated and Merrill Lynch. According to its prospectus, The China Fund targets 25 percent of its assets for direct investments in Chinese companies and 65 percent for China-related stock plays.

In April 1992, G. T. Management in Hong Kong says it became the first organization to launch a fund that invests solely in Chinese B shares. The $30 million (as of January 1993) GT Shenzhen & China Fund was set up as an open-ended vehicle and is marketed in Europe and Asia. At year-end 1992, the fund was about 95 percent invested, according to G.T.'s Oscar Wong.

In December 1992, Batterymarch Financial Management in Boston launched its $35 million closed-end Equity Fund of

China for U.S. institutional investors. In June 1993, the fund had about one-quarter of its assets in Chinese B shares and the rest in China plays listed outside the PRC.

To enhance its ability to buy shares in China, the firm has tightened contacts with high-level PRC officials. In return, Batterymarch instructs Chinese brokerage firms on services expected by international institutional investors. Among other liaisons, Batterymarch works with the Shanghai Investment Trust Company, a government-owned investment banking firm, as a consultant on potential investments, and the China Merchants' Group, a government-owned conglomerate, with which Batterymarch exchanges information on markets, products, and investments, Speidell says. Batterymarch also has "close relationships with representatives of the People's Bank of China in Beijing as well as in Shenzhen and Shanghai."

Some funds targeted to take direct stakes in Chinese companies have run into problems nailing down good investments. But the $60 million China Investment & Development Fund Ltd., managed by KB China Management Ltd., Hong Kong, has found an ample supply of possibilities, officials say. KB benefits from having the China International Trust & Investment Corporation, China's international merchant bank, as a shareholder in, and an advisor to, the fund.

Launched in October 1992, the fund takes direct stakes of 25 percent or more in Chinese companies that have the potential to be listed in four to five years. With holdings of 25 percent or more, the company qualifies as a Sino–foreign equity joint venture, and can claim tax and trading advantages in China.

As of June 1993, the fund had three investments: a 30 percent stake in Shanghai Intl Storage Battery Ltd. that cost $4.1 million, a 34.6 percent holding in Jiangxi Ceramics Co. Ltd. for $5.3 million and a 35 percent stake in Upsonic BVI Ltd., the offshore arm of a Taiwanese group that will set up a wholly-owned joint venture in China to manufacture and distribute uninterruptible power supplies.

Andrew Taylor, managing director of KB China Management Ltd., believes that taking direct stakes in China is better than buying B shares: "With our fund we think we get the best of both worlds. We invest in companies with lower market multiples than those of currently listed shares. Eventually, our holdings will go public. But in the meantime, these investments are still expected to produce a dividend flow."

Anna Tong, director, Aetna Investment Management (F.E.) Ltd., echoes his opinion. On one hand, she sees "good investment opportunities in some of the newly listed shares, and probably a few names among earlier listings are still attractive. But the return potential is higher from direct stakes in "good entrepreneurial companies." Once they list, "investors would get a windfall—more so than with B shares."

Investing in Hong Kong

Since China's markets are still small, many international stock investors have been playing their PRC card through the Hong Kong market. There they find much more substantial trading liquidity, better market and corporate disclosures, and a market that—unlike China's—imposes no limitations on foreign investments. Investors in Hong Kong have been able to choose from a wide array of stocks, rather than grab whatever has been available in China.

Anne Tatlock, executive vice president with Fiduciary Trust Company International in New York, believes that the riskiness of the Chinese market has made it unwise to invest clients' money in the earliest stages of these markets. "An intriguing market is opening up in China; and once the market widens it would be healthier and a more appropriate way to play the dynamic growth in China," she said in 1992. "But Shenzhen is both very limited in the types of investments, marketability of issues, and the number of shares traded," as well as weak on "the whole question of what you're dealing with in trading, settlements, taxation, currencies."

Moreover, in their early days, China's markets were "so speculative. People wanted in at any price, and that hasn't made sense to us," she said in early 1993. "But over the next two to three years, as China's market expands, we would want to be a part of that growing, dynamic market. And we will look at it in a serious way."

In the meantime, Fiduciary Trust was playing China through

the Hong Kong market. In 1991 the firm opted to overweight Hong Kong, with a portfolio exposure of about 10 to 12 percent. At year-end 1992, the firm was maintaining an approximately 10 percent weighting in Hong Kong shares.

Established in 1891, share trading has existed for over a century in Hong Kong. With a capitalization of about $171 billion (1992), that market is today the second largest in Asia. Although volatile, and certainly prone to jitters over political/economic activities—especially in China—it also reflects investors' enthusiasm over the current and future opportunities in both Hong Kong and China.

Hong Kong's economy real GDP growth, of 5.2 percent in 1992, could expand by 5 to 7 percent annually through 1997, believes Simon Ogus, an economist with G. T. Management. Among its attractions, this British territory has the highest per capita income in Asia outside of Japan. Even though Hong Kong loses 70,000 manufacturing jobs a year to China, it gains 1.2 service jobs for every manufacturing one lost, according to Ogus. With its less than 2 percent unemployment rate (1992), the territory needs to import labor to fill job openings.

While the territory suffers from high inflation, which was 9.4 percent in 1992, it is unable to raise interest rates to fight it, since Hong Kong's currency is pegged to the U.S. dollar. Indirectly, that's good news for the territory's stock market. With Hong Kong's fixed-income instruments producing negative real returns, equities become the obvious choice for securities investment in the colony.

Investors can choose from a wide range of Hong Kong–listed companies with significant PRC exposure. Among them: Café de Coral Holdings, a fast-food restaurant operator that has branched into China; Goldlion Holdings, manufacturer of brand-name men's apparel, which expects that by 1994, 64 to 65 percent of all sales will be to China; Hopewell Holdings, which, among other attractions, is developing a superhighway in southern China; and Tian An China Investments, a Sino–Hong Kong consortium that invests in and develops properties in China.

Nervousness continues about Hong Kong's future after it reunites with China in 1997. Officially, the territory will be treated as a Special Autonomous Region and will be permitted to run most of its own affairs. But lingering uncertainty about the implications of unification has encouraged some emigration and prompted many to seek foreign passports as future insurance policies. A number of Hong Kong pension funds have been moved to new offshore headquarters.

The market's price-earnings multiple has also reflected concerns about unification with China. In December 1992, its P/E ratio was about 11, compared with 18 for Singapore's market, about 15.3 for South Korea's, and 20 for Taiwan.

Hong Kong crowds protested loudly after the Tiananmen Square crackdown, which provoked Beijing to snarl back with threats aimed at what it called subversive elements in the territory. And that wasn't the end of Sino–Hong Kong tensions. Hong Kong's Governor Chris Patten infuriated the PRC by proposing in 1992 an expansion of democracy in the territory. For the 1995 elections, his plan calls for lowering the voting age from 21 to 18 and allowing every member of the Legislative Council—Hong Kong's governing body—to be directly or indirectly elected, thereby abolishing appointed seats.

The PRC's ire over this promotion of democracy clouded Sino–Hong Kong relations in 1993. And it stirred uncertainty in Hong Kong's business community. Some feared that a continued rift with China over the Patten program could possibly stall some development projects and erode confidence. Other sources of friction could also arise before Beijing officially reclaims Hong Kong in 1997. But in the end, the transition is likely to go smoothly. Hong Kong is already taking gradual steps leading up to this formal changing of the guard.

Whatever happens with China's Communist leadership, many agree that its economic advances cannot be permanently reversed. Nor would future leaders, acting in their own as well as the country's best interests, be likely to try to turn back the economic clock. Guangdong's successes are an achievement that Beijing's leadership wishes to claim and to replicate. Believing this, more and more international investors are exploring opportunities in this vast land.

These opportunities are spreading rapidly amid China's economic reformation. However rocky China's transition to a more market-oriented economy may be, its commitment to economic development is clear. From all appearances, the PRC is finally taking its Great Leap Forward.

24

The Commonwealth of Independent States

It would seem a match made in heaven. American manufacturers need new markets to which to sell their goods and services. Russia and the other states that made up the Soviet Union constitute a vast virgin market.

The former communist states need huge transfusions of cash to prop up their ailing economies. American investors are looking for deals, and willing to take at least a certain amount of risk in the expectation of future profit.

As Russia and the Ukraine phase in reforms, a capitalistic spirit is developing in their new commodities and stock exchanges.

"Today all countries without exception are working to attract foreign capital, and it is not considered a sellout of the homeland," is the way Nursultant Nazarbayev, the Kazakhstan President, explained this spirit to his parliament in 1991, as reported in *The Wall Street Journal*.

Shortly after the failed coup that established the Commonwealth of Independent States, Robert S. Strauss, then the U.S. ambassador to Russia, said: "If I were younger [he was 73 at the time], I would invest $100,000 in the old Soviet Union and run it up to $10 million. But if I had $10 million to invest, I would gamble only $100,000 of it." Strauss, a millionaire Texas lawyer, has earned a reputation as a shrewd trader.

Why then are American investors so cautious about joining in the transformation from Karl Marx to free markets? Why are they watching, waiting, and hedging their bets? The answer lies in history, and in 74 years of communist rule that opened a wide gulf between two of the greatest nations in the world.

The Cold War between the Soviet Union and the West was a 40-year nightmare, out of whose shadow we are only now emerging. It grew from fear that the Russians were preparing to spread their Communist doctrine and way of life to the rest of the world. The United States and its allies spent trillions of dollars to contain the Soviet Union behind an Iron Curtain and prevent it from using its military might in a third world war.

Today the countries that made up the Soviet bloc are no longer a threat. The enemy is not their military might but their weakness and unpredictability. Western governments and businesses are being asked to invest in the Commonwealth of Independent States (CIS), comprising the former Soviet republics, to prevent its collapse.

In return, the former Communist states have agreed to work toward establishing democracy and a free-market economy. They must accomplish this monumental task in a disintegrated state where the economy is in ruins and people have little or no experience with either capitalism or democracy.

The CIS is a phantom state made up of many of the former Soviet states, but the CIS has virtually no control. The CIS was the final compromise engineered by Mikhail Gorbachev, who set out to reform the Soviet Union and ended up presiding over its collapse. His partial reforms were not enough to turn a totalitarian economic system into a free-market economy, but he won the Nobel Peace Prize for trying.

The day before Gorbachev planned to sign a union treaty intended to keep several republics together, hard-line communists moved to overthrow him. The coup failed, and on December 8, 1991, the leaders of Russia declared that the Soviet Union had ceased to exist. The republics were invited to join with Russia in the CIS, and in short order most of them said they would. At one time or another those that have agreed to join have included the Ukraine, Belarus, Moldova, Georgia, Armenia, Azerbaijan, Uzbekistan, Turkmenistan, Tajikistan, Kazakhstan, and Kyrgyzstan, but a number have dropped out since or have only observer status. Each of the republics is a sovereign state that controls its own economy and natural resources and collects its own taxes, providing only minimal support to the CIS.

Boris N. Yeltsin, President of Russia, inherited the mantle of chaos. With the freeing of most prices on January 2, 1991, he staked his political life on the rapid creation of a free-market economy in Russia. The euphoria that followed the coup was swiftly followed by an assessment of the real state of affairs: GNP and foreign trade down, rampant inflation, recession, and unemployment. Many of the countries' industries, built to support the military, were no longer needed.

The Western nations agreed, and continue to agree, that the political stability of the CIS requires substantial infusions of cash credits and know-how, but they have been reluctant to provide it. The botched coup of hard-liners lasted only three days—August 19 to 31, 1991—but uncertainty about the union remains. The risks are that the reforms will not work and that there will be a return to the deep freeze of the Cold War. If Yeltsin were to be toppled, the result could be anarchy—strikes, riots, bloodshed, even revolution. Economic disintegration could send millions of refugees into Western Europe, further destabilizing that region.

There is a bright side to the picture, too. The CIS is a rich consumer market—of almost 300 million—waiting to be tapped. About 150 million live in Russia alone, where there are more proven oil reserves than in Saudi Arabia. The former Soviet states are rich in other resources as well—natural gas, coal, iron, gold, timber, nickel, potash, and manganese. Food and agricultural products include grain, dairy, meat, and fish. An infrastructure of roads, railroads, and harbors exists, albeit in rundown condition, to transport these materials. An outstanding educational system has produced a highly skilled work force, exceptionally well trained in math, engineering, and the sciences.

The quick collapse of the coup indicated strength and staying power for reform. But by the end of 1992, the impetus for reform in Russia—the state that made the most progress in that direction—

had stalled. Observers feared that Yeltsin would be forced out of office by radical nationalists who wanted to recreate the Soviet Union. So far, that hasn't happened. But although Yeltsin has thus far endured as Russia's reformist leader, ongoing political clashes in Russia—and in other CIS states—appear to be keeping many would-be investors at bay.

Westerners drawn to Russia and the other commonwealth states appear to be waiting cautiously for the wrangling between Yeltsin and his opponents to end, and the Russian state to create the clear legal basis they need to sink large amounts of capital into private ventures. Many are still not confident that Russia and other CIS states can now sustain market economies. Investors' immediate worries include instability, ethnic rivalries, changing and arbitrary tax laws, and a general lack of understanding of the free-market economy or the democracy that most Russians say they want to emulate.

The Transition: Hardships and Hopes

After years of halfway measures under Gorbachev, the coup gave renewed impetus to reform. But leaving the Lenin legacy behind brought new hardships to the general public—particularly to hard-pressed pensioners on fixed incomes, many of whom were worse off than before.

After Yeltsin freed controls, food disappeared quickly from the fixed-price state shops and became substantially more expensive in the black and open markets. To ease the pain of the transition, many necessities had to remain subsidized.

Meanwhile, the economy continued to shrink. After falling 8.9 percent in 1991, Russia's GDP declined 14.4 percent in 1992, according to Morgan Guaranty Trust Co. As hyperinflation struck in 1992, workers were understandably outraged that their already low pay levels were not keeping up with galloping prices in the open markets.

Life today for the average Russian is hard, but not entirely bleak. Food and clothing are scarce, but that is not new. Thanks to an ineffective distribution system, it was scarce under the

Soviet Union as well. An alternative economy made up of informal street sellers and embryonic entrepreneurs—with goods or services to barter—has sprung up to ease some of the shortages.

A new class of rich entrepreneurs feasts at banquet tables heaped high with caviar, *blini,* and other ethnic delicacies: Food isn't scarce for the few who can pay for it with hard currency. Most Russians, however, survive on informal exchanges among friends and family members; at this level, every transaction takes time and patience.

Adding to their financial woes, the breakdown of communist discipline that once held people together created a high degree of social unrest. During the summer of 1992, a year after the coup, lawlessness began to take over some elements of society, according to Celestine Bohlen, a correspondent in the Moscow office of *The New York Times.* In an article that appeared on August 30, 1992, she used a Russian word—*naglost,* meaning brazen insolence—to describe the prevailing atmosphere. "Naglost applies equally to the Moscow drivers, who think nothing of running red lights, and to the state factory director, who drives a Mercedes with government plates to a meeting where he attacks the government for failing to provide adequate subsidies to his floundering industry."

The upheavals created a kind of frontier mentality, Bohlen added. Bribery, corruption, and alcohol abuse were running rampant. Business contracts were signed and ignored, and white-collar crime increased. Car thieves, prostitutes, and guns appeared openly on the streets. In 1992, police reported a 30 to 35 percent rise in crime.

Unemployment soared, as industries serving the military tried to convert to civilian production. Health services were cut, and there was a sharp rise in infant mortality. Spending on education and scientific research was reduced. In short, it was not a climate to attract and reassure foreign investors, most of whom decided to opt for postponement.

Internally, Yeltsin needs to find a way to sustain economic relations among newly sovereign republics that are often at each others throats. Russia and the Ukraine are fighting over the Crimea region and the Black Sea Fleet of the former Soviet Navy. In the meantime, the Ukraine has delayed ratification of the Strategic Arms Reduction Treaty (START I), demanding that it first receive ample compensation and security guarantees against Russia. (START II, designed to eliminate the multi-warhead land-based missile, was signed by President George Bush on January 3, 1993.)

Other major problems continue to plague the CIS. As its leader, Yeltsin needs to find a way to control the money supply in the rubble zone where most of the republics want to handle their own monetary policy. He needs to find a way to integrate the economies of the former Soviet states into the global economy without exposing them to lethal foreign competition. And there are threats even within Russia itself. Many in Moscow fear that Islamic fundamentalism in central Asia could fuel calls for independence in restless ethnic regions of the country.

Although Yeltsin's popularity has diminished since that dramatic moment when he climbed up on a tank to rally his countrymen against the coup, he remains Russia's most powerful political figure. At the end of April 1993, he handily won a vote of confidence in a referendum on the country's future. He then moved forward with plans for a new constitution that would strength the presidency and create a new legislature, while abolishing the Congress of People's Deputies that had opposed him.

The Aid Debate

The failed coup and the breakup of the union into independent states created fresh problems for the international aid community. Its first task was to help the postcoup governments with food through the harsh winter of 1991. A second crucial need was for technical assistance to establish an effective distribution system. A longer-term need was to make the ruble convertible with other currencies. To do that, the management, finance, marketing, and accounting professions that support a market economy would have to be developed along Western lines, and commercial banks would have to learn the ways of capitalist banking.

In the United States, the aid debate that had raged since the advent of Gorbachev took on a new dimension. Former President Richard M. Nixon was among those who urged the

United States to provide economic aid to pro-reform republics of the new CIS. "Russia and the other republics that broke decisively with their communist past in 1992 deserve our help," he said. "To put it bluntly, Russian President Boris Yeltsin and those like him in other republics must not fail." Nixon reminded Americans that in the 1950s the hot button issue was "Who lost China?," but said: "If Mr. Yeltsin goes down, the question 'Who lost Russia?' will be an infinitely more devastating issue in the 1990s."

The International Monetary Fund (IMF) is the pivotal agency providing aid to Russia and the other independent states. The IMF is a "club" that a country may join on fund approval by paying a subscription, or quota, based on the size of its economy, participation in world trade, and foreign exchange resources. If the fund agrees, a member can draw on the quota to cover a temporary balance-of-payments deficit. These credits have to be repaid within three to five years. The borrower must agree to certain reforms—such as cutting the deficit and the growth of money supply, raising interest rates, restricting flow of credits to inefficient state-owned enterprises, and raising taxes—all within the context of a free-market economy.

These have been hard pills for Russia to swallow. For example, although Russia stood to receive $24 billion 1992, some of which was conditional on further change—it had received only $1 billion of the Western aid package by the end of that year. Another $3 billion was delayed because of the lack of agreement on monetary and budget policies.

Meanwhile, Russia told the IMF that it could not meet its financial targets in 1992 and needed relief in rescheduling its $86 billion in debt, including $20 billion owed to private creditors by the former Soviet Union. That effectively cut off the flow of credit to Russian factories, which need Western currency to buy the imports needed to revive industrial production.

Close observers pressed for privatizations as a vital remedy. "Russia needs an economic reform program that recognizes the primacy of entrepreneurial activity and that elevates the businessman over the bureaucrat," wrote Judy Shelton, a senior research fellow at the Hoover Institute, in an op-ed piece in *The New York Times*. "Private investment, not public assistance, is the key to Russia's salvation." Critics on the left maintained that the IMF medicine was too strong for Russia to swallow, and that the resulting unemployment might cause the death of the patient.

Privatization and Joint Ventures

The Russian version of privatization involves transforming state-owned enterprises into joint stock companies owned partly by the government and partly by private investors. According to the World Bank, about 47,000 medium and large industrial enterprises are to be privatized or liquidated within the next few years.

The Russian government has encouraged foreign investment in joint ventures as a way to create new productive capacity and modernize equipment and management. But foreign investors usually want to get their profits out in hard currency or valuable products like oil or cotton. Entering 1993, very little hard currency had left the country.

Bartered goods are another story. Tambrands, a leading tampon manufacturer with a joint venture in Russia, uses the rubles earned from its sales to buy local cotton, some of which it ships out of the country. PepsiCo, which has sold its namesake product in the Soviet Union for about 20 years, exchanges soft drink syrup for Stolichnaya vodka to sell on the world market.

After the aborted coup, an unprecedented burst of optimism swept through Russia to stimulate the pace of joint-venturing. Almost immediately, Procter & Gamble Co. announced a joint venture with a Russian company. Others giants followed. Philip Morris International said it would build a factory in the St. Petersburg area for producing Marlboro cigarettes. Sun Microsystems in Redwood City, California, announced a contract with a team of Russian computer experts to develop advanced software for use with its work stages.

These corporate biggies joined a thousand or so small, medium, and large foreign companies that have signed joint ventures with enterprises in the former Soviet republics. With developments so rapid and rampant, the U.S. Department of

Commerce suspects that only a small percentage of these ventures were actually up and running at the beginning of 1993. Approximately 300 of these embryonic cooperative projects are believed to involve American investors.

The task of evaluating a potential business partner, remains a daunting task for most Western companies. Among others, Ernst and Young, Coopers & Lybrand, KPMG Peat Marwick, and FYI International have been in the front line of American firms that are starting to help investors evaluate potential partners in the CIS. Their task is complicated by the Russians' understanding of pricing and private ownership—unsophisticated, by Western standards. And normal guidelines like stock prices, real estate, and labor costs don't apply.

To do joint venturing in Russia, a company needs deep pockets and a long view of time, says Joseph Condon, president of RJR Nabisco, Russia and the CIS. This unit of RJR Nabisco Inc. has an agreement with a Russian factory to produce up to 22 billion cigarettes a year. RJR Nabisco gets hard currency for its product from traders in the United States or Switzerland, who deposit dollars in a U.S. account before the product is shipped. The traders also handle distribution of the cigarettes within the CIS. Joint-venture agreements have been signed with two additional plants in the Ukraine, where RJR Nabisco would take an equity interest and put in new technology to increase the volume and improve the quality of production. As Condon put it in 1992: "The ruble is wild, and we expect the GNP to go down for at least two more years. We wouldn't be here if we weren't looking at least 10 years ahead. In 50 years, we expect this to be an enormous market."

Some of the most eagerly sought joint ventures involve exploration and development of Russia's vast oil fields. But that has been slowed by jurisdictional disputes and endless wrangling among the various states. In early 1993, the biggest project to date was Chevron's multibillion-dollar proposal to develop the giant Tenghiz oil field in Kazakhstan. After four years in negotiations, an agreement for a joint venture was almost complete in December 1992, but as of the following January some details remained to be ironed out and the deal had not been finalized. The company expects peak development of 700,000 barrels daily and an investment of $20 billion over 40 years.

Exxon and Mobil, not to be outdone, have signed an agreement to search jointly for large oil fields and natural gas in Western Siberia. (While production in the former Soviet Union has declined sharply because of turmoil and lack of capital, western Siberia still pumps about six million barrels of crude daily.) The two companies are seeking oil fields with a minimum of 300 to 500 million barrels of reserves.

Hazel R. O'Leary, the U.S. Energy Secretary, has said that she is interested in the modernization of the Russian oil industry. The Clinton administration's proposal to help the Russian oil industry is not new. James D. Watkins, the Energy Secretary whose aides led American oil executives to meet Russian oil leaders in Siberia in 1992, got such a program under way. But O'Leary's plan to make help Russian oil producers a priority would represent an important shift in policy.

Russian Markets

One sign of movement toward a market economy is the debut of exchanges dealing in commodities. A few even trade stocks. The Moscow Stock Exchange opened in 1990, the country's first since 1917. All exchanges had been closed, and trading in shares outlawed, following the Bolshevik revolution.

In 1991 the opening bell rang in the St. Petersburg Stock Exchange, a modern addition to the city that was once the financial capital of czarist Russia. Experts say there are now two stock exchanges in St. Petersburg. By American and European standards, the exchanges are primitive. Only a few stocks in private companies, commercial banks, and financial institutions have been added to the bulk of the business—contracts for future deliveries of products.

Russia's market activity took on wider dimensions in 1993, based on Yeltsin's ambitious plan to turn the Russian man on the street into a capitalist. In late 1992, the government began to distribute vouchers for 10,000 rubles (about $50, or twice the average monthly salary) to each citizen as his or her share of state-owned businesses being auctioned off. The vouchers could be bought, sold, or, for example, pooled to buy a small neighborhood store. There have been three main uses of these vouchers: holders can sell them to other individuals, including foreigners; they can give them to investment management companies (of which there were more than 200 that had been set up by mid-1993) in exchange for shares in the now closed-end funds; or they can use them to make bids for stock in the companies being auctioned off. Investment management companies accumulate vouchers so that they can invest in companies being privatized. However, a number of voucher owners have developed an affinity for trading. By mid-1993, hefty trading volume in vouchers had developed, and there was even a floor for trading vouchers at the Moscow exchange.

The voucher program is due to end at the end of 1993—although it could be extended. But even as that program was going on, Russia was taking steps to create an adequate system for share trading. Some experts predicted that by mid-to-late 1994, these systems would be operational.

Russia already has a number of fervent capitalists who operate out of 700 commodities exchanges. These range from small, single-product floors to the large and thriving Russian Commodities & Raw Materials Exchange, which handles everything from computers to coal and is spinning off major commodities such as oil, metals, and grain into specialized exchanges. Neither the high taxes on exchange entrepreneurs nor the borderline criminal element in some of the dealing has dampened the zeal of these traders.

Esther Dyson, publisher of *RelEast*, an East-West high-tech computer business report, keeps a close watch on the Russian business scene. Dyson points out that the commodities exchanges are not on the American model but closer to auction or wholesale markets. Suppliers use them to get the best price for their goods without the bother of having to differentiate their products. Customers come to buy, almost independent of quality. For that reason, she predicts that the Russian commodities markets are probably a temporary phenomenon, for the next few years only.

Richard P. Bernard, a New York attorney at Milbank, Tweed, Hadley and McCloy, is convinced that when the Russians get used to open trading, the commodities exchanges will be phased out and the stock markets will develop rapidly. Bernard is a member of the Soviet-American Securities Law Working Group, which is helping the former republics to codify their laws on stock market transactions. Russia, Belarus, Estonia, Latvia, and Kazakhstan have projects that will result in laws influenced by those that govern the U.S. stock market, Bernard says.

Early in 1993, President Yeltsin issued a decree to establish a securities commission in Russia. Subsequently, a committee was formed that would set up such a body. But although these seemed like promising steps, many international investors remained skeptical about opportunities in the short-run; to many—although not all—investors, Russia's political and economic woes were still too daunting. Held one market watcher, "You simply can't do passive investing in the Russian stock market at this time. You'd have to be out of your mind to hand over money that way."

Nonetheless, Richard Bernard has cited powerful investment opportunities in joint ventures and in subsidiaries with Russian management and American consultants, as they can contribute their technical and management skills to the business.

Investors

Russia's aborted 1991 coup resulted in an unprecedented mood of optimism among many international investors, some of whom saw alluring possibilities for long-term investment in the CIS. A number of business and investment groups began to organize tours to the new states, where participants heard leading government officials pledge that there would be no turning back from radical economic reform.

About 100 top officials from American public and private pension funds attended an October 1991 "Pensions in the Nineties" conference in Russia. The pension sponsors and managers were interested in future opportunities, not immediate investment. Said one pension fund manager: "I'm cautious when I go swimming. I stick my toe in; then maybe I go in up to my ankles, then my knees, and finally—if everything is okay—I may jump. Right now, I'm still standing looking at the water."

Batterymarch Financial Management of Boston had plans for

a Soviet Companies Fund. Dean LeBaron, Batterymarch's chairman, saw the fund as a vehicle for investing in joint stock companies formed from military conversion in Russia and the Ukraine. He identified at least six enterprises spun off from state-owned agencies in such fields as optics, avionic equipment, and household appliances. Batterymarch's method of operation was to help these companies privatize and attract investments from Western counterparts.

Although the fund's assets reached $150 to $200 million, it never closed. Says Marilyn Pitchford, chief financial officer of the fund: "We recognized that the people were not yet trading in conventional securities; there were no regulatory bodies that set standards; and the accounting system was based on a command economy, not a free market."

She says Batterymarch will look at initiatives in the CIS later in the decade, when fund managers see the development of a market mechanism, a stable currency, and successful privatizations.

However, several funds have been, or expect to be, established for regions of the CIS. Among them: the Framlington Group, and investment management organization based in London, expected in September 1993 to launch a $50 to $75 million closed-end Framlington Russian Investment Fund. As its strategy, the fund will make direct investments in companies specially formed by a joint venture between a Western company and a Russian organization to operate in Russia. It will also invest in private Russian companies. For diversification, the fund expects to invest in a range of sectors, targeting small to medium-sized companies.

The fund was expected to be marketed to institution investors in North America and Europe.

"We believe there is a fantastic opportunity to get in on the ground floor of investing in Russia," says Gary Fitzgerald, managing director of Framlington's closed-end fund division. The new fund is expected to invest in low priced companies with high growth possibilities.

In another example, Boston-based Claflin Capital Management Inc. has created a private placement Ukraine Fund that, at midyear 1993, had already completed two direct investments, and another two were close to being finalized. The initially targeted

$10 million fund had among its investors, the European Bank for Reconstruction and Development and the Bank of Boston as well as partners in the firm and other individual investors.

While other investment arrangements are possible, the fund primarily targets to invest in profitable, existing, privately held companies that are, in many cases, their sector's leaders. Since there is no stock market in the Ukraine, the fund expects to make money through cash flow from its investments.

At mid-year 1993, the fund had invested in Leading Ukraine Distributors, a large Kiev-based retailer and Aquaton, a marine supply company in Odessa. (Claflin is also exploring another 15 to 20 projects beyond its initial four. Within two years it planned to about double the size of the fund.)

The Department of Commerce has compiled a list of industry sectors in which U.S. firms have the best prospects for entering the Soviet market. They include computer and peripherals; equipment for food processing and packaging, medicine, telecommunications, construction, mining, and pollution control; oil and gas field machinery and services; and laboratory/scientific instruments.

Ray De Voe, a market strategist and publisher of the *De Voe Report*, cites telecommunications as a promising field. "When I was in Russia [in October 1991], I tried to send a fax and found there were only 80 circuits, less than in a large apartment house in New York City," he says. "To advance beyond an emerging state, Russia will need a first-class telecommunications system." De Voe is confident that once the legal structure and exit mechanisms allow investors to repatriate their profits, investment opportunities in the CIS will increase.

A major deterrent to investing in the CIS has been the scarcity and high cost of risk insurance. (The high risk in certain market sectors makes it essential to back private loans with government guarantees. That way, payment is still assured if the borrower defaults.) In 1992 the Overseas Private Investment Corp. (OPIC), an arm of the U.S. government, assumed some of that risk. Available coverage now includes risk of expropriation and political violence, ranging from cross-border activities to terrorism. Currency convertibility insurance will not be offered in the CIS until the ruble meets international standards.

"We are officially open in the CIS," said Jim Hall, a senior assistant in public affairs for the agency. Although the agency was flooded with requests, five requests were approved by January 1993. The projects include a manufacturing facility to produce power tools for domestic consumption, two timber processing plants, an oil and gas development investment, and a cable television system in Moscow. Hall cited restrictions, including a ceiling of 10 percent on insurance the agency can provide in any single country. The agency also has to check the impact of an investment on the economies of the United States and Russia, and on the global environment.

When will the timing be right to invest in the CIS? Roger S. Leeds, a partner in the Policy Economics Group of KPMG Peat Marwick, told a 1992 conference at Geonomics Institute that investors who are willing to take the risk should do it "in a measured way." Leeds quoted a well-known observer of the Russian scene on short-term challenges and opportunities.

"The observer noted that production was decreasing, economic ties were being disrupted, and state solvency had reached critical levels; crime was on the rise, and energetic measures based on broad consensus were needed," Leeds told his listeners. The well-known observer was Mikhail Gorbachev, in 1990. Midway through 1992, in Leeds' view, the prognosis was more optimistic.

Says Leeds: "The near term is coming to an end in the northern-tier countries of Eastern Europe, and although they are still risky environments, there are investment opportunities in those countries today for the cautious and intelligent investor. The republics of the former Soviet Union are far, far behind Eastern Europe, so the near term is more like five years than two or three years. But every investor knows that if you wait until everything is comfortable, you're going to miss the boat. There's going to be a lot of opportunity in this period of chaos."

How long will the period of chaos last? Will the green shoots of entrepreneurship and joint-venturing blossom fast enough to absorb the unemployed and avert further turmoil? No one knows the answer, but history makes certain lessons clear. The Russians have had to rely many times on their ability to perform under pressure, and their best qualities shine when they are confronted with adversity. The heroism of the Russian people was amply demonstrated when they fought the Nazis in World War II. Their ability to rise out of the ashes of Communism is also a tribute to their resourcefulness and strength.

Now, in the face of real hardships, they are transforming their country. Foreign investors are being asked to hold out a helping hand—in their own self-interest, and in the interest of global peace. Investors who are willing to take that risk may in the long run see their profits roll in with the force of a Siberian blizzard.

25

Where Else in the World?

When internationally known investor Jim Rogers of New York City spanned the world on his 57,000-mile motorcycle tour, he got a ground-level view of the more exotic emerging markets. Among the developing countries he invested in were Botswana, Argentina, Uruguay, Peru, Ecuador, Costa Rica, and El Salvador.

Botswana's was among Rogers' favorite markets. Observing that the country has a strong economic and political foundation, and that companies on the tiny exchange are cheap, he made investments in all of the stocks then listed. The experience must have been rewarding, for in late 1992 he revealed that he was "investing now in another African market," although he was keeping its identity under wraps.

Adventurous investors such as Rogers are the consummate value-seekers. Rogers calls himself the father of the Austrian stock market, having wisely invested there well before the crowd. He believes in discovering investment opportunities before the crowd arrives and reaping the highest reward. As more emerging markets become "discovered" by foreign investors, true value-seekers are pushing on.

The quest for new, hot markets is turning up ever more intriguing possibilities. In 1992, for example, Jamaica's market was the world's best performer, having shot up 202 percent in U.S. dollar terms, according to the IFC. Bangladesh, Vietnam, and Papua New Guinea are among the more exotic locales that are starting to catch adventurous investors' eyes. In general, the Middle East and Africa are beginning to look alluring, amid enhanced peace prospects and economic liberalizations. Although in the Middle East political/social/religious struggles continue, alert investors in 1992 also recognized the potential in the region—one blessed with ample financial resources—that is renewing and tightening links to the global marketplace.

Israel's Stellar 1992 Showing

In the Middle East, the prospect of peace is one factor helping to lure investors to the regional stock markets. In 1992, in U.S. dollar terms, the IFC's price index of the Jordan market gained 21.1 percent in dollar terms (Jordan's is the only Middle East market in the IFC's Composite Index), while Israel's market—the fourth best performer in the world in 1992—vaulted 75.2 percent in dollars. (While some investors do not consider Israel's markets to be "emerging," it is often not included in major indexes of developed markets.)

By 1992 the Holy Land, which only about a year earlier had suffered through Iraqi scud missile attacks and the fear of chemical weapons, was enjoying a breath of fresh air both politically and economically.

Josephine Jimenez, a managing director of Montgomery Asset Management in San Francisco, offers the following explanation for Israel's superb showing that year.

Besides progress in peace discussions during 1992—which later stalled after Israel expelled 400 Palestinians from the Occupied Territories—Jimenez cited Israel's 5.2 percent real GDP growth in 1991 and an expected 6 percent rise in 1992. With Israel's increased population (from high levels of Russian immigrants), consumption has increased and aggregate demand has risen. Companies have been investing aggressively to meet growing consumer demand even as the "government has been increasing expenditures for housing and social services to meet" the needs of the expanded population.

In addition, despite the boom in consumption, Israel's central bank has "done an incredible job preventing a pickup in inflation," holds Jimenez. "In 1992, inflation was due to be 10 percent, down from 17.4 percent the year before. In 1992, the U.S. government approved the $10 billion in loan guarantees Israel had sought." Although "those guarantees won't be pumped in all in one year," the development is distinctly positive. As Jimenez points out, "If Israel, whose total output is only $60 billion, uses just one-tenth of those guarantees a year, the multiplier effect could produce strong economic growth ahead."

Another positive sign: Israel's exports have been on the rise. Formalized diplomatic relationships with India and China "opened a vast avenue for Israel to export chemicals and technology. The agricultural chemical industry has done superbly," reports Jimenez. She points out that Israel obtains phosphates from its desert, and bromine from the Dead Sea, both of which are used in producing agricultural chemicals. In addition, says Jimenez, Israel has expanded its exports beyond the European Community and the United States, where the country enjoys most-favored-nation status.

In late 1992, Jimenez cited the agricultural chemicals, telecommunications, housing construction, and domestic consumer companies as being "better positioned for above-average growth than the defense and technology sectors." Among the stocks chosen by Montgomery Asset Management were: Clal Industries, a highly diversified company whose 1991 sales, according to Montgomery, rose 13 percent to $2.4 billion, led by a 17 percent growth in exports, and Israel Land Development Company, which is likely to enjoy continued demand from Israel's expanding population.

Montgomery Asset has also invested in Israel Chemicals, one of the world's leading natural resource companies, which supplies 5 percent of the world's total demand for potash, 60 percent of its demand for bromine, and 5 percent of its demand for phosphate rock, according to Montgomery.

A key problem with Israel's market: It became pricey after the 1992 surge. According to Montgomery Asset, as of October 1992 the market's price-earnings ratio stood at 19 times earnings.

Nonetheless, the Israeli market has been growing rapidly. As of late March 1993, the Tel-Aviv Stock Exchange had 378 listed companies, and 170 had announced plans to go public in 1993. As of December 1992, the value of Israel's market in shares, options, and convertible bonds was $30 billion, and the total value of securities traded including equities and bonds, reached $60 billion. As of May 1993, the stocks of 47—mainly high-tech Israeli companies—were publicly traded in the United States, often over-the-counter.

Jordan's Percolating Market

Elsewhere in the Middle East, Jordan's sleepy stock market awakened in 1992 with a 21.1 percent gain in dollar terms, followed by a 19 percent rise between January and June 4, 1993, according to the IFC. In 1991, the market had advanced by a modest 6 percent following declines during each of the previous 5 years. According to the IFC, Jordan has been "traditionally one of the less active emerging markets." Located in Amman, Jordan's stock exchange has a capitalization of about $3 billion.

But 1992 brought "an explosion in volume, with activity running well above any levels previously seen," says a Lehman Brothers report. Daily trading volume averages about $5 million, with trading exceeding $10 million a day on several occasions, the report says.

There were various reasons for the enthusiasm. Politically, by 1992, the small country—about the size of the state of Indiana— had regained favor with much of the west after its pro-Iraqi slant during the 1990–early 1991 Persian Gulf War. Not only did Jordan subsequently become an active participant in the Middle East peace talks, but the country's monarch, King Hussein, urged Iraqis in November 1992 to "put an end to" the government of Iraq's President Saddam Hussein.

In addition, an outpouring of support for Jordan's monarch, King Hussein, after he returned home from cancer surgery in September 1992, fueled sharp gains in the stock market. All the while the economy was rebounding from the effects of the Persian Gulf War. In 1990, Jordan's GDP fell 5.6 percent, and in

1991 it posted a less than 1 percent growth rate, according to the IFC. But in 1992, real GDP growth jumped nearly 11 percent, making Jordan's economy one of the strongest in the world that year. For 1993, Lehman Brothers was estimating 6 percent GDP growth. Beyond that, "the pace of spending on infrastructure will be the major determinant of growth. We think [a 5 percent real GDP growth rate] is sustainable," Lehman said in a January 1993 report.

The economic boom in 1992 was fueled by the influx of evacuees from Kuwait, including 300,000 Jordanians, as a result of the Persian Gulf War. The need for new housing triggered a boom in construction. Although the construction surge is expected to taper off, "thereafter private sector growth will be service-led, as a result of the higher levels of economic activity generated by the returnees," said a Lehman report, pointing to "business and financial services and the retail trade, [which] are all strong."

Recently, there have been other positive factors to point to. For example, indebted Jordan, whose aid from Middle East countries had diminished by the late 1980s, received new assistance, especially from Japan and Germany. In June 1993 the *Financial Times* reported that Jordan was about to reach a $1 billion debt restructuring accord with the London Club of commercial creditors. In addition relations with a number of moderate Arab states warmed, according to Kleiman International Consultants Inc., Washington, D.C., allowing Jordan's exports to the Gulf states to attain pre-war levels. Kleiman, in an October 1992 report, said:

> In other hopeful economic signs, industrial production...[now] stands at one-quarter of GDP. "Commodity producers have recorded a pick-up in business. Jordan Phosphate Mines recently signed two large international contracts to convert sulphur into fertilizer, which buoyed its share prices. The finance and banking sector, as well, is looking to emerge from the post-Gulf War doldrums." "For the year to June 30, 1992, leader Arab Bank revealed 12 percent rises in assets and deposits, while France's Societe Generale relocated its Middle East base from Bahrain to Amman in a move closely watched by international competitors.

Established in 1976, the Amman Financial Market (AFM—

Jordan's stock exchange) began trading at the beginning of January 1978. The Amman Financial Market is a government agency and, according to the AFM, has legal, financial, and administrative independence. As of this writing the AMF lists about 120 stocks, and it is open from Saturday through Wednesday. While the manufacturing and the financial sectors are the largest components of the market, other sectors include transportation, textile mill products, cement, chemicals, fabricated metals, and mining and power companies. In its *Emerging Stock Markets Factbook, 1993,* the IFC rates Jordan's accounting standards and investor protection as "adequate."

According to Lehman Brothers, foreign investors need approval of the prime minister's office, which can be obtained through a local broker. There have been attempts to restrict non-Arabs access to the stock market. But once approved, foreigners are "free to invest, subject to the restriction that non-Arab foreigners are not allowed to own more than 49 percent of most businesses. Capital and dividends can be repatriated through a bank without withholding, as long as foreign currency was brought in and declared for the original investment," said Lehman's January 1993 report.

Africa

For many reasons, Africa had been long neglected by international investors. Not only have many markets been closed to foreigners or hard to penetrate, but the war-torn and underdeveloped countries held little appeal for investors. In sub-Saharan Africa, for example, Mozambique's long, ravaging war has left the country impoverished. Foreign newspapers and TV frequently chronicle starvation and devastation in Somalia, while an estimated 5 percent of Uganda's 19 million people is reported to be infected with the AIDS virus. On top of these and other woes came a crippling 1991–1992 drought in Southern Africa, the worst in memory.

Political turmoil is widespread. After gaining their independence, many African countries became economically insular. Typically, the country's new ruler consolidated his power and created a one-party state. Eventually, as dictatorships began to crumble amid corruption and incompetence, and/or political pressure, the transition to democracy or majority rule involved violence. In South Africa, the tortured evolution to majority rule claimed some 7000 lives in 1992. The availability of foreign aid has decreased with the end of the Cold War. Russia and the U.S. now see less need to court the favor of African countries and to supply them with aid. "Dictators lost their ability to play the west versus the east. That hastened change and the demise of the old system, because countries couldn't get the aid," holds Anthony Newsome of Genesis Investment Management Ltd. in London.

As some countries of Africa wade through their transition period, at least a few international investors are studying opportunities. In its 1992 survey of 30 money managers, Kleiman International Consultants found that two respondents were already investing in Africa, "and some admitted keeping an eye on them because of the need to find the next Argentina," says Kleiman's Elizabeth Morrissey. The Aidoo Group Ltd., a New York financial advisory firm, in mid-1993 planned to launch a $30 to $50 million closed-end fund for investing in sub-Saharan Africa. To avoid illiquidity but remain opportunistic, the fund plans to invest in listed and unlisted stocks as well as some sovereign and corporate debt instruments.

Judith Aidoo, president of the Aidoo Group, sees the African continent as rich in opportunities. Attractions include the developing business skills and growing consumerism among the continent's 600 million people, as well as its abundant natural resources. There are some good companies, with often cheap stocks. She urges investors to look around while investment opportunities remain largely undiscovered, but to be aware of the sharp differences among Africa's countries, cultures, and markets. To take one example, in colonialist times far fewer white settlers came to West Africa than to the more climatically attractive East Africa. As a result, West Africa has better retained its cultural heritage.

Stock markets in Africa also have their separate personalities. While most of these markets are thinly traded, they diverge in size, capability, and openness to foreigners. For example, while Nigeria's $1.2 billion market is reasonably large for Africa, it remains largely closed to foreign investment, although that situation is expected to change in the near future. In 1993, Zimbabwe's stock market (capitalization of $628 million at the end of 1992) opened to foreign investments.

In all, the *Micropal Emerging Market Fund Monitor* reports that there are 13 African countries with operational stock exchanges. These countries are: Botswana, Cote d'Ivoire, Egypt, Ghana, Kenya, Mauritius, Morocco, Namibia, Nigeria, Swaziland, South Africa (often not categorized as "emerging"), Tunisia, and Zimbabwe. In addition, Uganda and Tanzania are planning to set up stock exchanges, while Gambia and Algeria are considering doing so, said the newsletter in May 1993.

This book profiles some of today's largest and/or most intriguing markets in the region.

Ghana

Times have changed for this small West African nation. Once an economic basket case, Ghana has transformed itself in recent years into one of Africa's premier success stories. This former British colony known as "the Gold Coast" gained its independence in 1957. But subsequent leadership embraced socialism and a centrally planned economy. Economic mismanagement, along with a fall in commodities' prices over time, produced economic decline. By the beginning of the 1980s, Ghana was in desperate economic straits. But a restructuring launched in 1983 brought economic renewal. Ghana, named after an ancient empire of West Africa, has been posting 4 to 5 percent real economic growth in recent years, reports Judith Aidoo.

Unfortunately, the country's nascent stock market hasn't yet advanced. Since the market opened in Accra in November 1990, trading has been thin. Nonetheless, there are good reasons to be optimistic for the future. John Taylor, an analyst with James Capel & Co. in London, sees Ghana as "one of the bright spots in Africa in the next few years."

Politically, in November 1992 the country held its first democratic elections since 1979, reports Judith Aidoo. Economically, Ghana was among the first African nations to adopt a structural adjustment program and a package of economic liberalizations.

The ongoing privatization program promises to bring greater depth to the fledgling stock exchange, where, as of 1992, there were approximately 15 listed shares and a market capitalization of about $74 million.

Ghana's economy is largely agricultural, and cocoa is the leading crop. Gold mining and timber production are the second and third largest industries, Aidoo reports. But shares on the Ghana Stock Exchange do not reflect the country's economic underpinnings in agriculture and mining. Instead, listed stocks mainly include a combination of banks, breweries, trading companies, and general consumer products. Unilever Ghana Ltd. has the largest market capitalization, followed by Standard Chartered Bank (Ghana) Ltd. and Pioneer Tobacco Co. Ltd.

Recent legislation now allows foreigners to invest in Ghana. But experts say that market liquidity is very limited, and like most African markets, the free-float of stock averages only about 10 to 15 percent.

Botswana

Since opening in June 1989, the Botswana Share Market, in Gaborone, has posted impressive results. The index, which was 100 when the market opened on June 19, 1989, stood at around 273 in mid-January 1993, having hit a peak of about 293.7 in August 1992.

Some international investors see Botswana, a South African country of 1.3 million people, as an attractive investment locale. Annual GDP growth has averaged 13 percent since 1966—the year Botswana gained independence—and the country features a stable, democratic government that enjoys good relations with its neighbors, including South Africa. "It's one of the real exceptions in Africa that" many of the people are members "of a single tribe," says Anthony Newsome of Genesis. "In the 19th century, they actually invited British protection from Afrikaners moving up from South Africa. As a result, Britain invested in the country," Newsome reports. Among its attractions, Botswana has also escaped black–white racial strife; indeed, Seretse Khama, the country's first president, was married to a white Englishwoman, Newsome points out.

While the economy has been heavily dependent on the diamond industry, there has been increasing economic diversification. But in 1992 a rise in interest rates, along with a ravaging drought, restrained economic growth.

As of mid-January 1993, Botswana's market had 11 listed shares. Its market capitalization was $294.62 million. The most actively traded stocks are: Engen Botswana Limited, with 25 percent of the volume; Pep Holdings Botswana Limited, with 13 percent of the volume; Sechaba Investment Trust, which accounts for 10.29 percent of activity; and Sefalana Limited, with a 22.5 percent share.

Stockbrokers Botswana Limited in Gaborone is the only firm authorized to trade on the Botswana Share market. The firm said that a stock exchange act might be forthcoming in 1993. That legislation would formalize the rules governing marketable securities trading and formalize the establishment of the Botswana Stock Exchange.

Foreign investors can purchase up to 49 percent of the free shares in any listed company in Botswana.

Kenya

Kenya became independent in December 1963. This ancient land, where some of mankind's earliest ancestors lived, is today touted as one of the brightest investment prospects of sub-Saharan Africa.

Kenya's economy is the third largest on the subcontinent, and its population is about 25 million. According to James Capel & Co., Kenya's attractions include: a well-developed private sector; an educated people with a strong entrepreneurial spirit; an infrastructure that surpasses most others' in Africa; and labor costs that are a fraction of those in South Africa. The country has also been implementing a number of structural reform measures destined to benefit its economy.

But Kenya has also been grappling with a myriad of political and economic problems, among them political corruption, high inflation, an economic downturn (the economy advanced only 0.4 percent in 1992), and the 1991 cutoff of about $400 million in aid from foreign donors. One condition for renewing aid—the

holding of the first multiparty elections in 26 years—was ful-
filled in late December 1992 and produced a victory for long-
time President Daniel Arap Moi. In fits and starts, Kenya has
subsequently reactivated some previously stalled economic liberalization measures.

Founded in 1954, the Nairobi Stock Exchange Ltd. has 54
listed companies covering a range of sectors. The most actively
traded stocks comprise 70 percent of the market's activity. In
order, these are the stocks of: Barclays Bank Ltd., Kenya
Breweries Ltd., Jubilee Insurance Co., Standard Chartered Bank,
B.A.T. Kenya Lt., Diamond Trust, ICDC, Total Kenya Ltd., Sasini
Tea & Coffee, and Kenya Commercial Bank.

Experts say market demand has been growing strongly. Share
prices advanced throughout 1992. And when the Housing
Finance Company of Kenya floated 126 million Kenyan shillings
of stock in October 1992 (as part of a much broader stock flotation
program) the cheaply priced issue was massively oversubscribed,
reports Elizabeth Morrissey of Kleiman International (about 63
Kenyan shillings = 1 U.S. dollar). There are no restrictions on the
amount of foreign ownership of shares in Kenya's market, and
foreign exchange rules have been eased considerably.

Although there is no capital gains tax, dividends are subject to
a 15 percent withholding tax.

Mauritius

Situated well offshore from continental Africa, in the Indian
Ocean, the small, democratic island nation of Mauritius, with its
population of 1.1 million, has been attracting increased attention. The Stock Exchange of Mauritius in Port Louis began operations on July 5, 1989. As of 1992 it had 21 listed companies, and
a market capitalization of roughly $360 million. The prospectus
for the Mauritius Fund Ltd. reports that, as of June 1992, $322
million of shares, representing 72 companies, were trading over
the counter. Although the stock exchange was still tiny in 1992,
"it will grow dramatically in the next couple of years as companies see the advantages in having access to relatively cheap
financing," predicts Anthony Newsome of Genesis Investment
Management.

Mauritius's real GDP growth annually averaged about 6.6 percent for the six years ended 1991. Newsome of Genesis Investment foresees an average of 5 to 7 percent GDP growth in coming years. While Mauritius's economy was once based on sugar production, the country some two decades ago decided to diversify into manufacturing, and in 1970 set up the Mauritian Export Processing Zone, which has been a significant contributor to economic gains on the island.

Attesting to the island's economic development, manufacturing as a percent of GDP has climbed from 14.9 percent in 1979 to 23.3 percent by 1991, according to the prospectus for the Mauritius Fund. Among its achievements, Mauritius has become the third largest exporter of wool sweaters.

Attractions for business investors have included tax breaks, affordable labor costs, and access to the European Community at preferential tariff rates, since Mauritius is a signatory to the Lome IV Convention, signed in 1989, which provides this benefit for 10 years.

But as wage rates climbed in the 1980s—GNP per capita was $2212 in 1991—many companies have moved their lower-value manufacturing offshore, particularly to Madagascar, one of the world's poorest countries. To diversify its economy at home, Mauritius, is, among other moves, promoting itself as an offshore banking and financial services center. The advent of the stock exchange is part of that process, says Newsome.

In 1993, the London-listed Mauritius Fund Ltd. became the exclusive foreign portfolio investor for 12 months in Mauritius and that period could be extended, says Newsome. The fund was expected to invest in listed, OTC, and prelisted securities, he adds. However, in the foreseeable future—most likely after the Mauritius Fund has been fully invested—additional foreign investment may be allowed.

South Africa

Is the anguish of South Africa finally coming to an end? As of this writing, the legacy of apartheid is crumbling, and the one-time international pariah is increasingly being welcomed into the world community.

Few investors are unfamiliar with South Africa's troubled history: the violence in black townships, the human rights violations, and the struggles for liberties by groups such as the African National Congress (ANC), the country's largest opposition party. South Africa's President F. W. de Klerk, who was elected in 1989, faced up to political and economic reality and set the stage for the transition to majority rule. That process has been far from smooth. But by mid-1993, leading political parties were nearing agreement on key issues, and multiparty elections are expected to take place in April 1994. After that, a coalition government is expected to hold power for five years amid the conversion to majority rule.

An improved political environment should also benefit what has been a weak economy. In 1992, according to press reports, South Africa was suffering from its sixth year of economic decline since 1982. In mid-1993, it was reported that the jobless rate in the formal economy stood at a staggering 46 percent. But some analysts see brighter days ahead for the country with the largest industrial base in Africa. After declining by about 1.5 percent in 1992, GDP was expected to rise between 1 to 1.5 percent in 1993. Future engines of growth should include the disbursement of World Bank loans, an expected pickup in commodities prices linked to economic gains around the world, and further easing of the world's trade sanctions against the country. But South Africa will need to keep its economic engines running: according to the *Financial Times* newspaper, the country's economy needs to grow 3.5 percent a year until the end of the century if it is to absorb new entrants into the labor market.

As of August 1993, the Washington, D.C.–based Investor Responsibility Research Center (IRRC) reported that 694 foreign companies had direct investments or employees in South Africa. The IRRC said that such investments had been on the rise since 1991, after several prior years of disinvestment from South Africa.

Many U.S. public pension funds have been barred from investing in the South African market, and from investing in companies that do significant business in or with South Africa. But in time, that situation may change. With multiparty elections planned for 1994, the ANC was expected to begin inviting foreign investment into South Africa sometime in 1993.

Before rallying in 1993, the Johannesburg stock market rode a tide of bad news in 1992. After a strong 1991 showing, in 1992 the market's all-share index fell about 2 percent in local currency terms, but was down sharply in dollars. However, 1993's gains in gold and platinum prices gave a boost to this market in which mining is heavily represented. Mining producers and mining finance together comprise 39 percent of the market's capitalization.

As investments, James Capel's John Taylor suggests Rustenburg Platinum Holdings and, as a mining house, Johannesburg Consolidated Investment Co. In mid-1993, he was also still recommending the gold sector, "including for brave persons, Freegold, which has the world's largest gold mine, and for the slightly more cautious, Vaal Reefs.

As of June 1993, the Johannesburg Stock Exchange had 665 listed companies and a market capitalization of $186.7 billion (converted at the commercial rate). The country has a dual currency system that includes the financial rand and the commercial rand. Buying and selling are done through the medium of the financial rand, the currency of foreign investments, while dividends and interest are paid at the commercial rand rate. As of February 15, 1993, the financial rand was valued at a 30 percent discount to the commercial rand.

While some experts categorize South Africa's as a developed market, it still suffers from limited trading liquidity. Domestic institutional investors—including pension funds and insurers—have tended to grab available shares in the market, since they have not been allowed to invest outside the country.

Nigeria and Zimbabwe

In 1992, the Lagos Stock Exchange in Nigeria had a market capitalization of about $1.2 billion and 153 listed companies. However, in its *Emerging Stock Markets Factbook, 1993*, the IFC rated Nigeria's market as "closed" to foreign investment—the only one of 28 emerging markets so designated. In 1992, Nigeria's market fell almost 39 percent in U.S. dollar terms, according to the IFC.

In mid-1993, Zimbabwe's market effectively opened to foreign investment. Previously, corporate/unit trust foreign investors were not permitted to invest on the Zimbabwe Stock Exchange, located in Harare, although foreign individual investors could apply to invest through the Investment Centre in Harare. Under the revised rules, foreign investors, using local brokers, can purchase up to 5 percent of a public company's shares, with aggregate ownership capped at 25 percent. Dividends and capital gains are freely remittable after taxes. Prior exchange control approval is not needed. Banks will convert foreigners' currency to Zimbabwe dollars, which are then forwarded to brokers for stock purchases.

In 1992, Zimbabwe's market plunged 61.6 percent in U.S. dollar terms, according to the IFC, making it the second year in a row that Zimbabwe's market was the world's worst performer. But in 1990, the market rocketed 84.6 percent in dollars.

Other Markets

Other markets catching investors' eyes include those of Peru, Sri Lanka, and, to a limited extent, Bangladesh. In Peru, rapid liberalizations and declining inflation were paired with positive political developments. On the political front, Abimael Guzman Reynoso, the leader of the Shining Path Maoist guerilla group, was captured in September 1992; in November, congressional elections kept Peru's President Alberto K. Fujimori in power. As investors saw this Latin American market as both attractive and cheap, its share price index soared 124.9 percent in U.S. dollar terms, according to the IFC.

In dollar terms, Sri Lanka's market tumbled 36 percent in 1992. Nonetheless, the politically strife-ridden South Asian island has been making considerable economic gains. After embarking in 1989 on an economic restructuring program with World Bank/IMF support, the economy grew 6.2 percent in 1990. 1993 brought the assassinations of two of the country's leaders, including President Ranasinghe Premadasa. But the government nonetheless vowed to push on with its economic enhancement program, which includes deregulation and a rapid privatization thrust.

The capitalization of Sri Lanka's market—the Colombo Stock Exchange—reached about $1.46 billion in 1992. Foreigners account for approximately 40 percent of the secondary market's trading.

Originated in 1896, the Colombo market has become what some experts call the most well managed and smoothly modernized exchanges in the realm of emerging markets. Among market reforms: the abolition of stamp duty and wealth tax on listed securities, and the elimination of both capital gains as well as withholding tax for nationals—although foreigners still pay a withholding tax of 15 percent, deductible at the source.

Foreign investment is restricted in several sectors. The restrictions are: a 49 percent limit on banking stocks; a maximum 40 percent holding in mining companies; a 40 percent limit in residential housing companies' stocks; and total restriction from investing in insurance companies.

Some experts believe that Bangladesh's tiny market, the Dhaka Stock Exchange, holds some promise for the future— although it remains too small and primitive for most international investors' tastes. When the $400 million (capitalization) market opened to foreign investors in September 1991, it was not "preceded by foreign exchange liberalizations," says one expert. "Taxation had not been well thought out, and there was a lack of understanding of how to attract and keep foreign capital. Domestic capital to fuel the market has also been limited." But spillover from the economic reforms and practices of its neighbors in South Asia may well give a boost to that country's market. Moreover, in early 1993, investors could "purchase shares at very attractive P/E ratios of under 7, with matching dividend yields," said an article in the *Micropal Emerging Market Fund Monitor.*

Papua New Guinea

Papua New Guinea (PNG), a mainly agricultural country located north of Queensland, Australia, was expected to post at least 10 percent GDP growth in 1993, after an expected 8 to 9 percent rise in 1992. Reserves of gold and oil are fueling PNG's explosive economic growth. According to William

Schmick, emerging markets director of Dillon, Read & Co. Inc., New York, this remote island nation, which gained its independence in 1972, was, as of this writing, about to begin mining what he calls the "largest [previously] undeveloped gold deposit in the world" on Lihir Island. In recent years two other gold mines, one in Misima and the other in Progara in the highlands of PNG, have gone into production. In the latter two cases, Placer Pacific, a company listed on the Australian stock exchange, operates and owns a substantial portion of the mines, Schmick says.

PNG is now also producing oil. In July 1992 the first 135,000 barrels of oil flowed in Kutobo. And according to Schmick, that outflow "is just the tip of the iceberg. There's probably 5 to 10 times that amount of oil in the area."

Of course, Papua New Guinea is not without its problems. In 1989, developmental projects had ground to a halt as violence flared over local landowners' claims to ownership rights on the Bougainville copper mine at Panguna. The mine had been an important source of gold and silver as well as copper. Ultimately it was shut down by the violence, which had also temporarily scared away would-be developers of PNG's oil and new gold discoveries.

But as developers' fears ebbed, projects came back on-stream, and investors' interest in PNG was renewed, Schmick observes. However, in 1992 new problems surfaced. When the government saw how fruitful some of the mines could be, it began seeking stakes as high as 30 percent in them, compared with its earlier-agreed holdings of about 10 percent. Private developers were incensed and felt that the government was acting unjustly. The move was seen as "increasing the risk that legal contracts wouldn't be honored," says Schmick. PNG's investors were given another reason for concern.

Clashes aside, however, PNG's economic boom does provide a compellng investment story. But to capitalize on the opportunity, portfolio investors must buy shares in Australia, since Papua New Guinea does not have its own stock exchange.

Besides Placer Pacific, two other names of PNG companies trading in Australia are Oil Search Ltd. and Niugini Mining. As for capitalizing on Lihir Island, Schmick reports that the project's majority owner is Rio Tinto Zinc, one of the world's largest mining houses based in the U.K. A minority stake is held by Niugini Mining, which in turn is 56 percent owned by the publicly held, U.S.-based Battle Mountain Gold.

Beyond Papua New Guinea, some investors are talking about opportunities in Central America and the Caribbean. As Kleiman's Elizabeth Morrissey explains, probing these locales is a logical next step for brokers and/or investors already exploring South America. In addition, more of Africa will be opening markets and competing for foreigners' investments. Eventually, if peace is maintained and more markets liberalize, the Middle East will draw more international investors. Already researchers are combing through locales such as Oman, and poking around Egypt's sleepy market. Interest in direct investing in Vietnam is also rising; but as of this writing, that country still did not have a stock exchange.

Which market will be "the next Argentina"? With more and more markets opening up, the question becomes harder to answer. It could be a brand-new market. Or investors may continue to bet on the "old" favorites in South America, Europe, and Asia. Tomorrow's hot ticket could literally be anywhere in the world. It could even again be Argentina!

NAFTA

The North American Free Trade Agreement is an accord designed to promote trade among the nations of Mexico, Canada, and the United States. The pact that was signed by the leaders of these three nations in December 1992 included the following areas of agreement:

Sectors

Agriculture

All U.S.–Mexico nontariff barriers to trade will be eliminated, either through conversion to tariff-rate quotas or ordinary tariffs. Mexican import licenses and duties on half the farm imports from the United States will be eliminated immediately. Within 10 years, all agricultural products except corn and beans will enter Mexico duty-free. Mexican tariffs on U.S.-imported corn and beans will be removed in 15 years, as will U.S. tariffs on Mexican sugar and orange juice.

Mexico and Canada will eliminate all tariff and nontariff barriers on their agricultural trade, except for dairy, poultry, eggs, and sugar. Tariffs on fruit and vegetables will be phased out over a 10-year period, with tariffs on some items being eliminated immediately. U.S. exports of grain, oilseeds, horticultural products, and meat will benefit.

Automotive

Mexico will reduce its tariffs by half (to 10 percent) on passenger autos and light trucks. Passenger auto tariffs will be phased out over 10 years, and on light trucks over 5 years. Remaining tariffs will be phased out over 10 years.

Duties on about three-fourths of U.S. parts exported to Mexico (now ranging from 10 to 20 percent) will be phased out over 5 years. For the first 4 years the agreement is in force, rules of origin will require origination in North America for a specific percentage of the parts used in building vehicles in NAFTA member countries.

Mexico will also immediately permit NAFTA partners to make investments of up to 100 percent in Mexican "national suppliers" of parts, and up to 49 percent in other automotive parts enterprises, increasing to 100 percent after 5 years.

Energy and Petrochemicals

Foreign production or sale of five basic petrochemicals (ethane, propane, butane, pentane, and hexane), as well as raw materials for lampblack and naphtha, will still be restricted. Mexico can provide performance incentives in service contracts for U.S. and Canadian companies active in Mexico.

U.S. firms will be able to sell to Pemex and CFE (Mexico's electricity commission) under full and open bidding, and foreign participation will be permitted in nonbasic petrochemical goods and in electric-generating plants.

Telecommunications

North American providers of voice, fax, modem, and packet-switching equipment and services will have full, nondiscriminatory access to Mexico's public telecommunications transport networks. All investment restrictions will be removed by 1995.

Textiles and Apparel

All North American trade restrictions will be eliminated. Mexican tariffs (20 percent on apparel and 15 percent on textiles) on 20 percent of U.S. imports will be eliminated immediately. Tariffs on the remainder will be set at 20 percent, and that tariff will be phased out over a 6-year period. Under rule-of-origin regulations, apparel and textiles qualify for duty-free treatment only if the fabric was woven from North American yarn spun in a NAFTA country.

Services

Financial Services

Equity and market-share restrictions in Mexico on U.S. financial services providers will be phased out. This applies to banks and securities firms, insurance companies, leasing and factoring companies, and nonbank lenders.

Banks and Brokerages

Upon enactment, U.S. and Canadian institutions will be able to establish and operate wholly owned branches that will receive the same treatment as Mexican-owned firms. They will also be able to provide investment services without relocating employees to Mexico.

The limits on the combined equity of foreign ownership as a percent of total equity will be scaled from 8 to 15 percent of the banking system, and 10 to 20 percent of the securities system, over 7 years. During the transition period, Mexico will apply individual market share caps of 1.5 percent for banks and 4 percent for securities firms. After the transition, bank acquisitions will be subject to a 4 percent market share limit on the resulting institution.

Insurance

U.S. and Canadian companies can form joint ventures with 30 percent ownership, and can increase their stake to 51 percent by 1998 and 100 percent by 2000. Existing U.S.–Mexican or Canadian–Mexican joint ventures can obtain 100 percent ownership by 1996. No aggregate or individual market share limits will apply. Insurers from nonmember nations can establish subsidiaries, subject to aggregate limits of 6 percent of market share, gradually increasing to 12 percent in 1999, and subject to market-share caps of 1.5 percent per institution.

Intermediary and auxiliary service companies will be able to establish subsidiaries with no ownership or market-share limits immediately, and U.S. companies will be able to provide cross-border reinsurance and cargo insurance.

Finance Companies

Canadian and U.S. finance companies can establish separate subsidiaries in Mexico to provide consumer lending, commercial lending, mortgage lending, or credit card services. They are limited to a share of 3 percent of the aggregate assets of all banks, plus all limited-scope financial institutions in Mexico (except automotive companies).

Factoring and Leasing

These will be subject to the same transition limits on aggregate market share in Mexico as apply to securities firms, but not to individual market-share limits. NAFTA warehousing and bonding companies, foreign exchange houses, and mutual fund management companies will be permitted to establish Mexican subsidiaries immediately, with no ownership or market share limits.

Transportation Services

U.S. and Canadian trucking companies will be allowed to use their own drivers and trucks to carry cargo across borders to contiguous states in Mexico by 1996, and will have complete access to all of Mexico by 1999.

In 1996, Mexico will permit 49 percent Canadian and U.S. investment in bus companies and truck companies providing international cargo services, scaling up to 51 percent by 1999 and then to 100 percent by 2003. The United States and Canada will permit Mexican truck companies to distribute international cargo, and the United States will permit Mexican bus companies to provide cross-border passenger service.

U.S. railroads will be able to operate and ship goods on Mexican rail. U.S. seaport operators will be allowed to invest in and operate land-side ports in Mexico. U.S. exporters and importers will have a guaranteed open, competitive land transport market, and increased efficiency in moving goods across the Mexican border.

Regulations

Dispute Resolution

A special trilateral commission will regularly review trade relations among the three countries. Five-member panels from a trinationally-agreed-upon roster of trade, legal, and other experts (not restricted to NAFTA members) would be created to resolve disputes involving interpretations of the NAFTA text, dumping, or duties. Each side can pick two members.

The chair, who is selected by agreement of both sides, may not be a citizen of the side making the selection, and is not required to be a NAFTA national. Disputes must be resolved within 8 months. The importing country's domestic law must be applied in reviewing a determination.

Determinations by these panels are binding, and an extraordinary challenge procedure exists to challenge a determination. If a country does not comply with panel recommendations or offer acceptable compensation, the affected country can withdraw equivalent trade concessions. Disputes involving investment can go directly to arbitration. For commercial disputes, each country must have legal mechanisms in place to enforce arbitration contracts and awards.

Environment

The United States can maintain its environmental, health, and safety standards. States and localities can enact tougher standards, and "upward harmonization" of standards is encouraged. None of the three countries can attract investment by lowering environmental standards. Mexico's antipollution statutes were toughened in 1988 and are now roughly equivalent to U.S. statutes. In February 1992, the EPA and SEDUSOL (its Mexican counterpart) completed a comprehensive plan for addressing air, soil, water, and hazardous waste problems in border areas. If a dispute arises, the burden of proof is on the complainant. Where the complainant has a choice of forums, the responding country can insist on NAFTA dispute resolution.

Food Safety

NAFTA-signer countries would be permitted to challenge one another's food safety standards if it could be proven that one country's import standards discriminated against another country's products.

Government Contracts

Mexico's state-owned enterprises and government agencies have traditionally reserved virtually all of their contracts for Mexican companies. The reserve will initially be limited to half the contracts, then scaled down to 30 percent over 8 years. After 10 years, no contracts will be reserved.

Intellectual Property

High-technology, entertainment, and consumer goods producers that rely heavily on protection for their copyrights, patents, trade secrets, service marks, and trademarks will have strong protection under NAFTA. It will limit compulsory licensing. Procedures for enforcing intellectual property rights are set forth, and these include provisions as to damages, injunctive relief, and general due-process issues, as well as safeguards to prevent enforcement abuse.

Maquiladoras

The *maquiladora* system of border-located assembly plants was begun in Mexico in 1965. It is second only to petroleum as a generator of foreign exchange. The majority are foreign-owned. They pay no duty, because parts imported are generally imported on a temporary, in-bound basis, and are assembled and then shipped either to the country of origin or to a third country. Duties are levied only on the value added in assembly or manufacture.

For the first 7 years, the present system will remain unaltered. Some requirements, such as local content and balance of payments, are eliminated. After that, *maquiladoras* can receive a duty drawback at the lowest value of either the total value of import duties paid in Mexico for materials incorporated in the final product, or the total value of the import duties paid in the United States or Canada on the final product. The temporary import system for machinery and equipment will be eliminated by the year 2000.

Temporary Work Visas

Business visitors (generally corporate executives), traders, investors, intracompany transferees, and certain categories of professionals (such as doctors, lawyers, biochemists, architects) who meet specific educational requirements or have alternative credentials and want to apply their training, will be able to live and work anywhere in North America with fewer bureaucratic formalities.

The United States presently limits entry of Mexican professionals to 5500 per year, but this statute will expire in 10 years. This limit is in addition to the number admitted under the U.S. law covering global admission. Canada has not set a numerical limit with respect to Mexico. Citizenship requirements for licensing of professionals will be eliminated in 2 years.

Index

Note: The *f.* after a page number refers to a figure.

About the Author

Margaret M. Price is the international editor of *Pensions & Investments*, where she writes extensively on emerging stock markets. She has 15 years' experience in business and financial journalism. Her work has appeared in such publications as *Industry Week*, *Financial World*, *Global Finance*, and *Bond Buyer*. She is a past president of the New York Financial Writers' Association.